Hiking the Old Dominion

The Sierra Club Totebooks®

The Best About Backpacking
The Climber's Guide to the High Sierra
Climber's Guide to Yosemite Valley
Climbing and Hiking in the Wind River Mountains
Cooking for Camp and Trail
Fieldbook of Nature Photography
Food for Knapsackers
Footloose in the Swiss Alps
Hiker's Guide to the Smokies
Hiking the Bigfoot Country
Hiking the Great Basin
Hiking the North Cascades
Hiking the Southwest
Hiking the Teton Backcountry
Hiking the Yellowstone Backcountry
Hut Hopping in the Austrian Alps
Starr's Guide to the John Muir Trail and the High
    Sierra Region
Timberline Country
To Walk With a Quiet Mind

A Sierra Club Totebook®

Hiking the Old Dominion

The Trails of Virginia

Allen de Hart

Sierra Club Books
San Francisco

The Sierra Club, founded in 1892 by John Muir, has devoted itself to the study and protection of the earth's scenic and ecological resources —mountains, wetlands, woodlands, wild shores and rivers, deserts and plains. The publishing program of the Sierra Club offers books to the public as a nonprofit educational service in the hope that they may enlarge the public's understanding of the Club's basic concerns. The point of view expressed in each book, however, does not necessarily represent that of the Club. The Sierra Club has some fifty chapters coast to coast, in Canada, Hawaii, and Alaska. For information about how you may participate in its programs to preserve wilderness and the quality of life, please address inquiries to Sierra Club, 530 Bush Street, San Francisco, CA 94108.

Library of Congress Cataloging in Publication Data
De Hart, Allen.
    Hiking the Old Dominion.
    (A Sierra Club totebook)
    Includes index.
    1. Hiking–Virginia–Guide-books.   2. Trails–
Virginia–Guide-books.   3. National parks and reserves–
Virginia–Guide-books.   4. Virginia–Description and
travel–1981–Guide-books.   I. Title.   II. Series.
GV199.42.V8D4 1984   917.55′0443   83-19586
ISBN 0-87156-812-8

Book design by Marianne Ackerman
Maps by Nancy Warner
Printed in the United States of America
10 9 8 7 6 5 4 3 2 1

To the volunteers who design, construct, and maintain the hiking trails in Virginia.

Contents

8 List of Illustrations
11 Acknowledgments
15 Introduction

33 Part One National Forest Trails

34 Chapter 1 Jefferson National Forest
35   Blacksburg Ranger District
45   Clinch Ranger District
50   Glenwood Ranger District
58   Mount Rogers National Recreation Area
73   New Castle Ranger District
80   Wythe Ranger District
82 Chapter 2 George Washington National Forest
84   Deerfield Ranger District
95   Dry River Ranger District
106   James River Ranger District
113   Lee Ranger District
129   Pedlar Ranger District
137   Warm Springs Ranger District

149 Part Two National Park System Trails

150 Chapter 3 Appalachian National Scenic Trail
161 Chapter 4 Blue Ridge Parkway
174 Chapter 5 Shenandoah National Park
192 Chapter 6 National Battlefield Parks
213 Chapter 7 National Historical Parks

218 Chapter 8 National Wildlife Refuges
230 Chapter 9 Other Trails in the National Park
System

243 **Part Three State Managed Trails**

244 Chapter 10 State Wildlife Management Areas
269 Chapter 11 State Parklands
271   Mountain Division
288   Piedmont Division
306   Coastal Division

319 **Part Four County and Municipality Trails**

320 Chapter 12 County Parks and Recreation Areas
350 Chapter 13 Municipal Parks and Recreation
Areas

397 **Part Five Regional, Military, College, and
Private Trails**

398 Chapter 14 Regional Parks
410 Chapter 15 US Army Corps of Engineers and
Military Areas
421 Chapter 16 Colleges and Universities
426 Chapter 17 Private Holdings

435 Maps
455 Resources

    Organizations and Clubs
    Agencies and Other Sources of Information
    Trail Supplies

474 Index

List of Illustrations

Photographs

Cascades National Recreation Trail, Jefferson National
    Forest
Piney Ridge Trail, James River Face Wilderness
Mount Rogers National Recreation Area
Shenandoah River, George Washington National Forest
South Range of Massanutten Mountain, George
    Washington National Forest
Appalachian National Scenic Trail
Mabry Mill, Blue Ridge Parkway
Skyline Drive, Shenandoah National Park
Petersburg Battlefield National Recreation Trail
Ridge Trail, Cumberland National Historical Park
Mason Neck National Wildlife Refuge
River Trail, Great Falls Park, George Washington
    Memorial Parkway
Highland Wildlife Management Area
Breaks Interstate Park
Lake Shore Nature Trail, Holliday State Park
False Cape State Park
Annandale Community Park
White Oak Trail, Newport News Park
St. John's Church, Old Dominion Trail, Richmond
Natural Chimneys Regional Park

Maps

The Counties and Regions of Virginia
Region 1 Northern Virginia
Region 2 Richmond
Region 3 Hampton Roads
Region 4 Roanoke-Lynchburg
Region 5 Southwest Virginia
Region 6 Shenandoah Valley
Region 7 Northern Piedmont
Region 8 Tidewater
Region 9 Petersburg-Hopewell
Region 10 Eastern Shore
Region 11 Southern Piedmont
The Washington, D.C. Area
The Richmond Area

Acknowledgments

David A. Tice, vice-president and consulting forester of the Mid-Atlantic Forestry Services, Inc (Charlottesville), is a specialist in forest management and environmental planning. In addition to having taken degrees in forest resources management and working in the field he also writes about it, and he has logged thousands of miles on Virginia foot trails. Without the access I had to his resource materials and without his generous support this book would not have been possible.

Personnel who provided assistance from the Jefferson National Forest (JNF) include Sara Patterson, office assistant, and Buford Belcher, of Blacksburg Ranger District; Charles Saboites, district ranger, and John C. Hinrichs, forester, of Clinch Ranger District; Joseph H. Hedrick, district ranger, and Bill Baggett, assistant ranger, of Glenwood Ranger District; Paul Dore, forestry technician, and Kirby A. Brock, area ranger, of Mt Rogers National Recreation Area; Robert W. Boardwine, district ranger, and David Pollock, other-resources assistant, of New Castle Ranger District; and Ronald L. Druien, resource forester, of Wythe Ranger District.

In the George Washington National Forest (GWNF) I received assistance from John Romanowski, land-use assistant, and James D. Thorsen, district ranger, of Deerfield Ranger District; Holden Mason, forester, of Dry River Ranger District; James D. Mattox, land-use assistant, and William B. Leichter, district ranger, of James River Ranger District; Tom Brady, forester, and Bill Kruszka, recreation technician, of Lee Ranger District; Harry Fisher, assistant ranger, of Pedlar Ranger District; and Kenneth Rago, silviculturist, of Warm Springs Ranger District.

Liz Hawk, trail coordinator, of the JNF headquarters (Roanoke), and Melvin L. Anhold, recreation staff officer, of the GWNF headquarters (Harrisonburg) had or found the answers to my many questions. Harry L. Baker, who is landscape architect for the Blue Ridge Pkwy of the National Park Service (Asheville, North Carolina), Chuck Schuller, who is trails coordinator of the NPS (Atlanta, Georgia), and Robert R. Jacobsen, who is superintendent of Shenandoah National Park (Luray) assisted in verifying trail locations under their supervision.

On the state government level, John R. Davy, Jr., chief of planning, Commission of Outdoor Recreation (Richmond), was a valuable and dependable resource adviser. For state parks information, Tom Blackstock, park interpreter (Richmond), and, for state forest information, W.C. Stanley (Charlottesville) provided counsel and assistance from their offices.

Without the help of Chris Bogert, trail planner of Fairfax County Park Authority (Annandale), and of Dorothy Werner, public information officer, and Ken Brundage, administrative assistant of Northern Virginia Regional Park Authority (Fairfax), I could not have completed investigating the 300 parks in their areas.

A number of families opened their homes for me as base points in my final three years of covering the state county by county. Among them are Dr. and Mrs.

Raymond Shultz (Roanoke), Mr. and Mrs. Lawrence Pitt (Mechanicsville), Mr. and Mrs. John Borum (Norfolk), Mr. and Mrs. Atlas Parker (Buena Vista), and Mr. and Mrs. Emmett Snead III (Fredericksburg).

Dr. Steve Croy, professor of biology at VPI and SU and director of the Virginia Natural Diversity Information Program of the Nature Conservancy (Blacksburg), contributed information from his research on the state's flora and fauna. And special support was received from Ed Page (Lynchburg), president of the Natural Bridge A.T. Club and the Virginia Trails Association; State Attorney General Gerald L. Baliles; Dr. Walter Cowen, director of the University Press of Virginia (Charlottesville); Ed Garvey, author of *Hiking Trails in the Mid-Atlantic States;* and Jeannette Fitzwilliams, president of the National Trails Council (Alexandria).

Throughout the years of my hiking and backpacking in Virginia many of my faithful companions have hiked with me in adverse weather, climbed frozen ridges, sweated through steamy summer bogs, pushed the measuring wheel, and kept log notes, sharing in the pleasure of hiking and often giving encouragement when I felt that this project could never be finished. Among them are Mike Ballance, Joyce Barbare, Steve Bass, Kim Bendheim, Tom Bond, John and Jimbo Borum, Dale Bowman, Chris Bracknell, Steven Cosby, Flora B. de Hart, Robert Dillon, Richard and Willie Lee Elgin, Greg D. Frederick, Nancy Freeman, Steve Guyton, Rudy Hauser, David Hicks, Billy Jones, Johnny King, Steve King, John LeMay, Jr., Jack A. Lewis, Walter J. May, Robert Old, Kevin Parker, Lawrence Pitt, John Rohme, Bill Ross, Chuck Satterwhite, Scott Smith, Emmett and Pam Snead, David Stinchfield, Kenneth Tippette, Ed and Seth Washburn, Dan Watson, Buster White, Charlotte G. Wicks, Rob Wilfong, Meredith Wilkins, Mary Willete, Darrell Williams, and Chuck Wilson.

Especially I appreciate one outdoor sports enthusiast, my brother Moir, who, until his death in 1979, was always my personal inspiration. Twelve years my senior, he took me on my first hike when I was five, teaching me early to love and to care for the natural environment. To him and to all those who gave of time, energy, and assistance, I express my gratitude.

Introduction

And this our life, exempt from
   public haunt,
Finds tongues in trees, books in
   the running brooks,
Sermons in stones, and good in
   everything.

—Shakespeare,
As You Like It, Act II

Virginia has 3,901 public outdoor recreational areas comprising 3,108,773 acres of land and water. Private outdoor recreational areas number 1,705, with 291,164 acres. Within these properties are 2,281 hiking trails—a total of 3,189 mi. And in addition there are 1,187 mi of bicycle trails, 998 mi of horse trails, and 750 mi of canoe trails.

The purpose of this book is to provide for you a definitive listing of, and an introduction to, the almost unlimited hiking trails of Virginia. To include such a wide variety in one book, it has been necessary to condense the voluminous research material to basics. The basics include trail length and difficulty, which US Geological Survey (USGS) topographical maps to use, trailhead locations, route directions, descriptions of the surrounding areas and, for some trails, addresses and telephone numbers for support facilities and further information. In presenting these fundamentals it is my objective to stimulate your interest in trails, to assure you of accurate access to them, and in the process to allow sufficient mystery about them to remain that you can pursue your own trail discoveries and surprises.

Sources of Information

In the past 40 years I have hiked all or a large portion of all the currently designated trails plus the old sections of the *Appalachian Trail* and numerous obsolete trails. Some of my favorite trails I have hiked frequently in all seasons; each time I can check the old characteristics and, in accordance with the law of succession, expect something new. For the past 12 years I have been collecting and filing trail information that now numbers more than 12,000 pieces of material. Since 1980 I have been rechecking, rehiking, and preparing the current list. From 1970 to 1980, David Tice, first while a student and subsequently with the Virginia Nature Conservancy, hiked and researched nearly 1,500 trails. Condensing and combining our sources has resulted in my coverage of 904 trails in this book. Of the remaining known total, the US Forest Service suggested that 361 not be included due to a lack of use or maintenance. Another 337 were deleted because of requests from private trail owners. An additional 38 trails are not included because they were under construction during the research period; examples are the 1.5-mi *Munden Point Park Trail* in Virginia Beach, the *Indian River Park Trail* in Norfolk, and the 12-mi *Sugar Loaf Mtn Trail* in Roanoke County, although the majority in this category of omitted trails are physical fitness trails, such as those under construction in Franklin and Staunton. The remainder were omitted for the reasons that some trails have become roads, or have been obliterated by urban development, or are used primarily by nonhikers.

Each trail was researched and hiked using information from governmental agencies and private land owners. Computer printouts from the US Forest Service were double-checked in the ranger-district offices and in the field. On the state level a computer printout from the Commission of Outdoor Recreation was used to delineate trail categories. From this source each county and city department of parks and recreation was contacted. With their assistance a new world of trails became known. The Boy Scouts councils and gardens clubs, as well as other local organizations, colleges, and forest-products companies, became sources of information for the private trails. Some of the published materials used for additional information are *The Virginia Outdoors Plan* (1979), by the state Commission of Outdoor Recreation; *A Guide to Virginia's Wildlife Management Areas* (1981), by the Virginia Commission of Game and Inland Fisheries; *Virginia State Parks,* by the Division of State Parks in the Department of Conservation and Economic Development; *Appalachian Trail Guide: Shenandoah National Park* (1977), by the Potomac Appalachian Trail Club; *Appalachian Trail Guide: Central and Southwest Virginia* (1981), by the Appalachian Trail Conference; *Hiking Trails in the Mid-Atlantic States* (1976), by Ed Garvey, Contemporary Sports Books; *Hiking Virginia's National Forests* (1977), by Karin Wuertz-Schaefer, East Woods Press; *Tidewater Trail Guide* (1980), by the Tidewater Appalachian Trail Club; *Happy Trails* (1983), by the Northern Virginia Regional Park Authority; and *Historic Garden Week in Virginia,* by the Garden Club of Virginia. And finally, some of the best sources I had were the local citizens at the country stores, hunting lodges, and farm homes.

How to Use the Book

To understand and receive maximum benefit from this guidebook, it is essential to become acquainted with the manner in which the trails and directions to them are described. Trails in the 12 districts of the national forests are generally grouped in designated areas, either for their connecting and circuit possibilities or for proximity to a campground, or both. Each combined group of trails has the total mileage listed. Where a long loop is outlined the description indicates any shorter routes for a return. Highway directions begin at prominent intersections or landmarks in an attempt to make only a state highway map and the book maps necessary.

An introduction precedes each national forest and park, state park and forest, and regional park. Addresses and telephone numbers for acquiring further information are listed after each. In each division of the state parks the parks are listed alphabetically. Cities and counties are listed alphabetically statewide, in chapters where they are the primary units. Private trail descriptions have introductions only if they are associated with parks or campgrounds. For trails where camping is not allowed and support facilities are nearby, the facilities are listed (as described in this Introduction under *Support Facilities and Information).*

Maps

Unless you are familiar with the Virginia area, a regular highway map is essential for locating trailheads. County maps are available at county courthouses or from the Dept of Highways and Transportation, which is in Richmond. See address for ordering maps in Resources. For the national forests the *Sportsman's Guides* are valuable maps. They are being updated and are available at any of the district ranger offices. Excellent maps accompany the *Appalachian Trail* and the Shenandoah National Park guidebooks from the Appalachian Trail Conference and the Potomac Appalachian Trail Club. The US Geological Survey (USGS) maps most commonly used and referred to in this guidebook are on the scale of 1:24,000 (1 in. = 2,000 ft); they are of considerable assistance in locating roads, residences, lakes, forests, streams, and, with the contour lines, in determining elevation. On a remote backcountry trail a contour map could be a lifesaver. If a local blueprint company does not have your desired topographical ("topo") map, write to Branch of Distribution, US Geological Survey, 1200 South Eads St, Arlington, VA 22202. As a charge is made for these maps (and the charge has increased), you may wish to first write for free information and an index to the maps of Virginia.

Because of the size of the state and the number of trails covered, it has been impossible to map each trail individually. However, a large-scale map of the state, broken up into eleven zones, with each trailhead marked and numbered on it, has been included. These numbers are also listed beside the trail names in the book, so by referring back and forth you can determine general locality.

Abbreviations

Abbreviations are used to save space. Some of the most frequently used are: *A.T.* (Appalachian Trail), ATC (Appalachian Trail Conference), BRP (Blue Ridge Pkwy), FR (forest development road or forest protection road), GWNF (George Washington National Forest), JNF (Jefferson National Forest), mp (milepost or milepoint in the SNP or on the BRP), PATC (Potomac Appalachian Trail Club), SNP (Shenandoah National Park), USFS (US Forest Service), USGS (US Geological Survey), WMA (Wildlife Management Area), VTA (Virginia Trails Association).

L (left), R (right), tel (telephone), rd (road), mi (miles), rt (round trip), ct (combined trails), m (meters), km (kilometers), yd (yards), ft (feet), jct (junction or intersection), sta (station), rec (recreation), fac (facilities), and rte (route).

Kinds of Trails

Trails in this book are described, according to condition or features, in a number of classifications. A *primary* or *main* trail is popular in usage and is blazed or marked and well maintained. A *primitive* trail is the opposite; infrequently cleared, it may be hard to find. It may also be called a *manway* requiring bushwhacking; these are recommended only for experienced hikers. A *side* or *spur* trail may or may not be in good condition. They frequently are used for a scenic point of interest or a connector route with other trails. An *inventoried* trail is on the computer print-out of government agencies, but they are trails usually overgrown with no effort made at maintenance. A *gated* trail can be on a graded and graveled forest road or on a forest road that is less maintained (known respectively as FDR and FPR; except, where information on level of road maintenance is nonessential, both are simply abbreviated FR.) A *jeep* trail is often rough and eroded, but hiking conditions on it, as on numerous horse trails, may be acceptable. A trail for people, horses, and wheels is often called a *multiple use* or *multi-purpose* trail.

Trails listed as *scenic* have impressive views from overlooks, waterfalls, or fine forest esthetics. A trail described as *historic* covers a significant point of interest in the heritage of an area. The increasingly common physical fitness trails, for example the par course or jogging track, are termed here as *recreational,* and trails constructed for the handicapped are described as *special use.* The *nature* trails, usually short in length, are interpretive and educational for the purpose of describing the flora and fauna. I have omitted another kind of trail title—the lost trail. Such a trail was explored, for example, when a lumberman in Nelson County told me to "hang a right," when it should have been a left. As a consequence, I got lost, fell off a precipice into a kudzu thicket with my measuring wheel and my backpack.

Finding the Trails

Virginians call every road, even an interstate, a *route.* This can be confusing to outsiders, and to some natives, who depend on multiple types of road systems as they drive to trailheads. It's not always clear, then, what sort of vehicle to use to reach the trailhead. In this book, roads are described according to the systems used by the

Dept of Highways and Transportation, as follows: **I** (interstate) **US** (federal-state arterial system, black and white shield), **VA** (major state primary system; black and white rounded, three-corner shield, numbered from 1 to 599), **SR** (state secondary system, "county roads," the bulk of the state's road system, paved or gravel; black and white rectangular signs numbered 600 and up, with numbers often changing at county lines or the same number repeated in multiple counties). There are also forest development roads (FDR), described under *Kinds of Trails*. These are open to the public but not shown on the county or state highway maps. Watch for the signs; they are small, rectangular, and inconspicuous, usually brown and yellow. Hunting roads, jeep roads, and logging roads may or may not be passable with any vehicle other than one with four-wheel drive. Where roads are difficult or gated, I have indicated the condition in the trail descriptions.

Once you have located the trailhead, the next decision is where to park. Parking areas are indicated, but a number of these have limited space. Unfortunately, a few of them have high rates of vandalism. As a result all valuables should be completely concealed and your vehicle locked when you are out of sight of it.

Trail Numbers and Markings

The numbers to the right of the trail names in this book's listings identify the trails' positions on the accompanying maps, as previously noted. These numbers should not be confused with trail numbers in other books or with the computerized US Forest Service numbers. The USFS numbers also are included, at the end of the trail write-ups; these are permanent numbers used by the USFS on its maps and records. However, neither number will be seen on trail posts, trees, or other markers.

The blazes and markings (these terms having the same meaning here) of trails are in almost every color and in a wide variety of shapes, squares, rectangles, diamonds, circles, and combinations. The *A.T.* blaze is always a 2-in.-by-6-in vertical white blaze. The Lee Ranger District has a number of purple-blazed trails connecting with others blazed in yellow, white, orange, and blue. Red blazes are rare because they designate the USFS boundary line markings.

Trail Length and Difficulty

A trail is often defined as a path or track made by the passage of persons or animals. I think of a trail as being a walkway for getting from one point to another point. With that interpretation of a trail I can support the increasing need for, and development of, urban trails, many of which are cement or asphalt.

Distance has been measured by the US Forest Service, the National Park Service, specific state government services, trail organizations, and myself. I have used a Model 400 Rolatape wheel. Whenever there was doubt in trail mileage accuracy, the trail was remeasured. Trail relocations may alter the trail lengths and where anticipated they are described in the guidebook.

Under the heading of each trail is the word length, followed by the numerical equivalent. Lengths may be a *loop* trail, which will bring you to your point of origin with no backtracking (an example is *Trimble Mountain Trail);* a *linear* trail, which requires backtracking *(Jerry's*

Run Trail); a *shuttle* trail, on which you have no interest in returning to the point of origin *(North River Gorge Trail),* or a *circuit* trail, which combines a network of trails (Iron Mountain South Area).

For some trails you will notice the abbreviations *rt* for *round trip,* or *ct* for *combined trails,* or both. A trail length with a *rt* means that you will have to backtrack or use a combination of trails to return to your point of origin. For example, the *Signal Knob Trail* has a USFS trail sign at the trailhead of 4.5 mi. The purpose for my describing the trail as having a *rt* of 9 mi is to point out that some forest, park and other officially listed or posted trail lengths give only one-way linear distance, the crucial factor in anticipating hiking time. If a *ct* follows the length, you will know that, as in the above example of the Iron Mountain South Area, your hike will include more than one trail in your total trail miles. Once you are in a location with a network of trails you will notice that you can make your own combination of trails to suit your plans.

Virginia's trails range in distance from the shortest, 88-yd *Stewart's Knob Trail* at mp 110.6 on the Blue Ridge Parkway, to the 543 mi of the *Appalachian Trail* from Damascus to Harpers Ferry. Some other long trails are the 55-mi *Big Blue Trail;* the 44-mi *Washington and Old Dominion RR Trail;* the 40-mi *Iron Mtn Trail;* the 38-mi *Shenandoah Mtn Trail;* the 26-mi *Wild Oak Trail;* and the 17-mi *Ridge Trail.* In the near future Virginia's Commission of Outdoor Recreation will re-evaluate one of its 1979 master plans for such proposed trails as the *Southside Virginia Trail, Trans-Virginia Trail, Rappahannock River Trail, Rivanna River Trail,* and the *Potomac Heritage Trail.*

Hiking time is not estimated in this book because it varies considerably with each hiker. A nature student or nature photographer can spend hours in one locale, whereas the through hiker must often rush to the next shelter before dark. More families are hiking, and more jogging is seen on the trails; both these styles of travel vary from the norm in time required. However, an average for many hikers with a backpack is 2 mi an hour on terrain of gradual contour.

The degree of difficulty listed for each trail—*easy, moderate,* or *strenuous*—is based on the ratings of average hikers, not professional hikers or athletes. Some hiking clubs have rated difficulty on a ratio basis of elevation and distance; others have made classifications according to age and weight. But, for the purpose of this guidebook, *easy* means that if you are in good health you can hike the trails without fatigue or exertion. *Moderate* ratings mean you should expect some exertion and may need to take some rests. *Strenuous* means that you will be climbing steep trails or taking a long hike where you will experience greater than average exertion; numerous rest stops may be necessary.

What You Can See on the Trails

This guidebook cannot attempt to include a description of all the geological formations and botanical and zoological species you can see on the trails. Where botanical references are made, species are generalized and common names used. For example, there are more than 11 species of rhododendron and azalea in the state, with every county in the mountains having *Rhododendron maximum,* commonly called rosebay, or great laurel; it has light pink or whitish blossoms. The *Rhododendron catawbiense,* with large purple flowers, is not found in all the mountain counties; its common name is Catawba rhododendron or purple laurel, not to be confused with mountain laurel, which is in the genus *Kalmia.* For the *Rhododendron calendulaceum* I have listed the common name as flame azalea. Along the *A.T.* in the Pedlar Ranger District the exceptionally fragrant mountain azalea *Rhododendron roseum* grows in profusion. For trees, the same principle of naming is applied. For example, there are 26 species of oaks and 8 species of pine in the state, and they are referred to generically except where there is a large concentration of a particular species.

Botanical listings in this book reflect what was representative of the flowering plants present while I was on the trails. Your hike during another season will provide a different and perhaps larger list. The state has more than 85 species of ferns and more than 3,400 species and varieties of other vascular plants. Some occur statewide, while most occur in only one or a few physiographic provinces. As Virginia does not have a comprehensive book dedicated to the vascular flora of the state, we must rely on books written for surrounding states. General books on wildflowers such as *Newcomb's Wildflower Guide,* by Newcomb, and the Peterson field guide on wildflowers will answer most questions if you are the botany-oriented hiker, but a more thorough treatment will be found in *Flora of West Virginia,* by E. L. Core. The *Atlas of the Virginia Flora,* parts I and II, by Harvill, Stevens, Ware, and Bradley, consists of maps showing the county-by-county occurrences of the known species of the state's flora and is useful for checking the plants' distribution. The nonvascular plants in Virginia consist of well over 25,000 species and include everything from algae, lichens, and fungi to liverworts and mosses. A number of guides cover these groups; an example is *Mushrooms of North America,* by O. K. Miller.

Fewer animals than plants are seen on the trails. From among the 75 species of terrestrial mammals known in Virginia you will be lucky to see a dozen in a single day, because most are nocturnal and many do not occur state-wide; a number live in specialized habitats. Your chances of seeing or hearing birds are much better, because most are active during the day and because they are so mobile. Approximately 400 bird species are known in Virginia, and most of these are breeders within the state. A few overwinter here during migration.

The state's herptofauna consists of 144 species and subspecies almost equally divided: 75 amphibians and 69 reptiles. Some occur statewide, but most have a rather limited distribution. The remaining group of vertebrate animals in the state, the fish, are known to occur in more than 200 freshwater species and in an almost equal number of marine and estuarine species. Finally, representing at least 90% of the animals in the state are the invertebrates. They include the insects and mollusks. A few of many recommended books for the hiker interested in wildlife are: *Amphibians and Reptiles in the Carolinas and Virginia,* by Martof, Palmer, Bailey, Harrison, and Dermid; *Virginia's Birdlife, An Annotated Checklist,* by the Virginia Society of Ornithology; and *Birds of North America,* by Robbins, Brunn, Zim, and Singer.

Virginia has a number of rare plants and animals, and I have referred to them if they are near the trails. Most are rare because of habitat destruction, not natural occurrences. A good overview of this subject is found in *Endangered and Threatened Plants and Animals of Virginia,* edited by D. W. Linzey.

If you hike in the mountains of SW Virginia you will become aware of the seven counties with bituminous coal on the Appalachian plateau. Other rock formations you may see in the state include slate, shale, limestone, feldspar, sandstone, granite, quartz, greenstone, gneiss, schist, and soapstone. Virginia is the only state in the nation that produces aplite, an acidic granite of quartz and feldspar. In a number of areas along the Blue Ridge chain you will see the remains of old iron mines and furnaces, which were prominent before the turn of the century.

Health and Safety

A recommended book on trail health and safety is *Wilderness Survival,* by Bernard Shanks. The inexperienced hiker should be familiar with the dangers of hypothermia, lightning, slippery rocks, snowstorms, flooded areas, being lost, poisonous snakes, and contaminated water. On the last: if you are in a national or state forest or park, use water officially designated as being safe. Designations may be posted on maps, trailhead signs, water sources, or ranger stations. You may also wish to ask forest and park officials for information on water supply and purity. A listing of springs, wells, and clear streams in this book does not mean the water is safe to drink. When in doubt use Globaline or Potable-Aqua tablets, or boil the water properly for purification. Always take a first-aid kit; a snake-bite kit in season is also recommended. For safety reasons, hike with a companion.

Support Facilities and Information

In describing the trails I have indicated where camping is allowed. For those where camping is not allowed, I have listed the support facilities of a commercial campground. These were chosen on the basis of proximity and full service and not on cost or recreational facilities. If *full service* is indicated it means the camp has sites for tenting and for trailers that need electricity, water, and sewage lines. Such camps also have hot showers, flush toilets, picnic areas, and public phones, and some have food and laundry facilities. Camping information is based on my 1982–1983 visits. In addition to the camping brochures that you can request from the national forests and state parks, a brochure is published by the Virginia Campground Association, Rte 1, Box 120, New Kent, VA 23124, on 100 private campgrounds. A recommended comprehensive directory is Woodall's *Campground Directory,* published by Simon and Schuster. Finally, addresses and telephone numbers for additional information have been included here so you can acquire the most direct and authoritative word on the trail areas.

Your Good-Hiking Checklist

If you plan to turn your hiking trip into a backpacking and camping trek, some advance planning and preparation, particularly for beginners, will be necessary. The following suggested checklist is presented to assist you in having a good time in the area of your choice.

1. *Planning Your Trip:* If you do not have a hiking and backpacking guidebook, I suggest *Walking Softly in the Wilderness: The Sierra Club Guide to Backpacking,* by John Hart. A smaller-size guidebook is *Backpack Hiking: The First Steps,* by Richard Eggert, published by Stackpole Books. Check your list for maps and directions, compass, backpack, clothing, footwear, sleeping bag, tent, food, canteen, tools of the trade, health and first-aid supplies, emergency equipment, backcountry permits, and extras (such as a camera). Your trail shop personnel (See Resources) can answer your questions on equipment quality, brand names, and specific outfitting needs.

2. *Camping:* Will you have a base camp? What are the regulations governing the occupancy of public open forests and of designated campgrounds, and governing sanitation, fires, firearms, pets, noise pollution, and security? For the Shenandoah National Park request the free brochure on *Exploring the Backcountry.* I have listed particularly pertinent information in this book and provided addresses from which you can request camping information.

3. *Protecting the Environment:* Build fires only where permitted, using only fallen deadwood. A small propane stove is recommended for food preparation. When possible leave no trace of your camping, and please remember that what we pack in we must pack out. Keep the water supply clean and use only biodegradable soap. Protecting the environment is easier when hiking with a small group. Join and be active in a hiking or outing club. You may wish also to become an activist in opposing policies of governmental agencies or conglom-

erate industries whose efforts are destructive of our remaining wilderness environment.

4. *Hunting and Fishing:* If you plan a hunting or fishing trip along with your backpacking excursion write for the *Hunter's Guide* and *Virginia's Fishing Regulations* from the Commission of Game and Inland Fisheries, whose address is listed under Resources.

Virginia Is for Trail Lovers

With this guidebook and other resources and with your plans all made, it is time to go. You will find and love each trail for its individual personality, its unique ambience. If you do not immediately sense its milieu, create one, by thinking of those who have preceded you, the timeless wind and shadows, the night cries and calls of wildlife, the ceaseless seasonal death and beauty of the forest—entrancing, illimitable. I hope that you will have as much pleasure hiking these trails as I have had in describing them to you. Welcome to the hiking trails of Virginia!

Allen de Hart
Woolwine, Virginia

Part One

National Forest Trails

1 · Jefferson National Forest

The Jefferson National Forest (JNF) has 680,000 acres, extending from the Tennessee–North Carolina border SW in Washington County to the James River NE in Rockbridge County. It has a vast expanse of recreational opportunities for camping, hiking and backpacking, cross-country skiing, horseback riding, and nature study. A source of timber—mainly Appalachian hardwoods sprinkled with pines—it also has abundant wildlife, such as deer, turkey, grouse, squirrel, and raccoon. Poisonous snakes are the rattler and the copperhead. Anglers have many miles of stocked trout streams. In addition to the many short trails, hikers have the *A.T.* winding for 316 miles across high peaks, meadows, and slopes from Damascus to Snowden. Camping is allowed throughout the forest, unless otherwise specified, and more than 30 campgrounds have facilities ranging from primitive to full service.

Two large areas in the forest are managed under special, legislated guidelines. In the SW is the 154,000-acre Mt Rogers National Recreational Area (Mt Rogers NRA), designated by Congress in 1966 to provide a wide range of recreational opportunities. It has five ranger districts. The other specially managed area, the James

River Face Wilderness, has 8,800 acres bordered by the James River on the NE. This large tract was formulated by the Eastern Wilderness Act of 1975.

Information: For district maps ($1 each) and for information, contact the offices of the five districts or the NRA, or contact the main office:

Blacksburg Ranger District, Rte 1, Box 404, Blacksburg, VA 24060; tel: 703-552-4641. On US 460, 1 mi W of Blacksburg.

Clinch Ranger District, Rte 1, Box 320-H, Wise, VA 24293; tel: 703-328-2931. On SR 646 in Wise, opposite Clinch Valley College.

Glenwood Ranger District, Box 8, Natural Bridge Station, VA 24579; tel: 703-291-2189. On VA 130, 0.5 mi W of Natural Bridge Station.

Mt Rogers NRA, Rte 1, Box 303, Marion, VA 24354; tel: 703-783-5196. On VA 16, 5 mi S of Marion.

New Castle Ranger District, Box 246, New Castle, VA 24127; tel: 703-864-5195. On SR 615, 1.5 mi E of New Castle.

Wythe Ranger District, Rte 4, Wytheville, VA 24382; tel: 703-228-5551. On US 11, W side of Wytheville.

Forest Supervisor, Jefferson National Forest Headquarters, 210 Franklin Rd SW, Roanoke, VA 24001; tel: 703-982-6270. Address on Franklin is in the Poff Bldg, Elm St Exit off I-581.

Blacksburg Ranger District

Note that 102.4 mi of the *Appalachian Trail* are available within the Blacksburg Ranger District of the Jefferson National Forest.

Mountain Lakes Area
Giles County

▼ WAR SPUR TRAIL, OLD CHESTNUT TRAIL   1–2

Length: 4.4 mi (7 km) rt, ct; easy to moderate. *USGS Maps:* Eggleston, Interior, Waiteville. *Trailhead:* Parking area on SR 613.

Directions and Description: From US 460 at Hoges Chapel turn on SR 613 to Mtn Lake at 4.8 mi. At 5.7 mi paved road becomes gravel. Pass L of University of Virginia Biological Station and park on R after 9.2 mi. (Another route from US 460 is SR 700, 6.3 mi from Ranger Station.) These trails are on a 1,583-acre tract set aside by the US Forest Service in 1960 to preserve the natural environment. It is part of the 6,900 acres included in the Wilderness Study Area here in 1975. No camping. Begin hike R on *War Spur Trail,* reaching overlook (3,650 ft) with impressive views into War Spur Hollow and John's Creek Valley at 1.3 mi. Backtrack for 0.2 mi and turn R; descend to War Spur Branch and a stand of virgin hemlock and spruce at 1.8 mi. At junction of *Old Chestnut Trail* turn R for 0.9 mi to *Appalachian Trail.* Return to parking area after 4.4 mi. Trail has generous understory of striped green maple, azaleas, ferns, carpets of wintergreen, and grassy trail floor. USFS trail numbers 56, 68.

Craig and Giles County

▼ POTTS MOUNTAIN TRAIL   3–4

Length: 5.5 mi (8.8 km); moderate to strenuous. *USGS:* Waiteville, Interior. *Trailhead:* SR 613 and *Appalachian Trail* junction.

Directions and Description: The trail can be approached from SR 636 at the Virginia–West Virginia state line or from SR 613 junction with the *A.T.* between Minie Ball Hill and Wind Rock. If the hiker chooses the trailhead at SR 613 and the *A.T.* junction, hike E for 2 mi on the *A.T.* to *Potts Mountain Trail* junction. Turn sharp L and follow along the ridge. After 1 mi on the ridge reach White Rocks and the state line. At 1.9 mi is junction with *White Rocks Trail.* (*White Rocks Trail* veers R leading down to SR 632. This could be a strenuous circuit route of approximately 12 mi back to SR 613 to reconnect with the *A.T.*) Continue NE along the ridge, where in some places the trail is overgrown. When in doubt stay on the ridge line. At 5.5 mi (plus the 2 mi of the *A.T.*) reach SR 636. This is the border between the Blacksburg and New Castle ranger districts. Deer are frequently seen in this area, and bear have been sighted. Vegetation is chiefly hardwoods. (For the 6.8-mi continuation of the *Potts Mountain Trail,* see the New Castle District description—Section 5.) Backtrack or use vehicle shuttle. USFS trail number 55.

Rocky Gap Area
Craig County

▼ JOHN'S CREEK MOUNTAIN TRAIL   5

Length: 3.5 mi (5.6 km); moderate. *USGS Map:* Waiteville, Newport. *Trailhead:* Parking area at junction of SR 601 and *Appalachian Trail.*

Directions and Description: From Newport go E on VA 42 for 1.1 mi, turn L on SR 601, and go 5.1 mi to

gravel road. After another 1.7 mi reach parking area at
A.T. Take the *A.T.* R and SE; ascend steadily for 0.5 mi on
old Kelly Knob fire-tower road. Reach the ridge crest,
notice trail sign, and turn L. Follow main ridge through
hardwood forest, passing rock outcroppings, to SR 658.
Wildlife is likely to be seen on this trail. (On SR 658 it is 1
mi E to VA 42, between Simmonsville and Maggie.)
Backtrack or use vehicle shuttle. USFS trail number 57.

▼ JOHN'S CREEK TRAIL   6

Length: 6 mi (9.6 km) rt; moderate. *USGS Maps:* Waiteville, Newport. *Trailhead:* End of FR 156.

   Directions and Description: Take SR 601 from Newport to junction with SR 632. Turn L on SR 632 and follow to beginning of FR 156. Park at end of road; old road
trail follows up John's Creek drainage on a generally
easy grade for 3 mi. Plenty of wildflowers and wildlife
along streamside. Backtracking is necessary.

Little Stony Creek Area
Giles County

▼ CASCADES TRAIL   7–8

Length: 3.8 mi (6.1 km) rt; moderate. *USGS Map:* Eggleston. *Trailhead:* Parking area.

   Directions and Description: At Pembroke on US 460
take SR 623 at the sign for 3.5 mi to Cascades Recreation
Area, and park. Follow directional sign on heavily used
trail for 0.2 mi to R, crossing footbridge over Little Stony
Creek (which is filled with rainbow and brook trout).

Cascades/National Recreation Trail, Jefferson National Forest. Allen de Hart.

Ascend over rocks and webs of tree roots, by rare wild-flowers. Cross another footbridge at 1.6 mi; turn R and reach the Cascades at 1.9 mi. Climbing the sidewalls of the falls is prohibited.

The Cascades is thought to be one of Virginia's most photographed waterfalls. Making a dramatic 65-ft fall into an oval pool, it is one of two major falls on Little Stony Creek, which begins 7 mi from the falls in a red-spruce bog not far from Lone Pine Peak. *Cascades Trail* is a national recreation trail, designated in 1979.

For a different view on the return to the parking area, take one of two routes downstream. At 0.2 mi from the falls, junction for downstream trail is straight ahead, passing footbridge; or, ascend 100 yds to old wagon road. At junction of old wagon road go L and, on a slope, parallel the downstream trail.

(Here at this junction with the old wagon road on the R is the trailhead for the *Conservancy Trail.* It is a 4-mi trail to Butts Mtn fire tower. Ascend on road through channel of rhododendron for 0.6 mi to fork and turn L. [The jeep road on R descends for a short distance to the Upper Cascades and Barney's Wall.] Immediately after this fork is a second fork. The wagon road goes straight ahead, and the *Conservancy Trail* turns L up old road over a mounded-earth tank trap. Pass two turnoff old roads on R, which lead to SR 714, as the trail continues NW to a R turnoff toward the fire tower. The correct turn is marked. Superb views from the fire tower. Backtrack and rejoin the *Cascades Trail* for a round-trip total of 11.8 mi to the parking area.)

Picnicking and fishing are other activities in the Cascades Recreation Area. No camping. USFS trail numbers 70, 7013.

White Rocks Area
Giles and Monroe Counties

▼ VIRGINIA'S NATURE TRAIL   9

Length: 1.5 mi (2.4 km); easy. *USGS Maps:* Interior, Waiteville. *Trailhead:* White Rocks Campground.

   Directions and Description: Take SR 635 SE of Pearisburg near New River Bridge US 460 for 16 mi to Kire intersection. Turn R on SR 613 for 1 mi, and turn L on FR 645 to White Rocks Campground. Area has drinking water, rest rooms, camping sites, and grills. From the camping area follow loop signs, crossing tributaries of White Rock Branch and traversing the Virginia–West Virginia state line. Vascular plants include oaks, maple, birch, hemlock, poplar, orchids, pitch pine, rhododendron, haw, alder, wild phlox, galax, and itchweed. To see numerous wildlife, choose a quiet occasion. USFS trail number 71.

Huckleberry Ridge Area
Giles County

▼ HUCKLEBERRY RIDGE TRAIL   10–13

Length: 8 mi (12.8 km); moderate. *USGS Map:* Interior. *Trailhead:* FR gate at Kelly Flats Rd.

   Directions and Description: Formerly called *Flat Peter Trail.* An excellent loop to choose for the beauty of the forest, creeks, wildflowers, and wildlife. Access is the same as to the White Rock Area (previous entry) on SR 635 from Pembroke at US 460, but near Interior. After passing by the Interior Picnic Area and crossing the *A.T.* go 1.9 mi to Kelly Flats Rd, SR 772, on the L. A "Glen

Alton" sign should be here. Turn L and follow gravel road for 0.2 mi to red gate, FR 942, and park.

From gate hike on the road for 0.4 mi to yellow-blazed trail and a sign on R. Enter young hardwood forest to North Fork Creek on R. Rock-hop the creek, following upstream for 1 mi to clearing. Cross creek again to old *Dixon Branch Trail.* Follow it upstream, rock-hopping, for another 1.7 mi. At source of stream is a virgin stand of hemlock. Cross a saddle to old *Dismal Branch Trail,* bearing L at 3.3 mi on slope of Huckleberry Ridge. (To R is ridge of *Allegheny Trail,* also in this section.) Proceed downstream through rhododendron slicks, sometimes hiking in the middle of the creek bed. Junction with old Kelly Flats logging road, P1040, is at 5.5 mi. Turn L, cross Laurel Branch at 6.5 mi, and continue on to US Forest Service gate at 7.9 mi. Turn L to beginning of loop for 8 mi. USFS trail number 52.

Dismal Creek Area
Giles County

▼ RIBBLE TRAIL   14

Length: 2.5 mi (4 km); moderate to strenuous. *USGS Maps:* Mechanicsburg, White Gate. *Trailhead:* E of Walnut Flat Campground.

Directions and Description: From Mechanicsburg on VA 42 go 3 mi E to SR 606; take L. Go 1 mi on SR 606, pass Trent's Store on R and turn R on FR 201. Follow to Dismal Falls on L and to Walnut Flat Campground on L. There are two entrances to the trail; the first is at red-gated FR P201, and the second is 0.2 mi up the creek to *Ribble Trail* sign on L. A "Honey Spring" sign may be here. Begin here on the blue-blazed trail. Ascend generally on a steep grade following in and out of coves, crossing two streams and going through sections of rhododendron, mountain laurel, and white pine. Reach Big Horse Gap and the junction with *Appalachian Trail* on Flat Top Mtn (4,066 ft) and Honey Spring Patrol Cabin at 2.5 mi. Backtrack or, for a circuit of 9 mi, return on the *A.T.* Elevation gain, 1,566 ft. USFS trail number 62.

Brush Mountain Area
Montgomery County

▼ PANDAPAS POND TRAIL   15–16

Length: 1 mi (1.6 km); easy. *USGS Map:* Newport. *Trailhead:* Parking lot.

Directions and Description: From the ranger station on US 460 go 2.7 mi NW and turn L onto FR 808 between Brush and Sinking Creek Mtns to parking lot. Hike the lake perimeter for view of wildflowers and wildfowl. (At the far end of the lake is the *Poverty Creek Horse Trail,* which follows along the creek for 4.8 mi to SR 708, and ascends SE of the lake for 1.4 mi to FR 188–2.) USFS trail number 74.

Peters Mountain Area
**Giles County, Virginia
and Monroe County, West Virginia**

▼ ALLEGHENY TRAIL   17

Length: 12 mi (19.2 km); moderate to strenuous. *USGS Maps:* Interior, Waiteville. *Trailhead: Appalachian Trail* at Pine Swamp Gap.

Directions and Description: This segment of the *Allegheny Trail* (also spelled *Alleghany*) is currently the southern end of a longer trail system planned to extend to Pennsylvania. Access to the SW trailhead is by the *A.T.,* and the most direct route to it is from SR 635. Drive from junction of US 460 and SR 635 for 10 mi on SR 635 to Stony Creek bridge (1 mi W of Interior Picnic Area and 0.2 mi E of Day's Grocery). From small parking area go 40 yds to *A.T.* and ascend L. (To R on the *A.T.* it is 2.1 mi to footbridge over Stony Creek and SR 635 crossing.) Reach Pine Swamp Branch Shelter at 0.4 mi. Continue upstream, pass spring on L at 0.9 mi, and ascend steeply over rocky terrain and underground stream to Pine Swamp Gap at 1.7 mi. In a unique area of clear pools, hemlock, and rhododendron, turn R on yellow-blazed *Allegheny Trail.* Go 0.3 mi to Virginia–West Virginia ridge line, turn R and at 0.8 mi the footpath becomes a jeep road. Water is infrequent on this trail. Vegetation includes hardwoods such as oaks, hickory, and maple with understory of azaleas, mountain laurel, wild plum, and cherry.

Follow jeep road for 3.2 mi to junction with FR P945 on R. (The rough FR P945 descends to SR 613, which leads to SR 635 at Kire intersection.) Continue ahead along crest of ridge to West Virginia boundary at 7.8 mi.

Follow hunting roads and footpaths up and down knolls. At 11.2 mi reach a spur trail R that leads 170 yds to abandoned Hanging Rock fire tower. Here are magnificent 360° views. Return to main trail, descend to driveway of private home on L, and exit at 12 mi near gated road and Gap Mills Rd, WV highway 15 to the trailhead. Vehicle shuttle is necessary. From NE trailhead drive 3.5 mi R to WV 17 and another 0.9 mi R to Waiteville. From Waiteville on WV 17 it is 4.9 mi to Virginia state line, where the route becomes SR 635. It is another 9.6 mi ahead to the *A.T.* parking area and point of origin. USFS trail number 1000.

Clinch Ranger District

Little Stony Creek Recreation Area
Scott and Wise Counties

▼ LITTLE STONY CREEK TRAIL   18–19

Length: 2.8 mi (4.5 km); moderate. *USGS Maps:* Coeburn, Dungannon. *Trailhead:* Hanging Rock Picnic Area.

    Directions and Description: Also known as *Bear Rock Trail.* Access is from the Hanging Rock Picnic Area on FR 805; L off VA 72 2.1 mi N of Dungannon. Enter a deep gorge that features three waterfalls, two 24 ft and one 8 ft, and spectacular rock outcroppings. Vegetation includes rosebay rhododendron, oak, poplar, dwarf iris, hemlock, birch, basswood, twisted stalk, wild ginger, papaw, fedder bush, and cucumber tree. Hike on a rocky treadway, often slippery, by the creek. At 1.8 mi pass waterfall, and reach FR 701 at 2 mi. Take the road R; at

0.1 mi is *Bear Rock Trail,* with a tremendous view, leading 0.7 mi to the site of Flatwood CCC Camp. Backtrack, or use shuttle. USFS trail number 331.

▼ KITCHEN ROCK TRAIL,
BARK CAMP LAKE TRAIL   20–21

Length: 3.7 mi (6.1 km) rt, ct; easy. *USGS Maps:* Fort Blackmore, Wise. *Trailhead:* Bark Camp Lake parking lot.

Directions and Description: It is 6.2 mi from Coeburn to Bark Lake Camp. For access, drive 2.8 mi S of Coeburn on VA 72 to junction with SR 664. Turn R on SR 664, then L on FR 700, following it to FR 933. Again turn L, pass camping area and park at the picnic area near the lake. *Kitchen Rock Trail* is a 0.5-mi loop on the N side of the parking lot in a hardwood forest. *Bark Camp Lake Trail* begins at the dam; cross to a well-designed path around the lake, walking in pleasant terrain for 3.7 mi. Hemlock is frequent and fragrant, and so are beds of ferns, wintergreen, running cedar. Wood ducks are obvious; beavers have been at work on the slopes and near the marshes, particularly near the boardwalk. Fishing is for species including bass, muskellunge, and sunfish. No swimming. USFS trail 209, 211.

High Knob Recreation Area
Wise County

▼ HIGH KNOB TRAIL, HIGH KNOB LAKE
SHORE TRAIL, MOUNTAIN FORK TRAIL   22–24

Length: 7.5 mi (12 km) rt, ct; easy to moderate. *USGS Maps:* Wise, Norton. *Trailhead:* Parking area.

Directions and Description: This recreation area has camping, swimming, fishing, picnicking, and hiking. From Norton, on US 58 Alt, take SR 619 S over the railroad bridge and for 4.5 mi, ascending to junction with FR 238 on L. Turn L and follow FR 238 for 0.6 mi, passing High Knob Tower. At FR 233 turn R; the recreation area is 0.3 mi. From parking area ascend on *High Knob Trail* for 1.5 mi to panoramic views from High Knob Tower (4,162 ft). Vascular plants along the way in addition to the usual mixed forest are hawthorn, elderberry, spicebush, and jewelweed. Backtrack to parking area. 0.5 mi *High Knob Lake Shore Trail* is well designed and maintained; alder, wild hydrangea, beds of wild lily of the valley, ferns, and black cohosh add to the beauty of large stands of hemlock and rosebay rhododendron. Cross bridge below the dam in picturesque view. Here, *Mountain Fork Trail* follows downstream for 2 mi to FR 204. Backtrack or use vehicle shuttle. USFS trail numbers 401–1, 401–2, 401–3.

Stone Mountain Area
Lee and Wise Counties

▼ STONE MOUNTAIN TRAIL, OLINGER TRAIL, KEOKEE TRAIL   25–27

Length: 15 mi (24 km) ct; moderate to strenuous. *USGS Maps:* Appalachia, Big Stone Gap, Keokee. *Trailhead:* Cave Springs Recreation Area.

Directions and Description: Access to the Cave Springs Recreation Area is from junction of US 58 Alt and US 23, in Big Stone Gap. From downtown, go 4.1 mi W on US 58 Alt to SR 621 on R. Follow SR 621 along Powell River for 6.9 mi to FR 845. Go R 0.3 mi to campground entrance. Another route is from US 58 Alt at Ely. Turn on SR 767, go 1 mi to SR 621, and turn R; then go 4.4 mi and turn L on FR 845. Begin hike on *Stone Mtn Trail* from campsite #21 or from the small pond. An exceptional example of stone masonry makes this trail unique. It leads to the cave with a subterranean stream at 0.2 mi and to an overlook at 0.4 mi. Continue ascending on switchbacks on graded trail.

At 1.3 mi trail becomes steeper and may be overgrown with summer vegetation. (Rare yellow flower here, difficult to classify.) Reach ridge at 2 mi, turning R on old woods road. (*Olinger Trail* extends L from here, but the 3-mi trail of switchbacks and steep grades down to the N Fork of Powell River has not been maintained. Bushwacking would be necessary.) Continue along the ridge to site of former fire tower (2,850 ft) at 3.1 mi. Ascend and descend over knolls and reach junction with *Keokee Trail* at 6.8 mi. (The *Keokee Trail* descends L from Olinger Gap for 1 mi to Keokee Lake dam, a good fishing lake accessible from SR 623.) Continue on the Stone Mountain ridge with occasional outcroppings for scenic views toward Kentucky NW and Powell Mtns SE. At 8.8 mi begin descent into Roaring Branch Roadless Area; pass waterfalls, cascades, and old large timber to the end of the trail at US 58 Alt and US 23 for a total of 15 mi. Use vehicle shuttle or backtrack. (The parking area here is dangerous, with traffic near the trailhead at Roaring Branch cascades.) USFS trail numbers 207, 327, 402.

Pine Mountain Area
Wise and Dickenson Counties

▼ PINE MOUNTAIN TRAIL   28

Length: 22.8 mi (36.5 km); strenuous. *USGS Maps:* Jenkins E, Clintwood, Hellier, Elk Horn City. *Trailhead:* Kentucky-Virginia state line on US 23, or FR 616.

Directions and Description: Although this trail complex has segments that are exciting, challenging, and scenic for the backpacker, the complete span planned, from US 23 to Breaks Interstate Park, continues to be only a dream. It has been a dream since 1954, when a proposal was made to have a trail follow the crest of Pine Mtn and other mountain ranges all the way along the Kentucky-Virginia border to Cumberland Gap National Memorial Park. But lack of money for the purchase of private property along the route has left large segments posted. Even the open sections in the Jefferson National Forest (JNF) cannot be maintained because of the lack of funds. However, for the hiker who wishes to explore this trail, there is an entrance to a more complete section; take SR 611 from Isom to FR 616. (Isom is 3 mi N on SR 631 from junction with VA 83 in Clintwood.) At the top of the mountain the road continues NE to Jesse Gap and the site of the old fire tower. From here it is 4 mi to the JNF boundary. Beyond this point check on posted signs before continuing. Backtracking is necessary. USFS trail number 201 (plus four spur trails).

The Clinch Ranger District monitors the trails in the Fork Pound Lake area W of US 23.

Glenwood Ranger District

James River Face Wilderness Area
Rockbridge County

The James River Face Wilderness is named for the steep and high slopes on the S side of the James River with elevations ranging from 650 ft to 3,073 ft at Highcock Knob. Wildlife includes bear, deer, grouse, rattlesnake, turkey, raccoon, and gray squirrel. The Wilderness is the northern range limit of the Carolina hemlock and the southern range limit of the paper birch. Wildflowers are abundant.

▼ BALCONY FALLS TRAIL,
   SULPHUR SPRING TRAIL   29–30

Length: 10.7 mi (17.1 km) ct; strenuous. *USGS Map:* Snowden. *Trailhead:* either at the end of SR 782 or from gated road on FR 35.

   Directions and Description: From junction of VA 130 and SR 759 near Natural Bridge Station, take SR 759 for 0.9 mi, turn E on paved SR 782, pass to James River Recreation Area, and continue straight on gravel road to FR 3093 for 1.5 mi; park. Follow switchbacks through hardwoods and pines, reach James River Face Wilderness at 2.3 mi for scenic views of the town of Glasgow and the James River Gorge. *Balcony Falls Trail* ends at junction with old fire road at 4.1 mi, and *Sulphur Spring Trail* begins. Elevation gain to this point, 1,450 ft.

   Continue ahead on old road, ascending. Cross *Appalachian Trail* at 5.5 mi, excellent views of the James River Gorge at 5.7 mi on easy grade, and reach junction with

Piney Ridge Trail on L at 7.6 mi. Continuing on Sulphur Spring Trail, cross the *A.T.* again at 7.8 mi, and descend into Sulphur Spring Hollow. Pass Sulphur Spring on R at 10.4 mi; reach the gate at FR 35 at 10.7 mi.

(If using vehicle shuttle, reach in advance the gated road ending the route by driving on SR 759 from VA 130 junction for 3.2 mi, then turn E on SR 781, which becomes FR 35, for another 3.2 mi. Gated road and parking is on L.) Total elevation change, 1,175 ft. USFS trail numbers 7, 3001.

▼ BELFAST TRAIL   31

Length: 5.6 mi (9 km) rt; strenuous. *USGS Map:* Snowden. *Trailhead:* Parking area on Elk Creek.

Directions and Description: At junction of VA 130 and SR 759 take SR 759 for 3.2 mi and turn L on SR 781. Go 1.5 mi on SR 781 to parking area near footbridge across Elk Creek. Hike across footbridge and ascend to Devil's Marbleyard, a large outcropping of loose boulders, on L at 1.4 mi. Pass ridge crest at 2 mi and the junction with *Gunter Ridge Trail* at 2.4 mi. At 2.8 mi is junction with *Appalachian Trail.* Backtrack or use the 4.6-mi *Gunter Ridge Trail* as a loop to SR 759 for vehicle shuttle. (Another loop is via the *A.T.* SW for 3.5 mi to Petites Gap; then descend 4.2 mi on FR 35 to the parking area for a combined 10.5 mi.) Elevation gain to *A.T.* junction, 1,650 ft. USFS trail number 9.

▼ GUNTER RIDGE TRAIL   32

Length: 9.2 mi (14.7 km) rt; strenuous. *USGS Maps:* Snowden, Arnold Valley. *Trailhead:* Parking area.

Piney Ridge Trail, James River Face Wilderness.
JNF/Allen de Hart.

Directions and Description: At junction of VA 130 and SR 759 take SR 759 for 1.5 mi to unpaved road on L after passing bridge over Elk Creek. Park near SR 759 or go 1.2 mi to the end of the road. Hike up blue-blazed, seldom used trail with switchbacks through a mixed forest with blueberry and mountain laurel understory. Skirt S of a knob and reach junction with *Belfast Trail* at 4.6 mi. Backtrack or use the *Belfast Trail* for vehicle shuttle. Elevation change 1,700 ft. USFS trail number 8.

▼ PINEY RIDGE TRAIL   33

Length: 7 mi (11.2 km) rt; strenuous. *USGS Map:* Snowden. *Trailhead:* On FR 54.

Directions and Description: From Blue Ridge Pkwy at US 501 go W on US 501 for 0.6 mi to FR 54; turn L. Road appears to be a private residence driveway. Go 0.6 mi, passing the Big Island Hunt and Fish Club, and park near entrance to trail on R. Trail sign is by yucca and Virginia pine. Follow up Piney Ridge, entering the James River Face Wilderness at 1.7 mi. Reach junction with *Sulphur Spring Trail* near the *Appalachian Trail* at 3.5 mi. Either return by same route or hike one of the other trails in the James River Face for vehicle shuttle. Elevation gain, 1,550 ft. USFS trail number 2.

Middle Creek and North Creek Areas
Botetourt County

▼ APPLE ORCHARD FALLS TRAIL/WEST   34

Length: 3.4 mi (5.4 km) rt; strenuous; *USGS Map:* Arnold Valley. *Trailhead:* End of FR 59.

Directions and Description: From I-81, N of Buchanan, take exit 48 E onto SR 614 and go to FR 59, which leads to North Creek Camp. Pass the camp and continue ahead on FR 59 to gate after 7.5 mi from I-81. Park here and begin hike past the gate on the road for 0.3 mi. Follow the trail sign off the road, ascend steeply in sections of the slope and cross the stream occasionally. At 1.7 mi reach the spectacular 200-ft Apple Orchard Falls. Backtrack, or continue steep climb for another 1.2 mi to Sunset Field Overlook at mp 78.7 on the BRP. USFS trail number 17. (See *Apple Orchard Falls Trail/East* under trails of the Blue Ridge Parkway.)

▼ CORNELIUS TRAIL   35

Length: 5.8 mi (9.3 km) rt; strenuous. *USGS Map:* Arnold Valley. *Trailhead:* End of FR 59.

Directions and Description: From I-81 as described above for the *Apple Orchard Falls Trail/West,* park near the FR 59 gate. Follow sign up W side of Backbone Ridge L of Cornelius Creek on old logging roads, making a sharp turn L over Backbone Ridge to ascend to the *A.T.* at 2.9 mi. Backtrack, or continue steep climb for another 1.3 mi to junction with *Apple Orchard Falls Trail/East* and to Sunset Field Overlook at mp 78.7 on the BRP. USFS trail number 18.

▼ BUCHANAN TRAIL,
COVE MOUNTAIN TRAIL   36-37

Length: 3.4 mi (5.4 km) rt; easy. *USGS Maps:* Arnold Valley, Buchanan. *Trailhead:* Private road off VA 43 near Buchanan and Arcadia.

Directions and Description: These two trails are lead-ins to the *Appalachian Trail.* For the *Buchanan Trail* go E on VA 43 for 1.2 mi, turn L on unnumbered private road, and after 1 mi watch for trail sign on R. Follow trail 1.6 mi to *Appalachian Trail.* For *Cove Mtn Trail* take I-81 exit 48, follow SR 614 to Arcadia, turn R on SR 622 to Arcadia Store, and park. Go 0.1 mi and turn L on trail, following old logging road to *A.T.* at 1.8 mi. USFS trail numbers 24, 23.

▼ LITTLE COVE MOUNTAIN TRAIL   38

Length: 2.8 mi (4.5 km); moderate. *USGS Maps:* Buchanan, Montvale. *Trailhead:* Footbridge at Jennings Creek.

Directions and Description: From I-81 exit 48 take SR 614 through Arcadia, past junction with N Creek Rd. Go 0.5 mi farther, past junction with Middle Creek Rd, and look for trail sign on R; park. Cross creek on footbridge; cross again a number of times before ascending to top of ridge at 1 mi. Reach *Appalachian Trail* at 2.8 mi. Back-track or turn R on *A.T.* and make a circuit to SR 614 and turn R to parking area. (Or, continue for 1.5 mi on the *A.T.* to Bearwallow Gap, junction of VA 43 and BRP, and use vehicle shuttle.) USFS trail number 25.

▼ WILDCAT MOUNTAIN TRAIL   39

Length: 3.8 (6.1 km); strenuous. *USGS Map:* Arnold Valley. *Trailhead:* Cove Mtn Campground.

Directions and Description: A loop trail developed principally for use of campers at Cove Mtn Lake. Terrain is rough and may be difficult to follow in summer vegetation—including nettles. Access is on SR 759, from VA 130 near Natural Bridge Station, to SR 781 R at Elk Creek and FR 780 near junction of SR 781 and SR 812. Go to the S end of Cove Mtn Lake on FR 780 and look for sign. USFS trail number 326.

Other Trails Off the Blue Ridge Parkway
Bedford and Botetourt Counties

▼ CURRY CREEK TRAIL   40

Length: 6.2 mi (9.9 km) rt; moderate to strenuous. *USGS Map:* Villamont. *Trailhead:* Blue Ridge Pkwy mp 101.5.

Directions and Description: A seldom used trail beginning at BRP mp 101.5. Ascend FR 191 for 0.7 mi to crossing of *Appalachian Trail.* Turn R on *A.T.* and reach Curry Creek at 1.5 mi. Turn L, and follow bank of creek down the mountain to private land at 3.1 mi. Backtrack. USFS trail number 20.

▼ HAMMOND HOLLOW TRAIL   41

Length: 2 mi (3.2 km); moderate. *USGS Map:* Montvale. *Trailhead:* SR 645 in Hanging Rock Hollow.

Directions and Description: On SR 640 along Back Creek between Buchanan and Troutville turn off SR 640 onto SR 645 and go 2 mi; look for trail sign and park. Ascend to *Appalachian Trail* at 2 mi. Another 0.7 mi N is Bobblets Gap on the Blue Ridge Pkwy. USFS trail number 27.

▼ HUNTING CREEK TRAIL   42–43

Length: 3.5 mi (5.6 km); moderate. *USGS Map:* Snowden. *Trailhead: Appalachian Trail* near Thunder Ridge Overlook.

   Directions and Description: (The only recommended foot trail on the E side of the Blue Ridge Pkwy in this district.) Begin where the *A.T.* crosses the BRP 0.5 mi S of Thunder Ridge Overlook. Follow the *A.T.* S 100 yds to trail on L. Descend to stream; at 1.2 mi is junction with FR 45 (to R FR 45 leads to *Terrapin Mtn Trail*). Continue L on FR 45 to SR 602 at 3.5 mi. SR 602 leads 1.5 mi to VA 122, 3 mi S of Big Island and US 501. Backtrack or use vehicle shuttle. USFS trail number 3.

▼ SPEC MINES TRAIL   44

   Length: 2.8 mi (4.5 km); strenuous. *USGS Maps:* Villamont, Montvale. *Trailhead:* Near junction of SR 640 and SR 645.

   Directions and Description: From W end of the town of Buchanan at junction of US 11 and SR 640 take SR 640 for 4.5 mi through Lithia and junction with SR 645 on L. Follow SR 645 for 0.5 mi to trailhead on R, and park. Ascend steeply for 2.8 mi to *A.T.* and to BRP 200 yds S of Montvale Overlook at mp 95.9. Scenic views of James River and Purgatory Mtn. Elevation gain 1,380 ft. Backtrack or use vehicle shuttle. USFS trail number 28.

North Mountain Area
Rockbridge County

▼ BLACKS CREEK TRAIL   45–46

   Length: 3 mi (4.8 km) rt; strenuous. *USGS Map:* Collierstown. *Trailhead:* End of SR 655.

Directions and Description: In S Lexington take VA 251 at junction with US 11, Main St, and go 10 mi to Collierstown. Turn L on SR 770 and go 0.4 mi to junction with SR 655, and follow it for 5.2 mi to end of road. A remote, rarely used and rugged trail, it follows an old fire road past gate. It ascends through hemlock, locust, and oaks from Blacks Creek to Blacks Gap on the ridge for a junction with *North Mountain Trail* at 1.5 mi. Backtrack. Alternatively, hike 5 mi on *N Mtn Trail* to FR 3081. USFS trail number 4.

Mount Rogers National Recreation Area

Stretching across Virginia's highest and most spectacular land masses is an enormous corridor 55 mi long and 5 to 10 mi wide, from W of Damascus E to the New River. It is the Mt Rogers National Recreation Area (Mt Rogers NRA), the finest section of the national forests in the state. Its scenic beauty and opportunities for varied recreation prompted Congress to designate this sleeping giant an NRA in 1966. Since that time 109,373 acres have been acquired, six campgrounds (including Raven Cliff on Cripple Creek, which opened in 1983) have been constructed, numerous new trails opened, and a master plan written. How intensively the area should be developed remains a question. Solitude is easy to find in this NRA. That, plus the natural quality and the 300 mi of trails, should place this area at the top of the list for Virginia's hikers and backpackers.

The NRA's habitat for wildlife varies widely. At least 156 species of birds have been sighted; such a large variety is due chiefly to the 4,000-ft elevation change.

The range of levels supports growth ranging from young succession to climax forests, from light understory to heath balds, and from hardwood stands at low elevations to magnificent Canadian spruce-fir on the crest zone. One estimate places the number of vascular plant species in this massive botanical garden at 325. The list of mammals includes bear, deer, fox, bobcat, raccoon, red squirrel, woodchuck, and the one seen most often— the chipmunk.

Although the Mt Rogers NRA's features are particularly scenic throughout, what sets it apart from many of the other Virginia mountain areas most significantly is the crest zone. This zone frames White Top Mtn (5,530 ft) in the W, Mt Rogers (5,729 ft) in the center, and the three peaks of Pine Mtn (4,859 ft) in the E with extensive mountain balds, dense red spruce and Fraser fir, dazzling displays of purple rhododendron, and matchless views from rocky crags. The weather is typically cool and moist; but it can change suddenly, a dangerous risk for hikers unprepared or inexperienced.

Because the NRA is so vast and honeycombed with trails and roads, for convenience in this guidebook it is divided into four areas. By narrowing trail selection to an appropriate area, as well as making a visit to the NRA headquarters on VA 16 near Sugar Grove for map brochures and trail-change updates, hikers and backpackers should be able to find trails to suit their desires.

In 1982 the NRA had 68 mi of the *Appalachian Trail,* 40 mi of the *Iron Mtn Trail,* 70 mi of the *Virginia Highlands Horse Trail* (plus 40 mi of other horse trails), and 162 mi of hiking trails on which some sections are also multi-purpose, for cross-country skiing or off-road vehicles. Some miles of trail are inventoried only on the NRA printout; being unmarked, overgrown, or unmaintained excludes trails from coverage in this guidebook. (Horses can be rented at the Fairwood Livery, Rte 1, Box 340, Sugar Grove, VA 24375; tel: 703-677-3688. It is located on SR 603, 2.8 mi W of Troutdale.) The NRA headquarters address is Rte 1, Box 303, Marion, VA 24354; tel: 703-783-5196, or (for emergencies) 703-783-7204.

Iron Mountain South Area
Washington and Smyth Counties

The Iron Mtn S area of the Mt Rogers NRA includes the SW range from Damascus, US 58, NE to Skulls Gap, VA 600. Base camp is the Beartree Recreation Area off US 58 on FR 837 at Bear Tree Gap, 3 mi W from the US 58 and SR 603 junction. It has 113 campsites, rest rooms, warm showers, fishing, and picnicking. (A new family campground is under development.) Open May through September.

▼ LUM MARTIN TRAIL, STRAIGHT BRANCH TRAIL, IRON MOUNTAIN TRAIL, FEATHERCAMP BRANCH TRAIL, BEECH GROVE TRAIL, SHAW GAP TRAIL   47–57

Length: 21.8 mi (34.9 km) rt, ct; moderate to strenuous. *USGS Maps:* Damascus, Konnarock. *Trailhead:* Near first rest room after Chipmunk Circle gate.

  Directions and Description: From US 58 take FR 837 3.8 mi to Chipmunk Circle and entrance to Beartree Campground, FR 837-A. (This point begins a counterclockwise circuit trail grouping. Another route begins at the entrance of gated FR 403 on *Straight Branch Trail,* near gate of Chipmunk Circle. This trail follows road for 1.5 mi to SR 600. Stand of wild orchids at second shale gravel pit. Hemlocks, oaks, wildlife. A turn L on SR 600 for 1 mi leads to *Iron Mtn Trail* at Skulls Gap; follow the trail 1.5 mi L to Straight Branch Shelter for a total of 4 mi to this point.)

Begin hiking NE on the purple-blazed *Lum Martin Trail,* found R of first restroom after entering gate at Chipmunk Circle, and follow up Straight Branch Creek for 1.1 mi through rhododendron and black birch to *Iron Mtn Trail* junction. (*Iron Mtn Trail* was formerly a section of the *Appalachian Trail* but is now a yellow-blazed trail-road used by equestrians and in some sections by motorbikers.) Turn L here near Straight Branch Shelter. (*Iron Mtn Trail* R goes 0.8 mi to SR 600 and another 0.7 mi to Skulls Gap.) Follow contour to ridge crest of woods road and Grosses Mtn with views of Mt Rogers and White Top to SE. At 4.3 mi descend to cleared Shaw Gap and junction with *Chestnut Ridge Trail,* R (which goes 1.8 mi to FR 615, joining the *Little Mtn Trail,* and 2.5 mi farther reaches SR 730), and *Shaw Gap Trail,* L (which descends 1.6 mi to FR 837 and Beartree Group-Tent Campground at FR 837-D).

Continue ahead on *Iron Mtn Trail* to grassy summit with panoramic view at 4.7 mi. Reach junction with FR 90 at 5.9 mi. (L on FR 90 leads 1.3 mi to US 58, and then R on FR 90 ascends 1.4 mi to Feathercamp Lookout Tower; *Rush Trail* is R for a loop of 1.5 mi.) At 6.1 mi reach spring and Sandy Flats Shelter. Cross Feathercamp Branch and junction with blue-blazed *Feathercamp Branch Trail* on L. (On *Feathercamp Branch Trail* it is 2.5 mi to US 58.) Skirt S slope of Feathercamp Lookout; but a 0.2-mi spur, *Feathercamp Ridge Trail,* on R, leads up to the lookout. (Slightly beyond this point is *Wright Trail,* ascending R to junction with *Creasy Hollow Trail.* On *Wright Trail* it is 3.4 mi to SR 605 along Buzzard Den Branch, and on *Creasy Hollow Trail* it is 3.5 mi on R fork to FR 287 and on to SR 605.) Continue ahead, descending gradually to pass *Beech Grove Trail* on R at 9.5 mi. (*Beech Grove Trail,* for motorcycles, goes R for 2.4 mi to SR 605, and to the L it goes S 1 mi, crossing the *A.T.* 0.3 mi from US 58.) Ascending, continue ahead to 10.8 mi and junction with the *A.T.*

Turn L on the *A.T.* and descend on graded trail for 2 mi to junction with the blue-blazed *Feathercamp Branch Trail.* Turn L on *Feathercamp Branch Trail* at 12.8 mi. (*A.T.* turns R for 0.1 mi to US 58 at parking and picnic area.) Follow along the Feathercamp Branch for 2.5 mi to Sandy Flats Shelter and rejoin the *Iron Mtn Trail* at 15.3 mi. Turn R, returning on the *Iron Mtn Trail* to Shaw gap at 17.5 mi. Here, turn R on *Shaw Gap Trail* for 1.6 mi to Beartree Group-Tent Campground and Recreation Area and FR 837 at 19.1 mi. Turn L on FR 837 and hike up the road to the circuit origin for a total of 21.4 mi. Or, continue to backtrack on the *Iron Mtn Trail* to *Lum Martin Trail* at 20.7 mi, turn R, and return on the *Lum Martin Trail* to origin at 21.8 mi. USFS trail numbers, in order of description, are 4544, 301-6, 4542, 4543, 4547, 4565, 4550, 4548, 4546, 4553, 169.

▼ BEARTREE GAP TRAIL, APPALACHIAN TRAIL, VIRGINIA CREEPER TRAIL, FEATHERCAMP TRAIL, IRON MOUNTAIN TRAIL, SHAW GAP TRAIL   58–59

Length: 14.9 mi (23.8 km) ct; easy to strenuous. *USGS Maps:* Damascus, Konnarock. *Trailhead:* Beartree Group-Tent Campground on FR 837-D.

Directions and Description: This is a clockwise circuit hike that includes parts of the trails described in the preceding entry and also includes the scenic N&W RR grade. From Beartree Group-Tent Campground on FR 837-D parking area, hike FR 837 SW for 0.5 mi to Beach Picnic Area by the lake. Follow the lakeside L by the Group Picnic Area, pass dam, and reach US 58 at 0.9 mi. (Or, take the lakeside R by a beaver dam to the lake dam, cross, and reach US 58 on purple-blazed *Beartree Gap Trail* at 1 mi.) Follow *Beartree Gap Trail,* here blue-blazed, for 0.3 mi to the *A.T.* Turn L on the *A.T.* in grassy field. (The *A.T.* goes R 4.3 mi to Feathercamp parking area on US 58.) Follow the *A.T.* for 1.8 mi L to old railroad grade and junction with the *Virginia Creeper Trail* for a total of 3 mi from origin of this hike. (Upstream, L 0.5 mi, is the scenic, 550-ft Whitetop–Laurel Creek N&W RR trestle.) Follow new trail R, downstream through hardwood, hemlock, and rosebay rhododendron to the community of Taylor Valley at 6.7 mi.

Make a horseshoe curve, returning to the *A.T.* at 7.2 mi. Follow the *A.T.* through the Whitetop–Laurel Creek Gorge, reaching US 58 at 9.3 mi. Cross US 58 to Feathercamp parking area, take blue-blazed *Feathercamp Trail,* and reach the Sandy Flats Shelter at 11.8 mi. Here, take the yellow-blazed *Iron Mtn Trail* on R, cross FR 90, and follow to Shaw Gap at 13.3 mi. Turn R on *Shaw Gap Trail* for 1.6 mi, and reach the campground for a total of 14.9 mi. (An additional easy-to-moderate circuit in this section is to follow the route as above—or from the Fisherman's Parking Area by the lake dam—to the *Virginia Creeper Trail.* After reaching the *A.T.* junction from the *Virginia Creeper Trail* at 7 mi, turn R and return on the *A.T.* to the *Beartree Gap Trail* and L to the lake for a total of 11.8 mi.) USFS trail numbers 4551, 1, (*Virginia Creeper Trail* not numbered), 169, 301–6, 4547.

Iron Mountain Central Area
Grayson and Smyth Counties

Trail connections in the Iron Mtn Central area of the Mt Rogers NRA do not make good circuits unless forest roads and the *Appalachian Trail* are used. Hurricane and Raccoon Branch campgrounds can be used as base camps. Access to Hurricane Campground is from VA 16 2.3 mi N of Troutdale to SR 650. On SR 650 go 1.5 mi to FR 84, turn L and go 0.3 mi to campground entrance. It has 29 campsites, rest rooms, warm showers, picnicking, trout fishing, and nature study. The *Hurricane Knob Nature Trail* is a scenic 1-mi loop within the campground. Access is across the road from the bulletin board at the L side of the rest rooms, or in a stand of maples and witchhazel by a large white pine near site #5. The campground is usually open from April to September 15. The Raccoon Branch campground is on VA 16, 2.3 mi S of Sugar Grove. It has 20 campsites, rest rooms, no showers, offers trout fishing, and is open all year.

▼ DICKEY GAP TRAIL, APPALACHIAN TRAIL, IRON MOUNTAIN TRAIL, VIRGINIA HIGHLANDS HORSE TRAIL   60–64

Length: 12.4 mi (19.8 km) rt, ct; moderate. *USGS Maps:* Troutdale, Whitetop Mtn. *Trailhead:* Hurricane Campground.

Directions and Description: From Hurricane Campground entrance, at junction of FR 84 bridge (confluence

of Comers Creek and Hurricane Creek), take the blue-
blazed *Dickey Gap Trail* through hemlock, birch, maple,
and rhododendron for 0.5 mi to junction with *A.T.* Turn
R and follow *A.T.* At 2.5 mi cross stream and at 3 mi turn
L onto jeep road. (Unblazed *Hurricane Creek Trail*
extends R for 0.6 mi to junction with Hurricane Creek
Rd, FR 84; after another 2.2 mi R on FR 84, reach campground for a loop of 5.7 mi.) After another 1.3 mi on
jeep road, turn R and ascend to ridge with gentle contour
in hardwood forest. Junction with yellow-blazed Iron
Mtn Trail at 4.6 mi in Chestnut Flats. (The *Iron Mtn
Trail,* which was once the *A.T.*, goes 17.4 mi from this
point to within 3.5 mi of the town of Damascus and
rejoins the currently designated *A.T.*) (The current *A.T.*
turns L at Chestnut Flats and descends 2.3 mi to paved
SR 603.) From Chestnut Flats follow the *Iron Mtn Trail*
to the crest of Flat Top Mtn (4,451 ft) at 5.6 mi; descend
to dirt road, turn R and after 0.1 mi turn L into forest. At
6.6 mi reach FR 828. (Cherry Tree Shelter and spring are
ahead at 0.3 mi on the *Iron Mtn Trail.* A blue-blazed trail
and FR 828 descends L for 3.2 mi to SR 603 and to
Grindstone Campground.) At this point leave the *Iron
Mtn Trail,* take a R on FR 828, the *Virginia Highlands
Horse Trail,* for continuing the loop back to Hurricane
Campground. After 1.8 mi reach Hurricane Gap and
junction with FR 84. After another 4 mi on FR 84, return
to entrance of Hurricane Campground for a total circuit
of 12.4 mi. USFS trail numbers 4518, 1, 301–5, 337.

Another moderate, short loop is to follow the *Dickey
Gap Trail* as described above to the *A.T.* But take the L
this time, passing Comers Creek cascades at 1.5 mi.
Enter thicket areas of rhododendron and then a stand of
open hardwoods. Reach VA 16 junction with SR 650 at

2.7 mi. Cross road and, after 0.8 mi on the *A.T.*, reach junction with *Virginia Highlands Horse Trail.* Turn L, following the horse trail for 2 mi to SR 650. Turn L on SR 650 for 0.1 mi to FR 84. Turn R and go 0.3 mi to entrance of campground for a total of 5.9 mi.

For a forest roadway circuit that's particularly scenic when in fall colors, begin downstream on unmarked *Comers Creek Trail* in the campground. Tall trees, mosses, ferns, and wildflowers make this an excellent nature study route. At junction with FR 643 after 1.2 mi, turn L, away from the creek. Follow gravel road around Bear Ridge for 2.3 mi to Barton Branch. Go upstream for 1 mi to junction with FR 870. Turn L on FR 870, go 1.8 mi between Seng Mtn and Bear Ridge to FR 84. Turn L again, and after 2 mi return to the campground for a total of 8.3 mi. USFS trail number 4526.

▼ DICKEY KNOB TRAIL,
RACCOON BRANCH TRAIL, APPALACHIAN TRAIL,
MULLINS BRANCH TRAIL   65–67

Length: 19.2 mi (30.7 km) rt, ct; moderate to strenuous. *USGS Map:* Atkins, Troutdale. *Trailhead:* Raccoon Branch Campground.

Directions and Description: At Raccoon Branch Campground, the *Dickey Knob Trail* and the *Raccoon Branch Trail* begin near campsite #4 and cross a sturdy wooden footbridge at the confluence of Dickey Creek and Raccoon Branch. Turn R to hike the 4-mi, round-trip *Dickey Knob Trail.* Back at the confluence again, this time take the L, proceeding upstream on Raccoon Branch for the circuit that's possible by taking the 3.3-mi *Raccoon Branch Trail* to the *A.T.*, and shelter. After reaching the *A.T.*, either backtrack or make the 8.5-mi loop from here on the *A.T.* to SR 672, with a return on the *Mullins Branch Trail*. For this loop, walk 0.8 mi on the *A.T.* to junction with *Mullins Branch Trail*. Continue L on *A.T.* for 1.7 mi to Trimpi Shelter. Reach SR 672 at another 1.4 mi. Turn R on SR 672, a gravel road, go 1.6 mi to R, and turn on former *A.T.*, the partly private *Mullins Branch Trail*. Follow upstream back to the *A.T.* for 2.4 mi. At 11.9 mi reach *Raccoon Branch Trail* for return to Raccoon Campground. Total route is 4 mi for first loop plus 15.2 for second; total, 19.2 mi. USFS trail numbers 346, 337, 1, 4513.

Iron Mountain North Area
Smyth, Grayson, Wythe, and Carroll Counties

The major trails in the Iron Mtn N area of the Mt Rogers NRA are the 40-mi *Virginia Highlands Horse Trail* and the 26.5-mi stretch of the *Iron Mtn Trail*. Use of these two trails and the other 10 short trails is less frequent than that of trails in the other areas of the NRA. The only campground now open is Comers Rock, with nine camp-sites, pit toilet, and limited picnic area, but by the time this book is published the new Raven Cliff Campground on Cripple Creek in Wythe County will be open. Al-though the tree is rare even here, this area has the few existing specimens of the round-leaf birch, an endan-gered species known no where else in the world. The species is protected by both state and federal law.

Long portions of the *Iron Mtn Trail* are overgrown in this segment, not maintained or marked; and parts re-main on private land. However the *Henley Hollow Trail*, extending from US 21, and the *Perkins Knob Trail*, from

US 21 and connecting the *Virginia Highlands Horse Trail* and the *Horse Heaven Trail,* have been maintained. A base camping area is Comers Rock Campground.

Access: From US 21, near the Wythe-Grayson county line, turn onto FR 57 and go W 3.5 mi to the campground. Open all year. The 1-mi *Unaka Nature Trail* begins R facing the picnic shelter and forms a loop through an extraordinary range of botanical species.

▼ IRON MOUNTAIN TRAIL,
HALE LAKE TRAIL   68–74

Length: 6.4 mi (10.2 km) rt, ct; moderate. *USGS Maps:* Speedwell, Cedar Springs. *Trailhead:* Campsite #7.

Directions and Description: Begin at campsite #7 and go 100 yds to the sign at the *Iron Mtn Trail.* Turn L on the Comers Rock Overlook spur trail. (Trail on R descends slope of mountain to West Fork of Dry Run and junction with the *Virginia Highlands Horse Trail* at 1.2 mi.) After 0.5 mi reach the panoramic views of Iron Mtn Range, Point Lookout Mtn, and Comers Rock Valley. Thick understory of striped maple and witchhazel are on the trail. Backtrack to the trail junction near the campsite and take a L turn on the *Iron Mtn Trail.* Hike through oaks, white pines, hemlock, and rhododendron for 2.2 mi. Cross FR 57-B and descend to Hale Lake at 2.5 mi. Circle the lake on *Hale Lake Trail* for 0.4 mi through pines, black gum, and tall sweetpepper bushes. (Former trails connecting at the lake have become overgrown.) Backtrack for a total of 6.4 mi, or have vehicle shuttle at parking area near dam on FR 57. USFS trail numbers 301–2, 342.

A circuit could be made from taking the R fork at the campground 1.2 mi to the *Virginia Highlands Horse*

Trail. Proceed R on old wagon road for 3 mi to US 21. From there take R, hike 1.2 mi on US 21 to FR 57, take R again, and hike the road back to camp for a total of 9 mi. A longer route would include the above, except, at the junction with the *Virginia Highlands Horse Trail* at the West Fork of Dry Run, take the *Little Dry Run Trail* for 3 mi to US 21. Cross the highway and enter *Henley Hollow Trail.* Ascend for 1.4 mi to *Horse Heaven Trail.* Take L, go 2 mi, turn R on FR 4009, go 1.3 mi to gate, cross FR 14, and take *Divide Trail* for 1 mi to junction with *Iron Mtn Trail.* Take R, and, after 3 mi, exit at Dry Run Gap on US 21 across the road from FR 57. Follow FR 57 for 3.5 mi back to camp. Total circuit is 16.4 mi. USFS trail numbers 337, 305, 306, 307, 309, 301–1.

*White Top Mountain, Mount Rogers, and
Pine Mountain Area*
Smyth and Grayson Counties

A number of excellent circuit trails can be made in this area of the Mt Rogers NRA, using the *Appalachian Trail* and trails in the adjoining Grayson Highlands State Park. Circuits can also be made with the trails of Iron Mt Central area of this section. Base camp is Grindstone on SR 603, 6.3 mi W of Troutdale. It has 108 campsites, rest rooms, and warm showers, and it is open May through December. A 0.5-mi interpretive trail, *Whispering Water Trail*, is on the SW corner of the campground 0.3 mi from entrance.

▼ MOUNT ROGERS NATIONAL
   RECREATION TRAIL   75–81

Length: 4 mi (6.4 km); strenuous. *USGS Map:* White Top. *Trailhead:* Grindstone Campground.

Mount Rogers National Recreation Area.
JNF/National Forest Service.

Directions and Description: Designated a national recreation trail in 1979, this trail has a 1,400-ft elevation gain from the Grindstone Campground to Deep Gap on the *Appalachian Trail.* Begin on the blue-blazed trail from the campground and go 0.3 mi to junction. Turn R on blue-blazed *Mt Rogers Trail.* (L is 0.2 mi to SR 603.) Ascend on switchbacks for 1.1 mi, and reach the top of Broad Ridge, along the Smyth and Grayson county line, at 2.3 mi. Junction of gray-blazed *Lewis Fork Trail* is L. (The *Lewis Fork Trail* descends downstream for 3.5 mi to SR 603. Along the way it has junctions with blue-blazed *Cliffside Trail* and other connecting trails E to both the

Virginia Highlands Horse Trail and the *A.T.*) Continue to ascend, passing a large outcrop, and enter a spruce and yellow-birch stand at 3.3 mi. At 3.8 mi begin gradual descent to the *A.T.* junction at 4 mi. (R is Deep Gap Shelter on part of *A.T.* leading to Elk Garden and SR 600.) To reach the summit of Mt Rogers turn L on the *A.T.* and descend to open meadow at 4.9 mi. Continue through Fraser fir to trail junction at 6 mi. Turn L on blue-blazed summit trail and go 0.4 mi to Virginia's highest mountain (5,729 ft). Dense forest here prevents panoramic views. Backtrack for 6.5 mi, or take a circuit ahead on the *A.T.* (See circuit-route description following.) USFS trail numbers 166, 4533–3, 4533–2.

A 19.2-mi circuit backpacking hike can be made, first following the preceding directions from Grindstone Campground to summit of Mt Rogers. Instead of back-tracking, continue ahead on the white-blazed *A.T.* for 1.5 mi to scenic Rhododendron Gap at 7 mi. At junction here take blue-blazed trail L (not to be confused with the blue-blazed *Rhododendron Trail* ahead to the Grayson Highlands State Park) along meadows and rocky knolls of Pine Mtn on the *Pine Mtn Trail* to rejoin the *A.T.* at 8.9 mi. (For a longer circuit, the hike on the *A.T.* could be continued R at Rhododendron Gap, descending into scenic Grayson Highlands, crossing Wilson Creek and Pine Mtn meadows for 6.6 mi extra to junction previously mentioned.) Turn L onto *A.T.*, and descend by switchbacks to Old Orchard Shelter at 10.8 mi. Continue descent to SR 603 and parking area at 14 mi. Here, the circuit can be completed by returning on SR 603 for 2 mi L to Grindstone Campground at 16.2 mi. Or, remaining on the *A.T.*, complete circuit by ascending to *Iron Mtn Trail* at 16 mi. Turn L on yellow-blazed *Iron Mtn Trail*, following gradual contour for 2.5 mi to the point called Flat Top on FR 828. Turn L on blue-blazed trail and descend to SR 603, across from Grindstone, for a total of 19.6 mi. (See Grayson Highlands State Park in Chapter 12 for more connecting circuit trails.)

Another circuit from Grindstone is to follow directions given for 4 mi to the *A.T.* and turn R (SW). After 0.2 mi reach Deep Gap Shelter (4,900 ft), with a spring, and reach paved SR 600 and parking area another 1.9 mi farther. Turn R on SR 600 and descend for 1 mi to junction on R for *Grassy Branch Trail.* Continue descent on old railroad bed—an excellent cross-country ski route in winter and wildflower display route in spring—for 3 mi, to SR 603. From here go R 0.9 mi on paved SR 603 to Grindstone Campground entrance. Circuit total is 11 mi. USFS trail number 4535.

▼ SUGAR MAPLE LOOP TRAIL,
HELTON CREEK LOOP TRAIL   82–83

Length: 8.5 mi (13.6 km) rt, ct; moderate. *USGS Map:* Whitetop Mtn. *Trailhead:* End of SR 783.

Directions and Description: From US 58, 6 mi W of Grayson Highland State Park, turn on SR 783 (1.5 mi E of SR 600) and go 1.5 mi to where road becomes FR 4032. Park in meadow where camping is allowed. Begin on purple-blazed *Sugar Maple Loop Trail* on R at first gate near old cement water trough; ascend and pass sites of old houses. At 0.3 mi turn R through fields, passing another gate, and at 0.8 mi enter woods. Ascend on switchbacks to contour grade.

Reach junction with *Helton Creek Loop Trail* at 2.3 mi. Option here to complete only *Sugar Maple Loop*

Trail, for 4.5 mi, by bearing L, or, continuing R for another 4 mi, to include the *Helton Creek Loop Trail.* If the latter, continue on gentle grade of old tram road for 1.1 mi to *Virginia Highlands Horse Trail* beyond the headwaters of Helton Creek. Follow horse trail to junction L in field, and begin descent to Helton Creek on old logging road. Rejoin the *Sugar Maple Loop,* and continue ahead on road to origin of trail at end of SR 783 at 8.5 mi. *Helton Creek Loop Trail* is open for hiking, horseback riding, and cross-country skiing. USFS trail numbers 4538, 4572.

New Castle Ranger District

Roaring Run Area
Botetourt County

▼ ROARING RUN TRAIL, IRON ORE TRAIL,
HOOP HOLE TRAIL   84–86

Length: 12.8 mi (20.5 km) ct; easy to strenuous. *USGS Map:* Strom. *Trailhead:* Either at Roaring Run Furnace Picnic Area or the parking lot at Stoney Run.

Directions and Description: Access to this desirable area is from junction of US 220 and SR 615 at Eagle Rock on the James River. Take SR 615 NW along Craig Creek for 6 mi to SR 621. Proceed R on SR 621 for 0.9 mi to Roaring Run Furnace Picnic Area on L, and 0.3 mi farther to parking area. *Roaring Run Trail* is a 1.4-mi round trip from the picnic area. It follows upstream to cascades and waterfalls and in a heavy canopy of hard-woods and hemlock. Stream is trout stocked. The furnace is across the creek from the picnic area. No camping here.

The yellow-blazed *Iron Ore Trail* ascends from the picnic area SW on old wagon road. Cross under power line at 0.4 mi, and turn L at 0.8-mi old road junction. Cross under power line again at 0.9 mi. Vegetation is young, mostly hardwoods and patches of pine. Fragrant trailing arbutus and snowy mountain laurel border the old roadbed. At 1.4 mi reach ridge crest and, at 1.5 mi, enter stand of large oaks. Ascend to another ridge at 1.8 mi and bear sharply L. Good campsite here, but no water. Ascend steeply in rocky section to summit area, where a forest fire has destroyed many of the mature trees at 2.2 mi. Begin descent at 2.4 mi, reaching junction with *Hoop Hole Trail* at 2.6 mi. Backtrack. Or, take *Hoop Hole Trail* either R or L. On R trail extends 5.6 mi across Pine Mtn Ridge W and descends S to SR 615. L, trail extends 3.4 mi S on a descent to SR 615. If L, follow slope on steep and brushy trail for 0.7 mi to spring. At 1.6 mi are tall trees with sparse understory. Cross small stream at 1.8 mi and reach junction with short loop of *Hoop Hole Trail* at 2.2 mi. Cross stream at 2.3 mi. This area is excellent for campsites. Continue downstream along Stoney Run by a treacherous ravine and towering hemlocks. Cross creek again at 2.6 mi, reach trail display sign at 3.3 mi, and parking area near SR 615 at 3.4 mi. Elevation change to this point, 1,530 ft.

Options here are to backtrack—a total of 6 mi—or ascend on strenuous long loop of *Hoop Hole Trail* to Pine Mtn (3,700 ft) and rejoin *Iron Ore Trail* for 8.2 mi, or hike back to the picnic area on SR 615 and SR 621 for 3.7 mi, a total of 9.7 mi. Another option? The easy one, a vehicle shuttle. USFS trail numbers 264, 5004, 5001.

The total mileage of the Hoop Hole Trail is 9 mi, the Iron Ore Trail is 2.4 mi, and the Roaring Run Trail is 1.4 mi.

▼ CRAIG CREEK TRAIL   87

Length: 2.1 mi (3.4 km), easy. *USGS Maps:* Strom, Oriskany. *Trailhead:* Parking area.

Directions and Description: This trail begins 10.6 mi SW from Roaring Run on SR 615 (toward Oriskany). Alternatively, access is from the SR 615 and SR 817 junction in Oriskany; take SR 817 0.4 mi to FR 5075, and turn R. Park at *Craig Creek Trail* sign. (This trail can also be hiked from parking space farther ahead near Craig Creek Picnic Area.) Follow yellow-blazed trail in young hardwood forest on L side of slope by a ravine to top of ridge at 0.2 mi. Area has laurel, woodmint, blueberry, buckberry, and sundrops. Deer and woodchuck are frequently seen. Reach scenic open grassy field at 1 mi and return to parking area on FR 5075, or make a loop by hiking the river road downstream to river junction. Here take L on old woods road, ascending to ridge and trail origin. USFS trail number 5006.

Patterson and Price Mountain Area
Botetourt and Craig Counties

▼ PATTERSON MOUNTAIN TRAIL, TUCKER TRAIL, HELMS TRAIL, LOOP TRAIL, ELMORE TRAIL, PRICE MOUNTAIN TRAIL, KELLY TRAIL, SULPHUR RIDGE TRAIL   88–98

Length: 27.3 mi (43.7 km) ct; easy to strenuous. *USGS*

Maps: Oriskany, New Castle, Catawba. *Trailhead:* Junction of FR 184 and FR 5013.

Directions and Description: Access to this network of trails is by SR 606, 9 mi W from US 220 in Fincastle to SR 612 and R on FR 184. (Or, from ranger station, go NE on SR 615 for 4.4 mi and turn R on SR 606 for 2.5 mi to SR 612 and FR 184, L.) Turn off SR 606 onto SR 612 for 0.4 mi, turn R on FR 184 and go around R of YMCA Camp to Little Patterson Creek. Park in area apart from gated road R and L.

Begin ascent on *Patterson Mtn Trail* L (1,250 ft). After 1.2 mi the trail is on a more gradual grade and R slope of the ridge. Hardwoods dominate, but mountain laurel and white and Virginia pine offer a contrast. At 2.6 mi is junction with *Tucker Trail* on R. (It leads down the ridge, steeply at first, for 1 mi to gated road FR 5015 and to FR 184.) Continue ahead on *Patterson Mtn Trail* for another 0.9 mi across a ridge spine to *Helms Trail* R. (In a slight sag *Helms Trail* descends 0.5 mi to junction with the *Loop Trail.* From here it continues descent for another 0.8 mi to FR 184.) Continue ahead again, slightly R of ridge crest, up and down over gradual terrain for another 1.2 mi to junction with *Elmore Trail* on R. (*Elmore Trail* also descends SE, but on a less steep descent, extending to the *Loop Trail* and to FR 184 for 1.5 mi.) *Patterson Mtn Trail* continues along the R, turning R and descending after 0.5 mi from *Elmore Trail* gate. Cross jeep road, and follow trail descending to FR 184. Turn R on FR 184 and go 1 mi to junction with yellow-blazed *Price Mtn Trail* on L. At this point either continue to hike the pleasant forest road back to the original trailhead, for 4.8 mi, or take the *Price Mtn Trail* for a longer loop as described below for a round-trip total of 11.3 mi.

If taking the *Price Mtn Trail* start near small drainage;

ascend the ridge, which is moderately steep in sections but more gradual in incline after the first mi, to the ridge crest. After 3.1 mi is junction with *Kelly Trail* on R. (This trail descends for 1.6 mi down steep slope to FR 184.) On the *Price Mtn Trail* follow the ridge crest, among mainly oaks, locust, birch, and scattered pine with mountain laurel and blueberry, to *Sulphur Ridge Trail* on R. (On this trail, an old woods road, it is 2.1 mi to SR 606, where one could hike on the roads for a circuit of 17 mi back to the original trailhead, or, with vehicle shuttle, finish hike for a total of 14 mi.) The *Price Mtn Trail* continues on the ridge, reaching a gap at 5.8 mi where SR 606 crosses the mountain. From here the trail becomes *Price–Broad Mtn Trail,* climbs the bank in a curve, and continues ahead in hardwoods, ascending and descending steep knobs and crossing wildlife clearings for 4.8 mi from SR 606 to junction with *North Mtn Trail* (at this point a lead-in to the *Appalachian Trail,* to L) and *Lick Branch Trail,* R. (*Lick Branch Trail* is 5 mi and has a spur, *Ferrier Trail,* extending 2.6 mi to R, that leads to gated FR 5026.) Backtrack to SR 606, for a total of 27.3 mi, or use vehicle shuttle to be picked up on FR 5026, 2.5 mi E of New Castle (by way of SR 616, 690, and FR 182 to FR 5026). USFS trail numbers 148, 191, 181,153, 151, 334, 182, 149. *Lick Branch Trail* is 262, *N Mtn Trail* is 263, and *Ferrier Trail* is 189.

Fenwick Mines Area
Craig County

▼ FENWICK NATURE TRAIL, LIGNITE TRAIL   99–100

Length: 8.3 mi (13.3 km) rt, ct; easy. *USGS Map:* New Castle. *Trailhead:* Parking area.

Directions and Description: From the ranger station go NE on SR 615 for 3 mi to SR 611—Barbours Creek Rd—and turn L. Go 0.2 mi, turn R on SR 685, which leads into FR 181 and continue on FR 181 for 1.8 mi. *Fenwick Nature Trail* parking area is on R, and the Fenwick Mines Picnic Area is 0.5 mi ahead on R. *The Fenwick Nature Trail* is a 0.7-mi loop, self-guiding trail beginning on an old railroad grade. An exceptionally attractive area, with unique rock formations appearing as steps for the waterfalls in Mills Creek and with wildflowers in profusion. A mixture of shade, sun, and mist create an excellent setting for the tall oaks, cherry, birch, and hemlocks. A beaver dam is upstream. From the *Nature Trail* take the *Lignite Trail* paralleling Mill Creek. Peaceful, historic, and bright with fall colors, this easy grade ascends gently in area where lignite has been mined. Reach Botetourt County line and FR 704 at 3.8 mi. Backtrack for a total of 8.3 mi, or for a different route take FR P229, R, after 1.5 mi on the return. It is a gated road leading back to the Fenwick Mines Picnic Area. USFS trail numbers 5007, 59.

North Mountain Area
Roanoke, Craig, and Botetourt Counties

▼ NORTH MOUNTAIN TRAIL/SOUTH   101–105

Length: 13.2 mi (21.1 km), moderate. *USGS Maps:* Looney, Catawba. *Trailhead:* VA 311 at McAfee Run.

Directions and Description: (The first 9 mi of this trail is a temporary section of the *Appalachian Trail.* Access is from VA 311, 2.5 mi W from Catawba. A parking area is nearby that also serves as the trailhead for the 1.2-mi

Dragon's Tooth Trail SW and its junction with the *A.T.* (From this point the *A.T.* follows a creek with impressive stands of Carolina hemlock to prominent outcrops on the top of Cove Mtn.) Begin the *N Mtn Trail* on switchbacks up N Mtn, reaching the crest at 0.9 mi after ascending 1,100 ft. At 2.4 mi is junction L with faint *Deer Trail,* which leads for 1.6 mi to FR 224. After another mile, in a saddle, reach *Grouse Trail,* a 1-mi trail also leading to FR 224 on L. Continue ahead on dry ridge through hardwoods and blueberries, ascending and descending over knolls.

At 6.2 mi on *N Mtn Trail* the 1.6-mi *Turkey Trail* descends L to FR 224. At 9 mi the *A.T.* extends R, and the *N Mtn Trail* continues straight ahead for 4.2 mi to Stone Coal Gap, FR 183, at 13.2 mi where across the road the trail leads to *Branch Trail* and *Price Mtn Trail.* For *Price Mtn Trail* information, see preceding Patterson Mtn trail description. Route on *A.T.* descends on rocky trail and crosses SR 779 after 1.4 mi. From here, it is 9 mi L to Daleville, and 9 mi R to Catawba. The *A.T.* continues across the road and, at 4.3 mi from *N Mtn Trail,* reaches Lamberts Meadow Shelter and stream. USFS numbers (not including the *A.T., Dragon's Tooth Trail,* or *Branch* and *Price Mtn Trail*), 263, 186, 187, 188.

Potts Mountain Area
Craig and Alleghany Counties,
Virginia and Monroe County, West Virginia   106–107

(The 11.5 mi *Potts Mtn Trail/W* from VA 311 to SR 636 and the 6.8 mi *Potts Mtn Trail/E* from FR 176 to SR 617 are not included here, because they are now categorized as a system off-road-vehicle road.)

Wythe Ranger District

Stony Fork Area
Wythe County   108–109

Wythe Ranger District has 77.7 mi of the *Appalachian Trail*. This includes public roads or lands managed by the National Forest Service. Many of the trails open during the 70s are no longer maintained or recommended for hiking. Some of the other trails became part of the relocated *A.T.* in the Burkes Garden–Brushy Mtn Area. And, further, the National Forest Service (NFS) does not plan to make the old *A.T.* along the Walker Mtn ridge crest a blue-blazed trail. (The shelters have all been removed to the new *A.T.* Because the old *A.T.* crossed a few sections of private land and the right-of-way agreements have expired, the NFS no longer recommends it; hikers on it would take the risk of trespass claims.) However, there do remain long sections of the 28-mi old *A.T.* that are within the NFS, which should be hiked and maintained. Consult the district ranger's office for conditions of these sections (which figure in the memories of many who have hiked the old *A.T.*). And, if another old circuit trail is desired, inquire about the 10-mi *Punch and Judy Creek Trail* in the Beartown Area.

Additional trails in the district are in two proposed Wilderness areas—Beartown on the western end of Garden Mtn and Kimberling Creek N of I-77. Both are extraordinarily wild and scenic, offering both solitude and challenge. Among the recreational areas in the district are Big Bend Picnic Area, Dark Horse Hollow Picnic Area, and Stony Fork Campground (which has *Stony Fork Trail,* a 1.5-mi self-guided trail, meandering from the S edge). Access to the campground is R on US 21–52, NW of I-81 at Wytheville, for 7.5 mi.

Information: Contact District Ranger, Wythe District, Jefferson National Forest, Rte 4, Wytheville, VA 24382; tel: 703-228-5551.

2 · George Washington National Forest

With more than a million acres and 30 developed recreational sites, the scenic George Washington National Forest (GWNF) spreads from the James River in the S to Front Royal in the N, and from the Shenandoah National Park in the E to the Monongahela National Forest, in West Virginia, to the West. In the center of this vast and resplendent forest is the idyllic Shenandoah Valley, where pioneers settled to create their farms and where heroic battles were fought in the Revolutionary and the Civil wars.

The forest is home to a wide range of vascular plants—hardwoods, pines, shrubs, wildflowers, and ferns. There are pockets of virgin timber, such as the oaks and hemlocks near Little Irish Creek. The forest is also home to abundant wildlife, including deer, bear, turkey, grouse, raccoon, squirrel, quail, bobcat, skunk, woodchuck, rattlesnake, and mallard. There are more than 160 species of songbirds, owls, and hawks.

Among the GWNF's many attractions are Crabtree Falls, the highest in the state; historic Warwick Mansion, in Hidden Valley; Camp Roosevelt, where the first Civilian Conservation Corps was established in 1933; and of

Shenandoah River, George Washington National Forest.
Virginia State Travel Service.

course the *Appalachian Trail.* A network of more than 275 other trails provides an adventurous experience for every age group.

Information: Contact the offices of the six districts or the main office:

Deerfield Ranger District, 2304 Beverley St (P.O. Box 419), Staunton, VA 24401; tel: 703-885-8028.

Dry River Ranger District, 510 N Main St, Bridge-water, VA 22812; tel: 703-828-2591.

James River Ranger District, 313 S Monroe St, Covington, VA 22426; tel: 703-962-2214.

Lee Ranger District, Windsor Knit Rd, Rte 1, Box 31-A, Edinburg, VA 22824; tel: 703-984-4101.

Pedlar Ranger District, 2424 Magnolia Ave, Buena Vista, VA 24416; tel: 703-261-6105 or 261-6106.

Warm Springs Ranger District, Rte 2, Box 30, Hot Springs, VA 24445; tel: 703-839-2521 or 839-2442. (Office is S of Hot Springs 1.8 mi on US 220.)

At headquarters for the forest, write Forest Supervisor, GWNF, 210 Federal Bldg, Harrisonburg, VA 22801; tel: 703-433-2491.

Deerfield Ranger District

North Mountain and Crawford Mountain Area
Rockbridge and Augusta Counties

▼ NORTH MOUNTAIN TRAIL/NORTH, COLD SPRING TRAIL   110–114

Length: 14.5 mi (23.2 km); strenuous. *USGS Maps:* Elliott Knob, Deerfield, Craigsville. *Trailhead:* Dry Branch Gap, SR 688.

Directions and Description: From ranger station in Staunton go W on VA 254 for 7.8 mi to junction of VA 42. After 0.7 mi on VA 42 turn R by Buffalo Gap Presbyterian Church on SR 688. Cross picturesque bridge after 2.7 mi on SR 688, Dry Branch Rd, and reach Dry Branch Gap after another 1.2 mi. Here the gated *N Mtn Trail/N* is L (S) on the ridge, and *Crawford Mtn Trail* extends R to US 250, 7.8 mi. The yellow-blazed *N Mtn Trail/N* follows the ridge crest; several springs are close to the trail, but overall the ridge is dry, and water should be carried. For the first 1.2 mi the trail is on and off an old logging road. (At 1.8 mi a side trail on R leads 0.2 mi to Buffalo Spring.) Continue on rocky ridge with the possibilities of seeing deer, grouse, or turkey. Oaks, white pine, birch, and locust are the predominate trees.

At 4.2 mi is junction with Elliott Knob road; turn R. (On L at 0.1 mi is spring and small pond among larch and spruce, a fine camping spot. Farther down the mountain the road goes 2.5 mi to VA 42.) On this road it is 0.2 mi, ascending, to Elliott Knob (4,463 ft, the highest peak in the George Washington National Forest). At top again turn R, walking 0.1 mi. Here is an outstanding panoramic view, near the TV relay station and at the old fire tower. Continue S on ridge through spruce; at 4.5 mi *Cold Spring Trail* is on R at junction. (The *Cold Spring Trail* descends into Deerfield Valley, with scenic rock outcroppings. On this trail, after 1.8 mi reach spring, then a creek, pass over mounded-earth tank traps, and at 2.2 mi reach parking area near old woods rd on FR 77, Cold Spring Rd; this is 3.5 mi S from SR 688, Dry Branch Rd.)

Continue ahead on ridge crest over Hogback Ridge, passing junction on R with *Chestnut Flat Spring Trail,* a 0.3-mi old woods road. At 8.1 mi cross FR 82, Hite Hollow Rd. (It is 6.5 mi R to SR 600 and 4.8 mi L to VA

42.) Hiking over a number of knobs, reach *Taylor Hollow Trail,* which leads to FR 388 L (E), at 10.1 mi. *Ferris Hollow Trail* junction is on R (W) at 11 mi. (*Ferris Hollow Trail* descends 1.7 mi to Calfpasture Creek near Marble Valley and SR 600 on private land of Dr. Vest.) Trail enters old road at 12.5 mi and continues descent to SR 687, Ramsey Draft Rd, at 14.5 mi. Use vehicle shuttle. From this point it is 1 mi W to SR 600 and 3 mi E to VA 42. USFS trail numbers are *N Mtn,* 443; *Crawford Mtn,* 485; *Cold Spring,* 445.

▼ FALLS HOLLOW TRAIL   115

Length: 6 mi (9.6 km) rt; moderate to strenuous. *USGS Map:* Elliott Knob. *Trailhead:* VA 42.

Directions and Description: From ranger station in Staunton go W on VA 254 for 7.8 mi; turn L on VA 42 and go 3.2 mi to *Falls Hollow Trail* entrance on R. Follow yellow-blazed trail on old jeep road through oaks, pines, poplar, maple, and locust. After 2 mi reach Buffalo Falls. Another 0.8 mi leads steeply in sections to Elliott Knob Rd. Backtrack (or continue R for 1.2 mi to Elliott Knob—4,463 ft—and then double back). Turn L on the road to make a loop to VA 42. USFS trail number 657.

▼ CHIMNEY HOLLOW TRAIL, CRAWFORD MTN TRAIL, CRAWFORD KNOB TRAIL   116–118

Length: 14.5 mi (23.2 km); strenuous. *USGS Maps:* Elliott Knob, W Augusta, Stokesville, Churchville. *Trailhead:* Dry Branch Gap, SR 688.

Directions and Description: Follow directions in preceding *N Mtn Trail* description to N entrance of *N Mtn*

Trail/N on SR 688. Climb steeply over earth hummock by wildflowers and through forest of mainly oaks, white pine, dogwood, haw, and sassafras on yellow-blazed trail. Reach top of Crawford Knob at 0.4 mi. At 2.4 mi is junction with *Chimney Hollow Trail,* L. (*Chimney Hollow Trail* leads 3.5 mi N, passing over rock outcroppings, descending along a stream, entering a stand of large white pines, and exiting at US 250. Here, parking is on N side of highway; it is 15 mi E to Staunton on US 250, and 3.5 mi R [E] to junction with terminus of *Crawford Mtn Trail.*)

Continue ahead on *N Mtn Trail* for 0.1 mi, past junction with side trail on R (which leads 0.3 mi through wildlife clearing to spring.) At 2.6 mi is junction with *Crawford Knob Trail,* R. (*Crawford Knob Trail* descends for 3.2 mi E to McKittrick's Rd, FR 1296, and 0.4 mi farther to SR 720 near Jerusalem Chapel, S of Lone Fountains on US 250. Follow trail through stand of bear oak, skirt N side of Crawford Knob, descend on switchbacks, follow along McKittrick's Branch, enter timber regeneration area, and exit at FR 1296.) At 4.7 mi is faint trail on L that leads to private property. Scenic views are along the rocky descent at 5.4 mi. Reach old road at 6.1 mi, turn R at 7 mi into forest regeneration area, and end at Dunlop Hunter Access Rd, off US 250, at 7.8 mi. Use vehicle shuttle. (It is 3 mi E on US 250 to Churchville.) USFS trail numbers 651, 487.

▼ WHITE OAK DRAFT TRAIL,
 DOWELLS DRAFT TRAIL   119–120

These two moderate trails have trailheads on US 250, 3.5 mi apart, and they exit 1 mi apart on *Wild Oak Trail* in the Dry River Ranger District. A loop of 10.5 mi could be made, including a 3.5-mi hike on the busy US 250.

Entrance to the *White Oak Draft Trail* is off a dirt road, R, 150 ft before US 250 crosses small bridge over Buckhorn Creek, 0.5 mi W of White's Store. Follow old road; at first fork go R, then cross creek twice, take L at 1 mi, and leave old road at 1.2 mi, turning R up a ridge. Ignore side trail at 1.7 mi, and reach *Wild Oak Trail* at 2.5.

The *Dowells Draft Trail* begins on US 250 on N side, opposite *Chimney Hollow Trail* on S side. From parking area ascend on graded slope W of ridge, through young hardwood forest, frequent patches of Indian pipe, and trailing arbutus. Reach crest at 0.4 mi. Follow ridge crest to *Wild Oak Trail* at 3.5 mi. Here, turn L for 2.4 mi to FR 96, or R 1 mi to *White Oak Draft Trail* on S side of Hankey Mtn. *USGS Maps:* W Augusta, Stokesville. USFS trail numbers 486, 650.

▼ BRALEY POND LOOP TRAIL, BALD RIDGE TRAIL,
BRALEY BRANCH TRAIL   121–123

The 0.6-mi *Braley Pond Loop Trail* circles the lake from the parking area through young forest of pine and oak, blueberry, birdfoot violet, and false downy foxglove. Fishing and picnicking allowed; no camping.

The *Bald Ridge Trail,* an 8.3-mi rugged trail, ascends to scenic rock outcroppings, passes The Peak, The Pinnacle, and tops Gordon's Peak (3,915 ft). It begins on the Braley Pond at Johnson Draft. As this trail receives little use, it may be difficult to find. Its terminus is on *Wild Oak Trail* in Dry River Ranger District.

The *Braley Branch Trail* along Braley Branch goes 1.9 mi from the locked gate R of the picnic area to end of FR

348.1. Access to this recreation area is from US 250 (21 mi from Staunton) and SR 715 junction at Elkhorn Lake sign (0.2 mi W on US 250 from *Chimney Hollow Trail* exit). Go 0.3 mi on SR 715 and turn L onto FR 348.1. *USGS Map:* W Augusta. USFS trail numbers 653, 496, 449. These new trails extend from the Braley Pond Area and do not connect. Look for trail sign information at the picnic bulletin board.

*Ramsey's Draft Wilderness
and Shenandoah Mountain Area*
Augusta and Highland Counties

▼ RAMSEY'S DRAFT TRAIL   124–128

Length: 13 mi (20.8 km) rt; moderate to strenuous. *USGS Maps:* W Augusta, Palo Alto. *Trailhead:* Ford on FR 68.

Directions and Description: From SR 715, which figures in the preceding trail description, go 5 mi W on US 250 to Ramsey's Draft Recreation Area and Mtn House picnic sign on R. Enter on FR 68 and after 0.8 mi on FR 68 park at ford. Rock-hop across the creek, following old road on the blue-blazed trail. *Ramsey's Draft Nature Trail,* a 1-mi interpretive trail, is on R. It has enormous virgin hemlocks, oaks, poplar, and beech. Ferns, mosses, lichens, wildflowers, and shrubs are prevalent. Continue upstream, fording it at least 15 times in the first 5 mi. At 1.5 mi is junction with *Jerry's Run Trail,* L. (*Jerry's Run Trail* ascends W, first along a stream, for 2 mi to junction with *Shenandoah Mtn Trail.* After 1.7 mi on the *Jerry's*

Run Trail reach the Sexton Cabin, maintained by Potomac Appalachian Trail Club and not open without reservations.) At 3.5 mi on *Ramsey's Draft Trail* take the R fork, entering a magnificent forest of exceptional beauty. Reach junction with *Springhouse Ridge Trail* at 5.4 mi near the top of the ridge, R. (This easy contour trail goes 1.3 mi E to connect with the scenic *Wild Oak Trail*.) Hiner Spring is on L. At 5.6 mi take the *Hardscrabble Knob Trail*, which ascends 0.4 mi L (S) to Hardscrabble Knob (4,282 ft) outcrop and site of former fire tower. Return to main trail, and reach junction with *Shenandoah Mtn Trail* at 6.5 mi. Backtrack on *Ramsey's Draft Trail*, or continue NE for 3 mi to FR 95 (see *Wild Oak Trail* in Dry River Ranger District), or follow the blue-blazed *Shenandoah Mtn Trail* for 7 mi SW to the Confederate Breastworks on US 250. From the breastworks it is 2.1 mi E on US 250 to the entrance of Ramsey's Draft Recreation Area and origin of hike. USFS trail numbers 440, 446, 441, 447, for the first 4 trails listed.

▼ SHENANDOAH MOUNTAIN
TRAIL/NORTH   129–130

Length: 14.2 mi (22.7 km) rt; moderate. *USGS Maps:* McDowell, W Augusta, Palo Alto. *Trailhead:* Near Confederate Breastworks on US 250.

Directions and Description: On US 250 go W 2.1 mi from Ramsey's Draft Recreation Area, to top of ridge and parking area on R. Ascend on blue-blazed Shenandoah Mtn Trail N for 0.3 mi to Confederate Breastworks. Turn R, following blue-blazed trail on generally even contour through mostly oak, white pine, and hemlock for the entire 7 mi to *Ramsey's Draft Trail* junction. At 2.4 mi *Jerry's Run Trail* extends R; it descends 2 mi to junction with *Ramsey's Draft Trail*. At 6.6 mi, junction with *Sinclair Hollow Trail* is on L. (This is a 1.6-mi side trail that leads to Shaws Fork Rd, FR 64, and SR 616, from which is 7 mi S to community of Headwaters on US 250.) Continuing on *Shenandoah Mtn Trail*, intersect with *Ramsey's Draft Trail* at 7.1 mi, and either backtrack for 14.2 mi or follow trails described above under *Ramsey's Draft Trail*. USFS trail number 447.

▼ SHAWS RIDGE TRAIL   131

Length: 6.3 mi (10.1 km); moderate. *USGS Maps:* McDowell, Doe Hill, Palo Alto. *Trailhead:* Junction of US 250 and SR 616.

Directions and Description: From the Confederate Breastworks parking area on US 250 (27.2 mi W from Staunton), go W for 3.2 mi to Headwaters and the junction with SR 616, and park. The trail ascends the road embankment N on yellow-marked graded trail in a hollow with shagbark hickory and banks of stonecrop. Follow ridge through Virginia pine, maple, and witchhazel, and descend to pass stream headwaters at 2 mi. Deer frequent this spot. At end of trail merge into FR 501 and go approximately 1.5 mi; exit is at Jones Hunters Access on SR 614, near Cowpasture River. USFS trail number 652.

Shenandoah Mountain Area
Augusta, Highland, and Bath Counties

▼ SHENANDOAH MTN TRAIL/SOUTH   132–136

Length: 23.6 mi (37.8 km); strenuous. *USGS Maps:* W Augusta, Deerfield, Green Valley, Williamsville. *Trail-*

head: Confederate Breastworks on US 250 (or SR 678 near Cowpasture River).

Directions and Description: From the gated entrance at the Confederate Breastworks on US 250, begin S on a hunter's road. Stay on ridge, avoiding other hunters' roads to R or L. (At 1 mi the 1.9-mi *Signal Corps Knob Trail* is L, E.) At 2.6 mi the hunter's road climbs around the W side of the ridge, but follows the trail, turning L, up the crest. Pass through stands of chestnut oak and rhododendron thickets and by rock outcroppings. Pass junction with FR 173 at 7 mi; E of knob, follow the L branch of trail. At 7.6 mi reach ridge top; at 0.2 mi farther, on R, is Phillip's Spring, 300 yds down the hollow. Skirt W of The Bump (3,634 ft) at 9.5 mi. Reach junction with *Nelson Draft Trail* at 11.3 mi. (*Nelson Draft Trail* descends 1 mi to Sugar Tree Rd, FR 394.) From 11.6 mi to 13.8 mi there are a number of open views.

At 17.5 mi enter W of clearing, skirting the mountain below Wallace Peak (3,795 ft). A major trail intersection is here. Jerkemtight Jeep Rd descends L (E) for 5 mi to SR 629, using part of FR 399 along Jerkemtight Creek. Another road runs 0.4 mi up to Wallace Peak. (*Bolshers Run Trail* connects here, but its E descent is to private property.) And a few yards ahead on the main trail is junction with *Marshall Draft Trail.* (The *Marshall Draft Trail* R, near a large black-cherry tree, descends steeply for 1.3 mi to Sugar Tree Rd, FR 394.) Continuing on the main trail, skirt E of N Sister Knob at 19.1 mi, and back to W side for views of Cowpasture and Jackson river valleys at 20.7 mi. Cross SR 627, Scottstown Draft R, at 21.2 mi, and follow old logging road. Descend on ridge to rear of cabin, and exit to SR 678 at 23.6 mi. Use vehicle shuttle. To drive to exit point, go 0.8 mi W on VA 39 from Millboro Spring; turn R on SR 678 and go 6.2 mi to second junction with SR 629. Continue on SR 678 for 3 mi to trailhead, which is 0.6 mi E on SR 678 from Cowpasture River bridge. USFS trail numbers 447 (no number for *Signal Corps Knob Trail*), 393-C, 442, 547.

Mill Mountain and Walker Mountain Area
Bath, Rockbridge, and Augusta Counties

▼ MILL MOUNTAIN TRAIL   137–138

Length: 8.3 mi (13.3 km); strenuous. *USGS Maps:* Green Valley, Craigsville. *Trailhead:* On SR 600.

Directions and Description: From VA 39, W of Staunton, take R on SR 600, 1.7 mi W of Goshen; go 1 mi to gravel road L, near NF sign. Park off road here. Follow gravel road for 0.6 mi to foot trail with orange blazes. At 1.3 mi reach ridge of Mill Mtn. For next mile, excellent views from rock outcrops. At 3.1 mi is road junction. R leads down to scenic Ingram Draft; L leads to Panther Gap Draft. Continue straight, passing through clearcuts. At 3.8 mi begin steep climb. Follow jeep road at top of ridge, and, at 6 mi, enter foot path near site of old fire tower. At 6.7 mi veer L at fork. Join old logging road L at 7.4 mi; follow it, descending, to Little Mill Creek terminus on Clayton Mill Rd, FR 61, at 8.3 mi. Use vehicle shuttle. From here L (S), it is 5.5 mi to Yost on FR 61 junction with SR 640. R (N) on FR 61, it is 1.6 mi to entrance of *Back Draft Trail*, L (see following entry). Elevation change: 2,385 ft. USFS trail number 492.

▼ WALKER MOUNTAIN TRAIL,
BACK DRAFT TRAIL   139–142

Length: 16.7 mi (26.7 km) ct; moderate to strenuous.

USGS Maps: Green Valley, Craigsville, Deerfield. *Trailhead:* FR 61.

Directions and Description: For the *Walker Mtn Trail* go to Yost at SR 640 junction with FR 61 (3.5 mi N of VA 39); follow FR 61, Clayton's Mill Creek Rd, up Little Mill Creek for 1.8 mi to hunter access sign and gated road on L. The entire trail is actually a hunter's jeep road, closed seasonally to vehicular traffic, and neither signed nor blazed. At 0.2 mi is spring on L. Bear R at 1.6 mi, ascending. Continue straight at jeep road junction at 6.9 mi and avoid road on R. At 9 mi is crossing with *Back Draft Trail*. (R on yellow-blazed *Back Draft Trail* at 0.1 mi is large rock wall. At 0.5 mi pass spur ridge; descend, and at 1.2 mi reach Clayton's Mill Creek Rd, FR 61. Going L on *Back Draft Trail*, pass rock outcrops at 0.2 mi, descend steeply around several spur ridges, and turn L at 1 mi. At 1.6 mi cross Back Draft and enter easy contour in forest of large poplar and oak. Exit at 2 mi on SR 641. Alternately, on *Back Draft Trail*, to L it is 1 mi to SR 629. Across SR 641 begins overgrown *Brushy Ridge Trail* with white pines, green striped maples, mountain laurel, oaks, and hickory. It goes 0.9 mi over low ridge to SR 629 in a grove of tall cedar and white pine. At this point *Short Ridge Trail* begins across SR 629, and goes 1 mi over low ridge to Jerkemtight Rd, FR 399. R on FR 399 leads to SR 629 in 0.8 mi. L is *Jerkemtight Creek Trail* on FR 399, which leads 4.2 mi to *Shenandoah Mtn Trail/S.*)

To continue on *Walker Mtn Trail* follow jeep road on even contour and reach trail fork at 13 mi. Veer R, descending on ridge line. At 13.4 mi take L fork and complete descent to SR 600, Bussard Hunter Access, at 13.7 mi. Use vehicle shuttle. L on SR 600 it is 1.3 mi to

Deerfield and junction with SR 629. USFS trail numbers 488, 546, 718, 717.

The Deerfield District uses diamond-shaped plastic markers on some trails. Yellow is used to designate foot travel only and orange to signify foot and vehicular traffic. Three diamonds mark trailheads, and two mean a turn.

Dry River Ranger District

North River Multiple-Use Area
Augusta County

Todd Lake Campground and N River Campground are good bases within a circumference of 40 mi of trail in the North River area. In addition to that 40 mi there are a number of connecting trails in the Dry River Ranger District extending from the Deerfield Ranger District to the S side of *Wild Oak Trail* circuit. Facilities at Todd Lake include beach swimming, fishing, picnicking, campsites with tables and grills, flush toilets, and cold showers. The 0.5-mi *Todd Lake Trail* (USFS trail number 376) is at the beach area.

Access: From Dry River Ranger Station in Bridgewater go 0.9 mi on VA 42 S to junction of SR 727. After 5.9 mi turn L on SR 730. Follow SR 730 for 6 mi and turn R on SR 718. Go 1 mi on SR 718 and turn left on FR 95. At 3.1 mi turn R on FR 523 to Todd Lake Campground.

▼ TRIMBLE MOUNTAIN TRAIL   144

Length: 3.8 mi (6.1 km); easy. *USGS Map:* Stokesville.

Trailhead: Across FR 95 from the camper dumping station.

Directions and Description: From Todd Lake Campground hike the road for 0.4 mi to trail entrance across the stream opposite the camper dumping station. At the fork veer R of borrow area. Ascend gradually on a well-graded trail to ridge with scenic views across Broad Run and toward Elkhorn Mtn at 1.2 mi. Continue circle through hardwoods and groves of mountain laurel around slope of Trimble Mtn saddle; here are more views, including views of N River Campground area. At 2.1 mi reach highest point on trail (2,476 ft; Trimble Mtn is 2,740 ft). At 3 mi notice rocks along the trail with remnants of tree fossils. Pass through the borrow area frequented by wildlife at 3.6 mi and return to FR 95 at 3.8 mi. USFS trail number 375.

▼ WILD OAK TRAIL   145–152

Length: 25.6 mi (41 km) rt; moderate to strenuous.
USGS Maps: Stokesville, Reddish Knob, Palo Alto, West Augusta. *Trailhead:* Entrance of FR 95 from SR 718.

Directions and Description: This trail was designated a national recreation trail in 1979. Its name represents the prominence of oak species on its circuit. When formed, *Wild Oak* replaced the names of such trails as *Chestnut Ridge Trail, Hankey Mtn Trail,* and *Lookout Mtn Trail.* This is an excellent trail for backpacking. Following mostly on ridge crests, its elevation varies from 1,600 ft at its termini to 4,351 ft on Little Ball Knob. Water sources are infrequent; hikers should plan accordingly. Although open all year and a superb trail for all seasons, it is not safe or tranquil during the big-game hunting season from mid October to the last of December. If hiking during this time, a blaze orange jacket should be worn. Passing through more than 40 species of trees, including 5 kinds of pines, the trail is bordered with more than 50 species of wildflowers. Wildlife includes bear, deer, raccoon, turkey, grouse, owls, hawks, fox, rattlesnakes, a wide range of songbirds, and the unmistakable chipmunk.

There are three points of entry—one is the trailhead listed, on FR 95 near SR 718; a second is Camp Todd, on FR 95 in Horse Trough Hollow; and a third is on FR 96, W of Hankey Mtn and N of US 250. For the purpose of making this a circuit hike the three sections reached by means of these entry points are combined. Begin at sign on R of FR 95, 0.1 mi after leaving SR 718. Follow the gray-white diamond blazes through hardwood forests, gradually ascending to Grindstone Mtn. At 2.3 mi enter stand of pitch pine and understory of mountain laurel. Pass timber road, Little Skidmore Trail, L at 2.6 mi. Trail becomes steep and rocky at 3.9 mi. At 4.6 mi is junction with *Grooms Ridge Trail* (USFS trail number 424, also called *Big Ridge Trail*) on R. (From here it is 4 mi down the mountain on *Grooms Ridge Trail* to FR 101 and 1 mi S to FR 95.) Continue ahead on wide trail, formerly *Chestnut Ridge Trail*, passing steep and rocky section at 5.5 mi. Turn L at 6.9-mi junction with Bald Mtn Rd. (Bald Mtn Rd runs R for 5 mi to FR 85, where the *Shenandoah Mtn Trail* intersects S of Reddish Knob. *Buckwheat Mtn Jeep Trail* is also on the Bald Mtn Rd, 2.5 mi from *Wild Oak Trail*.)

At 7 mi is Little Bald Knob (4,351 ft), the highest point on the trail. This area, particularly a few yards out on Bald Knob Rd, provides magnificent views. Begin descent, sometimes on rocky terrain, to N River and Camp Todd on FR 95 at 10.2 mi. After crossing the road near Camp Todd historical marker begin the exceptionally steep climb up Springhouse Ridge toward Big Bald Knob (4,100 ft). At 11.5 mi pass spring, and at 11.6 pass junction with Hiner Spring and *Ramsey Draft Trail*, on R. (It is 1.3 mi to Hiner Spring on *Ramsey Draft Trail,* and 0.7 mi farther to Hardscrabble Knob, at 4,282 ft.)

Reach Big Bald Knob, a wide, flat wildlife clearing of mountain laurel, oaks, pitch pine, and blueberries, at 12.4 mi. Pass grassy open area at 12.6 mi and descend to a wildlife clearing with pond at 13.1 mi. (At 13.2 mi *Bald Ridge Trail* from the Deerfield Ranger District comes in on R. It runs 8.3 mi across Gordon's Peak and The Pinnacle to US 250.) At 13.8 mi pass stream in rocky area, and at 15.4 mi reach FR 96 (2,312 ft). Cross road and climb steeply through white pines and oaks. At 16.7 veer R from side trail on L, and at 17.7 mi reach peak of Hankey Mtn (3,407 ft). (*White Oak Draft Trail* in Deerfield Ranger District is on R, descending 2.5 mi to US 250.)

Continue ahead on what was formerly called the *Hankey Mtn Trail* through areas of fallen and decaying trunks of the American chestnut. Wildflowers are abundant, particularly on and between the summits of Hankey Mtn. Reach the second peak of Hankey Mtn at 18.6 mi. Trail becomes a hunter's road, passing a number of wildlife clearings and surrounded by hardwoods and white pines. An overlook is at 20.4 mi, and another excellent view is at 21.3 mi, where power line crosses road. At 21.8 mi reach junction with *Bear Draft Trail* (USFS trail number 535), R, and a road on L that leads to North River Campground. (*Bear Draft Trail* descends 3 mi along Bear Draft Creek to SR 730 near Stribling Springs.)

Proceed ahead on what was formerly called the *Lookout Mtn Trail*. At 22.6 and 23.1 there are overlooks along the ridge that provide panoramic views. At 23.8 mi is an area of table mountain pine, oaks, maple, and berries. Descend; at points, steep and rocky. From 25 mi a side trail on L leads to Camp May Flather; continue ahead to fording of the N River at 25.5 mi on old fire road. Exit at 25.6 on SR 718 across the road from a one-lane bridge sign 0.2 mi before entrance to FR 95 and point of origin. USFS trail number 716.

▼ NORTH RIVER GORGE TRAIL   153

Length: 5 mi (8 km); moderate. *USGS Map:* Stokesville. *Trailhead:* N River Campground.

Directions and Description: From Todd Lake Campground area take FR 95 SW, at 1.5 mi passing junction with FR 95B, L. Continue 1 mi and cross N River bridge to N River Campground on L. Begin hike downriver at road gate at 0.2 mi. At 0.6 mi ford the river for the first of nine times. Although this is a spectacular river trail, descending through steep walls of Lookout Mtn and Trimble Mtn, the trail terrain is irregular, and spots are not in top condition. The trail is actually hazardous during high water. (Some hikers have said they carried an extra pair of shoes—such as tennis shoes—to be used in the fording.) Ford the river twice again by 0.9 mi. For the next 1.5 mi follow a large horseshoe curve on the N side before fording again at 2.4 mi. Because of the mist and the moist earth the vegetation is lush and dense. A wide range of trees, shrubs, and wildflowers can be identified. Ford the river again at 2.7 mi, 3 mi, 3.2 mi, and 3.5 mi.

On the R side of the river follow an old road to a crossing of the river at 4.5 mi. Cross, and follow road to gate at FR 95 for 5.1 mi, or continue downstream on old trail to river crossing at Camp Flathery near SR 718 at 5.6 mi. Vehicle shuttle necessary. USFS trail number 538.

Hearthstone Lake Area
Augusta County

▼ TIMBER RIDGE TRAIL   154–157

Length: 7 mi (11.2 km); strenuous. *USGS Map:* Reddish Knob. *Trailhead:* Tillman RD, FR 101, 0.8 mi NW of Hearthstone Lake.

Directions and Description: This trail ascends steadily 2,616 ft in elevation from near Hearthstone Lake to Reddish Knob and FR 85. Or the reverse route can be hiked to make the trail category *easy.* (If ascending, a circuit trail can be made; leave *Timber Ridge Trail* at 3.5-mi point, where *Sand Spring Mtn Trail* turns off—a sharp R—on the mountain of the same name. This trail runs 3 mi along the ridge, descending to Tillman Rd, FR 101. Here, turn R and return to the *Timber Ridge Trail* on FR 101 for a circuit of 8 mi. A larger circuit also can be made; take the *Timber Ridge Trail* for 4.3 mi, ascending to *Wolf Ridge Trail* on R, then descend for 5 mi along the Augusta-Rockingham county lines to Tillman Rd, FR 101, and hike the road back to *Timber Ridge Trail* for 2.8 mi for a complete circuit of 12.1 mi.)

Begin 7-mi hike 0.8 mi NW of Hearthstone Lake junction on FR 101 at a seeded road with large hummocks L in semiopen area. (Trail sign may be missing.) Cross stream at 0.2 mi and begin ascent gradually on the ridge. Skirt R of small pond and L of another small pond at 2 mi, continuing to climb to Sand Spring Mtn at 3.5 mi. (*Sand Spring Mtn Trail* junction is sharp R.) Continue ahead for 0.8 mi to junction with *Wolf Ridge Trail* on R. (*Wolf Ridge Trail* descends 5 mi to FR 101.) Proceed through saddle of two small peaks and ascend on sharp ridge with occasional knobs. At 6.5 mi is junction with *California Ridge Trail* (USFS number 436) on R. (*California Ridge Trail* leads steeply down to Briery Branch and to SR 924 NW of Briery Branch Dam for 4.6 mi.) Continue along ridge to Reddish Knob Lookout road at 7 mi. Turn L on road for a 0.1-mi walk to Reddish Knob (4,397 ft), which has spectacular 360° views. Some of the wildflowers seen on this trail are starry campion, milkweed, yarrow, mountain mint, gold star, bell flower, black cohosh, wild orchids, trillium, evening primrose, and mullein. Backtrack or use vehicle shuttle. USFS trail number 431.

Hone Quarry Recreation Area
Rockingham County

The area around Hone Quarry Campground, within the SW corner of Rockingham County (and adjoining Pender County in West Virginia), has a network of trails. A section around Bother Knob is the proposed Skidmore Wilderness, which has a virgin forest of hemlock, white pine, and hardwoods. There is also a younger growth of balsam. Campground facilities are limited to fishing, picnicking, and camping. Hone Quarry Run flows through the campground. (The Dry River District

George Washington National Forest Sportsman's Guide map for 1976 shows *Mines Run Trail* along the Hone Quarry stream, but that is in error; *Mines Run Trail* is a 3-mi picturesque trail on a trout stream up Mines Run, R of SR 924, immediately beyond Briery Branch Lake.)

Access: From Harrisonburg go on VA 257 W (or SR 727 and 613 to VA 257 from Bridgewater) to FR 62 on R, 2.5 mi beyond junction with SR 731 near Briery Branch. Follow FR 62 for 1.4 mi to picnic area and camping. It is another 1 mi up the rough road passing camping spots under hemlocks to the base of Hone Quarry Dam.

▼ HONE QUARRY RIDGE TRAIL   158–160

Length: 8 mi (12.8 km); strenuous. *USGS Map:* Reddish Knob. *Trailhead:* Near junction of VA 257, SR 924, and FR 101.

Directions and Description: From the Hone Quarry Campground go back to VA 257, turn R, and go 0.6 mi on VA 257 to private road on R before SR 924 and FR 101 junction. Pass houses and begin steep hike up ridge. After 2.2 mi pass obscure trail on L (which descends for 0.8 mi to SR 924). Reach a knob at 3.5 mi, where *Big Hollow Trail* forks R. (*Big Hollow Trail,* USFS trail number 430, leads 1.7 mi to campground road with terminus a few yards from the creek bridge near a "rough road" sign. This trail can be used as an alternate access to *Hone Quarry Ridge Trail.*) Continue ahead up the ridge, ascending knolls; pass an obscure trail on L at 4.5 mi (which descends for 1 mi to *Mines Run Jeep Trail* and out to SR 924). After another mile the trail becomes wider on a more frequently used hunter's road. Hike over a number of bald spots with heavy grass and shrubs. Wildflowers are profuse, and black birch, oaks, and white pine are commonplace. At 8 mi pass gate and junction with FR 85, the main ridge of Shenandoah Mtn. It is 0.8 mi L on FR 85 to SR 942 junction along the Virginia and West Virginia state line, and 1 mi on R of trailhead to road fork on FR 85 L for Bother Knob (4,344 ft). The R-fork road leads another 2 mi to *Slate Springs Trail/AA*. Backtrack or use vehicle shuttle. USFS trail number 435.

(If a circuit is desired back to camp, follow FR 85 R along ridge crest to *Slate Springs Trail/AA* and descend for 4.7 mi to campground for a circuit of 15.7 mi. By using *Big Hollow Trail* in the beginning, the circuit-hike mileage could be reduced to 14 mi.)

▼ SLATE SPRINGS CIRCUIT TRAILS   161–166

Length: 12 mi or 15 mi (19.2 or 24 km) rt; strenuous. *USGS Maps:* Briery Branch, Reddish Knob, Brandy-wine. *Trailhead:* Hone Quarry Campground.

Directions and Description: Five trails make up the Slate Springs circuit, most of them interconnecting on jeep roads. They have the USFS trail numbers of 428/AA, /BB, /A, /B, and C. Although known as the *Slate Springs Circuit Trails,* the last is a connector also called *Rocky Run Jeep Trail.* Another trail in this region, called *Slate Springs Mtn Trail,* is not part of the two circuits described here. The two suggested circuit routes may be confusing to hikers unfamiliar with the area; if in doubt, or concerned about becoming lost, remember that the clockwise directions on these trails should bring back to the camping area the hiker who always turns R. Both circuits leave from the Hone Quarry Campground.

The ridge areas have infrequent water sources.

Circuit #1: From the picnic and parking area follow the road up the creek for 1 mi to the base of the Hone Quarry Dam. Go around the R on jeep road; at 1.8 mi on *Slate Springs Trail/AA* pass hemlock grove. At 2 mi *Slate Springs Trail/B* junction is on R descending 1.5 mi from *Slate Springs Trail/A.* Continue ahead on jeep road, crossing creek by rock-hopping or wading at 2.1 mi. On R at 2.8 mi is *Slate Springs Trail/BB,* descending for 1.6 mi from *Slate Springs Trail/A* at Pond Knob. Continue straight, and at 3 mi turn R on a tributary to Hone Quarry Run. Begin steeper ascent, climbing from 2,200-ft elevation to 4,200-ft elevation on Slate Springs Mtn at 5.4 mi E of Flagpole Knob. Turn R, using care to stay on ridge. After following the jeep road to Meadow Knob for 1.5 mi turn R on *Slate Springs Trail/A* at 6.9 mi. (Trail ahead is a jeep road down the mountain to Maple Springs.) Proceed SE along ridge for 1 mi to trail junction at Pond Knob. (To R is *Slate Springs Trail/BB,* back to camp; to L is jeep trail down to Black Run and FR 225.) Continue ahead, descending to *Slate Springs Trail/B* on R at 8.6 mi. Leave *Slate Springs Trail/A* and descend R on *Slate Springs Trail/B* to Hone Quarry Run at 10.1 mi and return to camp by the dam for a total of 12 mi.

Circuit #2: Follow directions as above to junction of *Slate Springs Trail/A* and */B* at 8.6 mi. Here, instead of taking *Slate Springs Trail/B,* continue ahead on *Trail/A* ascending to Oak Knob (3,480 ft) at 9 mi. Descend for 0.2 mi to trail junction with Mud Pond jeep trail ahead. Turn R on *Slate Springs Trail/A* to junction with un- named trail on R fork at 9.8 mi. Keep L at this point, and begin steep descent to another fork at 10.8 mi. (The R fork descends steeply to *Rocky Run Jeep Trail*—USFS trail number 428/C—in a narrow gorge and exits to VA 257 at 12.6 mi.) Turn R and follow VA 257 to FR 62 and back to camp after a total of 14.2 mi. Or, on L fork at Rocky Run, follow *Slate Springs Trail/A* down, skirting N of a knob to Narrow Back Mtn ridge and trail junction at 12.2 mi. Ignore trail at sharp L along the ridge, but take either one of the other two. The one to the R will descend on exceptionally steep terrain. Both trails lead to a jeep road, where a R turn leads out to VA 257 at 13.4 mi. Turn R on VA 257 and follow to FR 62 for return to camp after a total of 15 mi.

▼ BLUEBERRY TRAIL,
MUD POND GAP TRAIL   167–169

Length: 5 mi (6.9 km) ct; moderate. *USGS Maps:* Briery Branch, Reddish Knob, Rawley Springs, Brandywine. *Trailhead:* Near old Union Springs resort.

Directions and Description: (These two trails can easily make a loop with 0.7 mi of FR 225 for a total of 5 mi or combine 4.5 mi of FR 225 with an old jeep trail for a total of 11.5 mi.) Access is off VA 257 at Briery Branch on SR 731. Go 1.6 mi to SR 742. Turn L and go 1.3 mi to SR 933. On SR 933 go 1.3 mi to FR 225. Drive on FR 225, which may be rocky in sections, passing the site of the historic Union Springs mineral-water health resort. At 1.8 mi is *Mud Pond Gap Trail,* USFS trail number 544, on L. (Hummocks on the trail prevent 4-wheel-drive vehicles, or at least are supposed to.) Up the road 0.7 mi on L is trailhead of *Blueberry Trail,* USFS trail number 544-A. As parking is more adequate at the ridge crest for *Blueberry Trail,* begin hiking here, on an old jeep road.

Ascend to two knobs before reaching Mud Pond on

grassy spotted ridge at 2 mi. (At the pond it is another 1 mi to *Slate Springs Trail/A* at Oak Knob.) Turn sharply L and return to FR 225 by descending on *Mud Pond Gap Trail* for 2.3 mi. Reach FR 225 at 4.3 mi, turn L, and return to vehicle. (A longer route is to follow *Blueberry Trail* to *Slate Springs Trail/A* for 3 mi, at Oak Knob. Turn R and go 1.1 mi to *Pond Knob Trail* junction; turn R again on jeep trail descending to Black Run for 2 mi more. Turn R on old road and go 0.9 mi to FR 225. Here, continue R and return to ridge crest and trailhead of *Blueberry Trail* for a total circuit of 11.5 mi.)

James River Ranger District

Longdale Area
Alleghany, Botetourt, and Rockbridge Counties

▼ NORTH MOUNTAIN TRAIL/CENTRAL   170–171

Length: 11 mi (17.6 km), strenuous. *USGS Maps:* Longdale Furnace, Collierstown. *Trailhead:* Longdale Recreation Area parking area.

Directions and Description: From junction of I-81 and I-64 at Lexington, go W on I-64 for 21 mi to exit 10 and take US 60 W for 2.2 mi to Longdale Recreation Area on L. (From Clifton Forge recreation area it is 8 mi on US 60.) Go 0.1 mi to forest road fork; take FR 172 and after 0.2 mi park in picnic area. Blue-blazed *N Mtn Trail/central* begins on L up steps.

At 0.3 mi reach junction with *YACC's Run Trail* on R at footbridge. (This trail is described in the next entry.) Continue ahead for 100 yds; cross FR 271, Tri-County

Rd; ascend over mounded-earth tank traps, and follow old road. (A hunter's and trail parking area is located on L up FR 271.) At 2 mi is a primitive camping area and access to FR 33, Simmon's Rd (1.5 mi to SR 770). Ascend, crossing streams through oaks, poplar, white pine, hickory, and ash, to crest of ridge at 3.8 mi. Turn L and reach top of N Mtn at 4.3 mi. (No water available along the ridge.) Expansive views from rock outcroppings at 6 mi, 7.5 mi, and 7.7 mi. Cross SR 770, Collierstown Road, at 8 mi where there is a parking area. (SR 770 also connects W to US 60, 1.7 mi E from the Longdale Recreation Area entrance.) Continue ahead on the Top Drive Rd, FR 447, to Top Drive Overlook with views of Lake Robertson and Peaks of Otter at 9.3 mi. At 11 mi reach trail terminus and a parking area for the dead-end spur *Cock's Comb Trail,* which extends 0.5 mi to L for an excellent view of the RARE II wilderness area of Rich Hole. (To approach this end of the trail by vehicle, turn off I-64 at the Goshen exit, SR 780, and turn L onto FR 447 for 5 mi.) USFS trail number 467.

▼ YACC'S RUN TRAIL, ANTHONY KNOBS TRAIL, BLUE SUCK TRAIL   172–174

Length: 6.3 mi (10.1 km) ct; moderate. *USGS Map:* Longdale Furnace. *Trailhead:* Longdale Recreation Area parking area.

Directions and Description: Using directions in preceding entry, follow the blue-blazed *N Mtn Trail/Central* for 0.3 mi and turn R over footbridge of the unmarked and unblazed *YACC's Run Trail.* Hike on N slope of ridge to clearing with border of silverberry; turn sharp R at 0.2 mi. Cross small stream at 0.4 mi, and reach knoll at

1 mi. Descend, cross a footbridge over a ravine, and cross a creek to a jeep road at 1.5 mi. (Jeep road R leads back to the picnic area; *Blue Suck Trail* follows the road L for 1.3 mi to junction with *Anthony Knobs Trail.*) Cross road and ascend by switchbacks to ridge crest and junction with *Anthony Knobs Trail* on L at 1.8 mi. If hiking back to the parking area at this point follow R on ridge of oaks and pines to scenic views at 2 mi and at 2.3 mi. At 2.7 mi begin descent, and at 3 mi reach paved FR 172, 0.1 mi from parking area on R. (Large white pine is the only point of recognition for trail entry or exit.) If the *Anthony Knobs Trail* is hiked, ascend and follow ridge L from description above to up-and-down knolls and junction with *Blue Suck Trail* after 1.5 mi. Turn R for 0.5 to FR 271, or take a L on the *Blue Suck Trail* for a return to the Longdale picnic area. Wild turkey, deer, and grouse often are seen by quiet hikers on these trails. USFS trail numbers 704, 666, 460.

▼ RICH HOLE TRAIL,
WHITE ROCK TOWER TRAIL   175–176

Length: 9.8 mi (15.7 km) ct; moderate. *USGS Map:* Longdale Furnace. *Trailhead:* Parking area on US 60.

   Directions and Description: From I-64 at Longdale exit 10, take US 60 E, ascending for 5 mi to parking area on L, near Rockbridge and Alleghany county line. (From Lexington take Goshen exit 11, onto US 60; drive W for 6.8 mi to parking area on R.) *Rich Hole Trail* entry is on unmarked but white-blazed trail on old wagon road. After 0.5 mi reach a good view to the S. At 0.8 mi the grade is steep and rocky until a saddle is reached on Mill Mtn, with a large cliff at 1.2 mi. (To the N are the head-

waters of Alum Creek and an old growth of hardwoods.)
At the saddle, turn L down the North Branch Hollow
into RARE II wilderness area. At 1.8 mi begin to follow
the creek in an area of rich, moist soil. Large fern beds
are here.

At 2.3 mi make the first of 13 crossings of the creek. At
4.4 mi the trail widens to an old road, and it meets FR 108
and junction with *White Rock Tower Trail* at 5.7 mi in a
stand of large oaks. (To the L on FR 108 it is 1.3 mi to US
60.) To continue the hike on unmarked and unblazed
White Rock Tower Trail, turn R up rocky FR 108 to
gated road and reach ridge crest at 1.4 mi. Turn L, following SW along crest in oak forest with scattered pines
to FR 333. Here is a parking area, where FR 333 leads on
a gated road L for 3.1 mi to SR 770. In another 0.6 mi
reach US 60 and junction with I-64, exit 10.

Potts Valley Area
Alleghany County

▼ MORNING KNOB TOWER TRAIL,
JINGLING ROCKS TRAIL   177–178

These unlinked neighboring trails are scenic, less used
than most, and unmarked; each is unique. To reach the
3.4-mi round trip *Morning Knob Tower Trail* go S on VA
18 from Covington for 9.1 mi to SR 614. Turn R on SR
614 for 2.7 mi to SR 600. Continue on SR 600 for 1.6 mi to
faint old road on L near Caststeel Creek at US Forest
Service boundary. Park and ascend on old road to rocky
summit. To reach the *Jingling Rocks Trail* (named for the
jingling sound from walking on the rocks), instead con-

tinue driving ahead on SR 600 for 2.4 mi to junction of
SR 613 and FR 175. Park here and hike for 1 to 3 mi on
FR 175 along ridge crest to discover areas of rocks that
jingle. *USGS Maps:* Alleghany, Jordan Mines.

▼ EASTERN NATIONAL
CHILDRENS FOREST TRAIL   179

Length: 0.3 mi (0.5 km); easy. *USGS Map:* Gordon
Mines. *Trailhead:* Parking area.

Directions and Description: Take VA 18 S of Covington for 11.7 mi to SR 613 on L. Go 3 mi on SR 613 to terminus, and turn R on forest road at sign. (FR 351 goes
straight ahead.) After 0.8 mi park on R for excellent
views of Potts Valley and Peters Mtn range. A stone
monument L of road with the 0.3-mi paved loop nature
trail and a time capsule honors the local children who
helped reforest Potts Mtn in 1972 after it was destroyed
by fire a year earlier. Wildflowers are prominent. USFS
trail number 626.

▼ POTTS MOUNTAIN TRAIL   180

Although hikers can use this 6.8-mi (or 10 mi) road, it is
now a system off-road-vehicle route traversing the
mountain ridge in the James River District—George
Washington National Forest, USFS trail number 630
—and in the New Castle District—Jefferson National
Forest, trail number 58. Sections heavily used in hunting
seasons. Access is from junction of VA 18 and SR 607 in
Potts Creek. Go 2.1 mi on SR 607 to FR 176. After 3.2
mi, trail road is on L. Exit is on SR 617, 1.9 mi S of
Alleghany and Craig county line.

Fore Mountain Area
Alleghany County

▼ FORE MOUNTAIN TRAIL, DRY RUN TRAIL   181–184

Length: 22.6 mi (36.2 km) ct; strenuous. *USGS Maps:* Clifton Forge, Covington, Healing Springs. *Trailhead:* Dolly Ann Work Center parking lot.

Directions and Description: From Covington go E 1 mi on US 60 to Dolly Ann Work Center on L. Begin hike from parking lot on white-blazed *Fore Mtn Trail,* ascending Fore Mtn in large stands of oaks. Range of elevation is from 1,200 ft to 3,000 ft on this isolated and sometimes rocky ridge trail. Follow crest NE past junction with *Dry Run Trail* on L at 6.1 mi. (*Dry Run Trail* follows old gated hunter's road to FR 125, crosses, enters another gated road, and at 2.6 mi reaches view of Bald Knob R. At 3.4 mi is view to N of Big Knob, 4,072 ft. This and Fore Mtn are among the highest in the Alleghany Mts. Continue the circle of the Dolly RARE II area. At 4.5 mi is junction with *Big Mama Trail;* a sharp R here leads to US 220. Trail may be overgrown. At 4.9 mi is junction with *Fat Pat Trail*, an overgrown hunter's trail on R. Reach top of Peters Ridge at 5 mi, and descend to Dry Run, a stream, at 6 mi. Exit at Dry Run Rd, FR 339, after another 1.8 mi to parking area on Cyprus St, near High Acres Trailer Ct in N Covington.)

To continue on the *Fore Mtn Trail* go straight ahead on ridge passing a number of views, including of rock outcrop at 9 mi (2,823 ft). Begin descent; reach parking area on White Oaks Flat Rd. (It is 0.7 mi on road out to SR 606.) Continue L, descending through forest on relocated trail to SR 606, McGraw Gap; cross road and

Smith Creek (may have to wade) at 10.3 mi. (It is 4.3 mi R on SR 606 and VA 188 to US 60–220 in Clifton Forge.) Ascend on steep switchbacks to scenic overlook of Clifton Forge and Rainbow Gap at 11.4 mi on Pine Spur Ridge. Reach crest of Middle Mtn at 13.3 mi and boundary of Bath and Alleghany counties (3,043 ft) at 14.8 mi. Backtrack to SR 606; or continue on *Middle Mtn Trail* for 8.8 mi into Douthat State Park (see Warm Springs Ranger District) parking areas for total of 22.6 mi. USFS trail numbers 473, 471.

Jerry's Run Area
Alleghany County

▼ JERRY'S RUN TRAIL   185

Length: 3.8 mi (6.1 km) rt; moderate. *USGS Map:* Jerry's Run. *Trailhead:* Parking area on FR 69.

Directions and Description: Not many trails have an interstate-exit sign exclusively for themselves, but at I-64, exit 1, sign points the route for *Jerry's Run Trail.* (The junction is 12.7 mi W of Covington from the junction with VA 154, exit 4, and 2 mi E from the Virginia–West Virginia state line.) Turn off I-64 onto FR 198, S, and go 0.6 mi to FR 69. In another 0.4 mi on FR 69 park in area on L.

To begin hike, cross road to "rough road" sign and follow white-blazed trail down to Jerry's Run, an excellent trout stream and camping area. Cross creek at 0.4 mi in area of hemlock, rhododendron, beech, maple, and white pine. Follow the creek until ascending on slope with switchbacks to scenic views from the state line at 1.9 mi. Backtrack. (An alternate for the experienced hiker is to continue along the state line for another 2 mi on national forest property to VA 311 and the Mtn Top Restaurant, 0.4 mi off I-64. Vehicle shuttle would require a turn around in White Sulphur Springs, another 3 mi, because I-64 exit 183 to VA 311 does not have an E exit.) USFS trail number 659.

Oliver Mountain Area
Alleghany and Bath Counties

The two *Oliver Mtn Trails,* 2.5 mi and 7.5 mi long, plus other trails in the Lake Moomaw region (which have become the management responsibility of the George Washington National Forest instead of the Virginia WMA), are scheduled for a system of improvement and marking. Hikers should consult the James River and Warm Springs ranger district headquarters for current trail conditions. (Also, see Gathright WMA in chapter 10.)

Lee Ranger District

The Lee Ranger District has a complex color-coded trail system and, in the last 10 years, has conducted a thorough research project to determine the condition of more than 75 trails and 180 mi in Virginia and 20 trails and 70 mi in West Virginia.

The Lee Ranger District's divisions, for the purpose of describing trail connections in this guidebook, number four. Three of the areas include parts of Massanutten Mtn, which is shaped like a large, slender wishbone; the

South Range of Massanutten Mountain, George Washington National Forest. National Forest Service.

R clavicle is Massanutten Mtn/E (MME), the L clavicle is Massanutten Mtn/W (MMW), and the prong base is Massanutten Mtn/S (MMS). The beautiful mountain range of which Massanutten is a part is between the S and N forks of the Shenandoah River. The fourth area of trails is the N Mtn range, W of the Shenandoah Valley and bordering West Virginia. In addition to the Lee Ranger District's trails in the four areas is one trail cutting across a large part of the whole district. The *Big Blue Trail* runs across the district from Bentonville, over the MME and MMW, between Woodstock and Strasburg, and, N of Mill Mtn, into West Virginia.

▼ BIG BLUE TRAIL   187

A new guidebook, *Guide to the Big Blue Trail,* by Elizabeth Johnston, was published by the Potomac Appalachian Trail Club in 1983. Maps were drawn by Lynn T. Gallagher. The book details 143 mi, 55 of which are in Virginia from a junction with the *Appalachian Trail* at Matthews Arm in the Shenandoah National Park to the West Virginia line. The trail continues through West Virginia to Hancock, Maryland. (The northern half of more than 100 mi ends, or begins, as the *Tuscarora Trail,* at a junction with the *A.T.* at Deans Gap near Donnellytown, Pennsylvania.) For information on the guide, and to purchase it, contact PATC, 1718 N St NW, Washington, DC 20036. Tel: 202-638-5306, weeknights 7–10 P.M.

Massanutten Mountain East Area
Shenandoah, Warren, and Page Counties

An excellent base camp from which to begin trails for this area is Elizabeth Furnace Campground. Access is from Waterlick, junction of VA 55 and SR 678 (5.2 mi E of Strasburg and 7.2 mi W of Front Royal on VA 55). Go 4.5 mi S on SR 678 to the campground (passing SR 619 on L at 1.3 mi, the group campground at 3.5 mi, and the Elizabeth Furnace picnic area at 4 mi—all on the L side of SR 678). At the picnic area are *Pig Iron Trail,* a 0.2-mi loop interpretive trail explaining how pig iron was made at the furnace, and *Charcoal–Passage Creek Trail,* a 0.6-mi loop interpretive trail explaining how charcoal was processed. USFS trail numbers 483, 483/A. 188–189

▼ MASSANUTTEN MOUNTAIN EAST TRAIL   190–200

Length: 23.1 mi (36.8 km); moderate to strenuous.
USGS Maps: Strasburg, Bentonville, Rileyville, Luray,
Hamburg. *Trailhead:* Elizabeth Furnace.

Directions and Description: From Elizabeth Furnace
picnic area (747 ft elevation) follow blue-blazed *Big Blue
Trail* L of the furnace downstream by Passage Creek for
0.4 mi. Vegetation includes basswood, oaks, azaleas,
phlox, spicebush, asters, and gold star. Ascend on
graded switchbacks to overlook at 1.5 mi, crossing old
wagon road occasionally. After steep ascent reach ridge
crest at 2.3 mi (1,700 ft). (Here is junction with orange-
blazed *Buzzard Rock Trail,* extending L along the ridge
spine for 1.6 mi. Another 0.5 leads to exit at SR 619 near
the Fish Culture Center, which is 0.4 mi E of SR 678. Or,
another trail at junction is yellow-blazed *Shawl Gap
Trail,* which descends E on old jeep road for 2.4 mi to exit
on SR 613, 3.2 mi S from the Fish Culture Center.)
Continue R on *Big Blue Trail,* which is also the *MME
Trail,* along rocky ridge on narrow tread. Forest is
mainly hardwoods.

After passing a number of overlooks reach Little
Crease Mtn at 5.2 mi, and descend into Mill Creek Hollow. At 8 mi reach Veach Gap; cross 17-ft-wide stream
and turn L. (Mill Run jeep trail with yellow blazes descends R for 1.1 mi along stream with large hemlocks to
gated FR 409 and parking area. From here it is 0.3 mi to
SR 744 and, on SR 744, 0.5 mi across Passage Creek to
SR 678.) At 8.1 mi is Little Crease Camping Shelter, 100
ft L from trail. Ascend on old rocky road—the *Veach
Gap Trail*, which was a Revolutionary War access road to
and from Fork Valley—for 0.9 mi to ridge gap. Here the

Big Blue continues straight ahead and descends; the orange-blazed *MME Trail* turns R on old woods road. (From here the *Big Blue Trail* and the yellow-blazed *Veach Gap Trail* go 1.7 mi conjointly to SR 613. At that point the *Big Blue* continues ahead to the low-water bridge crossing of the S Fork of the Shenandoah River. After another 12.2 mi the *Big Blue Trail* intersects with the *Appalachian Trail* near Matthews Arm in the Shenandoah National Park.) On the *MME* follow the ridge with successive ascents and descents on rocky conglomerate knolls; at 12.4 mi is Milford Gap and junction with *Milford Gap Trail*. (This trail, white blazed, descends for 1.8 mi R to Chalybeate Spring and then 0.9 mi to SR 758 near Passage Creek and out to Detrick. Also from this point *Milford Gap Trail* descends L for 2 mi to Hazard Mill Campground near the S Fork of the Shenandoah River; a hike downstream on SR 613 3.3 mi farther leads to *Big Blue* crossing. After 0.5 mi on the *Milford Gap Trail* from the *MME*, the *Tolliver Trail* forks R, descending for 2.3 mi to SR 717 at Burners Bottom near the S Fork of the Shenandoah River and E of the fire warden's home.)

At 13.8 mi on the *MME Trail* is junction with *Indian Grave Ridge Trail*, L. (The purple-blazed trail descends for 2.5 mi through oaks and pines to a parking area on SR 717, 3 mi from SR 684 junction near Goods Mill Falls on the S Fork of the Shenandoah River.) At Habron Gap (1,927 ft) cross *Habron Gap Trail*. (The E side is blazed blue; it descends by Keyser Path for 1.4 mi in locust and walnut stand to SR 684 near Fosters Landing of the S Fork of the Shenandoah River. The unblazed W side descends to SR 684 off SR 769 near Mt Zion Church.) Continue through numerous blueberry patches; cross

faint, unblazed *Stephens Trail* at 20 mi. Reach junction
with *Kennedy Peak Trail* at 20.9 mi on L. (This 0.3-mi
white-blazed spur trail ascends to Lookout Tower (2,560
ft) for outstanding view of Page Valley. Backtrack.) The
MME Trail skirts W of Kennedy Peak, but after 21.6 mi
partially follows old jeep trail to SR 675 (1,849 ft) at 23.3
mi, and end of *MME Trail*. To continue hiking S see
MMS Trail below. (It is 6.5 mi L to Luray and 1.4 mi R on
SR 675 to Camp Roosevelt Campground, the site of the
first Civilian Conservation Corps (CCC) camp in the
nation, operating April 4, 1933 through May 1942. Sign
here recognizes Henry Rich, first CCC member.) Camp
Roosevelt has campsites, restrooms, water, picnic facilities and dumping station. USFS trail numbers (except
unnumbered *Mill Run Trail* and *Stephens Trail*) in order
of directions, 404, 1013, 404/B, 406, 484, 560, 560/A,
567, 559, 404/A.

▼ LION'S TAIL TRAIL   201

This 0.3-mi loop trail for the visually handicapped was
designated a national recreation trail in 1979. Access is
from parking area on FR 274, Chrisman Hollow Rd; it is
0.9 mi S of junction of FR 274 and SR 675, and 1.3 mi S
from Camp Roosevelt. The unique trail with Braille
descriptions is maintained by the Lions Clubs of 13 cities
and towns in the area. USFS trail number 407.

▼ DUNCAN HOLLOW TRAIL   202–206

Length: 9.1 mi (14.6 km); moderate. *USGS Map:* Hamburg. *Trailhead:* Across road from Camp Roosevelt.

   Directions and Description: From entrance of Camp
Roosevelt (see preceding entry for *Massanutten Mtn E*

Trail) go E on SR 675 for 100 yds, enter on graded orange-blazed trail through oak forest to Duncan Creek, and proceed 3 mi to blue-blazed *Gap Creek Trail* junction. (*Gap Creek Trail* runs W over Catback, through Peach Orchard Gap to connect with red-blazed *Scothorn Gap Trail* in 1 mi. *Gap Creek Trail* continues descent to FR 274 for another mi at Passage Creek.) Continue ahead upstream on graded contour. At 4.6 mi leave Duncan Hollow, cross Middle Mtn at saddle, and descend to headwaters of Big Run at 5.2 mi. (Here yellow-blazed *Middle Mtn Trail* ascends R (N) for 0.6 mi to a bog at Scothorn Gap, where the red-blazed *Scothorn Gap Trail* goes N for 1.5 mi to *Gap Creek Trail* or SW for 1.3 mi to FR 274. At this point a circuit hike of 11.3 mi can be made in a clockwise direction back to *Duncan Hollow Trail* and Camp Roosevelt.) Continue ahead gradually descending; at 7 mi pass junction with *Waterfall Mtn Trail,* a white-blazed trail on R. (This trail ascends steeply over the mountain range to FR 274 for 1.3 mi.) After 2 mi of crossing a dozen small tributaries of Big Run, reach US 211 at 9.1 mi. (It is 0.9 mi W on US 211 to the New Market Picnic Grounds and beginning of *MMS Trail,* 1.7 mi W to the Massanutten Visitor Center, and an additional 3.8 mi W to New Market. Luray is 8.5 mi E.) USFS trail numbers 410, 409, 555, 555/A, 412.

Massanutten Mountain South Area
Page, Shenandoah, and Rockingham Counties

▼ MASSANUTTEN MOUNTAIN
SOUTH TRAIL   207–216

Length: 16.4 mi (26.2 km), moderate to strenuous.

USGS Maps: Hamburg, 10th Legion, Elkton W, Stanley.
Trailhead: New Market picnic area.

Directions and Description: (A visit to the visitor center is recommended. *Discovery Way,* a 0.4-mi paved self-guiding loop nature trail begins at the S end of center's parking area. Also, the *Massanutten Story Book Trail* is on Chrisman Hollow Rd, FR 274, 1.5 mi N from the center. This paved trail for the handicapped explains the geology of the mountains.) Begin the *MMS Trail* on W side of New Market picnic area (1,572 ft) entrance road, 125 yds from US 211. Ascend on orange-blazed *MMS,* pass spring at 0.1 mi, and pass junction at 0.2 mi with path R to visitor center. At 0.3 mi begin steep climb to ridge line. Follow crest through hardwoods, scattered conifers, and berries; pass huge overhanging rock at 0.7 mi on rocky trail and reach overlook at 1 mi. At 1.2 mi, overlook is outstanding.

At 2 mi is junction with white-blazed *Bird Knob Trail.* (This trail extends R 2.2 mi from here to FR 375. It does not go to 2,684-ft Bird Knob.) Continue, bearing L onto woods road. Pass large ant hills for next 0.7 mi. Wet weather springs are along trail. Reach FR 375 at 3.2 mi and bear R (FR 375 L ascends to WSVA-TV towers). Pass *Bird Knob Trail* R at 3.6 mi and junction with purple-blazed *Roaring Run Trail* on L at 3.9 mi. (This rocky and usually brushy trail first ascends Big Mtn, then descends for 3.7 mi to Catherine Furnace on FR 65 near SR 685 and 2.2 mi out to US 340.) Continue ahead on *MMS*—here also called FR 375—to Pitt Spring (1,751 ft) at 6.6 mi. (FR 375 descends through Pitt Spring Gorge for 2 mi to Catherine Furnace.) Leave FR 375, turn L on old woods road, seeded in places. At 7.4 mi white-blazed *Pitt Spring Lookout Trail* extends L, 0.3 mi. At 9.9 mi

cross Morgan Run and junction with *Morgan Run Trail,*
which extends L. (This 1.4-mi yellow-blazed trail
descends along a rocky and sometimes boggy stream area
to FR 65, Cub Run Rd.) Continue ahead, crossing a
number of streams frequented by wildlife for the next 2
mi. Reach Fridley Gap at 12.3 mi. (Blue-blazed *Fridley
Gap Trail* crosses; on L (E) descends steeply in places for
2.1 mi to FR 65, and on R (W) goes 0.7 mi to SR 868
along Mtn Run, with black birch, maple, mountain
laurel, pines, and wildflowers. For exit continue beyond
SR 868 1.1 mi to SR 722; 4.6 mi farther on state roads is
US 11.)

At 13 mi on *MMS* is overlook on L. Begin descent
from ridge at 13.9 mi, turning E, leaving Fourth Mtn to
Fridley Run and crossing the stream at 14.5 mi. Third
Mtn is ahead at 15.3 mi. At 15.6 mi is junction with *Shelton Trail,* a white-blazed crosstrail. (To R it is 1.6 mi to
Boone Run Trail and Boone Shelter. There, *Boone Run
Trail* goes R, SW, for 1 mi and descends, with view of
Page Valley; on L it goes for 0.7 mi along a stocked trout
stream to FR 65. Vegetation is hemlock, gum, poplar,
and oaks. The L, NE, direction of *Shelton Trail* goes 1 mi
to junction with *Fridley Gap Trail.*) Continue straight
ahead by wildlife clearing, climb Second Mtn, and
descend to FR 65 at 16.4 mi, the trail terminus. L, it is 7
mi to Catherine Furnace on FR 65; R is 2.1 mi to SR 636,
and is 2 mi farther to SR 602 at Greenwood (3.1 mi NW
of Elkton). USFS trail numbers 416, 416/B, 582, 584,
583, 419, 549, 579. Use vehicle shuttle.

Massanutten Mountain West Area
Shenandoah County

▼ SIGNAL KNOB TRAIL   217–218

Length: 9 mi (14.4 km) rt; moderate. *USGS Map:* Strasburg. *Trailhead:* Parking area.

Directions and Description: From VA 55 at Waterlick, drive S on SR 678 for 3.4 mi to parking area on R (0.6 mi N of Elizabeth Furnace picnic area). (The loop is less strenuous made clockwise; following white-blazed *Blue Spur Trail* L near gated road at parking area for 0.5 mi to *Big Blue–Bear Wallow Trail,* ascend for 3.4 mi to *MMW Trail,* turn R for another 1.5 mi to Signal Knob, and descend on *Signal Knob Trail* for 4.5 mi to parking area for a circuit of 10 mi.) To hike counterclockwise, follow the sign at the parking area on a yellow-blazed graded trail through hardwoods, scattered conifers, azaleas, blueberries, filberts, and wildflowers to spring on L at 0.4 mi. Weave in and out of rocky coves to Buzzard Rock Overlook at 1.5 mi. Excellent view of Passage Creek Gorge. Turn L and reach Fort Valley Overlook at 2.2 mi. At 3 mi Shenandoah Valley Overlook is R on short spur. Reach Signal Knob (2,106 ft), a Confederate and Union Civil War lookout point, at 4.5 mi. Elevation gain 1,334 ft. Backtrack; or use other trails, described for clockwise hike, for loop. USFS trail numbers 402, 563, 405/2, 408.

▼ MASSANUTTEN MOUNTAIN WEST TRAIL   219–224

Length: 11.5 mi (18.4 km); moderate. *USGS Maps:* Strasburg, Toms Brook, Rileyville, Edinburg. *Trailhead:* Signal Knob Trail.

Directions and Description: This trail has two sections; first from Signal Knob S 4 mi to Powell's Fort, and the second from Little Fort, SR 758 to Edinburg Gap for 7.5 mi. They are connected by FR 66 and FR 273. Before the Jawbone Gap wildfire of 1981, *Taskers Gap Trail* extended another 4.5 mi S to connect with trails to Massanutten Mtn E.

To begin the *MMW Trail* ascend on the *Signal Knob Trail* for 4.5 mi to Signal Knob. From here go S on orange-blazed *MMW Trail,* passing spring at 0.8 mi, and reach *Big Blue–Bearwallow Trail* L at 1.3 mi. (This trail crosses Green Mtn and descends to SR 678 parking lot for 3.9 mi, as described above under *Signal Knob Trail,* and continues to Elizabeth Furnace picnic area at 4.4 mi. Or, leads to Elizabeth Furnace Campground via 0.5-mi *Bear Wallow Spur Trail* at 3.8 mi. The *Glass House Trail* also forks R from the *Big Blue Trail,* descending to PATC-owned Glass House at SR 678.)

Continue ahead on the *MMW Trail,* passing the Strasburg Reservoir L at 1.8 mi. Bear R at 2.1 mi. At 2.3 mi manganese mine is L. Reach FR 66 and end of this section at gate at 4 mi. Powell's Fort Camp is R, and parking area is L.

To reach the second section of *MMW Trail* (also called *Powell's Mtn Trail*), hike or drive on FR 66 to Mine Gap, and then take FR 273 for 5 mi to Little Fork Recreation Area, Woodstock Gap. (It is 5.6 mi W to Woodstock and US 11 on SR 758 and 665. At Woodside Gap is *Wagon Rd Trail,* a 1.3-mi white-blazed loop trail to Woodstock Tower and SR 758. Scenic views of seven bends in the N Fork of the Shenandoah River are superb.) Continue on the orange-blazed *MMW Trail* halfway around camping loop on dirt road. Follow S, upstream, along Peter's Mill

Run, crossing examples of Coweeta dips (wide water bars) and passing autumn olives. At 0.9 mi pass spring followed by a number of wildlife clearings. Pass another spring at 2.4 mi, and a wildlife pond at 4.5 mi. Take R fork at 5.6 mi; 0.2 mi farther trail is rocky. At 6.2 mi begin descent, steep in spots, for 1 mi. Trail ends at 7.5 mi at Edinburg Gap on SR 675. It is 3.9 mi W to US 11 in Edinburg. Vehicle shuttle necessary. USFS trail numbers 408, 553, 402, 405/2, 562, 558, 552.

North Mountain North Area
**Shenandoah County, Virginia
and Hardy County, West Virginia**

Trails described in this area are those in VA or along the state line, NE of Wolf Gap Campground on SR 675, 11.3 mi W of ranger station in Edinburg.

▼ MILL MOUNTAIN TRAIL, BIG SCHLOSS TRAIL,
BIG BLUE TRAIL, LITTLE STONY CREEK TRAIL,
LITTLE SLUICE MOUNTAIN TRAIL,
CEDAR CREEK TRAIL   225–231

Length: 24.8 mi (39.7 km) ct; moderate to strenuous.
USGS Maps: Wolf Gap, Woodstock. *Trailhead:* Wolf Gap Campground.
   Directions and Description: Either take the route mentioned in preceding description of N Mtn N area or, from the junction of I-81 and VA 42 in Woodstock, take VA 42 W to Columbia Furnace for 7 mi and turn R on SR 675. Go 6.6 mi on SR 675 to Wolf Gap Campground (2,240 ft) on the Virginia–West Virginia boundary. Park in parking area. Begin on the orange-blazed *Mill Mtn Trail,* near

campsite #9. Ascend on wide jeep road for 0.9 mi to ridge crest. "Road" becomes more a rocky footpath; continue for 1 mi to junction of 0.3-mi *Big Schloss Trail*. *Big Schloss Trail* ascends steeply to a massive rock formation (2,964 ft). Views of Trout Run Valley in West Virginia and Little Schloss Mtn in Virginia are outstanding. Return to *Mill Mtn Trail,* turn R and continue along Virginia–West Virginia line. Reach Sandstone Spring and stand of hemlock at 4.5 mi. On a straight trail through oaks and mountain laurel ascend to an airway beacon (3,293 ft); descend gradually, and reach junction with the *Big Blue Trail* at 6 mi. (L on *Big Blue,* also called *Pond Run Trail,* it is 2.8 mi to Waites Run Rd and another 6 mi to Wardensville, West Virginia.)

Turn R on the *Big Blue Trail,* a jeep trail descending 0.6 mi to junction with *Peer Trail* on L and with yellow-blazed *Little Stony Creek Trail* on R. (Elevation at this point is 2,995 ft.) (If *Little Stony Creek Trail* is chosen, pass the locked Sugar Knob Cabin—owned by PATC; reservations required for use—and pass spring here and again at 1 mi as trail descends on the W slope of Stony Creek. Vegetation is hemlock, white pine, oaks, maple, poplar, and rhododendron. Because area is a watershed for the town of Woodstock, camping is forbidden near the stream. Reach FR 92 at 3.7 mi. A continuing loop can be made R on FR 92 for 3.3 mi to SR 675, and 1.5 mi R on SR 675 to Wolf Gap, for a circuit of 14.5 mi. A steep, unmarked cutoff from FR 92 to SR 675 is on R 2.8 mi from Little Stony Creek. It reduces distance by 1.5 mi.)

If continuing on the *Big Blue Trail,* go straight ahead over broad ridge of Sugar Knob, and reach junction of *Little Sluice Trail* on R after 0.9 mi from *Little Stony Creek Trail.* Here too is a possible round trip back to

Wolf Gap, by descending on purple-blazed *Little Sluice Trail* (primarily a hunter's dirt road) for 4.8 mi to FR 88. At FR 88 it is 0.5 mi R to FR 92, and another 3.4 mi to *Little Stony Creek Trail*. An additional hike on the roads as described for *Little Stony Creek Trail* makes a circuit total of 16.2 mi. Unless the hiker prefers walking on FR-designated roads, a vehicle shuttle is essential. (On FR 88 S from junction of FR 92 the road becomes SR 608 and goes 2.8 mi to SR 675. A turn L leads 0.5 mi to Columbia Furnace and VA 42.)

There is one more trail that could make a circuit—a longer one, with vehicle assistance. Continue ahead on the *Big Blue Trail* from junction of *Little Sluice Trail* for 3.7 mi to *Cedar Creek Trail,* R. Along the way the *Big Blue* climbs Little Sluice Mtn, passes a scenic quartz outcropping, switches back and forth from forest to old roads, fords creeks, passes access to remains of the Van Buren Furnace, and finally, after some wet tread, it forks upstream along Cedar Creek; here the *Big Blue* goes L and *Cedar Creek Trail* leads R. Follow the wet and sometimes soggy yellow-blazed *Cedar Creek Trail* for 2.8 mi to gated FR 88. Wildflowers are abundant. From here on FR 88 it is 2.2 mi to FR 92, and it is a combined total of 24.8 mi on trails and roads to Wolf Gap Campground. USFS trail numbers, in order of description, 1004, 1004/A, 1013, 571, 401, 573.

North Mountain South Area
Shenandoah County, Virginia and
Hardy County, West Virginia

Trails described in this area are those in Virginia or along

Mills Creek Trail. (Exits to shuttle vehicle could be at Blue Ridge Pkwy mp 22.1 at Bald Mtn Overlook, or at Torry Furnace on SR 664.) If L, go 3.1 mi to FR 162 (which is 1 mi from BRP), turn R on old road, *Stony Run Jeep Trail,* for 0.6 mi to *Mills Creek Trail.* Turn R and descend. From 7.7 mi *Mills Creek Spur* leads 0.8 mi to Mills Creek dam on L. Continue ahead to junction with *Torry Ridge Trail* at 10.2. (Ahead it is 0.4 mi to SR 664 and Torry Furnace.) Turn L and follow *Torry Ridge Trail* to junction with blue-blazed *Torry Ridge Spur Trail* on L at 12.2 mi. (From junction it is 0.8 mi down to FR 91 near park entrance.) Continue ahead to beginning spur trail N of Campground A and turn L at 13.1 mi. USFS trail numbers, in order of above listing, 518, 507, 518/A, 507/C.

▼ WHITE ROCKS GAP TRAIL,
SLACKS OVERLOOK TRAIL   249–250

Length: 10.2 mi (16.3 km) rt, ct; moderate to strenuous. *USGS Map:* Big Levels. *Trailhead:* Campground B.
   Directions and Description: From Campground B or C follow gentle, graded orange-blazed trail SW by Back Creek. At 2.0 mi is junction with *Slacks Overlook Trail* on R. (It is 0.5 mi ahead to White Rock Gap (2,549 ft) and end of *White Rocks Gap Trail.*) Proceed on blue-blazed *Slacks Overlook Trail* for 1.8 mi to Slacks Overlook at Blue Ridge Pkwy mp 19.9. Continue ahead for 0.8 mi to junction with *Torry Ridge Trail* for a total of 5.1 mi. Backtrack or use the *Torry Ridge Trail* for a shorter route back to camp. USFS trail numbers: 480, 480/C.

▼ BALD MOUNTAIN TRAIL,
MINE BANK TRAIL   251–252

Length: 9 mi (14.4 km) rt, ct; moderate. *USGS Map:*
Big Levels, Vesuvius. *Trailhead:* Campground, or Blue
Ridge Pkwy mp 23.

Directions and Description: These trails can be
approached from *Torry Ridge Trail* to FR 162, or
opposite Fork Mtn Overlook on BRP mp 23. *Bald Mtn
Trail* is 2.5 mi one way on N slopes on Bald Mtn (3,250
ft), and *Mine Bank Trail* descends N from BRP mp 23 to
St Mary's Trail for 2 mi one way. A loop could be made
by following *Stony Run Jeep Trail,* FR 478, to Green
Pond, taking a L on *St Mary's Trail* and another L up the
mountain on *Mine Bank Trail* for approximately 10 mi.
USFS trail numbers 500/E, 500/C.

▼ SAINT MARY'S TRAIL,
SAINT MARY'S FALLS TRAIL   253–255

Length: 12.6 mi (20.2 km) rt; moderate to strenuous.
USGS Maps: Big Levels, Vesuvius. *Trailhead:* End of
FSR 41.

Directions and Description: (This trail can be
approached from *Torry Ridge Trail,* but a vehicle shuttle
at the end of FR 41 or Blue Ridge Pkwy mp 23 would be
shorter.) From I-81 Raphine exit go E on VA 56 through
Steeles Tavern. Turn L on SR 608 and go 3 mi (passing
under railroad bridge) to FR 41 on R. Go 1.5 mi to gate,
and park. Begin hike up L side of river in areas of wildflowers, berries, sumac, ferns, hardwoods, and pines. At
1.4 mi turn L on *St Mary's Falls Trail* for 0.5 mi to
waterfall in river gorge. Spectacular scenery. Pass mining

sites, quartzite rock slides; reach junction with *Mine Bank Trail* at 3.6 mi, and continue to criss-cross the creek. Reach FR 478 at 6.3 mi. Backtrack, or follow R up *Stony Run Jeep Trail* to *Torry Ridge Trail*. Or, hike N for 4.5 mi on *Stony Run Jeep Trail* to FR 42. (The unblazed *Kennedy Ridge Trail* continues across the road from *St Mary's Trail*.) USFS trail numbers 500, 500/B.

▼ CELLAR MOUNTAIN TRAIL   256–257

Length: 5.8 mi (9.3 km) rt; moderate. *USGS Maps:* Big Levels, Vesuvius. *Trailhead:* Old road on FR 42.

Directions and Description: From junction off FR 41 and FR 42 go 1.2 mi on FR 42 to blue-blazed old road on R. Parking area sparse. Ascend in mixed forest with understory of chinquapin, blueberry, mountain laurel, deerberry, and azaleas. Pass huge ant hills. Reach another old road leading to *Stony Run Jeep Trail* at 2.9 mi. Backtrack. USFS trail number 501.

South Fork Tye River Area
Nelson County

▼ CRABTREE FALLS TRAIL   258

Length: 2.9 mi (4.6 km); moderate to strenuous. *USGS Maps:* Montebello, Massies Mill. *Trailhead:* VA 56 parking lot.

Directions and Description: The *Crabtree Falls Trail* passes what is considered to be the highest cascading falls in Virginia. Care should be taken to prevent sliding or falling on the trail in icy conditions. From the Blue Ridge Pkwy at Tye River Gap (2,969 ft) junction with VA 56, take VA 56 E to parking lot on R. Hike across 110-ft foot bridge for 0.2 mi to the first of four constructed over-looks designed to accent the splendor of the five major cascades. Reach other overlooks at 0.3 mi, 0.7 mi, and 1.4 mi. Reach Crabtree Meadows parking lot at 2.9 mi and the junction with SR 828. Use vehicle shuttle, or backtrack. At this point it is 0.5 mi S on SR 828 to the *Appalachian Trail.* USFS trail number 526.

Mount Pleasant Area
Amherst County

▼ MOUNT PLEASANT TRAIL,
  POMPEY LOOP TRAIL   259–260

Length: 6.7 mi (10.7 km); moderate. *USGS Maps:* Montebello, Forks of Buffalo. *Trailhead:* Hog Camp Gap.

Directions and Description: From junction of US 60 and SR 634 at Oronoco (1 mi W of *Appalachian Trail* crossing) turn on SR 634. Go 0.9 mi on SR 634, turn R on SR 755 NE for 1 mi, and proceed on FR 48 if road is passable. Park at or pass the Wiggins Spring campsite to reach the *A.T.* crossing at Hog Camp Gap. Begin hike here and follow blue-blazed trail along road, turn L in timber regeneration area at 0.4 mi. At 2 mi reach top of Pompey Mtn (4,032 ft). A side trail on the L at 2.8 mi leads to top of Mt Pleasant for 0.5 mi. Superb views at the summit (4,021 ft). Pass untested spring on R at 4.4 mi and L at 4.5 mi. Reach open space at 5.4 mi; return to Hog Camp Gap at 6.7 mi. Trail has copious wildflowers and berries. USFS trail numbers 701, 702.

Elephant Mountain Area
Rockbridge County

▼ INDIAN GAP TRAIL,
RESERVOIR HOLLOW TRAIL,
ELEPHANT MOUNTAIN TRAIL   261–263

Length: 6.1 mi (9.7 km) ct; moderate to strenuous.
USGS Map: Buena Vista. *Trailhead:* US 60 parking area.
   Directions and Description: Although this system can
be approached from Laurel Park, an undeveloped area
of city property at the end of 21st St, and from the end of
12th St via Pine Ave and Woods Rd in Buena Vista, the
preferred route is from Buena Vista E on US 60 for 2.8
mi to parking area. From here ascend on blue-blazed
Indian Gap Trail and cross two small streams. At 0.9 mi,
side trail L leads to Blue Ridge Pkwy; at 1.1 mi is junction with *Reservoir Hollow Trail.* Continue on *Indian
Gap Trail,* which turns R descending through area of regeneration hardwoods, to Laurel Park at 2.6 mi. Backtrack or use vehicle shuttle.
   At junction of *Reservoir Hollow Trail* continue ahead
for 0.6 mi to junction of *Elephant Mtn Trail* on R. A hike
up Elephant Mtn (2,101 ft) is strenuous; trail is steep,
rugged, and narrow in sections. Mountain laurel, pitch
pine, chestnut sprouts, and blueberries are here. Reach
summit at 1.2 mi. Views of Buena Vista and the valley are
outstanding. Backtrack.
   To continue on *Reservoir Hollow Trail* turn R after
descent from Elephant Mtn, reach good primitive campsite at 1.9 mi, and descend to gate at Woods Rd in Buena
Vista at 2.3 mi. USFS trail numbers 509, 509/A, 509/B.

Bluff Mountain Area
Rockbridge County

Three trails—*Belle Cove, Saddle Gap,* and *Little Rocky Row Run*—all lead to the *Appalachian Trail* and are accessible from US 501 in the southern tip of Pedlar District. The trails can connect with each other from the *A.T.* to form loops or to ascend to Bluff Mtn, where FSR 164 and SR 607 exit to Buena Vista. USFS trail numbers 511, 512, 703.

▼ BELLE COVE TRAIL   264

Length: 9.2 mi (14.7 km) rt; moderate. *USGS Maps:* Glasgow, Buena Vista. *Trailhead:* Parking area at Belle Cove Branch.

   Directions and Description: From Ranger Station in Buena Vista it is 5.4 mi S on US 501 to Belle Cove Branch; parking area on L is small. Follow old road, observing blue blazes, to Belle Cove Branch crossing at 1.1 mi. Continue upstream into Belle Cove Canyon, where wildflowers are abundant. Ascend to *Appalachian Trail* in Salt Log Gap (S) at 4.6 mi. Backtrack or take the *A.T.* route for vehicle shuttle. (It is 1.5 mi L and N to Bluff Mtn; 1.1 mi R and S to *Saddle Gap Trail;* and 3.6 mi to *Little Rocky Row Run Trail* S on *A.T.)*

▼ SADDLE GAP TRAIL   265

Length: 3 mi (4.8 km) rt; moderate. *USGS Maps:* Glasgow, Buena Vista. *Trailhead:* Near Amlite plant.

   Directions and Description: From US 501 near Snowden turn at Amlite plant sign on SR 812 and FR 36 for 2.8 mi to trail sign on L. No place to park here. Ascend over large mounded-earth hummocks into forest of hemlocks and hardwoods. Reach *Appalachian Trail* at 1.5 mi. Backtrack or use *A.T.* for vehicle shuttle. (It is 1.1 mi on *A.T.* N to *Belle Cove Trail,* and 2.5 mi S to *Little Rocky Row Run Trail.*)

▼ LITTLE ROCKY ROW RUN TRAIL   266

Length: 5.4 mi (8.6 km) rt; moderate. *USGS Maps:* Glasgow, Snowden. *Trailhead:* James River Overlook.

Directions and Description: From junction of US 501 and VA 130 go 2.5 mi E and park on James River Overlook at Amherst and Rockbridge county line. Hike back down the highway for 150 yds to trail on R. Ascend on switchbacks to ridge crest. Trail is festooned with azaleas, ferns, and chinquapins; rocks are laced with lichens and mosses. Reach power line at 0.6 mi. Magnificent view of James River and Williams Store at Snowden. Reach *Appalachian Trail* at 2.7 mi. Backtrack, or use *A.T.* N to Bluff Mtn at 8 mi, or take *A.T.* S down to US 501 for 4.1 mi.

Warm Springs Ranger District

Laurel Fork Area
Highland County

▼ LAUREL FORK TRAIL, BUCK RUN TRAIL, LOCUST SPRING RUN TRAIL, COLD SPRINGS RUN TRAIL, MIDDLE MOUNTAIN TRAIL, CHRISTIAN RUN TRAIL, BUCK RUN SPUR TRAIL, SLABCAMP

RUN TRAIL, LOCUST SPRING RUN SPUR TRAIL,
BEARWALLOW RUN TRAIL   267–276

Length: 28.2 mi (45.1 km) rt, ct; easy to moderate. *USGS
Maps:* Thornwood, Snowy Mtn, Hightown. *Trailhead:*
Locust Spring Campground.

Directions and Description: Laurel Fork, in the headwaters of the Potomac River, is an isolated high area,
elevation 2,600 to 4,100 ft. The steep slopes in the area
are circumvented by a network of easy, graded abandoned railroad beds and other trails. It is an ideal area for
hiking and nature study. *Laurel Fork Trail* extends SW to
NE somewhat centrally through the entire area, and
numerous trails branch out from it. To fully experience
this beautiful forest where regenerative power is demon-
strated, multiple circuit hikes are recommended. Access
to Locust Springs Campground is from the junction of
US 220 and 250 in Monterey, taking US 250 to highway
28 in West Virginia. Here turn R (N) and go 7 mi to
Locust Springs Picnic Area sign. Follow R on FR 142 to
campground. (From Harrisonburg take US 33 to WV 28
and go 16 mi S to FR 142 on L.)

Begin at Locust Springs on *Buck Run Trail,* E (or
Locust Spring Run Trail, SE for 3.1 mi), to the central
trail, *Laurel Fork Trail.* (*Buck Run Spur Trail* goes off R
from *Buck Run Trail* for 0.6 mi to connect with *Locust
Spring Run Trail.)* Pass a beaver pond and meadows and
stay on S side of the tributary along Buck Run, descending along the stream stocked with brook trout. Reach
Laurel Fork Trail at 3.3 mi; continue several miles on it,
or take either of two options.

One option at this point is to turn L, cross stream and
go 0.6 mi to *Cold Springs Run Trail* on R; follow it S for

1.3 mi, where it becomes *Middle Mtn Trail.* At 2.9 mi is *Christian Run Trail,* R. Follow it for a 1.5-mi hike looping back to *Laurel Fork Trail* and a total of 8.3 mi. A R turn down *Laurel Fork Trail* for 0.7 mi will connect with *Buck Run Trail* or *Locust Spring Run Trail* on L. A return on either trail to the campsite would total 12.3 mi for the circuit.

Another option from *Laurel Fork Trail* begins at junction of *Buck Run Trail;* turn R, going upstream on Laurel Fork stream. At 3.6 mi (from the beginning at the campground) reach the junction with *Slabcamp Run Trail* on the R. This trail leads up the tributary for 3 mi to junction with *Locust Spring Run Spur Trail,* then 1.5 mi to *Locust Spring Run Trail*—on which is a stand of red spruce and red pine—on the L for 1.5 mi and a return to camp for a total circuit of 9.6 mi.

Continuing upstream on the *Laurel Fork Trail* pass *Christian Run Trail* on L at 4 mi. Birch, oaks, cherry, maple, beech, hemlock, and spruce are on the trail. Wildflowers, ferns, and mosses are abundant. Animals are bear, deer, turkey, grouse, snowshoe hare, raccoon, mink, and considerable evidence of beaver in the tributaries. At 6.5 mi reach *Bearwallow Run Trail* on the R. (Continuing up the stream for 1.4 mi leads to SR 642 and limited parking area.) Bear R on scenic *Bearwallow Run Trail,* viewing beaver ponds and meadows, and after 2.7 mi on this trail reach FR 55 at 9.2 mi. Take a R on FR 55 to junction with *Locust Spring Run Spur Trail* at 11.2 mi. Go R on *Locust Spring Run Spur Trail* for 1.5 mi to junction with *Locust Spring Run Trail,* bear L, and return to the campground at a circuit total of 14.2 mi.

A route S to begin on *Middle Mtn Trail* is from FR 457.

This trail connects with all the others but has a different entrance. Access is at junction of US 220 and Forks of Water, SR 642. Go 10.3 mi on SR 642 (passing through Blue Grass community at 4.3 mi), turning N on FR 457 to the parking area. USFS trail numbers 450, 598, 633, 634/A, 634, 599, 598/B, 600, 633/A, 601.

Paddy Knob Area
Highland and Bath Counties

▼ PADDY KNOB TRAIL,
   PADDY KNOB SPUR TRAIL   277–278

Length: 5.9 mi (9.4 km) ct; moderate to strenuous. *USGS Maps:* Paddy Knob, Sunrise. *Trailhead:* Paddy Knob Overlook.

Directions and Description: From junction of US 220 and VA 84 at Vanderpool (3.5 mi S of Monterey) take VA 84 W to West Virginia state line and junction with Monongahela National Forest Rd 55. Go L on FR 55 for 3 mi to Paddy Knob Overlook. Trail follows ridge top E. Follow trail to small stream crossing at 0.8 mi and through wildlife clearing at 1.1 mi. At 1.8 mi descend steeply, almost a skid trail. Cross over to L side of ridge at 2.3 mi through mixed forest. Cross stream at 4.6 mi and reach SR 600 at 4.7 mi. Backtrack or use vehicle shuttle. Access here is 2.2 mi S on SR 600 from VA 84 near the Bath-Highland county line. The *Paddy Knob Spur Trail* is 1.2 mi and begins with directions as above, but after 0.3 mi turns L (N) on ridge top. After steep descent it exits on FR 55, N of the overlook. USFS trail numbers 636/O, 636/D.

Hidden Valley Recreation Area
Bath County

▼ HIDDEN VALLEY TRAIL,
BOGAN RUN TRAIL, MUDDY RUN TRAIL,
ROCK SHELTER TRAIL   279–282

Length: 17.3 mi (27.7 km) ct; easy to moderate. *USGS Map:* Warm Springs. *Trailhead:* Campground exit.

Directions and Description: Access to Hidden Valley Recreation Area is from the junction of VA 39 and SR 621 (3.2 mi W of US 220 in Warm Springs). Go N on SR 621 for 1 mi and turn L on FR 241. After 1.5 mi turn L to entrance of campground, which has 30 camp units open all year, in a hardwoods and white-pine forest. Water, pit toilets, and dump station are facilities.

To begin the trails leave the campground, hike 0.1 mi to area sign, turn L on road, and hike 0.3 mi to locked metal gate on R. (On L begins *Bogan Run Trail.*) After entering gate pass L of barn and house at 0.6 mi. At 2.3 mi the trail bears close to the trout-stocked Jackson River on a high bluff. Along the banks are sycamore, hemlock, birch, maple, beech and rhododendron. At 2.8 mi is junction with *Muddy Run Trail,* which extends R. (This trail is a wide spur up a tributary where hemlock, pine, and birch form a canopy over cascades. Deer are often seen in the wildlife clearings and hawthorn thickets. Backtrack after 1.1 mi.) Continue upstream on the road over high ledge; cross the river on a pedestrian swing bridge at 3.4 mi. Here is junction with *Rock Shelter Trail* that can be followed L for a circuit hike back to camp for a total of 6 mi. Follow upstream by large hemlock and heavy rhododendron stands. Cross the river at 5.6 mi. At 6.2 mi the road becomes FR 241-2 and is gated. Vehicle shuttle here would be 2 mi on SR 623 off US 220. Or, backtrack for round trip of 12.4 mi.

Bogan Run Trail bears L on road from the entrance to *Hidden Valley Trail* and goes 0.3 mi to parking area by Jackson River. After crossing the bridge it passes the Warwick House, spring, and cemetery, which are on the L. (The Warwick House, built in 1848, is listed in the National Register of Historic Places.) (*Rock Shelter Trail,* a spur trail of 2.3 mi, forks R here on FR 481-A paralleling the river to junction with *Hidden Valley Trail.*) Continue on FR 241-2 for 1.5 mi and turn L off the road; begin climb on switchbacks of Back Creek Mtn. After 1 mi reach the top of the ridge (3,000 ft) and Back Creek Mtn Rd. From here the trail descends on switchbacks through hardwood forest on old logging road, crossing Bogan Run, passing side trail on R at 7.2 mi, and ending at gate by SR 600 at 7.5 mi. Backtrack or have vehicle shuttle. It is 4 mi S on SR 600 to Mountain Grove on VA 39. USFS trail numbers, 481, 614, 481/B, 481/A (others not numbered).

Back Creek Gorge Area
Bath County

▼ BACK CREEK GORGE TRAIL   283

Length: 2.4 mi (3.8 km) rt; moderate. *USGS Map:* Mountain Grove. *Trailhead:* Blowing Springs Campground.

Directions and Description: A short but scenic hike downstream provides excellent white-water views, geology and wildflower study, and esthetic value. Walnut, hemlock, sycamore, and elm border the creek. Access is at gated S end of Blowing Springs Campground (which has spigot water and pit toilets) on VA 39, 9.5 mi W of Warm Springs. (Blowing Springs has its name from a forceful spring that releases strong air currents from beneath the earth's surface.) Backtrack. USFS trail number 516.

Piney Mountain Area
Bath County

▼ BEAR ROCK TRAIL, PINEY MOUNTAIN TRAIL, TOWER HILL MOUNTAIN TRAIL   284–287

Length: 13.6 mi (21.8 km) rt, ct; moderate to strenuous. *USGS Map:* Bath Alum. *Trailhead:* Two points along FR 465, one point along SR 624.

Directions and Description: The first two unblazed trails connect only by FR 465, but the road makes a fine hiking area. Access is from junction of VA 39 and SR 609 at Bath Alum. Take SR 609 for 2.6 mi to fork of SR 609 and SR 624. Turn L on SR 609, go 3.3 mi to FR 465 and turn L. After 1.3 mi *Bear Rock Trail* crosses road near rocky ravine. L descends 0.4 mi to SR 609; R ascends 1 mi to Warm Springs Mtn. (The 10-mi *Warm Springs Mtn Trail* is not maintained; reconstruction planned.) On FR 465 it is 2.8 mi, crossing cascading Bear Hole Run, to junction of *Piney Mtn Trail.* L descends 1 mi to Dry Run and SR 609; R ascends through young hardwood forest for 2 mi to top of Warm Springs Mtn. Backtrack. USFS trail numbers 635, 453.

Another trail nearby is the 2.4-mi *Tower Hill Mtn Trail,* reduced from 14 mi because of private-property boundaries. For access take SR 624, at the fork mentioned above, for 0.6 mi. Trailhead is L on blue-blazed trail by large white oaks and white pines. Ascend 0.5 mi to scenic Chimney Rocks and turn R (NE) to US Forest Service boundary. Backtrack. USFS trail number 452.

Douthat State Park Area
Bath County

▼ MIDDLE MOUNTAIN TRAIL, BRUSHY RIDGE TRAIL,
LITTLE MARE MOUNTAIN TRAIL,
GILLIAM RUN TRAIL, SANDY GAP TRAIL,
SALT POND RIDGE TRAIL, LITTLE MARE
MOUNTAIN SPUR TRAIL   288–294

Length: (See below), moderate to strenuous. *USGS Maps:* Clifton Forge, Healing Springs, Warm Springs, Bath Alum. *Trailhead:* (See below).

Directions and Description: All these trails connect, but not as a circuit unless FR 194 is used for a return. For the experienced or long-distance hiker, with a base camp in Douthat State Park (which has 40 mi of other trails), an exhilarating backpacking trip of 20 mi can be planned as follows: Take *Stony Run Trail* W in the park (4.5 mi) up to *Middle Mtn Trail* and turn R (N), proceeding for 5.5 mi; join *Brushy Ridge Trail* (3.9 mi), connecting with *Little Mare Mtn Trail* (6 mi) and making an exit 0.8 mi S of VA 39 on SR 683, for vehicular pickup. (With some bushwhacking for about 2 mi on the SW part of *Gilliam Run Trail*—not *Beards Mtn Trail,* SE—a circuit hike could be planned with directions as above, except, from the *Brushy Ridge Trail,* turn R on *Salt Pond Ridge Trail*

[3.3 mi] to SR 629; go N on SR 629 for 0.5 mi to *Gilliam Run Trail* R [2.3 mi], which is open and connects with *Mtn Top Trail* in Douthat State Park. Depending on where the hiker is camped in Douthat, the loop would be approximately 23 mi.)

Access to *Middle Mtn Trail* (unless from Douthat State Park) is on *Fore Mtn Trail* (described in James River Ranger District) as follows. Take VA 188 (which becomes SR 606) from downtown junction with US 60–220 NW in Clifton Forge for 4.3 mi. There, the white-blazed *Fore Mtn Trail* crosses road in McGraw Gap. Begin hike on R, crossing Smith Creek, and start up grade on switchbacks to scenic overlook of Clifton Forge and Rainbow Gap at 1.2 mi. Reach the ridge crest of Middle Mtn at 3.1 mi. Following ridge, enter Warm Springs Ranger District at 3.8 mi, where *Fore Mtn Trail* becomes *Middle Mtn Trail* near Alleghany-Bath county line. After 1 mi on *Middle Mtn Trail* (which may be partly obscured by brush) reach junction with *Stony Run Trail* on R. (It leads down to SR 629 in Douthat State Park for 4.5 mi.) After another 0.6 mi is junction with *Sandy Gap Trail* L. (It descends for 0.6 mi W to Smith Creek Rd, FR 125. It then crosses creek at 0.8 mi, ascends to large area of glacial rock slabs at 1.5 mi, and crosses stream at 2.1 mi. Continuing ascent and crossing of another stream near a spring at 2.4 mi, SR 703, Homestead Skyline Dr, is reached through a channel of purple rhododendron at 3.4 mi. There is outstanding scenery with views W over the Jackson River, and wildflowers, flame azaleas, locust, and mountain laurel decorate the area. Access to this point on road is 3.3 mi from SR 606. Bald Knob and Ingalls Airport are on road R.)

Continue on ridge. Signs may show that the *Middle Mtn Trail* is also *Salt Stump Trail,* but do not follow the *Salt Stump Trail* down from the ridge. It leads to Douthat Park. At 1.7 mi is view of Warm Springs Mtn. Ascend and descend on knolls. Reach excellent view at 4.2 mi. Among the oaks are some sections of pitch pine. Descend gradually along ridge, reaching Wilson Creek Rd, FR 125, at 5.5 mi. To the R it is 1 mi on FR 125 to SR 629 and Douthat State Park. Turn L on FR 125 and go 0.3 mi to entrance of *Brushy Ridge Trail* on R. Begin by crossing the mounded-earth tank traps on old logging road, then cross stream at 0.7 mi, and ascend gradually to junction with *Salt Pond Ridge Trail* on R at 2.5 mi. (*Salt Pond Ridge Trail* on R descends to SR 629 and to Douthat State Park for 3.3 mi. In its descent it passes a number of large boulder outcroppings, streams, and tank traps.) Continue L at the fork with *Salt Pond Ridge Trail* and follow it for 1.4 mi to Brushy Mtn Gap near Trappers Lodge. (Exit or entrance here can be made with a four-wheel-drive vehicle on steep, private Delafield Rd from Shady Lane junction with SR 658 near front entrance of The Homestead in Hot Springs. Ask office officials for permission to use the road, which is also used for horse traffic.) From here begin the *Little Mare Mtn Trail,* NE, on a downgrade, following the ridge generally all the way to SR 683. At 3 mi is junction with *Little Mare Mtn Spur,* L (which descends 0.7 mi to a road formerly called *Mare Run Trail*). Continue down the ridge in a hardwood forest and exit from old road to SR 683 at 6 mi, 0.8 mi S from VA 39 and 0.8 mi N from SR 629 junction. Backtrack, or have vehicle shuttle. USFS trail numbers (not including the park) 458, 637, 456, 620, 638, 417, 455/A.

Pads Creek Area
Bath County

▼ CRANE TRAIL, MILL MOUNTAIN TRAIL,
ORE BANK TRAIL   295–297

Length: 10.2 mi (16.3 km) rt, ct; strenuous. *USGS Map:*
Nimrod Hall. *Trailhead:* Parking area on FR 129.

Directions and Description: The 3-mi *Crane Trail* is on
isolated, rough, and demanding terrain. The W entrance
is 8 mi S from Millboro Springs (or 8.8 mi N from I-64)
on VA 42, across a wooden bridge over a stream. Ask
permission from resident to hike this direction. To reach
the E entrance on US Forest Service property go from
Millboro Springs SE on SR 633 to FR 129, R. Go 5 mi
along Pads Creek to gated road on R. Park here. To hike
Crane Trail go through the gate and follow road to C&O
RR tracks. Turn R and go 1 mi to the second small hollow
on the L. Trail follows the hollow steeply to ridge crest of
Rough Mtn, properly named for its rocky cliffs, at 1.2 mi
from C&O. Area is excellent to explore. Backtrack or
arrange for pickup after descending W to VA 42.

Mill Mtn Trail, formerly 9 mi, is now 1 mi. From
parking area cross road and go SE on unnamed stream.
Backtrack. The *Ore Bank Trail* trailhead is also at the
parking area. Go along Pads Creek on L following upstream for 1.2 mi. Backtrack. USFS trail numbers 454,
624, 625.

Part Two

National Park System Trails

3 · Appalachian National Scenic Trail

The 2,100-mile *Appalachian Trail* along the crest of the Appalachian Mtns from Georgia to Maine is the world's most famous trail. It traverses all or portions of 14 states and is protected by the National Trails System Act of 1968, to which supplemental amendments were made in 1970. Its maintenance, however, is essentially dependent on more than 32 organized Class A clubs, whose chief purpose is assisting the Appalachian Trail Conference in planning and maintaining sections of the *A.T.*, and hundreds of volunteer workers.

It was Benton MacKaye of Shirley Center, Massachusetts, who first conceived of such a supertrail. In response, clubs affiliated with the New York–New Jersey Trail Conference constructed the first section of the *Trail* in the Bear Mountain area of the Palisades Interstate Park in 1922. Interest in a contiguous trail spread to New England, where the venerable Appalachian Mountain Club and the Dartmouth Outing Club were influential in establishment of permanent trail connections.

In 1926 the leadership of Arthur Perkins of Hartford, Connecticut translated MacKaye's dream into reality, but it was Myron H. Avery of Lubec, Maine who, more

Appalachian National Scenic Trail. Allen de Hart.

than any other person, was instrumental in implementing and coordinating the agreement with government agencies (such as the Civilian Conservation Corps) and with thousands of volunteers to complete the *Trail.* He served as chairman of the Appalachian Trail Conference (ATC) from 1930 to 1952.

The 543.2 mi of the *A.T.* in Virginia is the longest section of the entire mileage. (Weaving between Virginia and West Virginia are 10 mi of trail on Peters Mtn in Monroe County and 15.5 mi in Jefferson County that add to the Virginia total.) Its highest point in the state is at Mt Rogers (5,729 ft) and its lowest point is at the Potomac River bridge (290 ft). Nine volunteer Class A clubs jointly assist the US Forest Service and the National Park Service in planning and maintaining the *Trail.* The Mt Rogers A.T. Club maintains 67.8 mi, from the Virginia-Tennessee line to VA 16, Brushy Mtn. From here the Piedmont Appalachian Trail Hikers maintains 42.1 mi, across Glade Mt and Walker Mtn ridges to Garden Mtn. The Virginia Tech Outing Club maintains the trail for the next 27.8 mi to SR 608, Brushy Mtn. Maintaining two sections is the Roanoke A.T. Club, with 29.1 mi from SR 608 to the New River in Pearisburg, and from Stony Creek Valley near Interior to Black Horse Gap on the Blue Ridge Pkwy for 87.5 mi. In between, the Kanawha Trail Club cares for 20.7 mi from the New River to Stony Creek Valley. From Black Horse Gap to the Tye River, the Natural Bridge A.T. Club maintains 87.2 mi, and the Tidewater A.T. Club cares for the next 9.9 mi to Reeds Gap. Starting at Reeds Gap, the Old Dominion A.T. Club has 15.4 mi to Rockfish Gap. Maintaining the longest segment in the state is the Potomac A.T. Club, with the strip from Rockfish Gap to the Potomac River, amounting to 155.7 mi.

In a 1982 land-acquisition report it was stated that 463 mi of the *A.T.* are still unprotected, of which 37 mi are in Virginia. A major advantage for the state is the length of trail segments running through the Jefferson and Washington national forests and the Shenandoah National Park, where protection is automatic.

Hikers on the *A.T.* should purchase the latest editions of *Shenandoah National Park, Southern Pennsylvania to Northern Virginia* and *Central and Southwest Virginia,* which have maps. If not available in bookstores, the guidebooks can be ordered from the Appalachian Trail Conference, PO Box 807, Harpers Ferry, WV 25425; tel: 304-535-6331.

The following list of milepoints is a reference description only of some of the major areas, such as shelters, support facilities, and distances of the *A.T.* in Virginia. USFS trail number 1.

Milepoint		Location and Description
From N	*From S*	
543.2	0.0	*Tennessee-Virginia state boundary*
539.5	3.7	*Damascus, Virginia (1,928 ft), US 58, lodging, groceries, restaurant, post office 24236*
536.0	7.2	*Feathercamp Ridge, yellow-blazed* Iron Mtn Trail *(extends 17.5 mi to Chester Flat, rejoins the* A.T.*)*
527.8	15.4	*Junction with* Bear Tree Gap Trail

Milepoint		Location and Description
From N	*From S*	

522.2	21.0	*Cross US 58, Summit Cut (3,160 ft)*
515.0	28.2	*Cross SR 600, Elk Garden (4,434 ft), White-top, VA 24292 (S), groceries*
513.1	30.1	*Deep Gap Shelter, water*
508.0	35.2	*Side trail, blue-blazed 0.5 mi (S) to Massie Gap in Grayson Highlands State Park*
500.1	43.1	*Old Orchard Shelter, water*
492.0	51.2	*Side trail 0.5 mi (NW) to Hurricane Camp-ground, Mt Rogers National Recreation Area*
489.9	53.3	*Cross SR 650 near VA 16 junction, Dickey Gap (3,313 ft), Troutdale, VA 24378, grocer-ies, restaurant (S)*
488.4	54.8	*Raccoon Branch Shelter, water*
485.9	57.3	*Trimpi Shelter, water*
475.5	67.7	*Pass Mt Rogers NRA headquarters and dis-trict ranger office, cross VA 16 (3,220 ft), Sugar Grove, VA 24375 (S), groceries*
468.6	74.6	*Glade Mtn Shelter, water*
464.9	78.3	*Motel, restaurant, US 11, Atkins, VA 24311 (W), groceries, laundry*
464.6	78.7	*Cross under I-81*
457.4	85.8	*Crawfish Valley camping area at Reed Creek (Old A.T. junction)*
452.7	90.8	*Cross VA 42, Ceres, VA 24318, groceries (E)*
450.4	92.8	*Knot Mole Branch Shelter, water*
441.3	101.9	*Summit of Chestnut Knob (4,409 ft)*
435.5	107.7	*Cross SR 623, Burkes Garden, VA 24608 (N)*

Milepoint		Location and Description
From N	*From S*	
430.5	112.7	*Hunting Camp Creek Shelter, water*
426.8	116.4	*Cross Little Wolf Creek here and 13 other places*
418.8	124.4	*Cross US 21-52, Bland, VA 24315 (S); Bastian, VA 24314 (N), restaurant, groceries, laundry, lodging*
418.6	124.6	*Cross over I-77*
405.5	137.7	*Cross SR 608, Lickskillet Hollow (2,200 ft), 0.8 mi N of Crandon, groceries*
400.7	142.5	*Cross SR 606, groceries*
393.7	149.5	*Wapiti II Shelter, water*
385.4	157.8	*Docs Knob Shelter, water*
379.6	163.6	*Angels Rest, Pearis Mtn, excellent views*
377.7	165.5	*Pearisburg, VA 24134; in the city, with lodging, laundry, restaurant, groceries*
359.5	183.7	*Reach source of Pine Swamp Branch and junction with* Allegheny Trail
358.2	185.0	*Pine Swamp Branch Shelter (2,530 ft), water*
355.7	187.5	*Cross Stony Creek Rd, SR 635*
354.1	189.1	*Bailey Gap Shelter, water*
346.3	196.9	*War Spur Shelter, water*
341.9	201.3	*Big Pond Shelter, water*
335.0	208.2	*Sinking Creek Covered Bridge*
334.4	208.8	*Sinking Creek Valley, cross VA 42, Newport, VA 24128 (W), camping area, groceries*
318.0	225.2	*Niday Shelter, water*

| Milepoint | | Location and Description |
From N	From S	
310.1	233.1	*Pickles Branch Shelter, water*
306.3	236.9	*Dragons Tooth with extraordinary views on Cove Mtn (3,050 ft)*
303.8	239.4	*Cross VA 311, Catawba, VA 24070 (E), groceries*
290.4	252.8	*Lamberts Meadow Shelter, water*
285.1	258.1	*Hay Rock, Tinker Ridge with superior views*
280.6	262.6	*Cross under I-81, US 220, Cloverdale, VA 24077, truck stop, lodging, restaurant, groceries*
276.6	266.6	*Fullhardt Knob Shelter, cistern*
271.0	272.2	*Wilson Creek Shelter, water*
268.2	275.0	*Blue Ridge Pkwy 97.7, Black Horse Gap, junction of FR 186 and SR 606*
263.3	279.9	*Bobblets Gap Shelter, water*
260.8	282.4	*Blue Ridge Pkwy mp 90.9, Bearwallow Gap, junction of VA 43 and SR 695, Buchanan, VA 24066 (W), groceries, restaurant, lodging*
257.7	285.5	*Cove Mtn Shelter, no water*
251.7	291.5	*Cross SR 714, Middle Creek, N Creek Rd, camping area, groceries*
246.4	296.8	*Cornelius Creek Shelter, water*
243.7	299.5	*Blue Ridge Pkwy mp 78, Parkers Gap Rd, FR 812*
241.8	301.4	*Thunder Hill Shelter, water*
232.2	311.0	*Junction with* Balcony Falls Trail *(W)*
229.4	313.8	*Matts Creek Shelter, water*

Milepoint		Location and Description
From N	*From S*	
226.8	316.4	*US 501, Big Island, VA 24526, 4 mi (E), groceries, cross James River Bridge, Snowden General Store 0.8 mi (W, may be closed)*
225.0	318.8	*Johns Hollow Shelter, water*
218.8	324.4	*Salt Log Gap, camping and water*
215.7	327.5	*Punchbowl Shelter, water*
215.0	328.2	*Robinson Gap Rd, cross SR 607, 7 mi W to Buena Vista*
206.9	336.3	*Brown Mtn Creek Shelter, water*
205.1	338.1	*Cross US 60, groceries 0.8 mi (W), 9 mi to Buena Vista (W)*
200.5	342.7	*Cole Mtn bald, (4,022 ft), granite rocks, excellent views*
199.1	344.1	*Hog Camp Gap, Wiggins Spring Shelter 0.5 mi (W)*
197.1	346.1	*Salt Log Gap, FR 63 out to SR 634*
194.5	348.7	*Lovingston Spring, camping*
190.4	352.8	*Fish Hatchery Rd, Montebello, VA 24464 (W), restaurant, groceries*
189.9	353.3	*Spy Rock, exceptional view on 0.1 mi side trail (E)*
189.6	353.6	*Maintop Mtn (4,040 ft)*
186.6	356.6	*Crabtree Farm Rd, SR 826, Crabtree Falls Trail junction, camping, 4.6 mi (W) to VA 56*
185.7	357.5	*The Priest Shelter, water*
185.2	358.0	*The Priest overlook (4,062 ft), exceptional views (W)*

Milepoint		Location and Description
From N	From S	
181.0	362.2	VA 56, Tyro, VA 22976 (E), groceries, cross Tye River on suspension bridge
178.6	364.6	Harpers Creek Shelter, water
172.7	370.5	Maupin Field Shelter, water
171.1	373.1	Reed Gap (2,645 ft) near Blue Ridge Pkwy, SR 664
162.9	380.3	Excellent views at Humpback Rock
158.5	387.5	Rockfish Gap, end of Blue Ridge Pkwy, US 250, I-64; Waynesboro, VA 22980 (W); Afton, VA 22920 (E), for lodging, restaurant, groceries
152.3	390.9	McCormick Gap, Skyline Dr mp 102.1 (2,434 ft)
150.5	393.6	Open Summit of Calf Mtn (2,974 ft)
147.7	394.9	Jarman Gap, mp 96.7
136.9	406.3	Blackrock Gap, mp 87.4
136.2	407.0	Blackrock Gap Hut, water
135.6	407.6	Blackrock scenic area (3,092 ft)
129.0	414.2	Loft Mtn Campground, Skyline Dr mp 79.5, groceries, May through October, camping, laundry
126.9	416.3	Ivy Creek Shelter, water
123.1	420.1	Pinefield Hut, Skyline Dr mp 75.2
114.8	428.4	Hightop Hut, water
111.4	431.8	Swift Run Gap, junction Skyline Dr mp 65.5 and US 33
108.9	434.3	South River Shelter, water
106.3	436.9	Summit of Baldface Mtn (3,600 ft)

Milepoint		Location and Description
From N	*From S*	
105.0	438.2	*Pocosin Cabin, picnic grounds, Skyline Dr mp 59.5*
103.2	440.0	*Lewis Mtn Campground, Skyline Dr mp 57.6, lodging, groceries, camp store*
101.2	442.0	*Bearfence Mtn scenic views*
94.9	448.3	*Big Meadows Lodge, restaurant, lodging, near picnic grounds*
93.8	448.4	*Big Meadows Wayside, camping open all year, lodging, restaurant*
90.9	452.3	*Rock Spring Hut, water*
90.6	452.6	*Hawksbill Mtn (4,050 ft, highest point in the Shenandoah National Park), Byrd's Nest Shelter #2*
84.4	458.8	*Hughes River Gap, Skyline Dr mp 38.6*
83.3	459.9	*Shavers Hollow Shelter, water*
82.2	461.0	*Pinnacles Picnic Grounds, Skyline Dr mp 36.7*
80.1	463.1	*Byrd's Nest Shelter #3, water*
78.8	464.4	*Mary's Rock with outstanding views (3,514 ft)*
77.1	466.1	*Thornton Gap, Skyline Dr mp 31.5, junction with US 211, restaurant*
75.9	467.3	*Pass Mtn Hut, near Pass Mtn (3,052 ft), water*
73.1	470.1	*Byrd's Nest Shelter #4, water*
68.4	474.8	*Elk Wallow Gap, Skyline Dr, mp 23.9*
66.2	477.0	*Junction with* Big Blue Trail *(W)*
62.6	480.6	*Gravel Springs Hut, water*
61.5	481.7	*S Marshall Mtn (3,212 ft) and N Marshall Mtn (3,368 ft) at 482.9*

Milepoint		Location and Description
From N	*From S*	
54.8	488.4	*Indian Run Shelter, junction with* Dickey Run Trail, *water*
52.7	490.5	*Tom Floyd Shelter and Wayside, water*
49.6	493.6	*Chester Gap (1,339 ft) (E), Lake Front Royal, US 522*
43.0	500.2	*Manassas Gap, cross VA 55, Linden, VA 22642 (E)*
39.6	503.6	*Manassas Gap Shelter, water*
33.2	510.0	*Sky Meadows State Park, water, camping*
30.6	512.6	*Ashby Gap, junction US 50 and SR 601, Paris, VA 22130 (E), groceries*
22.5	520.7	*Three Springs Shelter, water*
19.6	523.6	*Snickers Gap (1,060 ft), junction SR 601 and VA 7, Bluemont, VA 22012*
16.3	526.9	*Devils Racecourse, Raven Rocks (1,448 ft)*
6.1	537.1	*Keys Gap Shelter, Keys Gap, VA-WV 9 (6 mi W of Hillsboro, VA and 7 mi E of Charlestown, West Virginia*
2.2	541.0	*Blue-blazed* Loudoun Heights Trail *(W) descends to US 340*
0.9	542.3	*Split Rocks with outstanding views of Harpers Ferry*
0.0	543.2	*US 340, Virginia-Maryland state line, Harpers Ferry, WV 25425 (W), camping, groceries, lodging, restaurant, laundry, ATC Headquarters*

Information: For information on *A.T.* conditions, maintenance, changes, and relocations contact Mike Dawson, ATC Southern Field Officer, PO Box 124, Newport, VA 24128; tel: 703-544-7472.

4 · Blue Ridge Parkway

Blue Ridge Parkway Trail System

The scenic Blue Ridge Pkwy, America's first national parkway, traverses the crest of the Southern Appalachians in a link between the Shenandoah National Park and the Great Smoky Mountains National Park. Initial funding for the construction of the 470-mi "ribbon of beauty" was allocated in 1933 under authority of the National Industrial Recovery Act; three years later the park was established under the National Park Service. A major purpose was to preserve the natural resources and mountain folk culture within a corridor of 81,536 acres, 30,887 of which are in Virginia.

The chief recreational areas along the 217 mi of the BRP trail system in Virginia are at Humpback Rock, Whetstone Ridge, Otter Creek, Peaks of Otter, Roanoke Mtn, Smart View, Rocky Knob, and Mabry Mill. Activities include fishing, camping, bicycling, horseback riding, nature study, and hiking. In addition, historic exhibits, museums, and cultural displays are frequently encountered. Although some of the hiking trails ascend to lofty and ethereal points over 4,000 ft, the parkway's highest elevation is at Apple Orchard Mtn (3,950 ft), mp

Mabry Mill, Blue Ridge Parkway. Allen de Hart.

76.7, only 13 mi S of the lowest elevation, near the James River (646 ft) at mp 63.2. More than 32 trails branch out from the parkway, many forming loops, but a few join longer and more challenging trails into the George Washington National Forest or the Jefferson National Forest. Weaving and criss-crossing the parkway for 103 mi from Rockfish Gap to Fullhardt Knob, the *Appalachian Trail* offers the packpacker more exertive distances. Trails are listed here with N-to-S mileposts.

For information on the trail system, contact Blue Ridge Pkwy Superintendent, National Park Service, PO Box 7606, Asheville, NC 28807; tel: 704-258-2850. Campground and other information may be received from the Blue Ridge Pkwy, PO Box 1710, Roanoke, VA 24008 (Poff Federal Bldg, Second and Franklin Sts); tel: 703-982-6213.

Hikers who leave a vehicle outside campgrounds overnight should inform the ranger of vehicle make, license number, location, and names of hikers. No rock climbing is allowed on road cuts. No special trout license is required when fishing in BRP waters, but a state license is required for all fishermen 16 years or older. For emergencies, personnel can be contacted in the following areas: Montebello (804-377-2377); James River (804-299-5941); Bedford, Peaks of Otter (703-586-4357); Roanoke Valley (703-982-6490); Rocky Knob, Mabry Mill (703-745-3451); Fancy Gap (703-728-4511).

▼ MOUNTAIN FARM SELF-GUIDING TRAIL
(mp 5.9)   301

A 0.4-mi self-guiding trail from the Humpback Visitor

Center to a pioneer farmstead (2,353 ft elevation) with descriptive markers.

▼ HUMPBACK MOUNTAIN TRAIL (mp 6.0)   302

From the parking area (2,360 ft) on R it is 0.7 mi (S) ascending on the *A.T.* to the scenic "Rocks" and 2.1 mi to Humpback Mtn (3,650 ft), a total of 1,290 ft increase in altitude.

▼ COTOCTIN TRAIL (mp 8.4)   303

Turn L to Cotoctin Picnic Area. Trail is on farthest circle to R of *A.T.* sign. Walk to scenic overlook is 0.3-mi round trip. (It is 0.3 mi on blue-blazed trail to junction with *A.T.*)

▼ GREENSTONE TRAIL (mp 8.8)   304

Turn R to parking area, where signs for the self-guiding, 0.2-mi loop trail on R describe the greenstone geology formation of the Blue Ridge Mtns.

▼ THE PRIEST TRAIL (mp 17.6)   305

A short, 0.2-mi trail to a spectacular view of The Priest, a large mountain over which passes the *A.T.*

▼ WHITE ROCK FALLS TRAIL I (mp 18.5)   306

There is no parking area here, but the most likely place to park is on the R in small meadow. (Road to L goes to private property.) Trail entry is on L by large poplar at trail sign. It is 1.4 mi to White Rock Falls and 2.5 mi to Slacks Overlook.

▼ WHITE ROCK FALLS TRAIL II (mp 19.9)   307

Park at Slacks Overlook on R and hike across road L for 60 yds to trail sign down an embankment. A sign indicates the trail is primitive and recommended for experienced hikers. Descend on ground cover of wintergreen to stand of huge hemlocks, mountain laurel, and rhododendron. Cross stream at 0.3 mi, ascend ridge, and descend at 0.7 mi to rocky area by cliffs on L at 0.8 mi. Unless there is a sign here it is easy to miss the trail L by the cliff to the gorge and the cascades. Continue down switchbacks to stream crossing and begin ascending. Reach White Rock Gap and BRP at 2.5 mi.

▼ BIG SPY MOUNTAIN TRAIL (mp 26.3)   308

Grassy trail extends 0.1 mi to panoramic view (3,185 ft) of the Shenandoah Valley W and the Tye River Valley E.

▼ YANKEE HORSE TRAIL (mp 34.4)   309

A 0.2-mi trail on old narrow-gauge logging railroad where a million board feet of lumber was removed from the mountains in the early 1920s. Also, there is an excellent view of 30-ft Wigwam Falls in hemlock grove (3,140 ft).

▼ BOSTON KNOB TRAIL (mp 38.8) 310

A graded, 0.1-mi trail under black birch and dogwood to scenic view (2,523 ft).

▼ INDIAN GAP TRAIL (mp 47.5) 311

Within a 0.3-mi loop trail are large balancing rocks, oaks, and mountain laurel (2,098 ft).

▼ WHITE OAK FLATS TRAIL (mp 55.2) 312

From the picnic table at White Oak Flats Parking Overlook (1,460 ft) go S for 0.1 mi in open forest by a small stream.

▼ OTTER CREEK TRAIL,
OTTER LAKE TRAIL (mps 60.8, 63) 313–314

Length: 3.8 mi (6.1 km); easy. *USGS Map:* Big Island.
Trailhead: Otter Creek Campground (777 ft).
   Directions and Description: Begin hike downstream from Otter Creek Campground behind the restaurant, gift shop, and gas station. Follow the stream in a forest of oaks, hemlock, hackberry, hornbeam, rhododendron, poplar, and mountain laurel. Go under the BRP to Terrapin Hill at 0.6 mi. Continue ahead, passing under BRP again and crossing stream twice near VA 130. Reach Lower Otter Creek Parking Overlook at 1.9 mi. From here continue to Nathaniel Sledd cabin joining *Otter Lake Trail* at 2.4 mi. Go R or L around the lake, and reach the visitor center at 3 mi (3.8 mi if *Otter Lake*

Trail is included). Another hike of 2.6 mi may be taken upstream from the campground to the picnic area.

▼ JAMES RIVER TRAIL,
   TRAIL OF TREES (mp 63.6)   315–316

Length: 1 mi (1.6 km) rt; easy. *USGS Map:* Big Island.
Trailhead: Otter Creek Visitor Center (668 ft).

   Directions and Description: From the visitor center, at the N end of the James River bridge, proceed under the bridge to fork of *James River Trail* and *Trail of Trees.* Go L on elevated footbridge across the river to Kanawha Canal lock exhibit. Return at 0.4 mi. The R fork under the bridge ascends and descends gradually on a self-guiding trail passing more than 40 labeled trees, including papaw and the princess tree. Return on loop at 0.6 mi.

▼ APPLE ORCHARD FALLS TRAIL/EAST
   (mp 78.7)   317

Length: 2.8 mi (4.5 km) rt; strenuous; *USGS Map:* Arnold Valley; *Trailhead:* Sunset Field Overlook.

   Directions and Description: Only the first 0.2 mi is within the Blue Ridge Parkway boundary; the remaining 1.2 mi is in the adjoining Jefferson National Forest where the trail extends another 1.7 mi from the waterfall to FR 59 and to North Creek Campground. From Sunset Field Overlook (3,474 ft) go 0.2 mi on a blue-blazed trail to junction with the *Appalachian Trail.* Cross the *A.T.* and descend 1 mi to head of falls. Cross to L side and descend steeply in a rocky area for another 0.2 mi. Backtrack to Sunset Field Overlook.

▼ ONION MOUNTAIN LOOP TRAIL (mp 79.7)   318

A short, 0.2-mi trail in a deciduous forest with rhododendron and mountain laurel over lichen-covered rocks
(3,195 ft).

▼ FLAT TOP–FALLINGWATER CASCADES TRAIL
(mps 83.1, 83.5)   319–320

Length: 6 mi (9.6 km) ct; moderate to strenuous. *USGS
Map:* Arnold Valley. *Trailhead:* Fallingwater Cascades
parking area or Peaks of Otter picnic area.

   Directions and Description: Designated a national recreation trail in 1982, this trail has the scenic splendor of
cascades in a gorge and of panoramic views from a peak
more than 4,000 ft high. From Fallingwater Cascades
parking area follow signs and descend for 0.4 mi to the
cascades, where hemlock, green striped maple, and rosebay rhododendron form a partial cover. Cross the falls
four times, using care on slippery rocks in strenuous
flume area. After 0.3 mi by the cascades ascend for 0.6
mi to Flat Top parking area (2,512 ft), turn L, and return
to origin at 1.6 mi. Or, turn R, cross the BRP into tall
poplars, and follow the trail to mp 84. Here begin a
1,492-ft increase in elevation by switchbacks to Flat Top
Mtn. On the way a steep spur trail leads to Cross Rocks at
1.7 mi. After reaching Flat Top at 2.5 mi descend on
switchbacks to the Peaks of Otter picnic area at 4.4 mi.
(Vehicle shuttle necessary for *Flat Top Trail.*)

Peaks of Otter   321–324

The Peaks of Otter is a 4,200-acre recreational park on

the Blue Ridge Pkwy. Facilities include a trail system of 15 mi for viewing magnificent scenery and the study of at least 55 species of trees and shrubs. Among them are *Ailanthus,* Carolina hemlock, *Menziesia,* mountain ash, and fragrant thimbleberry. At least 60 species of wildflowers have been found here and more than 45 species of birds and other wildlife. The park has a visitor center, a picnic area, a 24-acre lake stocked with brown and rainbow trout, and a large 141-site campground (without hookups). A concessioner operates the 58-room Peaks of Otter Lodge and restaurant, open all year. (Address for the lodge is Virginia Peaks of Otter Co, PO Box 489, Bedford, VA 24523; tel: 703-586-1081.) In addition to the *Flat Top Mtn Trail* and the *Fallingwater Cascades Trail,* the *Sharp Top Trail,* a 3-mi round-trip steep and strenuous trail across the road from the visitor center, goes to the scenic peak of Sharp Top (3,875 ft). A spur trail of 0.4 mi to Buzzards Roost is scenic also. (This peak can be approached by a special tour bus from the base parking area.)

The 0.8-mi self-guiding *Elk Run Trail* begins behind the visitor center for a loop on easy contour. A pamphlet is available. Also beginning L behind the visitor center is the *Harkening Hill Trail,* a 3.3-mi loop that ascends 735 ft to a view of the Johnson Farm and to a unique balancing rock. On the way back, descending, the *Johnson Farm Loop Trail* is on the L. It is a restored pioneer farmstead. (The latter trail can be hiked directly R from the NE end of the visitor center for 1 mi.) (For an 8.1-mi hike on the *A.T.* within or near the BRP, go 5 mi SW on the BRP to mp 91. The *A.T.* crosses or parallels the BRP at mps 92.5, 95.4, 95.9, and 97, with a spur trail to Bobblet's Gap Lean-To from mp 93.1.)

▼ STEWARTS KNOB TRAIL (mp 110.6)   325

An 88-yd trail leads above the Blue Ridge Parkway to a
pedestrian overlook (1,275 ft) toward the city of
Roanoke.

▼ ROANOKE RIVER TRAIL (mp 114.9)   326

A river-view loop trail for 0.8 mi under the BRP bridge
leads to overlook of the Roanoke River in large stands of
hemlock and beds of dwarf iris. Dangerous to climb
rocky cliffs off the graded trail.

Roanoke Mountain Campground   327–328

Facilities at the Roanoke Mountain Campground include 105 campsites, the 18.5-mi *Roanoke Valley Horse
Trail,* picnicking, a panoramic view from Roanoke Mtn,
a spur road to the Mill Mtn Park with playhouse, lighted
100-ft Roanoke Star (commemorating the city's progress) and Zoo, and foot trails. Entrance is at mp 120.5.
The *Roanoke Mtn Loop Trail* is 0.4 mi through oaks and
mountain laurel with a rocky tread. Access is from mp
120.4 on a 4-mi motor loop restricted to vehicles without
trailers.

▼ CHESTNUT RIDGE TRAIL (mp 120.5)   329

Length: 5.4 mi (8.6 km); moderate. *USGS Map:* Garden
City. *Trailhead:* Chestnut Ridge Overlook.
   Directions and Description: From Chestnut Ridge
parking lot go R for 1 mi paralleling the road; turn R
across road at SR 672. At 2.1 mi junction with trail loop

spur R near campground and again on R at 3.1 mi. Cross Yellow Mtn Rd at 3.8 mi, and return to parking lot at 5.4 mi. The trail is well graded with gentle and moderate ascents and descents in a hardwood forest with mountain laurel and blueberries. Patches of galax, cat's claw, and woodland sunflower are frequent.

▼ BUCK MOUNTAIN TRAIL (mp 123.2)   330

Ascend 0.5 mi through hardwoods and scattered pines and mountain laurel from Buck Mtn Parking Overlook to summit of Buck Mtn for scenic view.

▼ SMART VIEW LOOP TRAIL (mp 154.5)   331

The *Smart View Loop Trail* begins at the parking lot near the picnic entrance. Follow sign across field to picnic area access at 0.3 mi. Continue through cattle pasture to S of Smart View Parking Overlook and then descend to stream. Large deciduous trees, abundant wildflowers, and elderberry grace the trail. Circle the picnic area, and pass the log cabin L at 1.4 mi. Cross Rennet Bag Branch (spur trail on R) and follow slope to E edge of park maintenance area. Complete loop at parking lot at 2.6 mi.

Rock Castle Gorge Campground

At mp 167 this campground offers 92 campsites—tent and trailer—from May through October. Picnic area and ball field are at mp 169, with the scenic Saddle Parking Overlook and Rocky Knob summit (3,572 ft) between the campground and picnic area. Housekeeping cabins are at mp 174; they are operated by the concessioner who operates the restaurant and gift shop at the famous Mabry Mill (mp 176). Backcountry camping is allowed here as described for Rocky Knob Recreation Area.

Rocky Knob Recreation Area

The Rocky Knob Recreation Area has 4,200 acres, mainly E of the BRP crest, with Rock Castle Gorge its primary geographic feature. Major usage is camping, picnicking, hiking, fishing, and nature study. It has more than 150 species of birds, and among the mammals are bear, deer, bobcat, raccoon, and fox. Reptiles include rattlesnake and copperhead. Seasonal changes may vary as much as three weeks because of altitude difference. Heavily wooded with the usual Appalachian species, it also has a large section of Carolina hemlock on the N slopes of the gorge. Early settlers named the gorge from the octagon-shaped quartz crystals with pyramid tips. At the Rocky Knob Campground (mp 167.1) there are 92 sites for tent or trailer, open from May 1 through October. (Permits from the ranger are necessary to camp at the primitive camp in the gorge.) At mp 174, SR 758 E leads to housekeeping cabins operated by the concessioner of Mabry Mill (mp 176.2).

▼ ROCK CASTLE GORGE TRAIL (mp 167.1)   332–333

Length: 10.6 mi (16.9 km); strenuous. *USGS Map:* Woolwine. *Trailhead:* Rocky Knob Campground.

Directions and Description: Designated a national recreation trail in 1982. From Rocky Knob Campground entrance, cross BRP to fence crossing and begin ascent on grassy bald. Follow white blazes for 0.8 mi to Saddle Parking Overlook. Here, join the *Rocky Knob Self-Guiding Trail,* which ascends for 0.2 mi to the summit of Rocky Knob (3,572 ft). Superb views of the gorge and VA 8 toward Woolwine. Continue on ridge until descent to the Parkway Overlook (mp 168.8) at 1.8 mi. Parallel the BRP in and out of woods and open spaces. At 3 mi reach Grassy Knoll (3,480 ft). Begin descent into deep defile with cascading stream and a canopy of large sugar maples, oaks, hickory, and virgin tulip poplar.

After numerous switchbacks reach an enormous 12-acre jumble of "bear rocks," a haven for wildlife. Cross Rock Castle Creek at 4.8 mi, turn L on old road bordered with rosebay rhododendron, cascades, and waterfalls. At least 28 species of ferns are known to grow in the canyon. Pass large vacant two-story house with an old-fashioned spring house on R, cross creek again and reach the primitive campground (1,720 ft), the site of a former Civilian Conservation Corps camp, at 7.4 mi. (Permit is necessary for camping.) Follow old road to where trail turns L up slope at 7.6 mi. From here the trail ascends in and out of mixed forest coves W of the Little Rock Castle Creek. Contour is more gradual at 9.5 mi. Return to road at the campground from a grassy field at 10.6 mi. (Vehicle approach to the primitive campground can be made to within 0.3 mi on SR 605 W, 0.7 mi from VA 8, near Rock Castle Creek bridge.)

▼ ROUND MEADOW CREEK TRAIL (mp 179.2)   334

From the Round Meadow Parking Overlook (2,800 ft) descend steeply on a 0.5-mi loop trail into an excellent cove of large hemlocks.

5 · Shenandoah National Park

Albemarle, Augusta, Greene, Madison, Page, Rockingham, and Rappahannock Counties

Containing 194,327 acres of the Blue Ridge Mtns, the Shenandoah National Park is a jewel of natural beauty and its Skyline Dr an engineering work of art. For 105 mi this scenic parkway weaves across or near the crest of 60 peaks ranging from 3,000 ft to 4,000 ft in elevation, with 75 overlooks to the historic Shenandoah Valley and the Piedmont. Paralleling this area of visual splendor for 95 mi is the *Appalachian Trail*. There are more than 15 major waterfalls, ranging from 25 ft to 93 ft; over 1,200 species of flowering plants, and numerous cascading streams stocked with trout. It is a sanctuary for bear, deer, fox, striped skunk, raccoon, and 200 varieties of birds. The park is 95% forested with more than 100 species of trees.

Authorized by Congress in May 1926, after years of extraordinary private and state governmental effort, Shenandoah National Park was fully established in December 1935—a gift of Virginia's citizens to the nation. The park is divided into three sections: the N Section is from Front Royal to US 211 (31 mi); the Cen-

Skyline Drive, Shenandoah National Park.
Virginia State Travel Service.

tral Section from US 211 to US 33 (34 mi); and the S Section from US 33 to US 250 and I-64 at Rockfish Gap (40 mi). The park is open all year, but lodge and cottage facilities are open April-October. Permits are required for hikers and backpackers who plan backcountry camping; permits are available at the park headquarters, entrance stations, visitor centers, from rangers, or by mail. (If requesting permit by mail use park address listed here at Information.)

The list of trails below was released by the park headquarters in 1982. Detailed directions and description are not part of this guidebook because all the trails are covered in two guidebooks by the Potomac Appalachian Trail Club. It is recommended that hikers purchase the *Appalachian Trail Guide: Shenandoah National Park* (with maps) and *Circuit Hikes in the Shenandoah National Park* from the Appalachian Trail Conference, PO Box 807, Harpers Ferry, WV 25425; tel: 304-535-6331, or from the Potomac Appalachian Trail Club, 1718 N St NW, Washington, DC 20036; tel: 202-638-5306. Another excellent book is *Guide to Skyline Drive and Shenandoah National Park,* by Henry Heatwole, available from Shenandoah Natural History Association, Luray, VA 22835; tel: 703-999-2243.

Information: For information on open facilities and weather, contact Superintendent, Shenandoah National Park, Luray, VA 28235; tel: 703-999-2266. For additional information and park business, tel: 703-999-2243.

Blue Blazed Foot Trails

Note: All trail listings are from N to S.

North District   335–358

SNP Number	Trail Name	Mileage	Termini and Milepost
2	Dickey Ridge	9.2	*Skyline Dr mp 0.1 – A.T. at Compton Gap (blazed both blue and yellow from Lands Run to Springhouse Rd)*
5	The Peak	1.9	*Bluff Trail – The Peak*
6	Big Devil Stairs	1.3	*Bluff Trail – park boundary mp 17.6*
8	Piney Branch	4.2	*A.T. at Piney River Ranger Station – Hull School Trail*
9	Little Devil Stairs	2.0	*Keyser Run Rd – park boundary mp 19.4*
149	Pole Bridge Link	1.0	*Piney Branch Trail – Keyser Run Rd (including upper connecting spur)*
106	Piney Ridge	3.2	*A.T. at Range View Cabin – Piney Branch Trail mp 22.1*
151	Fork Mtn	1.1	*Piney Ridge Trail – Hull School Trail*
157	Oventop Mtn	5.3	*A.T. –park boundary*
158	Butterwood Branch	0.5	*US 211 – Oventop Mtn Trail*

SNP Number	Trail Name	Mileage	Termini and Milepost
97	Jeremys Run	5.3	*A.T. at Elkwallow – Knob Mtn Trail mp 24.1*
150	Knob Mtn Cutoff	0.5	*Knob Mtn Trail – Jeremys Run Trail*
10	Elkwallow	2.0	*Matthews Arm – Elkwallow*
7	Overall Run	1.2	*Matthews Arm Trail – park boundary (distance is junction Big Blue to park boundary)*
143	Big Blue	6.2	*A.T. – park boundary*
344	Thompson Hollow	0.4	*Big Blue – park boundary*
146	Overall–Beecher Ridge	0.7	*Overall Run Trail – Beecher Ridge Trail*
333	Indian Run PATC Maintenance Hut	0.5	*A.T. – Indian Run Shelter*
334	Gravel Springs Hut	0.2	*A.T. – Gravel Springs Hut*
13	Pass Mtn Hut	0.2	*A.T. – Hut*
332	Possums Rest	0.1	*A.T. – Possums Rest View Point*
335	Hogback Spur	0.3	*Skyline Dr mp 21 – A.T.*
122	Compton Peak West	0.2	*A.T. – Compton Peak W View Point*
210	Compton Peak East	0.2	*A.T. – Compton Peak E View Point*
	TOTAL	47.7	

SNP Number	Trail Name	Mileage	Termini and Milepost
17	Buck Hollow	3.7	*US 211* – A.T. *mp 33.5*
160	Buck Ridge	2.4	*Buck Hollow Trail – Hazel Mtn Trail*
131	Sams Ridge	1.6	*Broad Hollow Trail – E park boundary*
129	Broad Hollow	2.2	*Hazel Mtn Trail – E park boundary*
167	Catlett Spur	1.1	*Hazel Mtn Trail – Hannah Run Trail*
128	Catlett Mtn	1.2	*Hazel Mtn Trail – Hannah Run Trail*
20	Hannah Run	3.7	*Skyline Dr mp 36 – Nicholson Hollow Trail*
166	Leading Ridge	1.1	*Skyline Dr mp 36.2 – W park boundary*
169	Crusher Ridge	1.8	*Skyline Dr mp 38.3 – W park boundary*
130	Hot Mtn–Short Mtn	2.1	*Hazel Mtn Trail – Nicholson Hollow Trail*
98	Corbin Cabin Cutoff	1.5	*Skyline Dr mp 37.9 – Nicholson Hollow Trail*
19	Nicholson Hollow	5.5	A.T. – *Corbin Cabin E park boundary mp 38.4*
171	Indian Run	1.6	*Old Rag Rd – Nicholson Hollow Trail*
172	Corbin Mtn	2.6	*Indian Run Trail – Nicholson Hollow*

SNP Number	Trail Name	Mileage	Termini and Milepost
173	Corbin Hollow	2.0	*Old Rag Rd – Weakley Hollow Trail*
174	Robertson Mtn	2.4	*Old Rag Rd – Weakley Hollow Trail*
100	Ridge	3.1	*Park boundary – Byrd's Nest Shelter #1*
27	Saddle	1.1	*Byrd's Nest Shelter #1 – Old Rag Shelter (road blue blazed only from Old Rag Shelter to Old Rag/Weakley Hollow/ Berry Hollow junction*
26	Whiteoak	5.0	*Skyline Dr mp 42.5 (Whiteoak Parking Area) – park boundary*
60	Limberlost	1.3	*Old Rag Rd – Old Rag Rd mp 43*
28	Cedar Run	3.5	*Skyline Dr mp 45.5 (Lower Hawksbill Parking Area) – Whiteoak Canyon Trail*
30	Naked Top	0.8	*Byrd's Nest Shelter #32 – Naked Top Summit*
118	Hawksbill	1.8	*Skyline Dr mp 45.5 (Lower Hawksbill Parking Area) – Byrd's Nest Shelter #2 – Upper Hawksbill Parking Area*

SNP Number	Trail Name	Mileage	Termini and Milepost
208	Rose River Loop	1.8	*Rose River Trail – Skyland/Big Meadows Horse Trail mp 46.7*
32	Dark Hollow Falls	0.9	*Skyline Dr mp 50.8 – Dark Hollow Falls*
33	Lewis Spring Falls	1.8	*A.T. at Big Meadows Lodge – A.T.*
176	Lewis Falls Spur	0.1	*Trail – Observation Point*
35	Mill Prong	1.0	*A.T. – Mill Prong Horse Trail*
187	Powell Mtn	2.9	*Skyline Dr mp 54.5 – park boundary*
191	Lewis Mtn West	2.5	*Skyline Dr mp 57.6 (Lewis Mtn) – W park boundary*
192	Lewis Mtn East	2.5	*Campground – Old farm site*
194	Hensley Church	1.0	*Skyline Dr mp 59.5 – W park boundary*
195	Pocosin Hollow	2.6	*Pocosin Trail – E boundary mp 60*
186	Laurel Prong	2.2	*A.T. – Fork Mtn Trail*
223	Staunton River	4.6	*SR 662 – Fork Mtn Trail (blazed both blue and yellow along Fork Mtn Rd)*
224	McDaniel Hollow	0.5	*Staunton River Trail – Jones Mtn Trail*

SNP Number	Trail Name	Mileage	Termini and Milepost
225	Jones Mtn Cabin	0.3	*Jones Mtn Trail – Jones Mtn Cabin*
189	Jones Mtn	4.8	*The Sag – Staunton River*
119	Betty's Rock	0.4	*Crescent Rock Overlook – Betty's Rock (includes unnamed connecting trail from A.T. to Betty's Rock Trail)*
64	Bearfence	0.8	*Skyline Dr – A.T.*
25	Millers Head	0.8	*Lower Skyland – Millers Head*
214	Crescent Rocks	1.1	*Skyline Dr mp 44.4 – Limberlost Spur*
226	Cat Knob	0.5	*Laurel Prong Trail – Jones Mtn Trail*
23	Little Stony Man	1.0	*Stony Man Nature Trail – A.T.*
63	Blackrock	0.2	*Big Meadows Lodge across Blackrock Overlook to A.T.*
336	Rock Springs Cabin	0.2	A.T. – *Rock Springs Cabin/Rock Springs Hut*
337	Bearfence Hut	0.2	A.T. – *Bearfence Hut*
338	Pocosin Cabin	0.1	A.T. – *Pocosin Cabin*
38	South River Falls	1.6	*S River Picnic Area – S River mp 63*
196	Saddleback Mtn	1.1	A.T. – *S River PATC Maintenance Bldg.*
	TOTAL	90.6	

SNP Number	Trail Name	Mileage	Termini and Milepost
111	Beldor Ridge	3.9	*US Highway 33 – Gap Run Trail*
121	Gap Run	2.2	*Rocky Mount Trail – Rocky Mt Trail*
42	Rocky Mt	5.4	*Gap Run – Skyline Dr mp 76.1*
43	Brown Mtn – Rocky Mtn	5.3	*Skyline Dr mp 77 (Brown Mtn Overlook) Big Run Trail Bridge*
200	Rocky Mtn Run	2.7	*Brown Mtn – Rocky Mtn/Big Run Trail*
46	Rockytop	6.0	*Big Run Portal Trail – Madison Run Rd*
47	Lewis Peak	2.6	*Park boundary (Lewis Run) – Rockytop Trail*
113	Austin Mtn	3.2	*Madison Run Rd – Rockytop Trail*
44	Big Run Loop	2.1	*Skyline Dr mp 81 (Big Run Overlook) – A.T. (includes yellow-blazed section between Big Run Portal and Rocky-top Trails)*
45	Doyle River	4.7	*Doyle River Parking Area – A.T. near Sky-line Dr mp 84*
112	Furnace Mtn	3.4	*Madison Run Rd – Trayfoot Mtn Trail*

SNP Number	Trail Name	Mileage	Termini and Milepost
227	Furnace Mtn Summit	0.5	*Furnace Mtn Trail – Furnace Mtn Summit*
48/ 217	Trayfoot Mtn	5.4	*Skyline Dr mp 84.7 – Paine Run Trail*
50	Riprap	4.4	A.T. *2.48 mi S of Black-rock Gap – park boundary*
228	Rocks Mtn	3.0	*Riprap Trail – Riprap Trail mp 90*
205	Wildcat Ridge	2.5	Riprap Trail – A.T. *Skyline Dr mp 92.1*
115	Turk Mtn	1.1	A.T. – *Turk Mtn Summit mp 94*
110	One-Mile Run	3.7	*Skyline Dr at Two-Mile Run Overlook – park boundary*
342	Ivy Creek PATC Maintenance	0.2	A.T. – *Ivy Creek PATC Maintenance Building*
219	Doyle River Cabin	0.1	*Doyle River Trail – Cabin*
49	Black Rock Hut	0.3	A.T. – *Black Rock Hut*
109	Hightop Rd	0.2	*Smith Roach Gap Rd – Hightop Hut*
340	Hightop Hut	0.1	A.T. – *Hightop Hut*
341	Pinefield Hut	0.1	A.T. – *Pinefield Hut*
	Ranger Station	0.2	A.T. – *Rockfish Entrance Station*
	TOTAL	63.3	

Yellow-Blazed Horse/Foot Trails

Note: All trail listings are from N to S.

North District   434–456

SNP Number	Trail Name	Mileage	Termini and Milepost
221	Jenkins Gap	0.8	*Skyline Dr mp 12.5 – park boundary*
4	Bluff	4.6	*A.T. – Mt Marshall Rd*
140	Harris Hollow	1.0	*Gravel Springs Hut – park boundary*
141	Browntown	2.3	*Skyline Dr mp 17.5 – park boundary*
145	Matthews Arm	4.7	*Matthews Arm Campground – park boundary*
144	Beecher Ridge	2.2	*Matthews Arm Trail – Heiskell Hollow Trail*
147	Heiskell Hollow	3.3	*Knot Mtn Trail – park boundary*
57	Keyser Run	4.4	*Skyline Dr mp 19.3 – park boundary*
11	Knob Mtn	7.6	*Matthews Arm – Jeremys Run*
152	Thornton River	4.0	*Skyline Dr mp 25.5 – park boundary*
153	Hull School	4.4	*Skyline Dr mp 28 – Keyser Run*
216	Mt Marshall	5.4	*Skyline Dr mp 12.6 – park boundary*

SNP Number	Trail Name	Mileage	Termini and Milepost
12	Neighbor Mtn	4.7	*A.T. – Jeremys Run*
97	Jeremys Run (part)	0.8	*Knot Mtn Trail – park boundary*
138	Hickerson Hollow	1.0	*Skyline Dr mp 9 – park boundary*
8	Piney Branch (part)	2.4	*Hull School Trail – park boundary*
156	Kemp Hollow	0.4	*Skyline Dr mp 30 – park boundary*
229	Jordan River	1.2	*Mt Marshall Trail – park boundary*
2	Dickey Hill (part)	0.5	*Hickerson Hollow Trail – Spring House*
54	Spring House Rd	0.5	*A.T. – Spring House*
230	Weddlewood	0.5	*Matthews Arm Trail – Heiskell Hollow*
52	Lands Run	2.0	*Skyline Dr mp 9 – park boundary*
53	Compton Gap	2.2	*Skyline Dr mp 10.5 – park boundary*
	TOTAL	60.9	

SNP Number	Trail Name	Mileage	Termini and Milepost
161	Old Hazel	1.4	*Hazel Mtn Trail – U.S. 211*
162	White Rocks	1.7	*Hazel Mtn Trail – park boundary*
164	Hazel Spur	0.8	*Hazel Mtn Trail – White Rocks Trail*
213	Hazel Mtn	5.2	*Skyline Dr mp 33.7 – Hot Mtn*
165	Hazel River	2.8	*Hazel Mtn Trail – park boundary*
170	Pine Hill Gap	1.7	*Hazel Mtn Trail – park boundary*
70	Skyland	3.2	*Skyland – park boundary*
58	Stony Man Horse Trail	1.5	*Skyland – Stony Man*
127	Skyland–Big Meadows Horse Trail	11.2	*Skyland – Big Meadows*
72	Old Rag	5.1	*Skyline Dr mp 43 – Old Rag*
186	Whiteoak Ranger Station	0.1	*Old Rag Rd–Whiteoak Ranger Station*
30	Weakley Hollow	2.4	*Old Rag Rd–park boundary*
187	Berry Hollow	0.8	*Old Rag Rd–park boundary*
103	Whiteoak Canyon	1.8	*Skyline Dr mp 45–Falls*

SNP Number	Trail Name	Mileage	Termini and Milepost
73	Red Gate	4.8	*Skyline Dr mp 50–park boundary*
120	Rose River	6.5	*Skyline Dr mp 50–park boundary*
177	Stony Mtn	1.1	*Rose River–Rapidan*
179	Upper Dark Hollow	2.0	*Rose River–Rapidan*
77	Rapidan	7.4	*Skyline Dr mp 51–park boundary*
62	Tanners Ridge Horse Trail	2.5	*Big Meadows Stables – Loop*
31	Tanners Ridge	1.4	*Skyline Dr mp 51.5–park boundary*
163	Camp Hoover	1.0	*Rapidan–Camp Hoover*
186	Laurel Prong (part)	0.6	*Junction Fork Mtn Trail–Camp Hoover*
185	Mill Prong Horse Spur	2.2	*Rapidan–Camp Hoover*
181	Fork Mtn Rd	2.8	*Rapidan–Fork Mtn*
222	Fork Mtn Trail	1.3	*Laurel Prong–Fork Mtn*
164	West Naked Creek Rd	1.8	*Rte 607–park boundary*
188	Conway	1.4	*Skyline Dr mp 55–park boundary*
25	Madison County Rte 649	1.8	*Park boundary–park boundary*
75	Graves Mill	0.5	*Rte 649–park boundary*

SNP Number	Trail Name	Mileage	Termini and Milepost
231	Meadow School	1.0	*Skyline Dr mp 56.8–park boundary*
190	Slaughter	3.8	*Skyline Dr mp 56.8–park boundary*
117	Pocosin	2.5	*Skyline Dr mp 62.5–park boundary*
184	Pocosin Horse Trail	1.6	*Pocosin Rd–park boundary*
82	Dry Run	1.9	*Skyline Dr mp 62.6–park boundary*
83	South River	1.4	*Skyline Dr mp 62.6–park boundary*
118	Big Bend	4.2	*US 33–park boundary*
	TOTAL	95.2	

South District   494–507

SNP Number	Trail Name	Mileage	Termini and Milepost
85	Smith Roach Gap	1.4	*Skyline Dr mp 68.7 – park boundary*
26	Simmons Gap – E/W	3.7	*Park boundary – park boundary*
201	Patterson Ridge	3.1	*Skyline Dr mp 78.8 – Big Run Portal*
203	Big Run Portal	4.2	*Big Run Loop – park boundary*

SNP Number	Trail Name	Mileage	Termini and Milepost
44	Big Run Loop (portion)	1.7	*Big Run Portal – Madison Run*
89	Stull Run	3.6	*Rockingham County Route 663 – park boundary*
90	Madison Run	5.6	*Skyline Dr mp 83 – park boundary*
91	Brown Gap	3.0	*Skyline Dr mp 83 – park boundary*
218	Paine Run	3.7	*Skyline Dr mp 87.3 – park boundary*
93	N Fork and S Fork Moorman River	6.9	*Skyline Dr mp 87.3 Skyline Dr mp 96.8*
204	Turk Gap	1.6	*Skyline Dr mp 94 – park boundary*
116	Turk Branch	2.1	*Skyline Dr mp 94.2 – South Fork Moorman River*
173	Gasline Rd	2.0	*Skyline Dr mp 96.2 – park boundary*
	TOTAL	42.6	

Nature Trails (Unblazed)   508–512

Note: The nature trails are not blazed; interpretive signs, brochures, or both are provided at the sites. Trail listings are from N to S.

SNP Number	Trail Name	Mileage	Termini and Milepost
220	Fox Hollow	1.0	*Dickey Ridge Visitor Center mp 4.6*
135	Traces	1.7	*Matthews Arm Campground – loop mp 22.2*
59	Stony Man	1.0	*Skyland – loop mp 41.7*
61	Story of Forest	1.8	*Byrd Visitor Center – Big Meadows Wayside mp 51*
136	Deadening	1.3	*Loft Mtn Wayside – loop mp 79.5*
	TOTAL	6.8	

Master List of SNP Trail Mileage Totals

Appalachian Trail Total	94.9 mi
Blue-Blazed Foot Trails	201.6 mi
Yellow-Blazed Horse/Foot Trails	198.7 mi
Nature Trails	6.8 mi
Paved Walks and Trails	14.0 mi
TOTAL	516.0 mi

6 · National Battlefield Parks

Colonial-Era Trails

Colonial National Historic Park
York and James City Counties

Yorktown is best known for the Yorktown Battlefield, the location of the last major battle of the American Revolution. It was on October 19, 1781 in the home of Augustine Moore, near the banks of the York River, that peace commissioners ratified the terms by which Lord Cornwallis surrendered to Washington's allied French and American forces. Jamestown Island is best known as the location of the first permanent English settlement, founded in 1607. Both of these historic sites, plus a 23-mile parkway connecting them through Colonial Williamsburg and the Cape Henry Memorial, are components of the 9,833-acre Colonial National Historic Park. The park was designated by an act of Congress in 1930. Since then two historic trails in the park have been established, sponsored in part by the Peninsula Council of Boy Scouts. These are the *Yorktown Battlefield Trail* and *Jamestown Colony Trail.*

Access: To reach Yorktown Battlefield turn off US 17 onto the Colonial Pkwy and go 0.6 mi to the visitor center parking area. To reach Jamestown follow the Colonial Pkwy W from Yorktown for 23 mi.

▼ YORKTOWN BATTLEFIELD TRAIL   513

Length: 12.5 mi (20 km); easy. *USGS Map:* Yorktown.
Trailhead: Visitor center.

Directions and Description: At the visitor center examine the exhibits and request a trail map from the information desk. (The trail can be hiked or cycled with or without the 3.5-mi French Artillery Park Loop.) When leaving the visitor center look for sign for "Hornwork," the main British defense line, on the L, and follow over the earthworks to a 5-point road junction. Cross the road, turn L, and continue walking on VA 238 E until reaching Surrender Rd, SR 704 junction. Turn R and go 0.2 mi to yellow-marked Goosley Rd. Proceed on Goosley Rd to W Tour Rd; turn L and reach reconstructed redoubt, an outer line of defense, at 1.2 mi. Continue ahead to the French Loop, marked by a brown sign R at 2.9 mi. (The French Artillery Park Loop through the French encampment is 3.5 mi.) On returning continue ahead to Washington's Headquarters area at 7.9 mi. From there follow the road over Beaver Dam Creek bridge, cross under US 17, and reach Surrender Field Pavilion at 10.2 mi. Here swords were formally exchanged by Gen O'Hara and Gen Benjamin Lincoln to signify the end of the war. From the parking lot follow the red-arrow tour across the road and through a wooded area; go to junction at SR 704. Cross road to Grand French Battery. From here cross through the Second Siege line (and cross VA 238) to redoubts of the British line #9 and #10. Visitor center is ahead L at 12.5 mi.

▼ JAMESTOWN COLONY TRAIL   514

Length: 5.5 mi (8.8 km); easy. *USGS Map:* Surry. *Trailhead:* Visitor center.

Directions and Description: Visit the visitor center before beginning the hike, then go to the monument behind the center and proceed around the Jamestown site, as a preliminary to the longer loop trail. Hike the Island Loop Dr on the grassy shoulder facing traffic, examining the exhibits along the way. Their subjects include colonial shipbuilding, agriculture, Indian trade, winemaking, medicine, household supplies, and brick making.

Support Facilities: Jamestown Beach Campsite, PO Box CB, Williamsburg, VA 23187; tel: 804-229-8366. Open all year, full service, excellent recreational facilities. Location: From junction of I-64 and VA 199, go 4 mi W on VA 199, then 4 mi S on VA 31.

Information: Contact Superintendent, Colonial National Historic Park, PO Box 210, Yorktown, VA 23690; tel: 804-898-3400 (in Yorktown) and 804-229-1282 (in Jamestown).

Civil War–Era Trails

There are seven Civil War battlefield parks in Virginia, at least 28 historic attractions, and more than 250 sites designated by state historical markers along the highways. They commemorate four years (July 21, 1861–April 12, 1865) of tragedy in 1,000 battles, engagements, skirmishes, and encounters; 60% of the entire war was fought in Virginia. (During the Civil War the number of men in battle was 4,137,304—1 in 8 of the population—and more than 617,000 died. In contrast, more than 120,000 died in WW I and 400,000 in WW II.) To hike the trails in these battlefields is to retrace and recount the heroic bravery and valor of the Confederate and Union soldiers. For the hiker to choose the season of the year in which the battles were fought provides an additional emotional awareness.

Manassas National Battlefield Park
Prince William County

The First Battle of Manassas was fought here on July 21, 1861 when Union general Irvin McDowell attacked a strategic E-W railroad junction over a stream called Bull Run. It was during this famous battle on Henry Hill that Confederate general Barnard Bee of South Carolina, in an attempt to rally his Third Brigade, used Gen. Thomas J. Jackson's brigade as an anchor. "Form, form," said Bee, "there stands Jackson like a stone wall, rally behind the Virginians." A few minutes later Bee was killed by Union gunfire. The battle ended in a rout for Gen. McDowell's troops and a Confederate victory. The Second Battle of Manassas, August 28–30, 1862, secured a place in history for Gen. Robert E. Lee as he defeated the 75,000 Union troops with his 48,327 Confederates. In the two battles the South lost 11,456 men and the North 17,170. These battles are commemorated in the 3,200-acre Manassas National Battlefield Park. Four interpretive trails, totaling 4.6 mi, describe in graphic detail the events of the battles. Other trails include a 10-mi bridle trail, a 20.5-mi *Boy Scout Historical Trail* (which combines parts of the interpretive trails), and a 12-mi driving tour. It is recommended that hikers visit the visitor center before their tours.

Access: From I-66 turn on VA 234 N, Sudley-Manassas Rd, and go 0.6 mi to park entrance and visitor center on R. From US 29–211 turn on VA 234 S and go 0.4 mi to park entrance.

▼ HENRY HILL TRAIL, STONE BRIDGE–VAN PELT TRAIL, DEEP CUT TRAIL, SUDLEY SPRINGS TRAIL   515–518

Length: 4.6 mi (7.5 km) ct; easy. *USGS Maps:* Manassas, Gainesville. *Trailhead:* See for each trail.

Directions and Description: The 1.2-mi loop *Henry Hill Trail* begins at the visitor center with interpretive signs, artillery positions, and seven push-button audio stations explaining in detail the fight to control the hill in the First Battle of Manassas.

Stone Bridge–Van Pelt Trail is a 1.4-mi interpretive loop trail that describes strategic maneuvers at Bull Run; it was here that the first shots were fired on the morning of July 21, 1861. The trail also has signs for a study of the local ecosystems, and along the bluffs of Bull Run the trail passes a biotic community usually found in higher elevations. (Access is from parking area on US 29–211 at the Prince William and Fairfax county line, 1.3 mi E of VA 234 junction with US 29–211.)

Deep Cut Trail is a 1-mi loop trail along an unfinished railroad where Gen Jackson deployed his wing of troops in an excellent defensive position in the Second Battle of Manassas, August 28–30, 1862. Here Gen John Pope, misjudging the Confederate defense, was defeated on

August 30. That night and all the next day it rained, preventing the Confederates from pursuing the retreating army. (Access is at parking lot on SR 622, 0.9 mi from US 29–211 and 1.4 mi E on US 29–211 from junction of VA 234.)

Another 1-mi interpretive loop trail memorializing the Second Battle of Manassas is *Sudley Springs Trail*, which follows the unfinished railroad to Bull Run and to the Sudley Spring Ford. The original Sudley Church here was used as a field hospital. (Access is from parking area on VA 234 N, 1.6 mi from junction with US 27-211).

▼ MANASSAS BATTLEFIELD
  HISTORICAL TRAILS   519–520

Length: 20.5 mi (32.8 km); easy to moderate. *USGS Maps:* Manassas, Gainesville. *Trailhead:* Visitor center.

Directions and Description: (No camping on these trails.) The *First Manassas Battlefield Trail*, 12.7 mi, is often hiked by Boy Scouts for educational credit. It begins at the visitor center and goes E to the ruins of the Van Pelt House. From there it descends to Bull Run using the interpretive *Stone Bridge Trail*. The trail then turns NW, proceeding to the Carter House Cemetery and to the Buck Hill Cannons. On reaching VA 234 (across from the picnic area) the trail turns S, crossing a hill before descending to the Stone House, which served as a field hospital in both Manassas battles. Ascending on a gentle grade, the trail reaches the *Henry Hill Trail,* following it for 1.2 mi. After a return to the visitor center the trail crosses VA 234 W, crosses Chinn Branch, ascends to NW end of Chinn Ridge, and descends to US 29–211. Here the trail crosses the highway and parallels VA 234 to the picnic area at 12.7 mi.

To complete the 20.5-mi route hike the 7.8 mi of the *Second Battle of Manassas Trail*. The trail extends R of the parking lot over gentle terrain to Battery Heights, where a bloody battle was fought on August 28. Continuing past an interpretive mural about an attack on Gen Jackson's forces, the trail then turns R to Dogan House and Groveton Confederate Cemetery. Here repose 50 known and more than 250 unknown Confederate soldiers. Again the trail crosses US 29–211, going to monuments honoring the Fifth and Tenth New York Regiments. After turning E the trail passes markers describing Longstreet's attack, the Chinn House Ruins, and the Hooe Family Cemetery. Before the trail's crossing of the Chinn Branch there is a monument to Col Fletcher Webster, who was killed here. He was the only son of US Senator Daniel Webster. Returning to VA 234, the trail passes a marker describing the retreat of the Union forces under Gen John Pope. Trail ends here after 7.8 mi. Vehicle shuttle is necessary. (More information on this trail may be received by contacting American Historical Trails, PO Box 810, Washington, DC 20044; tel: 703-281-1812.)

Information: Contact Park Superintendent, Manassas Battlefield Park, Box 1830, Manassas, VA 22110; tel: 703-754-7107.

Fredericksburg and Spotsylvania National Military Park
Spotsylvania and Orange Counties

This military park comprises 5,644 acres and seven

major historic sites, including four major battlegrounds: for the Battle of Fredericksburg, December 11–13, 1862; for the Battle of Chancellorsville and the Second Battle of Fredericksburg, April 27–May 6, 1863; for the Battle of the Wilderness, May 5–6, 1864; and for the Battle of Spotsylvania Court House, May 8–21, 1864. No other theater of war in America has had such fierce fighting and slaughter. The Union Army lost 70,000 men and the South lost at least 35,000.

The Fredericksburg Visitor Center and the Chancellorsville Visitor Center have museums, audiovisuals, and displays to acquaint the visitor with the history of the Civil War action. Hikers should visit these centers before taking the hikes. Two interpretive trails are at the Fredericksburg Visitor Center. The *Sunken Rd Trail* is along Telegraph Rd, where Confederates were entrenched behind the Stone Wall. By darkness on December 13, 1862 more than 7,500 Federal troops lay dead or wounded on the open space between the wall and the river. During the night Sgt Richard Kirkland from South Carolina responded to the anguished pleas for water from the wounded Union soldiers. His humanitarian act gave him the title of "Angel of Marye's Heights." Another walk from the visitor center ascends to Marye's Heights and the Fredericksburg National Cemetery, where there are graves for men numbering 15,243, of which 12,770 are unknown. The verses of Theodore O'Hara's "The Bivouac of the Dead" (written to honor Kentuckians in the Mexican War) are on metal plaques here:

> On fame's eternal camping ground,
> their silent tents are spread,
> and glory guards with solemn round,
> the bivouac of the dead

Access: From US 1 into downtown Fredericksburg on Lafayette Blvd between Sunken Rd and Willis St, or from US 1 Alt, take VA 3, Williams St, E for 0.3 mi to Hanover St. After another 0.7 mi turn R at Sunken Rd to parking area.

▼ LEE DRIVE TRAIL   521

Length: 5.2 mi (8.3 km); easy. *USGS Maps:* Fredericksburg, Guinea. *Trailhead:* Howison Hill parking area.

Directions and Description: From the Fredericksburg Visitor Center take US 1 S for 0.6 mi and turn L into Battlefield Park. At 0.2 mi farther is a paved foot trail, 350 yds, R to Gen Lee's Command Post. From here go 0.6 mi to Howison Hill parking area and exhibit; the dark-blue-blazed *Lee Drive Trail* begins behind the artillery site. At 0.5 mi pass behind the park maintenance area; cross Lee Drive and reach picnic area at 1.2 mi. Cross road again, following the well-graded trail through oaks and scattered pines with holly and dogwoods forming a light understory. Cross Deep Run at 1.7 mi, ascend on gentle terrain to road, and follow along the shoulder to Lansdowne Valley Rd, SR 638. Reenter the woods R at 2.9 mi, and arrive at Prospect Hill exhibit area and Gen Lee's defense line at 5.2 mi. Backtrack or use vehicle shuttle.

▼ JACKSON TRAIL   522–523

Length: 10.9 mi (17.4 km); moderate. *USGS Maps:* Chancellorsville, Brokenburg. *Trailhead:* Lee-Jackson Bivouac.

Directions and Description: From I-95 W in Fredericksburg, go first to the Chancellorsville Visitor Center, 8 mi away on VA 3, for examination of the exhibits and audiovisuals. Plans may allow for a vehicle shuttle at any of the trail points or intersections. Drive N on Bullock Rd for 0.8 mi to Apex of Gen Hooker's Last Line at Ely's Ford Rd, SR 610. Turn R and go 0.7 mi to Chancellorsville Inn ruins, an area captured from Hooker in an incredible victory by the Confederates on May 3, 1863. Cross VA 3, and go 1.1 mi on SR 610 to the Lee-Jackson Bivouac. It was here on the night of May 1, 1863 the Confederate leaders planned the Battle of Chancellorsville. Jackson began his flank march the next day; Gen Lee would never see him again. Here, the hiker—history buff or not—can hike the road following Gen Jackson's famous and risky flank march along Furnace Rd. Reach Catharine Furnace remains at 1.4 mi, turn L on *Jackson Trail/E* and reach Brock Rd, SR 613, at 4.2 mi. (Here, Jackson turned S as part of the plan to deceive Hooker's scouts of his intentions.) After 0.3 mi turn R on *Jackson Trail/W.* Cross the stream, a good spot to imagine what this trail must have been like with Jackson's army in a 7-mi column through the forest. Rejoin SR 613 at 6.7 mi, cross Orange Plank Rd, SR 621, at 7.9 mi and reach VA 3 at 9.4 mi. Turn E on VA 3 for 1.5 mi to the site where on May 2 Jackson surprised the Union Army with a flank attack. (The victorious march ended in tragedy for Gen Jackson when that night he was mistakenly shot by his own troops. He died of wounds and pneumonia eight days later at the Chandler Plantation in Guinea Station.) On May 3 the Confederates captured the Hazel Grove position. The *Fairview Trail,* on Stuart Dr 0.5 mi S from the visitor center, describes this significant artillery battle. Vehicle shuttle required for the *Jackson Trail*.

▼ SPOTSYLVANIA BATTLEFIELD HISTORY
   TRAIL   524–526

Length: 6.2 mi (9.9 km); easy. *USGS Maps:* Spotsylvania, Brokenburg, Chancellorsville. *Trailhead:* Sedgwick Monument.

Directions and Description: From Chancellorsville Visitor Center take SR 610, 612, and 613 S to Spotsylvania, or, if from Fredericksburg, take US 1 and VA 208 S. (At the time of the battle at Spotsylvania, a year had passed since the battle at Fairview, but this time the Federal Army was under the command of Gen Ulysses S. Grant. His intention was to push on to Richmond.) Begin the hike at Sedgwick Monument on SR 613 on a blue-blazed loop trail N paralleling the Grant Dr. (The Sedgwick Monument exhibit is the only place to get drinking water along this hike.) Cross the road at 0.6 mi along Upton's trace, and turn L over Dale's Salient at 0.9 mi. Cross Bloody Angle Dr to McCoull Spring and the McCoull House ruins at 1.6 mi. Turn L here through woods, and parallel Gordon Dr L to Bloody Angle Dr and the *Bloody Angle Loop Trail* at 2.5 mi. Here, on May 12, was the most intense and desperate hand-to-hand combat of the war. After hiking the *Bloody Angle Loop Trail* return to the McCoull House ruins at 4 mi, but take the R fork and cross the Gordon Dr. Follow S to Harrison House ruins, cross the Gordon Dr again, and reach SR 613 at 5.1 mi. A connecting loop to the Maryland Monument, across SR 613, and to the *Hancock Trail* returns the hiker to the Sedgwick Monument at 6.2

mi. Within the trail perimeter, more than 25,000 soldiers fell during May 8–21, 1864.

Information: Contact Superintendent, Fredericksburg and Spotsylvania National Military Park, PO Box 679, Fredericksburg, VA 22401; tel: 703-373-4461.

Richmond National Battlefield Park
Chesterfield, Hanover, and Henrico Counties

An area of 769 acres, the Richmond National Battlefield Park commemorates nine battlegrounds or other sites in the drive to capture the Confederate capital during the Civil War. Five were associated with General George McClellan's campaign in 1862 (Chickahominy Bluff, Beaver Dam Creek, Gaines' Mill, Malvern Hill, and Drewry's Bluff). In 1864 General Ulysses Grant led campaigns at Cold Harbor, Fort Harrison, and Parker's Battery. Other nearby battlefields, such as Fair Oaks, Savage States, and Glendale, are not within the park system but were part of McClellan's campaigns. A loop drive of 100 mi from the Chimborazo Visitor Center is necessary to visit all the historic battle areas, restored houses, cemeteries, and other park facilities scattered in a three-county area. Five designated hiking trails are in the park: a total of 3.6 mi. Before visiting or hiking go to the Chimborazo Visitor Center in Richmond. Here the visitor can acquire historical information and detailed maps on the motor routes. Also, each major battlefield has interpretive facilities, and both Cold Harbor and Fort Harrison have visitor centers.

Access: Southbound on I-95 in downtown Richmond take exit 10-A to Franklin St E; go 4 blocks to 18th St and turn L. After 2 blocks turn R on E Broad; Chimborazo Visitor Center is at 3215 E Broad St. Northbound traffic take exit 10 to E Broad St and follow directions as above.

▼ COLD HARBOR TRAIL,
BREAKTHROUGH POINT TRAIL,
FORT HARRISON TRAIL,
RIVER TRAIL, FORT DARLING TRAIL   527–532

Length: 3.6 mi (6 km); easy. *USGS Maps:* Drewry's Bluff, Seven Pine, Dutch Gap, Richmond. *Trailhead:* See below for each trail.

Directions and Description: The *Cold Harbor Trail* is 1.1 mi, a loop trail through Confederate and Federal earthworks involved in the Battle of Cold Harbor, May 31–June 13, 1864. The battle cost the Federal army 7,000 casualties in 30 minutes and was Gen Robert E. Lee's last major victory. (Cold Harbor is on VA 156 NE of I-295 and SR 615 junction).

Breakthrough Point Trail, a short loop trail of 0.2 mi, is near the Watt House. It follows a portion of the Seven Days Battle line to the point where Confederate forces broke through Federal defenses at the Battle of Gaines' Mill, June 27, 1862. (Access is a spur road from VA 156 at Cold Harbor.)

The *Fort Harrison Trail* is 1.4 mi, a loop with exhibits describing construction techniques and soldier life at Civil War field fortifications. (Access is off VA 5 S of Richmond at Fort Gilmer junction.)

Across the James River W are two trails at Drewry's Bluff. *River Trail,* 0.4 mi round trip on the site of Fort Darling and the Confederate Naval/Marine Training Center, leads to the James River. The *Fort Darling Trail* loops 0.5 mi to an overlook of the James River where Confederate artillery stopped a Federal fleet, including the ironclad *Monitor,* from steaming upstream to attack Richmond. (Access is 7.5 mi from Richmond on I-95 S to exit 7 and junction with VA 150 W. Go L (S) at junction with US 301-1 for 2.4 mi to Bellwood Rd, SR 656, on L. After taking SR 656 go under I-95 and make a sharp L on Fort Darling Rd.)

Information: Contact Superintendent, Richmond National Battlefield Park, 3215 E Broad St, Richmond, VA 23223; tel: 804-226-1981.

New Market Battlefield Park
City of New Market 533

The 160-acre New Market Battlefield Park and Hall of Valor is a Registered National Historic Landmark. It is administered by Virginia Military Institute as a nonprofit educational facility and was made possible by a gift from VMI alumnus George Randall Collins. The area honors the 247 teenage cadets under the command of Gen John C. Breckinridge, who with other batteries and companies on May 15, 1864 courageously forced the Federal units to retreat. (Each year, on the Sunday preceding May 15, the battle is reenacted.) Before hiking the trail visit the park museum for information and audiovisuals. The 1-mi loop trail from the parking lot at the Hall of Valor leads to the historic Bushong Farm, where Confederate wounded were treated after the battle. Among the 43 Confederates killed, 10 were VMI cadets. Pass exhibit markers around the "field of lost shoes" to Federal lines and scenic overlooks 200 ft above the Shenandoah River. Return

Petersburg Battlefield National Recreation Trail.
National Park Service.

along the cliffs through a border of cedar and redbud.

Access: From I-81, exit 67 W, junction of VA 211, follow signs. (Open daily 9–5.)

Information: Contact New Market Battlefield Park, New Market, VA 22844; tel: 703-740-3102.

Petersburg National Battlefield Park
Prince George County

Established as a national military park in 1926, the site of the Petersburg siege was designated a national battlefield in 1962. Its 1,536 acres extend to Fort Lee E, to US 460 and VA 109 S, and to US 301 W, with VA 36 running through the N edge. A 16-mi auto tour of the siege lines around Petersburg begins at the junction of US 301, Crater Rd, and the park's Siege Rd. The route includes nine of the major forts Gen Lee maintained during the 10-month siege, June 15, 1864 to April 2, 1865.

After Lee defeated Grant at Cold Harbor on June 3, 1864, Grant said that the key to taking Richmond was in Petersburg, but a series of Union fumbles on June 15 and 18 cost him 10,000 men and a long delay in the capture of the city. The delay became 10 months, the longest siege in American warfare. More than 70,000 died. During this time Gen Grant's Army of the Potomac with 100,000 men were well armed and supplied from the City Point (Hopewell) Military RR, on which 500,000 tons of material was transported. In contrast, Gen Lee's army of 60,000 men was far less well equipped for the battles of Fort Stedman and Fort Haskell. Finally, with his defenses crumbling, Gen Lee evacuated Petersburg on the night of April 2, 1865.

Besides the siege lines, the auto tour at the Petersburg National Battlefield includes Poplar Grove (Petersburg) National Cemetery, a tract of 8.7 acres SW of Fort Wadsworth. From mid-June to Labor Day the park has a living history program of artillery demonstrations and live exhibitions of soldier life of the Civil War. Comprehensive displays and audiovisuals are at the visitor center. There are 12 trails in the park; these total 11.3 mi, of which 7 mi are part of the *Petersburg Battlefield National Recreation Trail.* At the visitor center across from the parking area is a 225-yd interpretive trail for the visually handicapped with sweet gum, cedar, willow, oaks, and other trees and shrubs.

Access: From I-95 in Petersburg turn at signs on VA 36 E, E Washington St (and US 301 S and US 460 E), and go 1.8 mi to park entrance on R.

▼ PETERSBURG BATTLEFIELD
NATIONAL RECREATION TRAIL   534–542

Length: 7 mi (11.2 km) rt, ct; easy. *USGS Maps:* Petersburg, Prince George. *Trailhead:* Parking area on VA 109.

Directions and Description: Designated a national recreation trail in 1981, this loop trail (with two optional spurs) begins at the parking area on VA 109, Mahone Ave, junction with A Ave, 1.2 mi S from VA 36 and 1.6 mi NE from junction of US 460 and VA 109. The wide trail is exceptionally well designed and marked. Its surface is chiefly beds of pine needles, with spots of blacktop or gravel. The first major historic stop is at Meade Station, one of the key supply points for Grant's military railroad. At 0.5 mi turn L on Jordon Point Rd, go 125 yds, and turn R on *Branch Trail* to Siege Rd at 1.1 mi. (On the R is *Battery 5 Spur Trail,* which proceeds R along the multiuse lane to the visitor center and to the site of the famous 17,000-lb Union mortar, the "Dictator." Backtrack for a round-trip total of 1.7 mi. Along the way, near the park entrance from VA 36, is *Battery 7 Trail,* a round-trip side trail of 1.3 mi.)

After returning to *Branch Trail* follow it across the Siege Rd to Fort Friend and the *Friend Trail.* Cross Harrison Creek and reach junction L with Fort Stedman at 2.7 mi from beginning of *Petersburg Battlefield Trail.* (At this point those who wish to hike the *Short Loop Trail* should bear L to Fort Stedman exhibit, cross Siege Rd, and go to *Encampment Trail*; turn R. After 50 yds turn L, cross Harrison Creek, and follow *Harrison Creek Trail* for 0.6 mi to Attack Rd. Turn L, and reach Union Camp at Siege Rd. Turn R on old Prince George Courthouse Rd, returning to parking area for a total of 4.7 mi.)

Continue on *Petersburg Battlefield Trail* to Colquitt's Salient and to Fort Haskell at 3.9 mi. Here is an excellent example of the best-preserved fortifications. Cross and parallel Siege Rd past the Taylor House to railroad at 4.5 mi. (Here the *Crater Spur Trail* continues across the railroad to the site for the ironic and incredible plans of the 48th Pennsylvania Infantry to tunnel under the Confederate line. After a loop of 1.3 mi return to the *Petersburg Battlefield Trail.*) Follow the *Petersburg Battlefield Trail* E to the *Encampment Trail*, cross Taylors Creek, pass junction with *Short Loop Trail* at 5.6 mi, and return to trailhead and parking area for a total of 7 mi. (If spur trails are hiked the total round trip is 11.3 mi.)

Information: Contact Chief Ranger, Petersburg

National Battlefield, PO Box 549, Petersburg, VA
23803; tel: 804-732-3531.

Appomattox Court House National Historical Park
Appomattox County

After the Federal victory on April 1, 1864 at Five Points,
SW of Petersburg, Gen Lee realized the siege of Petersburg was over. The next day both Petersburg and Richmond were evacuated and retreat W began. He made a
skillful withdrawal but counted on supplies arriving at
Amelia for his tired and starving army. The supplies
never came, and valuable time was lost foraging for
food. Furthermore, 8,000 of his men, one-third of his
army, were wounded, killed, or captured on April 6 in the
swampy bottom of Sayler's Creek (now a Virginia Historical State Park on SR 617, 2 mi N of VA 307 near
Rice).Gen Lee set up his last headquarters about 1 mi E
of the Appomattox River on the old Richmond-
Lynchburg Stage Rd. The trail next described follows
Gen Lee's route from his headquarters to other significant points in the final days of the Confederacy.

After the end of the Civil War, the Appomattox Court
House village was neglected for 65 years—the former
McLean House was dismantled, the courthouse burned
in 1892, and other buildings were in decay. Even the bill
passed by Congress in 1930 to build a monument never
was honored. Finally, in 1934 the National Park Service
recommended complete restoration of the village, and in
1935 Congress passed a bill authorizing it as a national
historical monument. In 1954 it was also designated a national historical park. The park has 1,318

acres and a dozen major buildings that have been meticulously restored.

Access: From the town of Appomattox go E on VA 24 for 3 mi to entrance on L. From US 60 at Mt Rush, go W on VA 24 for 17 mi to entrance on R.

▼ APPOMATTOX HISTORY TRAIL   543–544

Length: 6 mi (9.6 km); easy. *USGS Maps:* Appomattox, Vera. *Trailhead:* Visitor center at the courthouse.

Directions and Description: A recommended beginning point for the hike is the visitor center at Appomattox Court House, following E by the jail to Surrender Triangle on the Old Richmond-Lynchburg Rd, where approx 28,000 Confederates laid down their arms on April 12, four years to the day after Fort Sumter. Descend on grassy ridge following trail arrow sign to the Appomattox River Wayside at 0.6 mi. Cross bridge by the marker honoring Joel Walker Sweeney, the inventor of the 5-string banjo, and reach the site of the Apple Tree. Here, Lee waited on April 9 for a response from Gen Grant to Lee's offer of surrender. Pass the *Appomattox National Environmental Study Area Trail* on R and follow VA 24 to the site of Gen Lee's last field headquarters at 1.5 mi. It was here that Gen Lee held his last council of war on the night of April 8. From this point follow the trail onto a woods road at 1.8 mi, enter a Virginia pine stand for 0.2 mi, and reach an open field at Alexander Sweeney's Prizery. Again enter the woods, cross the Appomattox River at 2.4 mi, and follow it up-river, for 0.4 mi to a sharp L uphill. Reach Prince Edward Court House Rd, SR 627, at 3.8 mi. Cross road and continue through forest of locust, oaks, poplar, sassafras, mountain laurel, hickory, maple, dogwood, and huckleberry.

At 5 mi reach North Carolina Monument honoring troops who distinguished themselves in three major battles—Big Bethel, Gettysburg, and Chickamauga—and who fired the final Confederate shots, at Appomattox. Go 0.2 mi to VA 24. (Here, a spur of 0.5 mi L along the highway leads to site of Gen Grant's headquarters.) Turn R to Confederate cemetery for 0.3 mi and follow old coach route to McLean House. Here, at 1:30 P.M. on Palm Sunday, April 9, General Lee met with General Grant to surrender in dignity and honor the Army of Northern Virginia. (When General Lee mounted Traveller to sadly ride away to his men, General Grant and his officers lifted their hats to him in respect. General Grant immediately ordered rations issued for the hungry men in gray and ordered paroles to be printed.) Complete the hike to the visitor center at 6 mi.

Support Facilities: For camping facilities see Holliday State Park, in Chapter 12.

Information: Contact Superintendent, Appomattox Court House National Historical Park, PO Box 218, Appomattox, VA 24522; tel: 804-352-8987. (Also, Blue Ridge Mtn Council, Boy Scouts of America, 116 Jefferson Ave, Vinton, VA 24179; tel: 703-345-7388.)

7 · National Historical Parks

Cumberland Gap National Historical Park
**Lee County, Virginia; Bell County, Kentucky;
and Claiborne County, Tennessee**

Before the American Indians made use of it along the
"Warrior's Path," Cumberland Gap had been the pass
for buffalo and deer that trampled across in large herds
seeking new pastures. It was the main pass on the wilderness trail that became the Wilderness Rd, marked by
Daniel Boone from Virginia to Kentucky in 1775. By
1792 more than 100,000 pioneers had crossed the gap for
Kentucky and beyond. Subsequently the route over it
became a significant artery of migration, trade, and
transportation to the West. In both the Revolutionary
and Civil wars it was an important military objective.
With such a rich history Congress deemed the area
appropriate for designation as a national shrine. Accordingly, in 1940 Cumberland Gap National Historical Park
was authorized; it has 20,270 acres, 7,526 of which are
in Virginia.

The park's chief features are a 160-site campground on
US 58, 45 miles of trails, an interpretive program, a
visitor center with exhibits, The Pinnacle area, and the
Tri-State Peak. Gates are open from 8 A.M. to 5
P.M. daily except for campers at the Wilderness Rd

Ridge Trail, Cumberland Gap National Historical Park.
Allen de Hart.

Campground. Only the trails in Virginia are covered here.

Access: In Virginia take US 58 W, and from Kentucky and Tennessee take US 25E.

▼ RIDGE TRAIL   545-547

Length: 17 mi (27.2 km); moderate to strenuous. *USGS Maps:* Middleboro S and N, Varilla, Ewing. *Trailhead:* Parking area at Pinnacle.

Directions and Description: (If overnight camping is planned, first secure a backcountry use permit from the park office.) Begin the hike at The Pinnacle parking area, ascend to the ridge, and follow an old fire road on the crest. Occasional rock outcroppings provide views into Kentucky and Virginia. Vegetation is mostly young hardwoods with understory of mountain laurel, dogwood, chestnut sprouts, and buck berry. At 2 mi pass *Lewis Hollow Trail* (also called *Skylight Cave Trail*) on R. Wildflowers such as Indian cucumber root, calicroot, wild orchids, and birdfoot violets are profuse. Ascend from gap and reach scenic area at 2.5 mi. Continue on the ridge, often grassy on moderate grade. Pass *Woodson Gap Trail* on R at 3.5 mi, and *Gibson Gap Trail* on R at 5.1 mi. (These trails, as *Skylight Cave Trail*, all lead down the mountain to the Wilderness Rd Campground.) Here at Gibson Gap is a primitive campsite.

Continue on old fire road under forest cover of oaks, hickories, locust, and birch. Frequent patches of woodland yellow sunflowers, purple phlox, lavender bee balm, red fire pink, white daisies, yellow fringed loosestrife, and blue Virginia spiderwort provide an extremely colorful wildflower garden. Wildlife is not equally abundant, but deer, grouse, raccoon, fox, squirrel, and the prevalent chipmunk may be sighted. There are no bears in the park area; however, care should be exercised in case of meeting the timber rattlesnake. At 11.1 mi reach trail on L that leads to Hensley Settlement, partially restored by the National Park Service. Martin Fork Campground is at 12.2 mi, and the trail to the R is a 1.3-mi exit to a state road in Chadwell Gap. At 16 mi pass trail on L to Sand Cave, and another 1 mi ahead is scenic White Rocks and a primitive campground. To exit and reach the Ewing trailhead, descend for 2.7 mi, passing gated road to the Civitan Club parking area. From here exit is to Ewing and US 58.

▼ LEWIS HOLLOW TRAIL, RIDGE TRAIL (SEC), GIBSON GAP TRAIL   548–549

Length: 10 mi (16 km), rt, ct; moderate to strenuous.
USGS Maps: Middleboro S and N, Varilla, Ewing.
Trailhead: Wilderness Rd Campground Registration parking area.

Directions and Description: Follow well-graded and much used *Lewis Hollow Trail*, ascending gradually to a gated cave entrance on R at 1.2 mi. Trail becomes steeper near the Skylight Cave at 1.3 mi. Enter with caution. Be sure to take a flashlight to examine the cave walls and ceiling. Continue climbing by a stream, and then reach the *Ridge Trail* at 1.8 mi. Turn R on old fire road, ascending gradually to excellent lookout on the Virginia side at 2.2 mi. Pass *Woodson Gap Trail*, also called *Mischa Moka Trail*, on R at 3.5 mi. (Here a steep descent can be made to *Gibson Gap Trail*, with a return to the campground at 6.1 mi for a loop.) Continue ahead, ascending and descending on knolls, to junction at 5.1 mi with *Gib-

son Gap Trail, and a primitive campground. Turn R and begin descent on the *Gibson Gap Trail,* passing junction with *Woodson Gap Trail* on R at 9.1 mi, and continue ahead, crossing creek to return at point of origin at 10 mi.

▼ GREEN LEAF NATURE TRAIL, HONEY TREE
SPUR TRAIL   550–551

Length: 1.8 mi (2.9 km) ct; easy. *USGS Maps:* Middleboro S and N, Varilla, Ewing. *Trailhead:* Near amphitheater.

Directions and Description: Follow trail signs L at *Green Leaf Nature Trail*, descending into a valley with high hardwoods. Reach junction with *Honey Tree Spur Trail* L and ascend on it, curving around the slope. Descend and rejoin the original trail near the fire road. Continue the figure eight by turning L on *Green Leaf Nature Trail,* and ascend to the campground. Trails are well graded.

▼ TRI-STATE TRAIL,
WILDERNESS ROAD TRAIL   552–553

Length: 3.4 mi (5.4 km) rt, ct; moderate. *USGS Maps:* Middleboro S and N, Varilla, Ewing. *Trailhead:* Parking area on US 25E in Cumberland Gap.

Directions and Description: Follow trail signs, ascending on wide graded trail, passing site of Fort Foote and Commissary to Tri-State pavilion at 0.9 mi. Area has exhibit information. Backtrack to junction of *Wilderness Rd Trail*, turn R, and descend steeply to Iron Furnace on old Wilderness Rd route. Backtrack.

Information: Contact Chief of Interpretation, Cumberland Gap National Historical Park, Box 840, Middleboro, KY 40965; tel: 606-248-2817.

8 · National Wildlife Refuges

The Fish and Wildlife Service of the US Department of the Interior owns four complete national wildlife refuges in Virginia—Back Bay, Chincoteague, Mason Neck, and Presquile. Another two—Great Dismal Swamp and MacKay Island—are each partially in North Carolina as well as Virginia. Totalling nearly 98,500 acres in Virginia, the refuges primarily are managed to benefit migratory waterfowl, though habitat is managed and protection afforded for other categories of species as well. Where compatible with wildlife management plans, recreational use is allowed; in some areas this includes hiking, picnicking, boating, swimming, fishing, and nature study.

Back Bay National Wildlife Refuge
City of Virginia Beach

Established in 1938, the 8,921-acre Back Bay National Refuge has been set aside primarily to protect the habitat of migrating waterfowl on the Atlantic flyway. Numerous species of birds have been recorded on the refuge—at least 259 avian species, including 30 species of waterfowl (ducks, geese, and swans). Three endangered species occur at the refuge—the American bald eagle, the loggerhead turtle, and the peregrine falcon. Hunting, fishing, camping, horseback riding, and use of motorized vehicles are prohibited, but nature study, photography, and hiking are permitted. Hiking S through the refuge is the only land access to the False Cape State Park, where, with a permit, camping is allowed. Biking is also allowed. Hikers and bikers should use caution, watching for venomous eastern cottonmouth snakes. Also, hikers and bikers are cautioned to take insect repellent for fending against the numerous biting insects. All drinking water must be carried in. Water at campsites may be used for cooking after 10 minutes of boiling.

Access: From downtown Virginia Beach go S for 5 mi to Princess Anne Rd and then 0.8 mi to Sandridge Rd. After 5.5 mi on Sandridge Rd turn R on Sandpiper Rd and go S 4.2 mi to Little Island Recreation Area. Access road to Back Bay/False Cape Natural Area is another 1.3 mi to the visitor center.

▼ EAGLE TRAIL   554

Length: 0.5 mi (0.8 km) rt; easy. *USGS Maps:* North Bay, Knotts Island. *Trailhead:* Parking area.

Directions and Description: Trail entrance is near S edge of parking area. Follow sign and walk on wide nature trail bordered with youpon, beach holly, myrtle, and live oaks to an observation deck at Buck Island Bay.

▼ BACK BAY TRAIL   555

Length: 10.8 mi to 17.2 mi (17.3 km to 27.5 km) rt; easy to moderate. *USGS Maps:* North Bay, Knotts Island. *Trailhead:* Parking area.

Directions and Description: Trail entrance is S through the gate on a sandy dike road; trail markers are posted. Observation deck of the Atlantic Ocean is on L at 0.4 mi. Pass maintenance buildings on R at 0.8 mi. Observe along the way the tracks of deer, raccoons, gray fox, mink, opossum, or otter. (The pig tracks are not those of wild boars but of trespassing swine. Neither are the cat tracks those of wild cats; they are only from domesticated felines adapted to the natural environment.) Reach False Cape State Park boundary at 5.4 mi. In another 0.7 mi arrive at Barbour Hill contact station, with primitive camping sites, pit toilets, boat dock, security lighting, and emergency phone. For other campsites continue S on sandy road trail to False Cape Landing at 7.5 mi. All campsites can be reached by boat from ramps on the W side of Back Bay, a distance of 2 to 6.5 mi. (See False Cape State Park.)

Camping is prohibited from the last Monday in October through the second Saturday in November due to game management programs. Apply in person for camping permits at Seashore State Park, 2500 Shores Dr, Visitor Center, Virginia Beach, VA 23451; tel: 804-481-4836.

Some of the vascular plants seen on this hike are marsh mallow, blue toadflax, meadow beauty, daisy fleabane, partridge pea, golden ragwort, red cedar, youpon, beach holly, *gaillardia,* bullrush, and live oaks.

Support Facilities: Open all year is the Holiday Trav-L-Park, 1075 Gen Booth Blvd, Virginia Beach, VA 23451. It is 2 mi S of Rudee Inlet. Full service, exceptional recreational facilities. Tel: 804-425-0249 for camping information.

Information: Contact Back Bay National Wildlife Refuge, 287 Pembroke Office Park, Virginia Beach, VA 23462; tel: 804-490-0505. Also, False Cape State Park, Box 6273, Virginia Beach, VA 23456; tel: 804-426-7128.

Chincoteague National Wildlife Refuge   556-557
Accomack County

The northernmost of Virginia's barrier islands is also one of the most fascinating. Assateague Island, 37 mi long and spanning the Maryland-Virginia line, was designated a national seashore in 1965. The Virginia portion consists of Chincoteague National Wildlife Refuge and a small National Park Service facility near the southern tip of the island. Established in 1943 with 9,460 acres, the ocean side has a beach for surfing, swimming, and fishing, but the NPS area is wild and unsupervised. A prime habitat for migratory waterfowl, the island has 262 species of birds, including geese, ducks, swans, herons, hawks, egrets, ibis, gulls, and terns. The wild ponies have made the island nationally famous with the "Pony Swim" and auction the last Thursday in July. During Thanksgiving week the refuge holds "Waterfowl Week" for observing the waterfowl at their peak in numbers. This is the only time the N-S Rd is open to private vehicles.

Access: From US 13 junction with VA 175, go 10.5 mi on VA 175 to Chincoteague. Turn L on N Main St for 4 blocks and then R on SR 2113 for 2.2 mi to refuge entrance.

The *Wildlife Trail* is also Wildlife Dr, a 3.5-mi loop for hikers and bikers (and for vehicles from 3 P.M. until dark) around the freshwater Snow Goose Pool. The trail begins at the visitor center and passes a number of nesting stands. (Although not listed as a trail, the experienced hiker may wish to backpack approximately 24 mi N to Assateague National Seashore campground and Assateague State Park in Maryland. Start at the visitor center; follow N on Wildlife Dr going straight ahead at the first curve. Cross the gate and pass through a service road of dunes, wetlands, and wash flats. Wildlife is likely to be seen. Reach a turnaround at 7.5 mi. By crossing over to the beach, continue N to the Maryland-Virginia line fence at 10.5 mi. Across the fence in Maryland is a hike-in campsite (reservation required from the Assateague National Seashore headquarters). It is another 9.5 mi N to Little Level Campground, and another 4.5 mi before reaching the Assateague State Park Campground. No camping in Virginia. There is no water on this route, and deadwood for a campfire is scarce. Shuttle vehicle necessary. USGS map is Chincoteague E, and Whittington Point).

(A drive to the beach from the Chincoteague Visitor Center connects with the southern tip of Assateague Island National Seashore and Visitor Center. From here drive or hike R to *Toms Cove Nature Trail*, a 0.6-mi interpretive trail about the animal life here and such flora as glasswort and sea oxeye.)

▼ SENSITIVITY TRAIL,
LIGHTHOUSE TRAIL, PONY TRAIL   558–560

Length: 2.1 mi (2.6 km) ct; easy. *USGS Map:* Chincoteague E-W. *Trailhead:* Parking area at visitor center.

Directions and Description: From the visitor center drive or walk to the E side of Snow Goose Pool to the

Sensitivity Trail. The short cabled path to an observation blind allows hikers to close their eyes and experience the sounds and smells of the area. Across the road W of the visitor center is the *Lighthouse Trail,* a 0.3-mi loop to the historic site overlooking Assateague Channel. The *Pony Trail* begins at a parking area off the Beach Rd between the refuge visitor center and the National Park Service visitor center. Hike for 1.6 mi, looping through pines and water oak to observation deck and open area where the wild ponies often graze. Sika deer may be seen here; also, this is a nesting and feeding area for the Delmarva fox squirrel.

Support Facilities: An area commercial campground is Camper's Ranch, Chincoteague, VA 23336; tel: 804-336-6371. Full service, excellent recreational facilities. Open Easter through Thanksgiving. Access is from S Main St onto Bunting Rd E.

Information: Contact Refuge Manager, Chincoteague National Wildlife Refuge, PO Box 62, Chincoteague, VA 23336; tel: 804-336-6122. Also, District Ranger, Assateague Island National Seashore, PO Box 38, Chincoteague, VA 23336; tel: 804-336-6577. And, in Maryland, Assateague State Park, Rte 2, Box 293, Berlin, MD 21811; tel: 301-641-2120.

Great Dismal Swamp National Wildlife Refuge
Cities of Suffolk and Chesapeake

Few places in Virginia invoke such legends and mystery as the Great Dismal Swamp. George Washington once owned it, calling it a "glorious paradise." Col William Byrd II cursed it as a "vast body of dirt and nastiness." He is said to have given the swamp its name, having nearly lost his life surveying the state line through it. The most recent private owner of much of the swamp, the Union Camp Corp, called it "a wonderland for the botanist . . . a contiguous area of separate ecosystems." In 1973, climaxing years of efforts by conservationists to preserve the swamp, Union Camp magnanimously gave their Great Dismal properties, totalling 50,000 acres and valued at $12 million, to the US Dept of the Interior, through the Virginia Nature Conservancy. The refuge currently totals 101,992 acres, 77,583 of which are in Virginia and 24,408 in North Carolina.

Lake Drummond, in the heart of the swamp, is a 3,000-acre circular pure-water lake that is kept pure by the tannic acid from the cypress and juniper. Its average depth is 6 ft. Among the flora and fauna are 8 species of turtles, 14 species of frogs, 15 species of snakes (including copperhead, canebreak rattler, and cottonmouth), 48 species of trees, 29 species of shrubs, 20 species of vines, and 177 species of birds. Bear, bobcat, and deer inhabit the swamp; speckles and blue gills are in the lake.

Refuge usage is limited to hiking, boating, and fishing. Camping and fires are prohibited. (One campground is in the swamp and is operated by the US Corps of Engineers. For information call 804-421-7401.) Trails at this time are limited to the old jeep trails alongside the ditches running through the swamp. By one estimate there are 100 mi of such passageways, but hiking some of the ditches would require bushwhacking. Two major ditches are described below. The Tidewater Appalachian Trail Club has recently made a proposal for an extensive trail system, the major goal of which would be establishing a N-S trail to connect Deep Creek near Portsmouth with Lake Drummond, the Corps campground, and the

North Carolina state parks.

Access to Refuge Office: From downtown-Suffolk junction of US 13, VA 32, and W Washington St (VA 337), go S on US 13–VA 32—Carolina Rd—for 2.4 mi to Refuge Office, L.

▼ WASHINGTON DITCH TRAIL,
JERICHO DITCH LANE,
BOARDWALK TRAIL   561–564

Length: 26.8 mi (42.9 km) rt, ct; easy to moderate. *USGS Maps:* Suffolk, Corapeake, Lake Drummond, Lake Drummond NW. *Trailhead:* Off Washington Ditch.

Directions and Description: The most direct and most used route to Lake Drummond is by the Washington Ditch. From junction of US 13, VA 32, and VA 337 in downtown Suffolk go E on US 13–VA 337 to R fork of SR 642—White Marsh Rd—for 0.7 mi. Follow White Marsh Rd S for 0.8 mi, passing *Jericho Ditch Lane* on L. Continue S on White Marsh Rd for 4.5 mi to Washington Ditch on L. Turn L on new two-way-traffic gravel road for 1.5 mi to *Boardwalk Trail*. Park and follow the signs on the 0.8-mi trail into the swamp and near the Dismal Town site. From here hike or bicycle in to Lake Drummond for 3.6 mi. (A good but less-used 5.7-mi hiking route is begun by continuing to drive S on White Marsh Rd for 1 mi to Desart Rd, SR 604. Here is *RR Ditch Trail* at gate. Hike 2 mi on Railroad Ditch E to West Ditch and turn R. Follow West Ditch S for 1.7 mi and turn L (E) onto Interior Ditch for 2 mi to Lake Drummond.)

The longest and most exploratory route to Lake Drummond is on *Jericho Ditch Lane.* Follow directions above to Jericho Ditch, and proceed on dirt road to gate. The route is approximately 9.5 mi in a straight line. After 1.8 mi pass Hundall Ditch, L, and pass Lynn Ditch, R, soon thereafter. At 5.3 mi pass Camp Ditch on L and, at 5.9 mi, Middle Ditch on R. After reaching Lake Drummond, the return trail could on the *Washington Ditch Trail,* using a vehicle shuttle at the gate.

Information: Contact Refuge Manager, Dismal Swamp National Wildlife Refuge, PO Box 349, Suffolk, VA 23434; tel: 804-539-7479.

MacKay National Wildlife Refuge
City of Virginia Beach

The MacKay National Wildlife Refuge has only 1,000 acres in Virginia but has 6,055 acres in North Carolina. It is on an island between Back Bay National Wildlife Refuge N and Currituck Sound S. The refuge has three trails (the 0.5-mi loop *Wildlife Trail,* a 1-mi loop *Nature Trail*, and an 8-mi loop dike road in a mixed forest and marsh), all in North Carolina.

Access: On SR 615, Princess Anne Rd, S from junction SR 672 and Indian River Rd at Pungo.

Information: Contact Refuge Manager, MacKay Island National Wildlife Refuge, PO Box 31, Knotts Island, NC 27950; tel: 919-429-3100.

Mason Neck National Wildlife Refuge
Fairfax County

The 1,118-acre Mason Neck Refuge, only 18 mi S of Washington, DC, was established in 1960 for the main purpose of protecting our national symbol, the bald

Mason Neck National Wildlife Refuge. Allen de Hart.

eagle. But more than the bald eagle is protected by this blend of upland forest, bogs, and river-front marsh. Thousands of waterfowl use the 285-acre Great Marsh on the Atlantic flyway, and the refuge hosts more than 211 bird species. Hikers are likely to see deer in the refuge, since hiking is the only recreational use allowed. The protected area does not allow camping.

Access: From US 1 junction with VA 242 (near Lorton) drive 4.3 mi on VA 242 to High Point Rd on R. Turn at sign and go 0.7 mi on gravel road to parking area on L.

▼ WOODMARSH TRAIL   565

Length: 3 mi (4.8 km) rt; easy. *USGS Map:* Fort Belvoir. *Trailhead:* Parking area on High Point Rd.

Directions and Description: Follow trail signs, using brochure supplied at trail entrance sign, along a log-bordered trail. At 0.8 mi turn L at fork on loop trail to Eagle Point. Pass two connector trails, *Hickory Pass* and *Fern Pass,* on R, and pass a beaver dam on the L. At 1.7 mi reach a display shed between interpretive points 13 and 14. Continue loop, rejoining the trail at the fork for a return to the parking lot. Among the plants in addition to the hardwood and pines are yellow pond lily, duck-potato, wild rice, rose mallow, cattails, and ferns.

Information: Contact Refuge Manager, Mason Neck National Wildlife Refuge, 9502 Richmond Hwy, Suite A, Lorton, VA 22079; tel: 703-339-5278.

Presquile National Wildlife Refuge
Chesterfield County

Established in 1952, the Presquile Refuge has 1,329

acres, of which 800 are tidal swamp, 250 are tidal marsh, and 279 are upland. The 1-mi *Presquile Nature Trail* is designed to feature the flora and fauna along an oxbow bend in the James River. Access is limited to use by government-owned ferry or private boat. Visitors should make prior arrangements with the refuge office.

Access to the Ferry: From VA 10 (across the Appomattox River W from Hopewell) to SR 827; on SR 827, go 3.4 mi.

Information: Contact Refuge Manager, Presquile National Wildlife Refuge, PO Box 620, Hopewell, VA 23860; tel: 804-~~458-7541~~

~~Office~~ 530-1397 —
Island

Office — 733-8042
7:30 – 4 pm M-F
Call first

9 · Other Trails in the National Park System

Assateague Island National Seashore
Accomock County, Virginia and Worcester County, Maryland

With 39,630 acres, the 37-mi Assateague barrier island is a haven for migratory waterfowl, wild ponies, and students of nature studies. Of the island's total acreage, 17,377 acres are federal property, with 6,897 of them in Maryland and 10,479 in Virginia. For hiking opportunities see (in Chapter 8) Chincoteague National Wildlife Refuge, which includes 9,021 acres under the park system's supervision.

Access: From the town of Chincoteague at junction of VA 175 and SR 2113, follow SR 2113 for 2.2 mi to Refuge Information Center.

Information: Contact Superintendent, Assateague Island National Seashore, Rte 2, Box 294, Berlin, MD 21811; tel: 301-641-1441.

Booker T. Washington National Monument
Franklin County

This national monument is in honor of Booker T. Washington (1856–1915), who was born a slave on the James and Elizabeth Burroughs plantation. The story of his life, in *Up From Slavery,* is one of a childhood of poverty and illiteracy and an adulthood that included graduation from Hampton Institute, the founding of the Tuskegee Institute, and distinction as an American educator whose advice was sought by Presidents William McKinley, Theodore Roosevelt, and William H. Taft. The monument area has a visitor center, primitive campground, picnic area, Environmental Education and Cultural Center, nature tours, and hiking trails. The set of trails was designated a national recreation trail in 1981. The park is open year round.

Access: From Rocky Mount junction of US 220 Bypass and VA 40, go 1.1 mi to VA 122. Turn L on VA 122 and go 12.3 mi to the entrance of the monument on the R.

▼ PLANTATION TRAIL   566

Length: 0.5 mi (0.8 km) rt; easy. *USGS Map:* Redwood. *Trailhead:* Parking area at the visitor center.

Directions and Description: Follow the trail from the visitor center to the historic slave cabin and to the tobacco barn at 0.2 mi. Return by the pigpen, hen house, and horse barn. Five areas have audio interpretive stations.

▼ JACK-O-LANTERN BRANCH TRAIL   567

Length: 2 mi (3.2 km) rt; easy. *USGS Map:* Redwood. *Trailhead:* Parking area at the visitor center.

Directions and Description: Follow the plantation

road W of the visitor center to the Environmental Education and Cultural Center at 0.2 mi. After a visit there, follow S through the middle of a field and enter the forest at 0.5 mi. Pass primitive campground on R at 0.6 mi, reach Gills Creek at 0.8 mi, and turn L along the creek bank. The area is rich in wildflowers such as orchids, bloodroot, asters, soapwort, and mandrake. Some of the trees are cedar, Virginia pine, walnut, poplar, red maple, sycamore, and ironwood. At 1 mi turn L, following wide, clear trail on L side of Jack-O-Lantern Branch. Reach the tobacco barn and a junction with the *Plantation Trail* at 1.8 mi. Continue on the *Plantation Trail* to the visitor center. (It is believed that the Jack-O-Lantern Branch received its name from foxfire—an eerie phosphorescent light caused by a luminous fungus in decaying wood—visible along the stream at night.)

Information: Contact Resources Manager, Booker T. Washington National Monument, Rte 1, Box 195, Hardy, VA 24101; tel: 703-721-2094.

George Washington Birthplace National Monument
Westmoreland County

Pope's Creek Plantation, which the Washington family acquired in 1718, was the first home of George Washington, who was born there February 22, 1732. After 3½ years his father, Augustine, and his mother, Mary Ball, moved the family to the Little Hunting Creek Plantation —later named Mount Vernon. Four years later they moved near Fredericksburg. George was age 11 when his father died. His half brother, Augustine II, inherited Pope's Creek Plantation, but young George frequently returned for stays at his birthplace.

In 1858 the commonwealth acquired the area, but the Civil War delayed restoration. With the assistance of the Wakefield National Memorial Association in 1923 and John D. Rockefeller in 1931, the commonwealth was able in 1932, the 200th anniversary of Washington's birth, to officially transfer the 394 acres with buildings to the federal government. Open daily, except December 25 and January 1. (To reach Monroe Hall, the birthplace of James Monroe, drive W 2.8 mi on VA 3 to Oak Grove, then take VA 205 to the historic site.)

Access: From US 301 junction with VA 3 (36 mi from I-95 in Fredericksburg), go E 12.5 mi. Turn L on VA 204; on VA 3 the visitor center is 1.8 mi.

▼ WASHINGTON HISTORIC TRAIL
WASHINGTON NATURE TRAIL   568–569

Length: 2 mi (3.2 km) rt; easy. *USGS Map:* Colonial Beach South. *Trailhead:* Visitor center.

Directions and Description: From the visitor center walk on the gravel trail along the edge of the cliffs to the birthplace site. On the way pass through an exceptionally large grove of aging cedars. Circle on trail to kitchen house, memorial house, barn, and farm area, and back to the visitor center. The 1-mi *Nature Trail* is at the picnic area, accessible by driving back to the granite monument and turning R. Follow the trail signs in a loop to interpretive plaques about the trees, shrubs, flowers, nuts, berries, soil, animal life, and history of the area.

Information: Contact Superintendent, George Washington Birthplace National Monument, Washington's Birthplace, VA 22575; tel: 703-224-0196.

George Washington Memorial Parkway
Arlington and Fairfax Counties and City of Alexandria

The George Washington Memorial Pkwy is a landscaped river-front limited-access parkway that links many of the landmarks associated with George Washington. Established in 1930, it connects Mt Vernon with the Great Falls on the Potomac and sites through the heart of Alexandria. Within the 7,141 acres are natural, historical, and recreational facilities, including Turkey Run Farm, Theodore Roosevelt Island, Arlington House, and Fort Hunt Park. Of particular interest here are the 17-mi *Mt Vernon Trail*, a limited-access urban trail paralleling the parkway for hikers, bicyclists, and joggers.

The Great Falls Park is a landscaped river-front connector from Mount Vernon to the Great Falls along the Potomac and to the Chain Bridge on the Maryland side. The park has a visitor center, special tours, picnicking, fishing, horseback riding, and rock climbing. Four designated trails total 12 mi for hiking and exploring.

For 300 mi the water of the Potomac flows to this last major falls, thundering and sending up a mist from its white water in a deep and narrow chasm only 15 mi from the peaceful Tidal Basin at the Jefferson Memorial in the nation's capital. The falls can be seen from four overlooks along the *River Trail*. Visitors and hikers are warned to stay away from the rocky edges of the gorge, which are extremely slippery when wet. There are an average of seven deaths annually from falls and hazardous water sports. No camping.

Access to *George Washington Memorial Pkwy:* Termini are at Mt Vernon and near Lincoln Memorial.

Access to *Great Falls Park:* From I-495, Capital Beltway, exit 13, take VA 193 NW (Georgetown Pike) for 3.9 mi to junction with SR 738, and turn R into the park.

▼ MOUNT VERNON TRAIL   570

Length: 17 mi (17.2 km); easy. *USGS Maps:* Mt Vernon, Alexandria, Washington W. *Trailhead:* Mt Vernon parking lot.

Directions and Description: At Mt Vernon, drive to the last parking lot, where a sign indicates recreational vehicles. Begin hike at mp 0 on a paved, descending forest route to Little Hunting Creek at mp 1. Here is Riverside Park, a place to fish and picnic. At 2.9 mi cross parkway; on the L is trail diversion to Forest Hunt Park for picnicking and for restrooms and drinking water. Continue on L side of parkway to mp 5 at Alexandria Ave, and cross over. Enter the 240-acre Dyke Marsh at 5.6 mi, where 250 species of birds have been seen. Water and restrooms are at Belle Haven, another picnic area, at 7.2 mi, where a spur trail goes to the Dyke Marsh shoreline. Cross Hunting Creek and pass Jones Point Lighthouse, named in honor of a fur trader whose cabin was here in 1692.

At 8.9 mi leave the wooded area and enter the historic city of Alexandria. Continue to 11.4 mi, where the 107-acre Daingerfield Island begins. Picnicking, sailing, fishing, and a restaurant are here. After crossing Four-Mile Run pass through the W side of the National Airport from 12.6 mi to 14.3 mi. Reach Gravelly Point at 14.5 mi for an excellent view of the nation's capital. Follow along the edge of the Potomac past vegetation, including a stand of white pines, to the Lyndon B. Johnson Memorial Grove at 15.9 mi. Food, water and restrooms are here. Reach the Arlington Memorial Bridge, the symbol of a nation united, at 16.5 mi; turn R across the bridge and reach the northern terminus of the trail at 17 mi near the Lincoln Memorial.

Information: Contact Superintendent, George Washington Memorial Pkwy, Turkey Run Park, McLean, VA 22101; tel: 703-285-2591.

▼ RIVER TRAIL, RIDGE TRAIL,
OLD CARRIAGE TRAIL,
PATOWMACK CANAL TRAIL   571–575

Length: 12 mi (19.2 km) ct; easy. *USGS Maps:* Seneca, Vienna, Falls Church. *Trailhead:* Visitor center parking area.

Directions and Description: From the parking area at the visitor center examine the trail diagram and hike up or downriver on the blue-blazed scenic *River Trail* for 3.8 mi. (The *River Trail* continues upriver to Riverbend Park, a Fairfax County recreational park. Downriver it connects with the red-blazed *Ridge Trail,* which goes upriver but at a more westerly angle, to River Bend Rd, for 3.3 mi.) The yellow-blazed *Old Carriage Trail* also goes up and down the river, passing W of the old canal; it totals 4.1 mi. It also joins an equestrian trail in Riverbend Park. Parts of the *River Trail* and the *Ridge Trail* are not open to horse traffic, and the 0.8-mi *Patowmack Canal Trail* is for foot travel only. It follows the remains of the Patowmack Company canal, which operated from 1784 to 1810. A number of undesignated footpaths are spurs from the trails just listed. Also, the *Difficult Run Trail* in Fairfax County connects with the *Ridge Trail* near the S tip of the park. Except for the area around the visitor

River Trail, Great Falls Park, George Washington Memorial Parkway. Allen de Hart.

center, all trails are in dense, mature hardwood forests.

Information: Contact George Washington Memorial Pkwy Office, Turkey Run Park, McLean, VA 22101; tel: 804-285-2591.

Prince William Forest Park   576–577
Prince William County

Designated in 1948 as Prince William Forest Park, this 18,571-acre tract is the forested watershed of Quantico Creek. It is forest in succession; the major hardwoods and pines have replaced barren, worn-out farmland used as early as the 17th century. In reclamation it provides a habitat for deer, fox, beaver, raccoon, squirrel, skunk, woodchuck, turkey, grouse, songbirds, fish, and reptiles—including the copperhead. It has more than 89 species of trees and shrubs, and 152 species of birds. Granite, schist, and quartzite are part of its geology. An environmental study area is reserved for educational field trips. The park is open all year, and recreational activities include hiking on 35 mi of fire roads, creek trails, and interpretive trails; biking; fishing for trout, bass, bluegill, and perch; and picnicking. Camping areas with hookups are provided for tents and trailers, and a primitive campground (Chopawamsic) is provided for backpackers. The primitive campground is from 0.5 mi to 1.5 mi from the main trailhead area. Use permits are required and are available either by mail or from the park headquarters.

Three short, self-guiding loop trails, two of which are at the park headquarters, emphasize the flora and fauna and ecosystem. *Pine Grove Forest Trail*, with trailhead on W side of the parking area at park headquarters, is paved for the easy access of the physically handicapped. Some of the trees prominent here are oaks, beech, poplar, locust, pine, and ironwood. The 0.3-mi *Living Forest Trail* is located at the Travel Trailer Village and cabin camp entrance off VA 234, 2.7 mi W from junction at I-95 (2.5 mi N on I-95 from SR 619 and main park entrance). The 15 markers are keyed to illustrate vegetation in succession. Longer trails are described below.

Access: From I-95 junction with SR 619 W near Quantico and US Marine Corps Reservation exit, take SR 619 W and immediately turn R into main entrance.

▼ FARM TO FOREST TRAIL   578

Length: 1.2 mi (1.9 km); easy. *USGS Map:* Joplin. *Trailhead:* Oak Ridge Campground.

Directions and Description: Drive from the park headquarters to the Oak Ridge Campground; park. Follow yellow-blazed trail NE, examining 18 marked, keyed points about trees, birds, and topography. Halfway around the loop an environmental-study-area loop trail extends R for 2 mi. This area has small stands of bigtooth aspen.

▼ DEER RIDGE TRAIL,
  BOBCAT RIDGE TRAIL   579–580

Length: 1.6 mi (2.6 km) ct; easy. *USGS Maps:* Quantico, Joplin. *Trailhead:* Primitive camp area.

Directions and Description: From park headquarters go back to entrance and turn R on SR 619. Go 2.1 mi and turn L on Breckenridge Rd, opposite Liming Lake Fire

Rd and Moose Lodge sign. Go 0.7 mi on gravel road, taking first R fork to 430-acre Chopawamsic primitive camp area for backpackers. Camping is by permit from park headquarters only. All water must be carried in. Minors (under 18) must be accompanied by a parent or guardian. Fishing in the Breckenridge Reservoir is allowed with a valid fishing license.

▼ T-TRAILS   581–591

Length: 21.8 mi (35 km) ct; easy to moderate. *USGS Maps:* Quantico, Joplin. *Trailhead:* Parking areas.

   Directions and Description: Seven T-Trails provide a network in the park, particularly in the eastern half, to connect with the park headquarters, the trailer village camp, Turkey Run Ridge Campground, nature center, and Oak Ridge Campground. *Trail #1* is a 1-mi yellow-blazed loop connector from park headquarters to white-blazed *Trail #8*, a lead-out for 0.7 mi NE to Quantico Creek and other trails, and NW for 8.4 mi up South Branch Quantico Creek to Oak Ridge Campground. Another trail, red-blazed *Trail #3*, goes from the park headquarters by the ball field and picnic area NE to Quantico Creek for 1 mi to connect with *Trail #7*. The latter trail leads to the trailer camp. Circuit trails can be arranged on all trails except *Trail #8*, which extends 3.8 mi beyond the last connector, Trail #10. Because the *T-Trails* criss-cross paved park roads and at least eight fire roads, routes of almost any desired length can be designed by the hiker. A park-brochure map will assist in orienting and choosing. Trail guideposts with labels are on cement pillars.

If hiking *Trail #8*, leave on *Trail #1* from the park headquarters parking area and at 0.5 mi junction with Orenda Fire Rd, turn L on *Trail #8*, an excellent white-blazed forest trail. (R on *Trail #8* goes 0.7 mi to Pyrite Mine.) Follow trail across Mary Bird Branch and reach junction with *Trail #11* after 1.8 mi. At 2.2 mi cross paved park road, meandering up South Branch Quantico Creek and crossing the road twice more, passing junction with *Trail #7* in between. At 5.3-mi junction with *Trail #10*, R, pass small lake L, and at 6.6 mi cross Mawavi Fire Rd. Continue winding on a well-graded trail among oaks, pines, birch, poplar, wild azaleas, and wildflowers to exit at Oak Ridge Campground at 9.1 mi. Vehicle shuttle necessary.

Information: Contact Park Naturalist, Prince William Forest Park, Box 208, Triangle, VA 22172; tel: 703-221-7181.

Part Three

State Managed Trails

Of Virginia's 25.5 million acres of land, 4 million acres are public lands, and this includes 175,000 acres in 30 Wildlife Management Areas (WMA's). The following WMA descriptions primarily emphasize trail usage, although some other facilities are described as well. The Virginia agency responsible for developing and preserving a wildlife heritage for sportsmen and recreational enthusiasts is the Commission of Game and Inland Fisheries. From the mountains to the sea, the state areas described here are distinctive and diverse; a source of pleasure and education to hunters, fishermen, trappers, naturalists, hikers, and others who love the outdoors. Since facilities and their regulations vary, the hiker may wish to contact supervisors for specific WMA's.

Information: For general information about WMA's contact the state office at 4010 W Broad St (Box 11104), Richmond, VA 23230; tel: 804-257-1000. For information applicable to specific WMA's contact the supervisors listed for each park.

Amelia WMA
Amelia County

With more than 3 mi of frontage along the Appomattox

River, ponds, and considerable diversity of vegetation, Amelia WMA is an excellent wildlife habitat. And the adjoining lands of WESTVACO and Chesapeake Corp significantly expand its recreational opportunities. The 2,200-acres of state land, purchased in 1967, include 100 acres of water, 850 acres of fields, and 1,250 acres of woods that has young timber. Hunting is chiefly for small game, but deer are becoming more abundant. Anglers can expect bass, bluegill, channel catfish, crappie, and walleye pike.

Access: From US 360 E of Amelia take SR 604 and go 7 mi to Masons Corner. Turn L on SR 616 for 1.5 mi and turn R on SR 652 to the WMA entrance.

▼ WOODCOCK TRAIL   592

Length: 4 mi (6.4 km) rt; easy. *USGS Map:* Chula. *Trailhead:* Parking lot on SR 652 at entrance.

Directions and Description: From the parking lot follow old winding trail partly along a small stream for 2 mi to the Appomattox River. Backtrack.

▼ LAKE TRAIL, BUNNY TRAIL   593–594

Length: 3.2 mi (5.1 km) rt; easy. *USGS Map:* Chula. *Trailhead:* Parking area at boat ramp.

Directions and Description: Turn off SR 652 and park near the lake under huge oaks. The *Lake Trail* is not maintained at all points. At the beginning of the hike, take it L, following the lake boundary S. After 1.4 mi cross the *Bunny Trail*, which goes 0.7 mi L, to SR 692. This is a serene environment. Follow the lake boundary to the dam, and return through woods or take the road back to the parking area.

▼ MARSH POINT TRAIL   595–596

Length: 2 mi (3.2 km) rt; easy. *USGS Map:* Chula. *Trail-head:* Main parking area on the ridge of SR 652.

Directions and Description: From the parking lot pass the *Fire Trail* (which leads to the lake) at 0.2 mi on the L, and continue R along a ridge to a split at 0.7 mi. Both legs lead down the hill to the bottomland and banks of the Appomattox River. Backtrack.

Support Facilities: Amelia Family Campground; tel: 804-561-4772. Full service, recreational facilities. Open all year. Access is from VA 153, 0.5 mi S from junction of VA 153 and US 360.

Information: Contact Area Supervisor, WMA, Rte 4, Amelia, VA 23002, tel: 804-561-3350.

Briery Creek WMA
Prince Edward County

Briery Creek WMA has 2,775 acres of typical Piedmont topography about evenly divided on either side of Briery Creek. Formerly farmlands for grain, tobacco, dairy, and livestock operations, the area is returning to its natural environment. There are pure stands of loblolly pine among the basic hardwoods. Biologists rate the area as one of the state's most productive wildlife management areas per acre. Wild game includes deer, turkey, dove, woodcock, and rabbit. An 814-acre impoundment is planned. Explore on the high grounds or on old roads. No trails are named or maintained at this time.

Access: On US 15 go 10 mi S from Farmville and turn R on SR 705, or SR 701.

Chickahominy WMA
Charles City County

The Chickahominy River wetlands have been identified as one of the state's most important wildlife habitats needing protection. With the aid of the Nature Conservancy, the Game Commission has now purchased more than 4,300 acres, with an equal amount proposed for future acquisition. The area's chief timber is beech, oak, hickory, and pine. Marshlands support beavers and wood ducks. Higher ground has deer, quail, snipe, and turkey.

There are no named or maintained trails, but at the first parking area on SR 623 (see *Access*), near Morris Creek and N of it, there is a 0.7-mi old road that serves as a trail. And, at the parking area near the end of SR 621, old road trails follow the ridges into the Morris Creek wetlands. To the E, down the second L turnoff along SR 621, is Eagle Bottom, a marsh intriguingly named after the endangered bird occasionally spotted in the area.

Access: From the town of Rustic, take VA 5 to junction with SR 623 (9 mi E of Charles City Courthouse); go N on SR 623 for 4.2 mi to SR 621. Turn R on SR 621 and proceed to termini of old roads described.

Information: Contact Area Supervisor, WMA, Rte 1, Box 115, Charles City, VA 23030; tel: 804-829-5336.

Clinch Mountain WMA
Smyth, Russell, Tazewell, and Washington Counties

The 22,000-acre Clinch Mtn WMA is remote, scenic, high, and rugged. Laurel Bed Lake, a 300-acre manmade lake, is excellent for trout fishing. Adjacent to the lake is a unique stand of black cherry that has been designated a natural area by the Society of Foresters. The trees in the cove are nearly 3 ft in diameter and 80 ft high. Big Tumbling Creek—heavily stocked with trout—forms falls and pools through deep gorges to the North Fork Holston River W of Saltville.

Facilities include those for picnicking, horseback riding, boating, canoeing, birding, hiking, and berry picking, and a number of permits are issued annually for "herbing." Camping is allowed at a designated campground from April 1 through Labor Day.

Access: From I-81 turn off at the Glade Spring exit on VA 91 and go 5.2 mi into Saltville. In the center of Saltville take SR 634 on L; cross the Holston River bridge and proceed to the junction with SR 613. Go L on SR 613 for 4 mi to SR 747. Turn R up Tumbling Creek Road for 2 mi to parking area.

▼ LAUREL BED CREEK TRAIL   597

Length: 8 mi (12.8 km) rt; moderate. *USGS Map:* Saltville. *Trailhead:* Laurel Bed Lake parking area.

Directions and Description: Cross below the dam from the parking area to a trail junction; turn L. (The R fork is a 0.5-mi trail down Laurel Bed Creek. The trail up the mountain is the *Clinch Mtn Trail.*) Follow along the lakeside for 1.2 mi, continuing up the creek for another 2.8 mi. Backtrack. Vegetation is chiefly oaks, basswood, poplar, and hemlock.

▼ CLINCH MOUNTAIN TRAIL   598

Length: 2.4 mi (3.8 km); strenuous. *USGS Map:* Saltville. *Trailhead:* Laurel Bed Lake parking area.

Directions and Description: Cross below the dam from the parking area to the trail junction. Continue ahead up the mountain at the edge of the Black Cherry Natural Area. (R and L trails follow the Laurel Bed Creek.) Ascend steeply for 1 mi to ridge crest (3,800 ft), then descend on switchbacks to Little Tumbling Creek and the campground road at 2.4 mi. (It is 1.5 mi L on the road to the campground, where the W terminus of the 7.4-mi *Little Tumbling Creek Trail* connects. Its E terminus is at the junction of VA 91 and SR 607.)

▼ LITTLE TUMBLING CREEK TRAIL   599

Length: 7.4 mi (11.8 km); easy to moderate. *USGS Map:* Saltville. *Trailhead:* Either the campground or VA 91.

Directions and Description: From the campground follow the rocky area along stream for 7.4 mi to the E terminus at the end of the WMA boundary and to the junction of VA 91 and SR 607. Area has mixed hardwoods, hemlock, rhododendron, and wildflowers. Vehicle shuttle is necessary, or backtrack. (See next entry for possible loop arrangement with *Fire Trail*.)

▼ FIRE TRAIL   600

Length: 8 mi (12.8 km); moderate to strenuous. *USGS Map:* Saltville. *Trailhead:* Flattop Mtn gate on VA 91, 1.1 mi S of junction with SR 607.

Directions and Description: From the Flattop Mtn gate on SR 91 ascend on the old road trail and along the ridge of Flattop Mtn. Vegetation is mixed forest with displays of mountain laurel. At the end of the trail (4,300 ft) either backtrack to trailhead or bushwhack R and NW down the mountain to the campground. Some sections of rhododendron and laurel make descent difficult. This trail can tie in with the *Tumbling Creek Trail* at the campground for a loop of approximately 15.5 mi.

▼ RED BRANCH TRAIL   601

Length: 8.4 mi (13.4 km) rt; moderate to strenuous. *USGS Map:* Saltville. *Trailhead:* Trout holding pond at WMA entrance.

Directions and Description: On the W side of SR 747, near the trout holding pond at the entrance, the trail begins up a hollow, traverses the mountain gradually uphill, then enters the Red Branch Hollow at 2.6 mi. Following Red Branch the trail ascends, steep in places, for another 1.6 mi to the WMA boundary. Directly W is the top of Beartown Mtn (4,700 ft). Hikers may wish to hike to the top because it has numerous plant species, including red spruce, normally found much farther N. Backtrack.

Access: Take exit 7 from I-81 into Abingdon; go N on US 19–Alt 58 for 8 mi to the town of Holston. Turn R on SR 611 and go 2.5 mi E. From here it is 14 mi E on SR 611 to SR 747, which leads into the WMA.

Support Facilities: Riverside Family Campground, Rte 6, Box 377, Abingdon, VA 24210; tel: 703-628-5333. Full service, recreational facilities. Open May 1–September 15.

Information: Contact Area Supervisor, WMA, Rte 2, Box 218, Saltville, VA 24370; tel: 703-944-3434.

Crooked Creek WMA
Carroll County

This area of 1,596 acres was acquired as one of the Game Commission's fee fishing areas. Crooked Creek is an excellent trout stream on the Blue Ridge plateau; fishing trails lead along parts of the creek. Otherwise, there are no maintained trails. Camping is not permitted, but a campground is located nearby on US 58 between Wood-lawn and Hillsville. *USGS Map:* Woodlawn.

Access: From junction of I-77 and US 58–221 go W on US 58–221 for 3 mi and turn L on SR 620 at Woodlawn. Follow S on SR 620 for 5.7 mi to the parking area beyond the fish tank.

Elm Hill WMA
Mecklenberg County

Much of this 1,000-acre section below Kerr Dam is open land managed for waterfowl and small game. Two ponds, wooded stream banks, and 1.5 mi of Roanoke River frontage at the back end of Lake Gaston provide an attractive area for field trail exploring. An old railroad bed provides another trail. Vegetation is mainly oak-hickory mixtures, ash-gum mixtures, and loblolly pine. Facilities include picnicking, horseback riding, birding, and hiking.

Access: From the junction of US 58 and VA 4, take VA 4 S for 4 mi to Castle Heights and turn L to entrance. (The John H. Kerr Dam is 1.4 mi ahead on VA 4.)

Information: Contact Area Supervisor, WMA, Rte 2, Box 109-A, Clarksville, VA 23927; tel: 804-374-5407.

Fairy Stone WMA
Patrick and Henry Counties

Fairy Stone Farms adds 5,286 acres to the public land in the area of Philpott Reservoir and Fairy Stone State Park. These three areas, in excess of 12,000 acres, compose one of the largest recreational regions in the state. Hiking in Fairystone Farms is chiefly on fire roads beginning at the gates. (See trail information on Philpott Reservoir and Fairy Stone State Park in Chapter 12.)

Access: Approach gated roads from VA 57 across the road from junction of VA 57 and SR 822, which is 7.5 mi W from Bassett. Or, park near gated road on SR 687, which is 1.3 mi W from VA 57. Exit off VA 57 at Stone's Store. Another section of the WMA is on SR 704, which is off VA 57 approximately 0.2 mi W of the Fairy Stone State Park entrance.

Information: Contact Area Supervisor, WMA, PO Box 704, Bassett, VA 24055; tel: 703-629-5902.

Gathright WMA   602
Bath County

The Gathright WMA is a showplace of conservation and recreational use in the rugged Alleghany Highlands bordering West Virginia. Three government agencies have been responsible for the management of the area since Congress authorized the Gathright Dam on the Jackson River in 1947. Finally in 1965 the US Corps of Engineers began construction; completion was in 1981, and recreational use began in 1982. In 1978 Congress renamed the 2,530-acre lake in honor of Benjamin Moomaw, an area citizen whose efforts made the project possible. The WMA's original 18,000 acres became 13,428 as forest land, including Bolan Mtn and the lake and its borders, became the responsibility of the George Washington National Forest. The Corps retains jurisdiction over the dam and the spillway area.

Recreation includes boating, fishing, swimming, picnicking, camping, nature study, and hiking. Although new trails and connections are being designed, some of the old fire roads continue to make nearly 20 mi of trails available. For example, the *High Top Fire Trail* leads to the ridge of the Alleghany Mtn and FR 55 to connect with the *Allegheny Mtn Trail*. Greenwood Point, a primitive campsite, can be reached from Lake Moomaw Beach. Because of the changes in WMA borders, the hiker should check with the area supervisor before setting out.

Access: From Springs take VA 39 W for 3 mi to junction with SR 687. Turn L on SR 687 and go 2.5 mi to SR 603 on R. Go 3 mi to boundary of WMA and Supervisor's office on the L.

Information: Contact Area Supervisor, WMA, Bacova, VA 24412; tel: 703-839-2635.

Goshen-Little North Mountain WMA
Rockbridge and Augusta Counties

The combination of the Goshen WMA to the S, the Little N Mtn WMA, and the Goshen Pass Natural Area, which connects the two WMAs, forms a tract of 34,000 acres of state-owned land stretching 35 mi from US 60 W of Lexington to Buffalo Gap W of Staunton. A scenic area of sandstone and limestone, of rugged mountain terrain and an abundant variety of flora and fauna, this large tract offers the hiker alluring trails for solitude and at least eight primitive campsites. (At the Goshen Pass foot-bridge across the Maury River, 11.8 mi from I-81, is a scenic short, unnamed trail ascending part of Round Mtn for views of the gorge.)

Access to Goshen Pass Area: From I-81 exit 53, at junction of US 11 N of Lexington, take US 11 N for 1 mi to junction of SR 716 W, and turn L. Go under I-81 on SR 716 W and proceed 3.5 mi to VA 39. Turn R on VA 39 and go 6.4 mi to Laurel Run Picnic Area.

Access to Little N Mtn Area: Continue NW on VA 39 to Goshen and turn R on VA 42 NE to the access points. (Or go SW from Buffalo Gap on VA 42 for 3 mi to Shill-ings Access, L). The Jackson Access point is L 5 mi S of Buffalo Gap, and the Denfield Access point begins 6.5 mi S of Buffalo Gap at Augusta Springs, where SR 601 forks L toward Estaline and parking area.

▼ LAUREL RUN TRAIL   603

Length: 4.2 mi (6.7 km) rt; moderate. *USGS Map:* Goshen. *Trailhead:* Junction of Laurel Run and VA 39.

Directions and Description: Park at the Goshen Pass Wayside picnic area, cross the road, and walk downriver to gated hunter's jeep road on R. Follow up road by a tumbling creek in a channel of aureate rosebay rhododen-dron, oaks, maples, and hemlock for 2.1 mi. Backtrack.

▼ GUYS RUN TRAIL, PINEY MOUNTAIN TRAIL, MEADOW GROUND TRAIL   604–606

Length: 23.6 mi (37.8 km) rt, ct; moderate to strenuous.

USGS Maps: Goshen, Millboro. *Trailhead:* Guys Run parking area on VA 39.

Directions and Description: Permit from the Virginia Game Commission is needed for camping, hunting, fishing, or trapping in the area. Drive up the gorge on VA 39 from Laurel Run picnic area for 3.6 mi to Guys Run Access Rd and parking area. (Goshen Pass footbridge is on R 1.9 mi after leaving Laurel Run.) If camping on this potentially long hike use care that vehicles do not block access roads.

Begin *Guys Run Trail* at gated road from the parking area heading SW. (At 2 mi an old road extends L; it crosses the stream, traverses Forge Mtn and crosses other tributaries for about 1.5 mi to the bluffs over the Maury River and Goshen Pass. Backtrack to *Guys Run Trail*.) Follow upstream and at 2.3 mi meet *Piney Mtn Trail* on R. It leads steeply R of Piney Branch for 2 mi to the top of Bratton Mtn (more than 3,000 ft). After returning continue upstream along Guys Run, fording it several times and observing the potential campsites along the way. At 4.2 mi *Meadow Ground Trail* and a campsite are on the R at trail fork. The R fork leads 2.1 mi to the top of mountain gap called The Loop, 6.3 mi from VA 39. The L fork steadily ascends the ridges, reaching the firetower area at Big Butt (more than 4,400 ft) at 7.8 mi from VA 39. The view is spectacular. Backtrack.

▼ LITTLE NORTH MOUNTAIN TRAIL   607

Length: 11.4 mi (18.2 km); moderate to strenuous. *USGS Maps:* Goshen, Augusta Springs. *Trailhead:* Denfield parking area.

Directions and Description: Take SR 682 E to the top of the mountain, and from here go N along the ridge. (Trail overgrown in spots.) After 4 mi reach Pond Gap, where a jeep road crosses the mountain, connecting with SR 601 to the L. Trail conditions improve beyond this point, and at 5.1 mi on *Little North Mountain Trail* a trail from Jackson Access comes in from the L. Continue ahead; at 7.1 mi the trail forks, the L fork leading down the mountain 1.5 mi to the Shilling Access. (Good camping spots are located at both of these access points.) Continue N on the ridge. (At 8.9 mi another trail to the L leads down to Shilling Access. At this same point, Kings Gap, a trail to the R leads to Trimble Mill Access off SR 705 on the E side of the mountain at Swoope.) *Little North Mtn Trail* ends at VA 42 in Buffalo Gap for a total of 11.4 mi. Vehicle shuttle necessary.

Information: Contact Area Supervisor, WMA, Box 32, Swoope, VA 24479; tel: 703-885-1702.

Hardware River WMA
Fluvanna County

Purchased in 1972, the Hardware River WMA is about 1,000 acres at the confluence of the Hardware and James rivers. The timber—black gum, hickory, maple, oaks, and sourwood—is young, and the terrain is generally rolling hills. Fishing, hunting, and hiking are the current sports. No camping is allowed.

From the W entrance parking lot the old farm roads make excellent hiking trails. For example, *Trail #1* starts at the parking lot and extends S to Dobby Creek, and the Kidd Mill Rd goes to site of old homestead. The E entrance parking area provides access to both rivers. Although not named, a 1.2-mi route up the James River is open. If hiking along the old railroad bed on the Hardware River, use caution at fallen bridges and eroded banks. *USGS Map:* Scottsville.

Access: Take VA 7 E of Scottsville for 3.5 mi to SR 611 on R. Follow SR 611 to terminus for WMA's W area. For E area follow VA 6 another 3 mi past junction with 611 and turn R on SR 646. Go 2.7 mi to terminus.

Information: Contact Area Supervisor, WMA, Rte 3, Box 150, Powhatan, VA 23139; tel: 804-598-3706.

Havens WMA
Roanoke County

The rugged Havens WMA is the oldest wildlife area still in Game Commission ownership. Located on Fort Lewis Mtn and purchased in 1930, the 6,290-acre area suffered a severe fire in 1953, evidence of which is still prevalent. The area is lightly visited in the off-season due to rough terrain and lack of easy access. Animal life includes bear, deer, turkey, grouse, and squirrel. *USGS Map:* Glenvar.

Trails are mainly fire roads leading along the ridge of Fort Lewis Mtn, past a fire tower and radio station. This area can also be reached through Owens-Illinois Corp land adjoining Havens to the SW. A challenging, strenuous trail ascends to top of mountain from SR 622, Bradshaw Rd, 4 mi NW from the town of Bradshaw on SR 622. Trail may be a manway, requiring bushwhacking, in sections.

Access: From I-81 in Salem turn off on VA 112 N,

which becomes SR 619 along Horners Branch. Look for gated roads on R. Or, enter on SR 700 from Mason Cove off VA 311 and SR 864.

Hidden Valley WMA
Washington County

Hidden Valley WMA is a scenic high mountain area, excellent for hiking, and has a 60-acre lake nestled in the headwaters of Brumley Creek (3,000 ft). Except during hunting season, few people are seen on the trails. Camping is permitted around the lake. The lake has a boat ramp.

Access: In Abingdon take US 19–Alt 58 NW for 10.3 mi to SR 690 on the R, and go 2 mi up a steep but paved road to Hidden Valley.

▼ BRUMLEY CREEK TRAIL 608

Length: 6 mi (9.6 km) rt; easy to moderate. *USGS Map:* Brumley. *Trailhead:* Parking area.

 Directions and Description: From the parking area by the lake follow the trail to the end of the lake, pass the dam, and take the trail to the L at the fork. (The trail to the R is *Long Arm Hollow Trail*.) Follow downstream through oaks, hickory, maple, birch, locust, cherry, and hemlock for 3 mi to a junction with Little Brumley Creek and a picturesque waterfall on the L. Backtrack.

▼ LONG ARM HOLLOW TRAIL,
BRUMLEY RIM TRAIL 609–610

Length: 9.5 mi (15.2 km) rt, ct; moderate to strenuous.

USGS Map: Brumley. *Trailhead:* Parking area.

Directions and Description: From the parking lot follow the trail to the dam and take the R fork below the dam. Ascend, following the creek, for 2.5 mi to the ridge top. Several trails converge. (The trail to the R runs to an FAA tower at 0.5 mi. Farther ahead you can descend for another 1.3 mi to the entrance road, and from there you can take a R and go 1 mi back to the parking area.) The *Brumley Rim Trail* turns L, following the ridge for 3 mi. Turn L at trail junction and descend to Stagger Hollow for 1.7 mi. When you reach the *Brumley Creek Trail* turn L and, after another 2.3 mi, return to the parking area. (A number of other unnamed trails descend from the *Brumley Rim Trail* toward Poor Valley; unless familiar with the area, topo maps are advised.)

Highland WMA
Highland County

The Highland WMA encompasses some of the best high mountain land in this remote corner of the state. The 13,978 acres are divided into two large tracts, plus a smaller one. The largest tract lies on Jack Mtn and includes 4,400-ft Sounding Knob, the best-known landmark in the county. The mountaintop includes a grazed open area, maintaining a bald appearance. The other large tract is scenic Bullpasture Mountain, bordering the edge of Bath County and the Bullpasture Gorge.

Access to Sounding Knob: From Staunton take US 250 W to McDowell, and after 2 mi turn L on SR 615. Continue on SR 615 to the *CCC Fire Trail* shortly beyond Davis Run.

Highland Wildlife Management Area. Aubrey Shaw, Jr.

Access to Bullpasture Mountain: Take US 250 to McDowell and turn L on SR 678 to the Bullpasture Gorge parking area. From the S, take VA 39 from I-81 N of Lexington; from VA 39 take SR 625 to Williamsville, then SR 678 through Bullpasture Gorge to the parking area.

▼ CCC FIRE TRAIL   611

Length: 10 mi (16 km) rt; strenuous. *USGS Maps:* Monterey SE, Williamsville. *Trailhead:* Junction of SR 615 and *CCC Fire Trail* (Rd).

Directions and Description: (This fire road is open to traffic as well as hiking.) Follow on L of Davis Run for 1 mi. (At this point a 2-mi exceptionally steep trail leads L, ascending to the W slope of Buck Hill and into remote Jack Mtn.) Continue on the road to a gap in the ridge; turn R, following the ridge (a private road comes in from the L side of the mountain), and go N to Sounding Knob. As the road skirts the knob, take a side trail to the L at 1 mi from the gap, ascending steeply to the knob. Return and continue to WMA boundary at 5 mi. Backtrack.

▼ BULLPASTURE MOUNTAIN TRAIL   612

Length: 7 mi (11.2 km); moderate. *USGS Maps:* Monterey SE, Williamsville. *Trailhead:* Bullpasture parking area.

   Directions and Description: Explore this area by crossing the river from the parking area and following gated trail along the river and up the mountain. At 2 mi an optional trail to the R leads up a hollow to the top of Bullpasture Mtn and, at approximately 2 mi, to SR 614 on the other side. Back on *Bullpasture Mtn Trail*, at 3.5 mi another trail L leads across the mountain also connecting with SR 614. It roughly parallels the other trail for approximately 2.5 mi. Backtrack (unless crossing the mountain for vehicle shuttle at SR 612, 613, or 614).

   Information: Contact Area Supervisor, WMA, Rte E, Box 25, Monterey, VA 24465; tel: 703-468-2419.

Hog Island Wildlife Refuge
Surry and Isle of Wight Counties

Acquired in 1953, the 3,200 acres of Hog Island have become one of the prime waterfowl areas along the James River. In recent years some 10,000 Canada geese and 15,000 ducks have been on the refuge at peak times, plus herons, egrets, and dozens of other species. The waterfowl benefit from an intensive management program of the Virginia Game Commission. The controlled ponds are drained in the spring, and millet is grown through the summer. As the fall waterfowl migration starts the areas are flooded. The spectacle of birds coming in to feed in the refuge is outstanding and impressive. Woodlands in the area are chiefly loblolly pine. Hiking in this area is allowed only during the daytime; no camping.

Access: From VA 10 at Bacon's Castle, take SR 650 to entrance gate, having passed VEPCO's Surry nuclear power plant and the Carlisle Tract on the R.

There are at least four loop trails, with parking areas at the beginning of each. The first trail reached on the refuge road leads a short distance—0.3 mi—into the woods. The loops are 1.7 mi, 3 mi, 4.2 mi, and 3.2 mi, in combinations of trails around the lakes. Also, at the refuge headquarters, a 0.6-mi trail extends NW to the edge of the James River.

Information: Contact Area Supervisor, WMA, RFD, Surry, VA 23883; tel: 804-357-5224.

Horsepen Lake WMA
Buckingham County

This WMA was formerly the Lee Experimental Forest of the US Forest Service. Much of the 2,600 acres has been cut over but the current diversity is ideal for wildlife. Numerous logging roads and access trails interconnect for short distances—up to 1 mi. Trees are chiefly oaks, hickory, poplar, pine, and gum. Animals are deer, beaver, raccoon, and mink. The lake has bass, bluegill, pumpkinseed, and warmouth. Access is by SR 638, 2 mi S of US 60 from the town of Buckingham Courthouse. *USGS Maps:* Buckingham, Andersonville.

C. F. Phelps WMA
Fauquier County

Named in honor of the former Game Commission executive director, the Phelps WMA was formerly known as the Rappahannock WMA. With 3,900 acres of gently rolling hills and hardwood forest, it offers the diversity of canoeing on the 5-mi strip of the Rappahannock and also hiking on 11 mi of unnamed trails that are fire roads and all interconnect. No camping.

Access: Drive approximately 16 mi N on US 17 from Fredericksburg to SR 651, near village of Summerduck. On SR 651 use the first parking area and entrance to the lake.

Information: Contact Area Supervisor, WMA, Rte 2, Box 50-B, Remington, VA 22734; tel: 703-439-8506.

G. Richard Thompson WMA
Fauquier, Warren, and Clarke Counties

Formerly known by the name of Apple Manor Wildlife Management Area, reflecting the orchard on the property and nearby orchards, this 3,810-acre mountain area provides a number of fine trails and 11 access points. The *Appalachian Trail* crosses along the western border, and several trails lace the larger of the two tracts that make up an eastern slope. A 12-acre lake with bass, sunfish, and catfish is at the lower elevations along SR 688. Wildflowers are abundant—especially large zones of trillium. The smaller of the tracts off the Blue Ridge Mtns is adjacent to the new Sky Meadows State Park.

Access: Enter the preserve from SR 638 N, near Linden, or from SR 688 N, near Markham. Both routes are from VA 55, E of Front Royal.

Information: Contact Area Supervisor, WMA, Rte 1, Sperryville, VA 22740; tel: 703-825-3653.

Powhatan WMA
Powhatan County

This 5,000-acre tract 30 mi W of Richmond, on the rolling central Piedmont plateau, is ideal for the hiker. Dispersion is easy with 13 trails dipping into copses, winding around lazy brooks, and rising on gentle ridge crests. The area is 75% forest, with fields near the six stocked lakes. Hunting for turkey, dove, and quail is popular. Bluegill, bass, and catfish are in the lakes. Powhatan Lakes, two of the WMA's largest, are N of US 60 with entry on SR 625. Around the perimeter of the S tract, between US 60 and VA 13, are seven access points at which to park and begin the trails.

Access: For main access point drive 1.5 mi S of US 60 on SR 627 (4 mi W of US 60–522 junction), then turn L and go 0.5 mi to parking area on Deer Ln, SR 622.

▼ FESCUE TRAIL, SQUIRREL RIDGE TRAIL, NATURE TRAIL, ARROWHEAD TRAIL, HOLLY TRAIL, PINE TRAIL, CCC TRAIL, DOGWOOD TRAIL, FRANKLIN TRAIL, REDBUD TRAIL, WHITE OAK TRAIL, RED OAK TRAIL, POWER LINE TRAIL   613–625

Length: 15.6 mi (25 km) ct; easy. *USGS Maps:* Trenholm, Powhatan. *Trailhead:* Parking area on Deer Ln.

Directions and Description: No trails are blazed, and some are not marked by signs. The *Fescue Trail* trailhead is on the L, 0.25 mi after entry on SR 622, Deer Ln. This trail runs 0.7 mi to crossing of Sallee Creek, making a junction at 1.7 mi with the *CCC Trail* and ending at Salmon Creek at 2.1 mi. Backtrack, or turn L on the return at the *CCC Trail* for connections to other trails in making a loop. Begin this labyrinth of trails by descending from the parking area between the two lakes R. Follow grassy open space to a stand of large oaks on a knoll L. (Grassy road to R goes 0.5 mi to parking area across the road, SR 627, from the Cozy Acres Campground.) From the knoll on *Squirrel Ridge Trail* descend and ascend through open area to forest road. Here is part of the *Nature Trail.* After 0.4 mi junction with *Arrowhead Trail* and take the L on a wide avenue, partially open, bordered with a magnificent display of redbud. At 1.2 mi is junction with *Holly Trail*, which goes R.

At junction of *Arrowhead* and *Holly Trails*, there are three options. The shortest is to go L on *Arrowhead,* bearing L at clearing near Sunfish Pond; cross the dam at 1.4 mi among fennel, sumac, and alder; and follow *Pine Trail* to parking area for a loop of 2.1 mi. Option two is to follow *Arrowhead Trail* E, without taking the shortcut to the lake. This route will cross Sallee Creek, reach junction with the *CCC Trail* at 1 mi, and offer two choices of a loop back to the parking area; if R on the *CCC Trail* go 0.5 mi to the *Dogwood Trail*, take another R for 0.8 mi, and turn R again at junction with the *Holly Trail*. From this junction go another 0.8 mi back to *Arrowhead,* follow the directions across the dam, and return to the parking area for a total of 5.2 mi. Or, if L on the *CCC Trail*, the hiker can follow for 1.1 mi to junction of *Fescue Trail*. Turn L here and return to parking area on the *Fescue Trail* for a total of 5.5 mi.

For the third option mentioned for routes from the

junction of the *Holly Trail* and the *Arrowhead Trail*, bear R on the *Holly Trail*, and go 0.8 mi to junction with the *Dogwood Trail*. Turn L, cross Sallee Creek, pass *Franklin Trail* on R, and reach a fire road after another 0.8 mi. (To the R is an access road and the game-manager residence, and to the L is access to the *CCC Trail* and the short *Redbud Trail*.) Continue straight ahead across the fire road, entering on *White Oak Trail*, which after 0.7 mi becomes *Red Oak Trail*. Follow *Red Oak Trail* for 0.6 mi to another fire road, and turn L on the *Arrowhead Trail*. Follow *Arrowhead Trail* straight west to its original junction with *Holly Trail* (crossing only the *CCC Trail*) for 1.8 mi. Backtrack or go R across the Sunfish Pond and turn L on *Pine Trail* to the parking area at the original trailhead. Total loop is 6 mi. (The *Power Line Trail* extends from a parking area on SR 601, 0.5 mi from junction of US 60 and SR 684.) Combined mileage of all options is 15.6 mi. No camping on these trails.

Support Facilities: Cozy Acres Family Campground, Rte 3, Box 22, Powhatan, VA 23139; tel: 804-598-2470. Open April 1 through December 31. Full service, recreational facilities. Location: From junction of US 522 and US 60 in Powhatan, go W on US 60 for 4 mi to junction of US 60 and SR 627. Go S on SR 627 for 2 mi to entrance on R.

Information: Contact Area Supervisor, WMA, Rte 3, Box 150, Powhatan, VA 23139; tel: 804-598-3706.

Rapidan WMA
Greene and Madison Counties

The 9,000-acre Rapidan WMA has 10 separate tracts,

chiefly in Madison County N of Standardsville and approximately 25 mi SW of Culpepper. Four of the parcels are mortised into the Shenandoah National Park, with Fork Mtn, Doubletop Mtn, and Bluff Mtn being the most popular for hiking. It is a scenic, rugged, and forested area, and the Rapidan River cascades between two parcels of the WMA. Near its beginning is the confluence of Mill Prong and Laurel Prong. The major trails originate in the SNP. (For descriptions of *Staunton River Trail, Jones Mtn Trail, Laurel Prong Trail, Doubletop Mtn Trail,* and fire roads, consult the *Shenandoah National Park A.T. Guide,* published by the Potomac Appalachian Trail Club, 1718 N St, NW, Washington, DC 20036; tel: 202-638-5306.) Other recreation in the WMA is fishing for brook trout and hunting for bear, deer, and wild turkey.

Access to the Rapidan River Area: From Criglersville take SR 670 1 mi to SR 649, turning L. Go fo 3 mi to SNP boundary, and continue to junction with SR 622; turn R, following SR 622 up the river.

Information: Contact Area Supervisor, WMA, Rte 1, Sperryville, VA 22740; tel: 703-825-3653.

White Oak Mountain WMA   626
Pittsylvania County

The 2,715-acre White Oak Mtn WMA is 12 mi NE of Danville and 5 mi E of Chatham. A low mountain range (800 ft), it is bordered on the NW for 4.5 mi by the quietly flowing Banister River. It has 11 ponds, the largest of which is Pete's Pond, off the road from the area headquarters on SR 707. A number of old gated roads and a fisherman's trail on the Banister can be used for hiking. No camping.

One named trail, *Hiawatha Nature Trail*, is 1.1 mi round trip. It was formerly maintained by the Pittsylvania County school system, but its 33 interpretive posts, many with numbers intact on an unmaintained trail, continue to challenge the hiker. From the parking area on SR 649, 1.6 mi S of SR 832, cross the road, enter gated road, and immediately turn R onto white-blazed trail. At 0.5 mi reach Banister River and turn L. Vegetation includes river birch, oaks, trout lilies, mountain laurel, and silverberry. Climb rocky bluff to scenic view of the river at 0.7 mi. Turn L, circle small lake and return on seeded road to SR 649.

Access: From junction of US 29 Bypass and SR 832 in Chatham, go E on SR 832 for 3.9 mi. Turn R on SR 649 and go 1.6 mi to first parking area on L. Another route is from Danville N on US 29 to SR 640 on R. Turn R on SR 640, go 7.8 mi to SR 649 on L, and go 0.9 mi to parking area on R.

Information: Contact Area Supervisor, WMA, Rte 1, Box 76-G, Chatham, VA 24531; tel: 804-432-1377.

11 · State Parklands

All of Virginia's 17 state parks that are developed for recreation have hiking trails. Two other parks, the Shot Tower Historic Park and the unique Breaks Interstate Park, also have trails, and trails are planned in at least three more state parks now under development: Sky Meadows, Lake Anna, and Smith Mountain Lake. Trails in Caledon and Leesylvania state parks are expected to open in 1984. In addition, 30 mi of the *Appalachian Trail* is under state control. (At the time of research for this book the state had a foot trail system of approximately 200 miles; bridle and bicycle trails had approximately 30 mi each.)

The Virginia Division of Parks is organized with a director, a commissioner, an assistant commissioner, and, to administer the parks program, four division branches —for information, administration and management, maintenance and operation, and design and construction. There is a continuous process of operating and acquiring sites for recreational needs, historic shrines, museums, scenic trails, and natural environmental areas. Although visitors are welcome in the 32 state parks all year, the period when most facilities are fully operational and available is from Memorial Day weekend through Labor Day weekend.

In 10 of the parks—Chippokes, Claytor Lake, Douthat, Fairy Stone, Grayson Highlands, Hungry Mother, Pocahontas, Seashore, Staunton River, and Westmoreland—a small parking fee is charged from Memorial Day to Labor Day. Free reservation service is offered for campsites and housekeeping cabins. During crowded seasons and at popular parks, reservations for overnight (or week-long) visits should be made to guarantee space. The usual fee has been $5 to $6.50 for each campsite per a maximum of six people and one motor vehicle. A small extra charge is made at Fairy Stone, Hungry Mother, Occoneechee, and Westmoreland for electrical hookups. Housekeeping cabins are at Claytor Lake, Douthat, Fairy Stone, Goodwin Lake–Prince Edward, Hungry Mother, Seashore, Staunton River, and Westmoreland. Pocahontas has group cabins, and only Douthat and Breaks Interstate have motor lodges. Hikers are advised to request a detailed brochure and reservation application from Ticketron Reservations Terminal, PO Box 62221, Virginia Beach, VA 23462; tel: 804-490-3939, before planning an overnight stay.

Hikers who wish to fish should be sure a Virginia state fishing license has been acquired. Some areas require an additional permit, in some cases a daily one, for trout fishing. Swimmers are protected only at parks with special beaches and lifeguards. Only Seashore State Park rents bicycles, and only Staunton River has tennis courts. A few parks provide horse rentals; only one park, Grayson Highlands, allows privately owned horses on designated trails. There is a charge for boat launching and for boat rentals in the parks with lakes. Regardless of which facility and activity are chosen, hikers should remember to protect the natural environment so that others may enjoy it also.

Information: Contact the appropriate park by using the address listed at the end of each park description, or contact the Division of State Parks, 1201 Washington Bldg, Capitol Square, Richmond, VA 23219; tel: 804-786-2132.

Mountain Division

Breaks Interstate Park
Dickenson County

In 1954 the 4,500-acre Breaks Interstate Park was created by joint action of the Kentucky and Virginia legislatures to protect controlled areas of natural beauty and to open them for recreational use. An allotment of land with legend, history, and spectacular scenery, the park also has complete facilities. Among them are an Olympic-size swimming pool; forest campsites with full services; grounds designated for picnicking, hiking and bridle trails; cabins; motor lodge; restaurant, visitor center with exhibits, and a playground. One area is for horseback riding. Other activities include fishing and nature studies. Some of the facilities and activities are open year round, but the regular schedule is from Memorial Day to Labor Day. The Russell Fork River has carved out what is often called the "Grand Canyon of the South," a 1,600-ft-deep gorge extending 5 mi, leaving the "Towers" —sandstone natural skyscrapers. All trails are marked and blazed. The forest is chiefly hardwoods, with

Breaks Interstate Park. Virginia State Travel Service.

abundant wildflowers, ferns, lichens, and mosses on the forest floor.

Access: From Haysi in Virginia take VA 80 N for 8 mi and turn L to entrance. From Elkhorn in Kentucky take KY 15, then VA 80 for 7 mi to entrance on R.

▼ CHESTNUT RIDGE TRAIL, GEOLOGICAL TRAIL, GRASSY OVERLOOK TRAIL, OVERLOOK TRAIL, TOWERS TRAIL, TOWER TUNNEL TRAIL 627–632

Length: 5.2 mi (8.3 km) rt, ct; easy. *USGS Map:* Elkhorn City. *Trailhead:* Any of the overlook parking areas.

Directions and Description: All of these are blazed rim trails designed to provide scenic views of the canyon's river, rock formations, faults, and vegetation. They can be interconnected, among themselves and with the following two sets of trails. For an educational tour take the *Chestnut Ridge Trail* loop with the *Geological Trail*, with information about trees, shrubs, wildflowers, rock outcrops, caves, fossils, rock faults, and rock formations.

▼ CENTER CREEK TRAIL, GRASSY CREEK TRAIL, LAUREL BRANCH TRAIL, LOOP TRAIL, PROSPECTORS TRAIL, RIVER TRAIL 633–638

Length: 9.1 mi (14.6 km) rt, ct; moderate to strenuous. *USGS Map:* Elkhorn City. *Trailhead:* At the visitor center or Stateline Overlook parking areas or at Tower Tunnel Parking.

Directions and Description: Each of the three trailheads offers connection to any of these trails. It is recommended the hiker secure a trail map from the visitor center. On descent, parts of the trails are steep; exceptions are part of the *Laurel Branch Trail* and the *Loop Trail*. A challenging loop trail arrangement is to park at the Stateline Overlook, hike the *Ridge Trail* for 0.5 mi to the Notches, descend for a few yards to the *Prospectors Trail*, make a L turn on it and go another 0.8 mi. Turn R on the exceptionally steep *River Trail*, and descend for another 0.3 mi. Turn R, following riverbank for 0.3 mi to the confluence of the Russell River and Grassy Creek. Turn R, ascend slightly, and reach the *Laurel Branch Trail* 0.4 mi farther. (*Center Creek Trail* turns L here to the Center Creek Picnic Area.) Turn R; ascend steeply for 0.5 mi to the Notches. From here turn R on the *Geological Trail* for 0.4 mi to the Stateline Overlook for a total loop of 3.2 mi. Distance for all trails combined is 9.1 mi.

▼ LAKE TRAIL, COLD SPRING TRAIL   639–640

Length: 2 mi (3.2 km) rt, ct; easy. *USGS Map:* Elkhorn City. *Trailhead:* Visitor center parking area.

Directions and Description: These trails connect and provide entry to the Laurel Lake area, which has a swimming pool, or connect via the *Laurel Branch Trail* with the other trails in preceding two entries. *Cold Spring Trail* may be wet and rocky.

Information: Contact Superintendent, Breaks Interstate Park, Breaks, VA 24607; tel: 703-865-4414.

Claytor Lake State Park
Pulaski County

Claytor Lake State Park, established in 1946, has 472

acres of woodland and a 21-mi-long lake. Activities and facilities include boating, water skiing, and fishing from a modern marina; swimming at a sand beach with bathhouse; and camping with full services, or in vacation cabins. Other activities include nature study, horseback riding, picnicking, and hiking.

Access: From exit 33 on I-81 between the towns of Radford and Dublin, take SR 660 SE for 2 mi to the park entrance.

▼ CLAYTOR LAKE TRAIL,
   OVERLOOK TRAIL   641–642

Length: 3.5 mi (5.6 km) ct; easy. *USGS Map:* Dublin. *Trailhead:* Marina parking area.

   Directions and Description: The *Overlook Trail*, orange-blazed, starts at the Campground Contact Station and runs along the shoreline, but for easier parking start from the marina parking, 0.2 mi off SR 660 on the road to the Game Commission ramp. The 1.5-mi trail leads to two rock overlooks at the lake, then becomes blue-blazed *Claytor Lake Trail*. The 2-mi lake trail continues along the lake, then splits; the R fork leads to the rental cabins and park road, the L fork passes through a pine plantation, paralleling the horse trail and ending at the park road near the swimming area. Backtrack or use vehicle switching. Vegetation includes pine, sycamore, locust, oaks, maple, and sumac.

▼ DEER TRAIL   643

Length: 0.9 mi (1.4 km); easy. *USGS Map:* Dublin. *Trailhead:* End of picnic parking area.

   Directions and Description: Enter loop trail slightly

uphill by maples and white pines, following the 10 markers. Chances of seeing deer are good when hiking quietly. Vegetation includes poplar, sassafras, oaks, rhododendron, sourwood, wintergreen, berries, wild grape, and wildflowers.

Information: Contact Park Superintendent, Claytor Lake State Park, Dublin, VA 24084; tel: 703-674-5492.

Douthat State Park
Bath and Alleghany Counties

Deep in the Allegheny Mtns Douthat State Park has 4,493 acres (one of the state's three largest acreages) of scenic high ridges, more miles of hiking trails than any of the state's other parks, and a 50-acre lake stocked with trout. Its facilities include a visitor center with exhibits, restaurant, camp store, vacation cabins, and swimming beach with bathhouse; activities include boating, fishing, picnicking, camping, nature study, and hiking. Trails are color coded and generally in good condition. A hiking map from the visitor center is recommended for long hikes. The campgrounds are open from the Monday nearest April 1 to the Monday nearest December 1.

Access: From Clifton Forge at the junction of I-64–US 60 and SR 629, go N 5.5 mi on SR 629 to the visitor center.

▼ STONY RUN TRAIL, TUSCARORA OVERLOOK
TRAIL, MIDDLE MOUNTAIN TRAIL, SALT STUMP
TRAIL, BACKWAY HOLLOW TRAIL, HUFFS TRAIL,
BLUE SUCK TRAIL   644–655

Length: 13.1 mi (21 km) rt, ct; easy to strenuous. *USGS Map:* Healing Springs. *Trailhead:* Visitor center.

Directions and Description: These trails are on the W side of Wilson Creek, forming a connecting system for a long loop that ascends to the Middle Mtn Ridge and the George Washington National Forest and descends on the N end of the park, where connecting trails S provide a return to the visitor center.

Begin from the visitor center, hiking down the road 0.5 mi to the trailhead for orange-blazed *Stony Run Trail* on R. (Or take *Beards Gap Hollow Trail*, which is closer to the visitor center.) Ascend; at 1.4 mi pass junction with *Locust Gap Trail* on the R. Continue ahead for another 1.1 mi to Stony Run Falls on the L. For the next 2 mi ascend on switchbacks to junction with *Middle Mtn Trail* and the yellow-blazed *Tuscarora Overlook Trail* at 4.5 mi. Take the R fork on the *Tuscarora Overlook Trail* to a scenic view at 5 mi. At 5.9 mi make sharp L turn and after a few yards make sharp turn R to be on the white-blazed *Middle Mtn Trail.* (A turn R at the 5.9-mi junction, on *Blue Suck Trail,* would lead down the mountain for 3 mi to the visitor center.)

Follow the ridge trail to the edge of the park boundary at 7.7 mi to begin *Salt Stump Trail.* Descend, passing *Pine Tree Trail* on R at 8.7 mi, and reach *Backway Hollow Trail* on R at 10.3 mi. (Vehicle shuttle could be arranged near here at the campground.) Follow the *Backway Hollow Trail* for 0.7 mi to the junction on the R with *Huffs Trail.* Take the *Huffs Trail*, passing *Laurel View Trail* on the R and then the *Middle Hollow Trail* intersection, and reach *Blue Suck Trail* at 12.2 mi. Turn L on *Blue Suck Trail*, pass *Tobacco House Ridge Trail* on the R and then the group camping area, and return to the visitor center at 13.1 mi. Forest cover along the trails is chiefly hemlock, oaks, Virginia pine, white pine, poplar, maple, beech, and birch. Some of understory is redbud, dogwood, sassafras, mountain laurel, rhododendron, buck berry, and sourwood. Wildflowers and berries are plentiful.

▼ BRUSHY HOLLOW TRAIL, MOUNTAIN TOP TRAIL,
ROSS CAMP HOLLOW TRAIL,
WILSON CREEK TRAIL   656–661

Length: 8 mi (12.8 km) rt, ct; easy to strenuous. *USGS Map:* Healing Springs. *Trailhead:* Visitor center parking area.

Directions and Description: These trail combinations are on the E side of Wilson Creek. Use a vehicle to the trailhead for *Brushy Hollow Trail* near Wilson Creek. Inquire of trail adviser at the visitor center for best area in which to park, as space is limited. Hiker must ford the creek (actually a river; if the water is high, a better route would be to take the *Beards Gap Trail* from the visitor center).

Begin the trail across Wilson Creek, and after 1 mi begin a long series of switchbacks NE and N extending to junction with *Beards Gap Trail* on the L at 3.2 mi. (*Beards Gap Trail* descends steeply for 1.1 mi to the visitor center.) Continue ahead, passing excellent overlooks W into the Wilson Creek valley. At 3.5 mi pass junction on L with *Buck Hollow Trail*, which has an outstanding overlook 0.5 mi W on its 1-mi descent to *Wilson Creek Trail*. Continue ahead a few yards to junction with *Mtn Side Trail* on the L and *Mtn Top Trail* on the R. (*Mtn Side Trail* goes 1.4 mi N on the W side of the slope to rejoin the *Mtn Top Trail*.) Turn R on *Mtn Top Trail*, ascending switchbacks, and pass scenic views at 5.2 mi.

Turn sharply L, descend, and pass junction with *Mtn Side Trail* on L at 5.8 mi. At 6.6 mi, near the last rental cabin, veer R and take either the *Guest Lodge Trail* or the *Ross Camp Hollow Trail* to the *Wilson Creek Trail*. Continue on the *Wilson Creek Trail*, paralleling the park road—SR 629—and passing a picnic area and, on the R at 7.5 mi, junction with *Buck Lick Interpretive Trail*. Immediately beyond the junction is the *Buck Hollow Trail* on the L, mentioned previously. Continue ahead on the *Wilson Creek Trail* to the amphitheater and to the visitor center at 8 mi.

▼ BUCK LICK TRAIL   662

Length: 0.3 mi (5 km); easy. *USGS Map:* Healing Springs. *Trailhead:* Parking area near restaurant.

   Directions and Description: From the parking area near the restaurant follow the red-blazed markers on a unique trail, constructed by the Civilian Conservation Corps, that has 17 interpretive signs about geological features, deciduous trees, wild animals, crustacean life, forest succession, lichens, and water cycles.

   Information: Contact Superintendent, Douthat State Park, Box 212, Millboro, VA 24460; tel: 703-862-0612.

Goshen Pass Natural Area
Rockbridge County

At one of Virginia's most scenic spots for white water, the turbulent Maury River twists and cuts its way through Goshen Pass in the N Mtns. Highway 39 turns with the river, providing exciting views. Picnicking is allowed, but parking space is along the highway, and limited. At the *Laurel Run Trail* site where Laurel Run joins the Maury River, for example, vehicles should be parked so as not to block trail or road. *Laurel Run Trail* is 4 mi round trip, and easy to follow. (See Goshen Wildlife Management Area, Chapter 10.) At the west end of the gorge, a 150-ft suspension bridge for pedestrians crosses the Maury River so hikers can explore the Round Mtn area. With the natural area and the WMA the state has a total of 33,000 acres in the Little N Mtn range. Adjoining national-forest land adds more recreational opportunities.

The Maury River was named after the famous oceanographer Matthew Fontaine Maury, the first man to chart the seas of the world. He retired in Lexington, and upon his death his body was carried through Goshen Pass, as he had requested, by VMI cadets before burial.

Access: From junction of VA 39 and VA 252 (9 mi N of Lexington), go W on VA 39 for 5.5 mi to Goshen Pass.

Information: Parks and Recreation, Washington Bldg, 8th and Franklin Sts, Richmond, VA 23219; tel: 804-786-1405.

Grayson Highlands State Park
Grayson County

Virginia's highest park (5,090 ft) and probably the one most magnificent, is a 4,754-acre preserve amid rugged peaks of igneous rock, alpine meadows, waterfalls, and spruce-fir forests. An area of mountain grandeur, it borders the crest zone of Mt Rogers, whose mile-high peak is the center of attraction for both the state park and the adjacent Mt Rogers National Recreation Area (see national-forest section). Solitude is easy to find in this park. Facilities in the park include campgrounds, rest rooms and hot showers, horse trails, hiking trails, and a visitor center with exhibits; activities include hiking, picnicking, and nature study.

Access: On US 58 between Volney and Damascus turn on VA 362 to park entrance.

▼ WILSON CREEK TRAIL, APPALACHIAN TRAIL, RHODODENDRON TRAIL, BIG PINNACLE TRAIL, TWIN PINNACLES TRAIL, STAMPERS BRANCH TRAIL   663–667

Length: 10.6 mi (17 km) ct, rt; easy to strenuous. *USGS Maps:* Whitetop Mtn, Troutdale, Park, Grassy Creek. *Trailhead:* Campground.

Directions and Description: (This connecting-trail arrangement is recommended for a hike of a full day; take a day pack with lunch, a camera, and—just in case —rain gear. Park regulations require all hikers to be off the trails at sundown.) From the campground follow the *Wilson Creek Trail* sign, descending to Wilson Creek in a forest of red maple, beech, and yellow and black birch, with an understory of striped maple and ferns at 0.6 mi. Follow upstream with cascades on R, and reach a 25-ft waterfall at 1 mi. Ash and rhododendron decorate the area. At road junction turn sharp R, follow old logging road, and cross Quebec Branch at 1.3 mi. Pass through open meadow, reaching the *A.T.* near Wilson Creek at 1.7 mi. Turn L, cross stile, and follow white-blazed *A.T.* through thick grass spotted with flame azalea, mountain laurel, and large sweet blueberry bushes. Cross Quebec

Branch again at 2.7 mi and ascend to rocky ridge crest at 3.4 mi. At 3.9 mi is a sign on the L to the Massie Gap parking area. Continue ahead following an old open cattle road; cattle and ponies may be grazing nearby.

Cross stile at 4.4 mi, leaving Grayson Highlands State Park. Follow the *A.T.*, veering L at fork with blue-blazed *Rhododendron Trail* at 4.5 mi. After 1.1 mi more come to junction with *Rhododendron Trail* again on a huge rocky peak of Wilburn Ridge. (From here it is 2 mi on the *A.T.* to the summit of Mt Rogers (5,729 ft), Virginia's highest mountain. The summit has no view and is covered with the only spruce-fir forest in the state. Fog often surrounds its green and fragrant beauty.) Follow the blue-blazed trail R to an enormous array of boulders with a 360° view at 5.9 mi. Vegetation, dwarfed by strong winds, is rhododendron, mountain ash, azaleas, and conifers. Descend to junction with the *A.T.* at 6.8 mi, and follow the *Rhododendron Trail* to the Massie Gap sign at 7.2 mi. Continue the descent to the Massie Gap parking area at 7.7 mi.

Cross the parking area and begin the steep climb— gaining 400 ft in elevation—on *Big Pinnacle Trail* to the summit of Big Pinnacle (5,068 ft) at 8.1 mi. Views are spectacular, the sights including Mt Rogers and White Top Mtn (Virginia's second highest peak) and the valleys of Virginia, North Carolina, and Tennessee. Wild-flowers, ferns, and lichens are abundant. From here continue through dense grass, scattered spruce, and hawthorn bushes on the *Twin Pinnacles Trail* to Little Pinnacle (5,089 ft) for more scenic views at 8.6 mi. Descend to junction with the *Stampers Branch Trail* at 8.9 mi and turn L, but not before a visit to the visitor center nearby. Continue descent on *Stampers Branch Trail*, crossing main road, Stampers Branch, and Wilburn Branch, and reaching a log cabin near the campground for a complete loop of 10.6 mi.

▼ CABIN CREEK NATURE TRAIL   668

Length: 1.9 mi (3 km); moderate. *USGS Maps:* Whitetop Mtn, Troutdale, Park, Grassy Creek. *Trailhead:* Massie Gap parking area.

Directions and Description: Follow the sign, descending for 0.6 mi to Cabin Creek—named for the cabins built by pioneers in the hollow. Near the base of the trail is rare big-toothed aspen. Frazer fir and magnolia are also here, with red spruce. Pass a 25-ft waterfall and, after 1 mi, begin the return to the parking area on an old railroad grade.

▼ LISTENING ROCK TRAIL   669

Length: 1.8 mi (2.9 km); moderate. *USGS Maps:* Whitetop Mtn, Troutdale, Park, Grassy Creek. *Trailhead:* Visitor center parking area.

Directions and Description: Follow trail signs on the R of the parking lot opposite the visitor center. This is a loop trail; it goes by the Buzzard Rock with excellent views of the valleys below. From here trail descends to the Listening Rock (also called Wildcat Rock) and more outstanding views. Vegetation includes both deciduous trees and conifers.

▼ ROCK HOUSE RIDGE TRAIL   670

Length: 1.8 mi (2.9 km); easy. *USGS Maps:* Whitetop Mtn, Troutdale, Park, Grassy Creek. *Trailhead:* Picnic area parking.

Directions and Description: Follow the sign from the parking area to the Jones homestead and cemetery. A number of outbuildings, including a spring house, provide an example of the way homesteads used to be. This loop trail receives its name from a huge, leaning shelter-type rock, which probably provided shelter for the Indians.

Information: Contact Superintendent, Grayson Highlands State Park, Rte 2, Box 141, Mouth of Wilson, VA 24363; tel: 703-579-7092.

Hungry Mother State Park
Smyth County

Excellent mountain scenery, a picturesque lake, and well-planned trails make the 2,180-acre Hungry Mother State Park a popular recreation area. More than 12 mi of trail make hiking very pleasurable. The paths were largely established by the Civilian Conservation Corps (CCC) in the 1930s. Most of the park is a designated natural area. Facilities and activities include campgrounds, vacation cabins, visitor center, restaurant, and hiking, horseback riding, picnicking, swimming, paddleboating, fishing, and nature study.

Access: Take exit 16 on I-81 at VA 16 into Marion. Follow the signs and proceed 3 mi N of Marion on VA 16 to the park entrance.

▼ MOLLY'S PIONEER TRAIL, MOLLY'S KNOB TRAIL, CCC TRAIL, LAKE TRAIL, SPILLWAY TRAIL, RIDGE TRAIL   671–676

Length: 10.5 mi (16 km) rt, ct; easy to moderate. *USGS*

Maps: Marion, Chatham Hill. *Trailhead:* Visitor center parking area.

Directions and Description: All these trails connect, but backtracking is necessary to connect one to another in order to form loops. *Molly's Pioneer Trail* is a short loop of 0.6 mi, red blazed and interpretive in nature, to educate about the wild animals, trees, shrubs, and flowers. Halfway around this trail *Molly's Knob Trail* (1.6 mi) begins. Follow *Molly's Knob Trail* to the summit (3,270 ft) for views of Marion, Mt Rogers, and White Top Mtn to SW. Backtrack, or descend to junction of *CCC Trail*, orange blazed, for 1.1 mi to Campground D. This route requires vehicle shuttle. Another route from *Molly's Knob Trail* could be to take the *CCC Trail* to junction with *Lake Trail* (3.1 mi) and loop back to the visitor center. Or, to make yet another loop, take the *Spillway Trail* (1.1 mi) from *Molly's Knob Trail* to the *Lake Trail.* A shorter route from Molly's Knob could be taken by picking up the *Ridge Trail* (0.7 mi) on the L 0.8 mi from the Knob and then connecting with the *Lake Trail.* Whatever the loop arrangements, a trail map from the visitor center would assist in planning and could prevent extra climbing or unexpected long connections. Signs are posted at the intersections. Wildlife in the area includes deer, raccoon, fox, squirrel, grouse, and wild turkey. Flora includes pines—Virginia, pitch, shortleaf, white—and the usual Southern Appalachian hardwoods, with banks of wintergreen and trailing arbutus, wildflowers, ferns, and Indian pipe amid the forest-floor duff.

▼ RAIDER'S RUN TRAIL,
OLD SHAWNEE TRAIL   677–678

Length: 1.5 mi (2.4 km); easy. *USGS Maps:* Marion,

Chatham Hill. *Trailhead:* Restaurant parking area.

Directions and Description: Follow the blue-blazed *Raider's Run Trail* from near the restaurant parking area for 0.4 mi to the *Old Shawnee Trail*. Both trails combined make a double loop.

Information: Contact Superintendent, Hungry Mother State Park, Rte 5, Box 109, Marion, VA 24354; tel: 703-783-3422.

Natural Tunnel State Park
Scott County

Established in 1967, the Natural Tunnel State Park has 40 acres currently available for recreation and nature study, with plans for expansion of this allotment to the full 527 acres. The park has a campground, with hot showers; an exhibit of railroad artifacts in the visitor center; picnic area; and well-graded trails with awesome views of the immense karst, one of the most impressive in North America. Over millions of years an enormous cave was formed in Hunter Valley by groundwater, with carbonic acid dissolving the sections of limestone and dolomitic bedrock. Since then, as the water table lowered, Stock Creek has flowed through to join the Clinch River.

Access: On US 23 at Clinchport go N for 2 mi, turn R on SR 871, and go 0.6 mi to park entrance.

▼ UPPER TRAIL, TUNNEL HILL TRAIL, LOWER TRAIL   679–681

Length: 1.7 mi (2.7 km) rt, ct; moderate. *USGS Map:* Clinchport. *Trailhead:* Visitor center parking area.

Directions and Description: Following trail signs—notice sign about extreme danger—take graded *Upper Trail* for 0.3 mi to Lovers Leap. Views into the gigantic amphitheater span 3,000 ft around the rim and 400 ft down to the chasm floor—deep enough for a 35-story skyscraper. A view into the valley shows the route taken by Daniel Boone in 1769. (Between points 1 and 3 on the trail *Tunnel Hill Trail* takes off to the NE, eventually crossing SR 696 and leading to the picnic area. Another trail near Lovers Leap leads to the campground.) Return from Lovers Leap to the junction with the *Lower Trail*, descend along it on steep switchbacks to the railroad, and turn R. Enter the nine-story tunnel at 0.4 mi, using care to stay on the trail in the event a Southern Railway train should come through. Return by the same route after tunnel exit. Some of the vegetation is ash, papaw, walnut, sycamore, poplar; wildflowers include columbine and ladies tresses.

Information: Contact Superintendent, Natural Tunnel State Park, Rte 3, Box 250, Clinchport, VA 24244; tel: 703-940-2674.

Shot Tower Historical State Park
Wythe County   682

In 1785 Thomas Jackson, an Englishman, came to America; he and David Pierce jointly owned the Lead Mines in Austinville, near the New River. Jackson built the 70-ft-high Shot Tower for processing lead shot for firearms in 1807, and he operated it until his death in 1824. In 1964 the Lead Mines Ruritan Club donated the tower to the commonwealth. After extensive renovation it was opened to the public in 1968. Tours may be arranged. Facilities include a picnic area, rest rooms, and the 0.7-mi *Shot Tower Historic Trail* around the tower and along the riverbank to US 52.

Access: At exit 4 on I-77 turn off at Poplar Camp; take VA 69 E to US 52, and go 1.5 mi N on US 52 to the park entrance.

Information: Contact Superintendent, Claytor Lake State Park, Rte 1, Box 267, Dublin, VA 24084; tel: 703-674-5492.

Piedmont Division

Bear Creek Lake State Park
Cumberland County

Centered in the heart of the Cumberland State Forest, the peaceful and serene 150-acre Bear Creek Lake State Park was established in 1939. Activities include boating, fishing, picnicking, hiking, swimming (at facilities that include a bathhouse) and camping. The main fish species are blue gill, big mouth bass, and pickerel. (Directions for the *Willis River Trail*, which is near the E edge of the park in the Cumberland State Forest, end of this chapter.)

Access: From the town of Cumberland go E 0.5 mi on US 60 and turn L on SR 622. Go 3.3 mi to SR 629 and turn into the park area. Drive 0.9 mi farther, and park near the park headquarters.

▼ RUNNING CEDAR TRAIL, PINE KNOB TRAIL, LAKESIDE TRAIL   683–685

Length: 1.7 mi (2.7 km) rt; easy. *USGS Map:* Gold Hill.

Trailhead: Parking area near park headquarters.

Directions and Description: Follow the blue-blazed *Running Cedar Trail* over large beds of running cedar in a large grove of tulip poplars, crossing a bridge near the parking area at the bathhouse. At 0.5 mi is junction with the green-blazed short loop *Pine Knob Trail*. Return to the bridge at 0.9 mi; reach junction with the *Lakeside Trail* at 1.1 mi, pass through Campground C at 1.4 mi, and reach the spillway at 1.5 mi; return through Campground A to parking area at 1.7 mi.

Information: Contact Superintendent, Bear Creek Lake State Park, Rte 1, Box 253, Cumberland, VA 23040; tel: 804-492-4410.

Fairy Stone State Park
Patrick and Henry Counties

Fairy Stone State Park, established in 1936, is a 4,570-acre natural preserve in the foothills of the Blue Ridge Mountains. It has a 168-acre lake fed by the Smith River, which flows into the adjoining Philpott Reservoir. The park is named for the famous lucky hexagonal crystals found in the southern tip of the park boundary. The crystals, called staurolite, are composed of iron aluminum silicate in small tan-brown and gray-blue forms of the Roman, Maltese, and St. Andrew's crosses. They have been formed by intense heat and pressure during the folding and crumpling of the Appalachian mountain chain.

A wide range of facilities include those for swimming, boating, fishing, horseback riding, hiking, bicycling, nature study, and tent and trailer camping. Also, housekeeping cabins are rented on a weekly basis from Monday to Monday and are exceptionally popular. Some facilities exist for the handicapped.

Access: From Bassett go 9 mi W on VA 57 and turn R on VA 346. Go 1 mi to the park entrance and information center. (VA 57 continues W to VA 8, leading to Stuart and Woolwine.)

▼ OAK HICKORY TRAIL   686

Length: 1.3 mi (2.1 km) rt; easy to moderate. *USGS Maps:* Charity, Philpott Reservoir. *Trailhead:* Picnic area near park entrance.

Directions and Description: Near the park entrance turn R on paved road and park near picnic area. Where the road crosses the stream look for the red-blazed trail sign and go R or L on the 1.3-mi loop trail. Large trees include beech, oaks, poplar, white pine, and maples. Parts of the trail are mossy, with a rhododendron canopy. Deer are often seen in this area.

▼ IRON MINE TRAIL   687

Length: 1 mi (1.6 km) rt; easy to moderate. *USGS Maps:* Charity, Philpott Reservoir. *Trailhead:* Parking area on VA 346.

Directions and Description: From the park entrance drive 0.7 mi on VA 346 to the parking area on the L for the *Iron Mine Trail* system. Climb up well-graded trail through periwinkle beds, fire pinks, redbuds, and mixed young forest. At 0.2 mi is junction with blue-blazed *Whiskey Run Trail*. Continue L through remains of iron mines and pass junction with orange-blazed *Stuart's*

Knob Trail at 0.5 mi. At 0.7 mi is superb view of the park beach and bathhouse. At 0.9 mi reach interpretive sign #17 at an open-shaft mine. Return to the parking lot at 1 mi.

▼ STUART'S KNOB TRAIL   688

Length: 1.7 mi. (2.7 km) rt; easy to moderate. *USGS Maps:* Charity, Philpott Reservoir. *Trailhead:* Parking area on VA 346.

Directions and Description: Follow the *Iron Mine Trail* for 0.5 mi and take the *Stuart's Knob Trail*, ascending steeply to the peak. Although the knob is rocky it has heavy vegetation, preventing scenic views. Descend along graded trail via the *Iron Mine Trail*.

▼ WHISKEY RUN TRAIL   689

Length: 2 mi (3.2 km) rt; easy to moderate. *USGS Maps:* Charity, Philpott Reservoir. *Trailhead:* Parking area on VA 346.

Directions and Description: Follow the *Iron Mine Trail* for 0.2 mi and take the *Whiskey Run Trail* R on a blue-blazed, well-graded trail. Circle the base of Stuart's Knob for 1.5 mi. Rejoin the *Iron Mine Trail* at park overview, and descend on the *Iron Mine Trail* to the parking lot at 2 mi.

▼ DAM SPILLWAY TRAIL   690

Length: 1 mi (1.6 km) rt; easy. *USGS Maps:* Charity, Philpott Reservoir. *Trailhead:* Parking area near nature center.

Directions and Description: From the nature center go 0.4 mi to the *Dam Spillway Trail* and hike along the edge of the lake on an orange-blazed trail through a mixed forest. Return to the nature center after 1 mi.

▼ HANDICAPPED TRAIL   691

Length: 0.1 mi (0.16 km), easy. *USGS Maps:* Charity, Philpott Reservoir. *Trailhead:* Parking area on VA 346.

Directions and Description: From the park entrance and information center go on VA 346 for 0.9 mi and park on the R. The cement-paved trail borders a cove of the lake and has a picnic table for the physically handicapped. Some of the plants are skunk cabbage, hornbeam, sycamore, pines, periwinkle, thimbleweed, and chickweed.

Information: Contact the Park Superintendent, Fairy Stone State Park, Rte 2, Box 134, Stuart, VA 24171; tel: 703-930-2424.

Goodwin Lake–Prince Edward State Park
Prince Edward County

Located in the state's central Piedmont, the double-lake, 270-acre Goodwin Lake–Prince Edward State Park adjoins the Gallion State Forest. Goodwin Lake with 40 acres and Prince Edward Lake with 30 acres provide a tranquil area where the hiker can circle either body of water or, with a connector trail, both. Wildlife is chiefly deer, quail, raccoon, beaver, squirrel, and wild turkey. The forest is mixed, but oaks, maples, hickory, and dogwood predominate.

Facilities include campgrounds and vacation cabins, swimming beaches, bathhouses, and areas for boating, fishing, picnicking, nature study, and hiking.

Access: From the junction of US 460–360 at Burkeville, go 3 mi SW on US 360 to SR 621 and turn R. Go 1 mi on SR 621 to junction of SR 697 and SR 621, where a large park sign gives directions. Proceed L for 0.5 mi to the parking area at Prince Edward Lake.

▼ TWIN BEECH TRAIL   692

Length: 0.5 mi (0.8 km) rt; easy. *USGS Map:* Greenbay. *Trailhead:* Parking area.

Directions and Description: Follow the *Twin Beech Trail* sign on a self-guided, graded loop trail that has 14 interpretive stops through a forest of beech, poplar, maple, sourwood, dogwood, hickory, ferns, and mayapple.

▼ OTTER'S PATH TRAIL   693

Length: 2.4 mi (3.8 km) rt; easy to moderate. *USGS Map:* Greenbay. *Trailhead:* Parking area.

Directions and Description: In either direction follow the orange markers around the lake. If hiking L from the boathouse, pass boat ramp and cross bridge near an active beaver dam at 0.2 mi. Trail winds around coves, up and down steep banks, and over mossy patches. Cross a cascading stream at 1.1 mi. At 1.8 mi reach junction with yellow-marked, 0.5-mi connector trail on the L to Goodwin Lake. Continue ahead; cross bridge over the dam and follow the orange markers through a mixed forest to the parking area at 2.4 mi.

▼ GOODWIN LAKE TRAIL   694

Length: 1 mi (1.6 km) rt; easy. *USGS Map:* Greenbay. *Trailhead:* Parking area at Goodwin Lake.

Directions and Description: From the parking area descend on slope to the picnic area and hike R or L. If L follow the blue markers through a mixed forest to the head of the lake, where there is evidence of beavers. Cross bridges at 0.5 mi and 0.6 mi; turn R at paved road, cross dam, and return to the picnic area and parking lot at 1 mi.

Support Facilities: In addition to camping facilities in the park, the nearest commercial campground is Amelia Family Campground, Rte 3, Box 26, Amelia, VA 23002; tel: 804-561-4772. Full service, with recreational facilities including marked nature trails. Open all year. Location: East of Amelia; from junction of US 360 and VA 153 go 0.5 mi S on VA 153.

Information: Contact Park Superintendent, Goodwin Lake–Prince Edward State Park, Rte 2, Box 70, Green Bay, VA 23942; tel: 804-392-3435.

Holliday Lake State Park
Buckingham and Appomattox Counties

Established in 1939, the peaceful, 250-acre Holliday Lake State Park lies within the Buckingham-Appomattox State Forest. The park's major attraction is a 150-acre lake, offering boating and fishing as well as swimming at a spacious beach area. There are two campgrounds with facilities, picnic areas, visitor center, bathhouse, and a lake trail for hiking. Open April 1 to December 1.

Lake Shore Nature Trail, Holliday State Park.
Allen de Hart.

Access: On VA 24 E of the town of Appomattox and US 460, go 8 mi to SR 626 R. Follow SR 626 for 3.5 mi, turn L on SR 640 for 0.3 mi, and then R on SR 692 for 2.9 mi.

▼ LAKE SHORE NATURE TRAIL   695

Length: 4.7 mi (7.5 km); easy. *USGS Map:* Holliday Lake. *Trailhead:* Parking area near boat dock.

Directions and Description: From the boat dock and bathhouse area begin the *Lake Shore Nature Trail* either L or R for a loop. If L, follow the initial dark-blue marker with subsequent orange arrow signs around the lake. Vegetation includes Virginia pine, shortleaf pine, oaks, hickory, poplar, mountain laurel, red cedar, alder, white pine, green ash, dogwoods, and numerous wildflowers. Reach lake overview at 0.4 mi on exceptionally well graded trail. At 0.6 mi pass yellow-marked Campground B trail junction on L. Cross small streams at 0.8 and 1 mi. At 1.1 mi a shortcut bridge over Forbes Creek is R. (Trail upstream goes for 0.4 mi to point where rock-hopping across allows circle back to bridge.)

After crossing bridge continue R to clearing and views of lake on R at 1.5 mi, and at forest road junction at 1.6 go straight ahead. Cross small tributary, and reach rocky bluff with huckleberries at 2.7 mi. Descend steeply to scenic cement bridge over the dam at 2.8 mi. Cross small stream in a cove, and follow upstream for 0.2 mi. Turn away from stream bank and reach paved gated road at 3.9 mi. (R is entrance to 4-H Educational Center.) Climb steps across road, descend to stream bank, follow through mature forest with beds of running cedar, and reach bridge at lake at 4.5 mi. L is junction with orange

sign to Campground A. Follow along lakeshore for
another 0.2 mi to parking area.

Information: Contact Superintendent, Holliday Lake
State Park, Rte 2, Box 230, Appomattox, VA 24522; tel:
804-248-6308.

Occoneechee State Park
Mecklenburg County

Leased from the US Army Corp of Engineers in 1968, the
2,690-acre Occoneechee State Park adjoins the John H.
Kerr Reservoir near Clarksville. The park is named after
the powerful Occoneechee Indians, who, in the period
from 1250 to 1676, lived in the area. They, like the Saponi
and Tutelo Indians, traded furs from now-inundated
islands until the rebel Nathaniel Bacon in 1676 massacred
many of them—thereby breaking their stronghold. The
survivors scattered into what is now North Carolina.

Facilities include 142 campsites, picnicking, boating,
hiking, and summer interpretive programs. Bass fishing
is a popular sport in the reservoir.

Access: From the junction of US 58–15 and VA 49
across the bridge from Clarksville, go E on US 58 for 0.6
mi and turn R at park sign. Follow VA 364 for 0.5 mi to
the park headquarters.

▼ OLD PLANTATION TRAIL   696–698

Length: 0.8 mi (1.3 km) ct; easy to moderate. *USGS
Maps:* Clarksville N and S, Tungsten. *Trailhead:* Terrace
Garden parking area.

Directions and Description: From the park headquarters go S 0.1 mi to the first paved road on the R, and park at the Terrace Garden parking area. Follow the red-blazed *Old Plantation Trail,* by the site of the Occoneechee plantation home of Dempsey G. Crudup, into a forest of black and honey locust, black walnut, red maple, red cedar, and oaks. Pass junction at 0.2 mi with *Mossy Creek Trail,* which extends right (and leads 0.7 mi up to a large white-oak stand and to the road at park headquarters). Continue on *Old Plantation Trail,* by stream and near beechnut, pines, and sweet gum and pass junction with orange-blazed *Warrior Path Trail,* a trail leading 0.2 mi R to parking area on the lakeshore. Continue on *Old Plantation Trail* for another 0.1 mi, passing junction with yellow-blazed *Big Oak Trail* on R. At 0.6 mi ascend through periwinkle groundcover to terraces lined with boxwood. Return to parking area at 0.8 mi.

▼ BIG OAK TRAIL   699

Length: 1.1 mi (1.7 km); easy to moderate. *USGS Maps:* Clarksville N and S, Tungsten. *Trailhead:* Terrace Garden parking area.

Directions and Description: From the Terrace Garden parking area descend on the *Old Plantation Trail* through the terraces lined with boxwoods to the yellow-blazed *Big Oak Trail* at 0.3 mi, and turn L. Climb steep bank to road, go L on road, and enter forest again near a huge white oak at 0.2 mi. Reach exit of trail in group of large red and white oaks at 0.6 mi on Campground C road. Turn L and follow road back to parking area at Terrace Garden. (A former long trail connecting Campground C with Campground A is no longer open or maintained.)

Support Facilities: Park camping facilities for tents and trailers are open from April 1 through December 1, but they do not have hookups.

Information: Contact the Superintendent, Occoneechee State Park, Box 818, Clarksville, VA 23927; tel: 804-374-2210.

Pocahontas State Park
Chesterfield County

Centered in Chesterfield County, slightly west of Richmond and Colonial Heights, and halfway between them, 1,783-acre Pocahontas State Park was established in 1946. Considered an outdoor laboratory, it is part of the 7,600-acre Pocahontas State Forest. A 156-acre lake fed by Swift Creek is used for boating and fishing. Also provided are a large swimming pool, bathhouse, areas for camping and picnicking, bridle trails, bicycle trails, hiking trails, wildlife exhibits, visitor center, and a playground.

Access: From the junction of VA 10 and SR 655 at Chesterfield Courthouse follow the park signs and go W on SR 655 for 3.8 mi, then turn R into park entrance on SR 780. Park office and parking area are another 1.5 mi away. (Access via I-95 is from exit 6; go W 7 mi on VA 10 to Chesterfield Courthouse and SR 655.)

▼ BEAVER LAKE NATURE TRAIL   700–703

Length: 2.6 mi (4.2 km) rt; easy. *USGS Maps:* Chesterfield, Beach. *Trailhead:* Visitor center.

Directions and Description: Follow the blue-blazed

trail down to Beaver Lake, which is bordered with tag alder; at 0.1 mi, turn R and hike through forest of large poplar, loblolly pine, oaks, beechnut, and holly with a groundcover of periwinkle. Pass old spring at 0.2 mi. Junction with yellow-blazed *Ground Pine Nature Trail,* extending R, is at 0.3 mi.

Continue through beds of ground pine and running cedar to lake overlooks at 0.5 mi and 0.7 mi. Cross boardwalk near large walnut, poplar, and sycamore stand at 0.8 mi. At 1.3 mi reach junction with *Third Branch Trail* and Old Mill Site. Turn L, cross stream, and continue circuit of the lake through a mixed forest. Arriving at the picturesque dam and spillway at 2.3 mi, descend, and cross footbridge below the dam. From there, a return to the visitor center can be made on the 0.3-mi *Awareness Trail,* which is marked in red, paved, and graded for wheelchair use; or, return can be made on the 0.1-mi spillway route to the junction with the *Beaver Lake Trail.*

Another route, for a circuit of 3.8 mi to include half of the *Beaver Lake Trail,* is to follow the trail signs for *Beaver Lake Trail* from the visitor center to the junction with the *Ground Pine Nature Trail* at 0.3 mi. Turn R on the *Ground Pine Nature Trail* and go 0.2 mi to Crosstic Rd, a bicycle trail. Turn L and follow the green-blazed bicycle trail across a cut L to Horner Road. Turn L again on Bottoms Rd and, 2.2 mi from the visitor center, turn L off the bicycle trail onto *Third Branch Trail.* Go 0.2 mi and make connections with the *Beaver Lake Trail.* At that point you may turn R or L for the return to the visitor center.

Support Facilities: Full camping facilities are open in the park from April 1 through December 1. A commercial campground nearby is Green Acres Campground, at Rte 4, Box 499C, Petersburg, VA 23803; tel: 804-732-9875. Open all year, full service, no recreational facilities. Location is 4 mi S on US 1 from the junction of I-85 and US 1.

Information: Contact Park Superintendent, Pocahontas State Park, 10300 Beach Rd, Chesterfield, VA 23832; tel: 804-796-4255.

Staunton River State Park
Halifax County

Containing 1,287 acres of forest, meadows, and shorelines, the Staunton River State Park forms a peninsula into the 48,000-acre John H. Kerr Reservoir (also called Buggs Island Lake). By boat, it is about 15 min upstream from the Occoneechee State Park. The park's history is associated with the Occoneechee Indians, who once controlled the area but were almost all annihilated or driven into North Carolina by Nathaniel Bacon in 1675. Bacon's marauders were taking revenge on Indians in general for the Jamestown Massacre. Also in the park area, on June 25, 1864 a Union attack on the Richmond-Danville RR at the Staunton River Bridge was defeated by a Confederate group of old men and boys. And in the late 1880s the Christian Social Colony settled on the peninsula, but it failed to find the expected utopia. Rich in history, the park was established in 1936, one of the six original state parks formed during the Great Depression. The park and river are named in honor of Capt Henry Staunton, who commanded a company of soldiers to protect the early settlers from Indian attacks before the Revolutionary War. Multiple facilities include campsites, vacation cabins, an Olympic-size swimming pool, bathrooms, boat rentals and ramps, playgrounds, a visitor center, and nearly 10 mi of hiking trails. Also, activities include picnicking, fishing, tennis, interpretive tours, and nature study.

Access: From US 58 and VA 304 junction E of South Boston, go N on VA 304 for 5.3 mi to SR 613. Turn R on SR 613 and go 2.8 mi to Scottsburg. Turn R on VA 344 and go 8 mi to the park entrance.

▼ RIVER BANK TRAIL   704–710

Length: 7.3 mi (11.7 km) rt; easy to moderate. *USGS Map:* Buffalo Springs. *Trailhead:* Parking area near the end of peninsula.

Directions and Description: From entrance of the park drive 1.7 mi to parking area in picnic area near the end of the peninsula. Begin hike on the blue-blazed *River Bank Trail* toward the tip of the park at 0.3 mi. Views of the lake and shoreline are outstanding in all seasons. Follow the blazes R on a wide trail along the Dan River side of the lake through walnut, pines, locust, sourwood, hickory, cedar, and sweet gum. Spring and summer wildflowers flourish.

At 1.3 mi pass the *Tutelo Trail* on R (which leads 0.1 mi to a parking area and information center). At 1.4 mi and 1.8 mi pass through picnic areas. At 2.3 mi pass the *Crow's Nest Trail* on R (which leads 0.4 mi to VA 344 in the center of the park). At 2.8 mi pass the *Robin's Roost Trail* on R (which leads 0.5 mi through a stand of pines to VA 344 in the park). The trail curves away from the lake at 3.3 mi, crosses VA 344 at 4.8 mi, and reaches a junction with the *Loblolly Trail* at 5.5 mi. (The *Loblolly Trail* goes R for 0.6 mi to VA 344.) Continue ahead E along the

Staunton River side of the lake at 6.2 mi, and pass junction with the *Campground Trail* on R (which leads 0.1 mi to Campground A). At 6.4 mi pass the *Capt Staunton's Loop Trail,* with white markers (which goes R for 0.5 mi to loop's trailhead at VA 344). Continue along scenic riverbank to park water plant and boat dock at 7.1 mi. Cross road and return to parking area where hike began at 7.3 mi.

In addition to deer, raccoon, wild turkey, and squirrel, the park also has several varieties of snakes; the copperhead is the only poisonous one. Snapping turtles and eastern box turtles also are seen in the park. During the early spring evenings a hiker can hear an orchestra of frogs—pickerel, bullfrogs, gray treefrogs, and spring peepers. Several species of waterfowl and wading birds, including geese, puddle ducks, diving ducks, osprey, and occasionally a great blue heron, can be seen.

Information: Contact Chief Ranger, Staunton River State Park, Rte 2, Box 295, Scottsburg, VA 24589; tel: 804-572-4623.

State Forests

Virginia has nine state forests, and the central Piedmont has four of them, with a total of more than 50,000 acres. The forests are managed for the purpose of multiple usage to include recreation, timber production, hunting, fishing, watershed protection, and forestry research. Within these forests are several state parks for hiking, camping, picnicking, and swimming. The parks are Holliday Lake, in the Appomattox-Buckingham State Forest; Goodwin Lake–Prince Edward, in Prince Edward–Gallion State Forest; Pocahontas, in the Pocahontas State Forest; and Bear Creek Lake, in the Cumberland State Forest. Of all the state forests, only the last named—Cumberland—has a designated trail system; it has the 10.4-mi *Willis River Trail,* which will extend nearly 20 mi when complete. (Other trails are planned in some of the state forests.) The *Willis River Trail* is a joint project of the Virginia Division of Forestry and Richmond's Old Dominion A.T. Club.

Cumberland State Forest
Cumberland County

▼ WILLIS RIVER TRAIL   711

Length: 10.4 mi (16.6 km); moderate. *USGS Maps:* Gold Hill, Whiteville. *Trailhead:* FR junction with SR 624.

Directions and Description: From US 60 in Cumberland go N on SR 622 for 1.8 mi to junction of SR 623, and take R fork on SR 623 for 2.6 mi to junction of SR 624. Bear R on SR 624 for 1 mi to gated FR on L. Park without blocking gated road. Go through gated road for 40 yds; turn L, following white-blazed trail, and descend on gentle contour to bank of Willis River at 0.5 mi. Veer L upstream on alluvial floodplain through large oaks, poplar, river birch, and sycamore with abundant papaw and spice bush as understory. (Papaw has ripe edible fruit in early September.) Follow along riverbank for 0.4 mi; turn L, following boundary line of 27-acre Rock Quarry Natural Area. At 1.3 mi cross dry stream bed, and at 1.5 mi reach turnaround of seeded road. Turn L on road to gate at 1.7 mi on Rock Quarry Rd. (Here is an exit L on Rock Quarry Rd, extending 0.4 mi to SR 623. A loop on SR 623 and 624 to origin is a total of 4 mi.)

Turn R on seeded road, following trail for 0.2 mi to

cul-de-sac. Enter forest and descend through oaks and beech to bluff and to Willis River at 2 mi. Bear L, leaving river's edge, and go 0.4 mi before returning to river bank. Again bear L from the river; pass an enormous oak, and go through a floodplain with light understory for 0.1 mi to the riverbank. Follow upstream, turn L on seeded road, go 180 yds, turn R off road at 2.9 mi, and reach Horn Quarter Creek. Follow along the edge of the scenic rocky stream to a crossing. Ascend to cul-de-sac of seeded road. Turn L and follow road past a large oak and grazing field on R and deep pit on L. Turkey, deer, pheasant, dove, and quail are often seen here. Turn R off road with pines at 3.5 mi, onto overgrown road. Reach SR 622 at 4.2 mi. Turn L for 65 yds to junction of SR 622 and SR 623. Follow on paved rd, SR 622 (or under power line if not overgrown), for 0.5 mi, to junction of SR 629 at 4.7 mi. (Here, SR 629 leads 0.8 mi to Bear Creek Lake State Park and 3 mi S on SR 629 to trailhead at Winston Lake.) Follow white-blazed path SE into tall stand of pine. Cross *Forest Trail 24* at 5.4 mi. (To R is 0.3 mi to Bear Creek Lake State Park.) At 6 mi begin parallel of the Little Bear Creek; cross it at 6.6 mi. Area has numerous patches of pinesap, ladies tresses, and papaw. Large oaks, beech, river birch, and sycamore are prominent. Raccoon, deer, squirrel, and a wide variety of songbirds have been seen in this area.

Follow around a steep bluff, return to edge of Little Bear Creek, turn R, and pass an open spring under large beeches at 7.3 mi. At 7.4 mi cross Bear Creek FR. (From here a loop can be made for 5.2 mi back to Park Entrance Station by turning R for 1.8 mi to SR 629, then R again.) Cross Bear Creek at 7.6 mi, where large bunches of liverwort are on the rock ledges. Follow open gated FR to Booker FR, turn L, and reach paved SR 628 at 8.5 mi.

Cross and descend gradually to damp area with patches of yellow root and cardinal flowers near a brook at 8.8 mi. At 9.8 mi cross stream in rocky area near old field of young saplings, gentian, and asters. Proceed L (S) of 10-acre Winston Lake on slope through acres of running cedar in mixed forest. At junction with old Civilian Conservation Corps walkway turn R; descend on steps, and cross footbridge to parking and picnic area at 10.4 mi. To the L is SR 629, on which a R turn leads, at 1.2 mi, to junction of SR 628 (a L here leads to forest headquarters); at 2.2 mi to Bear Creek Lake State Park; and at 3 mi to junction of SR 629 and SR 622.

Support Facilities: (See Bear Creek Lake State Park for information on camping facilities.)

Information: Contact Forest Resource Planner, Dept of Conservation and Economic Development, Div of Forestry, Box 3758, Charlottesville, VA 22903; tel: 804-977-6555. Also, State Forest Superintendent, Cumberland State Forest, Rte 1, Box 139, Cumberland, VA 23040; tel: 804-492-4121.

Coastal Division

Chippokes Plantation State Park
Surry County

Chippokes Plantation State Park was established in 1967, but its 1,683 acres across the James River from Jamestown have an agricultural history of more than 350 years. When Captain William Powell first patented the land, in 1612, he named the area in honor of an Indian chief, Choupouke, who had befriended the Jamestown settlers.

Through the centuries the plantation area has retained its original boundaries and plantation atmosphere. It fronts the James River and has more than 600 acres of cultivated and grazing lands. The large, antebellum Mansion was constructed in 1854.

Facilities are for public day use only, with emphasis on the historical interpretation of the area. The park has a visitor center and areas for picnicking, fishing, hiking, and bicycling. The historic buildings and formal gardens also are open for visitors.

Access: From the town of Surry go E on VA 10 for 1.5 mi and turn L on SR 634, which leads for 3.5 mi to SR 664 and the park area.

▼ CHIPPOKES PLANTATION LOOP TRAIL   712

Length: 2.2 mi (3.5 km); easy. *USGS Maps:* Surry, Hog Island. *Trailhead:* Parking area near the Mansion.

Directions and Description: From the Mansion's front yard enter the gate and turn R. Pass brick chimney on the R as you follow the fence on the L. Enter next gate, designed only for walkers. Continue straight ahead, meandering through the woods, and come out above the cliffs overlooking the James River at 0.8 mi. Follow along the cliffs L through pastures and up to the Powell House. Continue SE, returning toward Mansion. (Bald eagles have been seen along this trail.)

▼ LOWER CHIPPOKES CREEK TRAIL   713

Length: 1 mi (1.6 km); easy. *USGS Maps:* Surry, Hog Island. *Trailhead:* Parking area near Mansion.

Directions and Description: Begin this walk to the R of the brick chimney at the Mansion and go E for 1 mi to

Lower Chippokes Creek. Another trail, to the L at the brick chimney, goes N toward Lower Chippokes Creek. Either trail must be backtracked.

Information: Contact Chippokes Plantation State Park Ranger, Rte 1, Box 213, Surry, VA 23883; tel: 804-294-3625.

False Cape State Park
City of Virginia Beach

The 4,321-acre False Cape State Park (as well as nearby Barbours Hill Wildlife Management Area) is one of the few remaining undeveloped areas on the Atlantic Coast. A haven for wildlife, it is part of the Atlantic flyway, which aids a huge migratory bird population. It provides the hiker an exceptional opportunity to observe the natural environment; access is only by foot or bicycle through Back Bay National Wildlife Refuge, or by boat across Back Bay. Overnight permits are required; applications must be made in person at Seashore State Park, 2500 Shore Dr, Virginia Beach, VA 23451, at the visitor center. During the warm and hot seasons hikers should take adequate insect repellents. All drinking water must be carried in.

Access: Take SR 629 in Sandbridge S to the parking area in the Back Bay National Wildlife Refuge. Hike 6 mi through the refuge to False Cape. If you come with a boat, drive S on SR 615 (Princess Anne Rd) from Pungo to SR 622. Follow SR 622 (Mill Landing Rd) to Back Bay boat ramp. Or, continue S on SR 615 and turn L on SR 699 (Back Bay Landing Rd) to Pocahontas Trojan Headquarters boat ramp. Another boat ramp is farther S on SR 615 to Public Landing Rd on the L and to Bay Haven

False Cape State Park. Virginia Division of Parks.

Camp. It is approximately 6 mi across the bay to the park landing at Barbours Hill Boat Dock and False Cape Landing Boat Dock. (Wash Woods Boat Dock in the park is not open to the public.)

▼ FALSE CAPE TRAILS   714

Length: 7 mi (11.2 km); easy. *USGS Map:* Knotts Island. *Trailhead:* Either at Back Bay Refuge parking area or boat ramps off Princess Anne Rd.

Directions and Description: After entry into the park, hike the central trail by Sprett Cove with three spurs to the beach. Backtracking or looping may add extra miles to a hike.

Information: Contact Superintendent, False Cape State Park, PO Box 6273, Virginia Beach, VA 23456; tel: 804-426-7128.

Gunston Hall
Fairfax County

Gunston Hall, the colonial home and plantation of George Mason (1725–1792), is famous for its splendid architectural beauty. Its Palladian room, designed by William Buckland, has been called "the most beautiful room in America." The historic site also includes a number of service buildings, a schoolhouse, and formal gardens. The house and 556 acres were deeded to the commonwealth by Mr. and Mrs. Louis Hertle. Since 1950 it has been open to the public, and in 1961 it became listed on the National Register of Historic Places. Mason is the "Father of the Bill of Rights" for the US Constitution; he drafted a number of documents that have influenced human rights internationally. In the Virginia Declaration of Rights in 1776 he stated "That all men are by nature equally free and independent and have certain inherent rights . . . namely, the enjoyment of life and liberty. . . and pursuing and obtaining happiness. . . ." The facility is managed by the National Society of the Colonial Dames of America.

Access: From US 1 junction with VA 242 (near Lorton) go 3.5 mi on VA 242 to Gunston Hall on L.

▼ BARN WHARF TRAIL   715

Length: 1.7 mi (2.7 km) rt; easy. *USGS Map:* Fort Belvoir. *Trailhead:* W of gardens.

Directions and Description: Follow signs around Deer Park, and on a 25-point interpretive nature trail. After 0.4 mi in the forest take a R to the Wharf Overlook at Gunston Cove. Return to the nature trail on R and back to the formal gardens. Among the plants on this trail are cedar, oaks, pecan, maple, poplar, persimmon, walnut, dogwood, and numerous wildflowers. Some of the animals in the area are mink, otter, turkey, raccoon, bald eagle, and deer. Songbirds are prominent.

Information: Contact Director, Gunston Hall, Lorton, VA 22079; tel: 703-550-9220.

Seashore State Park
City of Virginia Beach

Established in 1936, the Seashore State Park, remarkably preserved in metropolitan Virginia Beach, is one of the state's six nationally designated natural areas. Additionally a national landmark, designated by the US Department of the Interior in 1965, it is also a part of the national recreation trails system, so designated in April 1977.

Rich in ecological succession, the 2,770-acre park has more than 350 species of plants, and the numerous animal species provide an unusual mixture of northern and southern wildlife. The area is also rich in history. Near the park's campground are the Cape Henry Memorial Landing Place of the English in 1607 and the Cape Henry Lighthouse, the first built by the Federal government (1791). Both are in the Fort Story Military Reservation.

Facilities include those for boating, fishing, hiking,

picnicking, bicycling, and nature study; a visitor information center; a large area of 220 campsites for tents and trailers; housekeeping cabins; and a grocery store. The visitor center is open from 8 A.M. to 8 P.M. in the summer. Contact the center for hours during the other seasons.

Access: From the junction of US 60–13 in Virginia Beach go E on US 60, Shore Dr, for 4.5 mi. At a traffic signal turn R on VA 343; or, if entering the campground, turn L.

▼ BALD CYPRESS NATURE TRAIL   716

Length: 2 mi (3 km) rt; easy. *USGS Map:* Cape Henry. *Trailhead:* Parking area at the visitor center.

Directions and Description: Using a guide booklet from the visitor center, follow the red-coded self-guiding-trail signs behind the center, where 40 markers along the trail explain the uniqueness of the water forest, lagoons, plants, fish, birds, reptiles, and dunes. At 0.3 mi pass junction with *Osmanthus Trail*, and at 0.5 mi pass junction of *Lagoon Trail*. At 1.8 mi the yellow-coded *High Dune Trail* is a connector trail of 0.3 mi to the *Main Trail*.

▼ OSMANTHUS TRAIL, LAGOON TRAIL   717–718

Length: 3.2 mi (5.1 km) rt; easy. *USGS Map:* Cape Henry. *Trailhead:* Parking area at the visitor center.

Directions and Description: From the visitor center follow the trail diagram on the boardwalk: first on the *Bald Cypress Trail* for 0.3 mi, and then turn L at the beginning of the blue-coded *Osmanthus Trail*. The trail is wide under heavily draped sections of Spanish moss. At 1.5 mi cross bridge and begin the return on the green-coded *Lagoon Trail*. Rejoin the *Bald Cypress Trail* at 2.7 mi.

▼ MAIN TRAIL   719–721

Length: 10 mi (16 km) rt; easy. *USGS Map:* Cape Henry. *Trailhead:* Parking area at the visitor center.

Directions and Description: Marked with a green code, this wide multipurpose trail is for bicycling and hiking. From the visitor center a section of trail goes N and NW to Broad Bay, returning for a round trip of 2.2 mi. The other section goes SE from the visitor center, passing intersections with the *Bald Cypress Trail* at 0.4 mi, the white-coded, 0.7-mi *King Fisher Trail* on the R at 1.2 mi, and the pink-coded, 2-mi *White Lake Trail* on the R at 2.4 mi. Reach the Campground Contact Station on the R near 64th St at 3.5 mi, cross the road, and follow R along Broad Bay to Narrows Boat Ramp at 5 mi. Backtrack or use vehicle switch.

▼ LONG CREEK TRAIL   722–723

Length: 8 mi (12.8 km) rt; easy. *USGS Map:* Cape Henry. *Trailhead:* Parking area at the visitor center.

Directions and Description: From the visitor center go back on the entrance road (passing 0.5-mi gold-coded *Fox Run Trail* connector trail on the L) to the sign of *Long Creek Trail* on the L. Take the *Long Creek Trail* orange-coded route toward Broad Bay. Cross bridge at 0.5 mi, and after 1.4 mi pass white-coded, 0.7-mi *King Fisher Trail* on L. Turn sharp R at 1.7 mi, the junction with *White Lake Trail*. (*White Lake Trail* continues ahead for 2 mi to connect with the *Main Trail*.) Reach Long Creek signpost at 3.5 mi, a fence at 3.9 mi, and 64th St at 4 mi. It is 0.5 mi L to the *Main Trail* and 1 mi R to the Narrows Boat Ramp. Backtrack or use vehicle switch.

Information: Contact the Park Superintendent, Seashore State Park, 2500 Shore Dr, Virginia Beach, VA 23451; tel: 804-481-2131, office, and 804-841-4836, visitor center.

Westmoreland State Park
Westmoreland County

The 1,295-acre Westmoreland State Park is located on the northern edge of the Northern Neck, a peninsula between the Rappahannock and Potomac rivers in the coastal plain. The area is rich in geological history—a story beginning about 127 million years ago—with remains of ancient marine life found in the beach sediments. The area is also rich in Virginia's political history. Adjoining the park on the E is Stratford, home of the Lees and birthplace of Robert E. Lee. And 8 mi W in Wakefield is the birthplace of George Washington. Early owners of the park property, which the state established in 1936, were Nathaniel Pope, about 1650, and Thomas Lee, in 1716. Facilities in the park include a visitor center, nature center, interpretive programs, campgrounds (but no hookups), vacation cabins, swimming and bathhouse, amphitheater, boat-launching ramp, picnic areas, playgrounds, boat rentals, grocery store, restaurant, and areas for swimming, fishing, and hiking.

Access: From junction of US 301 and VA 3 go 17.5 mi

to VA 347 (5 mi NW from Montross) and take VA 347
into the park.

▼ BIG MEADOW TRAIL,
TURKEY NECK TRAIL   724–726

Length: 4 mi (6.4 mi) rt; easy to moderate. *USGS Map:*
Stratford Hall. *Trailhead:* Parking area near nature
center.

Directions and Description: A brochure from the park
office keyed to the descriptions on the 18 numbered
stakes will provide assistance for the *Big Meadow Trail*.
Hike 0.2 mi on the road from the parking area between
the restaurant and the nature center to a sign for *Big
Meadow Trail* with a red-blazed arrow. Follow old
logging road through forest, which has by succession
returned to being a broadleaf area. Trees such as beech,
oaks, cherry, poplar, sweet gum, hickory, and a few
scattered pines make up the forest. Understory is chiefly
maple, dogwood, sassafras, holly, papaw, and laurel.
Descend steeply near Horsehead Cliffs, and at 0.6 mi
reach the sandy beach of the Potomac River. Area is easy
to explore. Return to the observation deck in "Yellow
Swamp," a term used because of yellow hue in summer. A
biological paradise, area has the sound of numerous
shorebirds, and the American bald eagle nests in the
vicinity. Flowering plants include white mallow, arum,
water roses, and sweet pepperbush.

From the observation deck return on *Big Meadow
Trail*, or take the blue-blazed *Turkey Neck Trail* L up the
swamp. On this trail a R turn can be made at the end of
the boardwalk for a climb to a patch of laurels and,
taking all R turns, a return to the parking area for a

round trip of 2.3 mi. Or, for a shortcut, continue from the boardwalk up the swamp for 0.7 mi to *Beaver Dam Trail* (yellow blazes for 0.3 mi) on R. A complete hike ahead on the *Turkey Neck Trail* completes the circuit to the parking area at 4 mi.

▼ LAUREL POINT TRAIL, RIVER TRAIL,
BEACH TRAIL   727–729

Length: 4.2 mi (6.7 km) rt; easy. *USGS Map:* Stratford Hall. *Trailhead:* VA 347 across from Campground C.

Directions and Description: From the western boundary of the park, enter on the road across from Campground C (VA 347) 0.4 mi from parking area, near restaurant. Hike on orange-blazed trail through forest similar to forest described in previous entry. At 0.6 mi reach Rock Spring Pond on L. Continue ahead through patches of laurel, ending at the park road near the boat launching area at 2 mi. Backtrack, or take road to point of origin for 3 mi. If on the road, go 0.2 mi to picnic area on L for a hike of 0.4 mi on the white-blazed *River Trail*, on R, to vacation-cabins area. From here return to point of origin for total of 3.2 mi round trip. The yellow-blazed *Beach Trail* is a 1-mi round-trip hike from the restaurant parking area to the beach and swimming area on an easy trail.

Information: Contact Superintendent, Westmoreland State Park, Rte 1, Box 53-H, Montross, VA 22520; tel: 804-493-8821.

York River State Park
James City County

York River State Park has 2,505 acres of an area rich in

archeological potential and has a rare estuarine environment. The hiker may wish to examine the exhibits in the visitor center before exploring the natural beauty of dense hardwood forests and marshlands. Facilities include those for boating, fishing, picnicking, and hiking. No camping.

Access: From I-64 (11 mi N of Williamsburg) take Croaker exit N on SR 607; go 1 mi, and turn R on SR 606, continuing 2 mi to park entrance. Visitor center is 1.9 mi farther.

▼ MUSKRAT RUN TRAIL,
TASKINAS CREEK TRAIL   730–731

Length: 2 mi (3.2 km) rt, ct; easy. *USGS Map:* Gressitt. *Trailhead:* Parking area.

Directions and Description: From parking area look for trail signs. The *Muskrat Run Trail* (0.4 mi) circles the visitor center with views from the bluff and from the York River beach. There is also a view of Taskinas Creek. The *Taskinas Creek Trail* (1.6 mi) forms a loop from the S end of the parking area, crosses a marsh on a boardwalk at 0.8 mi, and returns.

Support Facilities: KOA Williamsburg, Rte 4, Box 340B, Williamsburg, VA 23185; tel: 804-565-2907. Full service; recreational facilities; open all year. Access, from the park, is by SR 606 L and to SR 646 R. From I-64 and SR 646 junction take SR 646 N on Lightfoot Rd toward park for 1.5 mi.

Information: Contact York River State Park, Rte 4, Box 329-F, Williamsburg, VA 23185; tel: 804-564-9057.

Part Four

County and Municipality Trails

Wallops Park   732
Accomack County

The Accomack County Parks and Recreation Dept maintains a 0.5-mi loop, *Wallops Park Nature Trail*, in Wallops Park. The trail has mainly beech, poplar, holly, and pines.

Access: Leave VA 175 E of Wattsville, following sign to NASA (Wallops Island Station) on Wallops Rd for 0.3 mi. Park is on L.

Information: Accomack County Parks and Recreation Dept, Accomack, VA 23301; tel: 804-787-3900.

Albemarle County

Albemarle County has four parks—Chris Greene (183 acres), Mint Springs (445 acres), Beaver Creek (190 acres), and Totier Creek (180 acres). All have picnic areas and lakes stocked with bluegill, red-eye sunfish, bass, and channel catfish. A state fishing permit is required for fishing. Swimming is permitted at Chris Greene (N of Charlottesville Albemarle Airport) and Mint Springs (near Crozet) beaches. Paddleboating is allowed on all four lakes. Parks are open from 8 A.M. to

sundown. No camping or hunting. Only Mint Springs has a hiking trail system.

Mint Springs Valley Park

The valley, with a series of three small, terraced lakes, is surrounded by mountains on three sides. The water supply for the town of Crozet flowed from this valley until 1971, when Beaver Creek Reservoir was constructed. Since then the park has become an excellent area for hiking the serene old mountain roads through ruins of old cabins and orchards.

Access: From I-64, exit 20—US 250 junction—go 1.7 mi on US 250 to VA 240 junction. Turn L, go 1.4 mi to Crozet; pass under railroad bridge, turn L, and go 1.8 mi on SR 788, which becomes SR 684, to reach Mint Springs Park on L.

▼ LAKE TRAIL, FIRE TRAIL, BIG SURVEY TRAIL, HOLLOW TRAIL   733–736

Length: 3.6 mi (5.8 km) rt, ct; moderate. *USGS Map:* Crozet. *Trailhead:* Behind beach area.

Directions and Description: The loop *Lake Trail* is 0.5 mi from the picnic shelter, passing to the S of all three lakes. For the *Fire Trail*, begin NW of beach area, ascending on wide trail past cottonwood trees and old stone chimney. At 0.5 mi is junction with *Big Survey Trail* on R. (*Big Survey Trail* is a 0.8-mi loop up a rocky slope of Bucks Elbow Mtn; it rejoins the *Fire Trail*.) Continue ahead on two saddles and a knoll to another junction of *Big Survey Trail*, and begin descent. Junction

with *Hollow Trail* is at 1.1 mi. (*Hollow Trail* is a 0.5-mi connector trail from the picnic area along a stream between Bucks Elbow Mtn and Little Yellow Mtn.) Continue to 1.4 mi where a sharp descent begins for return to the picnic area. Some of the forms of vegetation, in addition to numerous wildflowers, are locust, walnut, oaks, wild cherry, poplar, maple, and tree of heaven.

Support Facilities: Montfair Campground, Rte 2, Box 383, Dept W, Crozet, VA 22932; tel: 804-823-5202. Full service, excellent recreational facilities. Open all year. Access is from downtown Crozet; at junction of VA 240, SR 788, and SR 810, take SR 810 N 9 mi.

Information: Contact Albemarle County Parks and Recreation, 401 McIveire Rd, Charlottesville, VA 22901-4596; tel: 804-296-5845.

Arlington County

Arlington County, the state's smallest (26 sq mi), formed in 1920, is land ceded to the federal government as part of the District of Columbia in 1789, then retroceded to Virginia in 1846. Rich in history and national landmarks —The Arlington House (Custis-Lee Mansion), Arlington National Cemetery, Fort Myer, the Washington National Airport, and the Pentagon—it also has some outstanding recreational areas. For example, the Washington Golf and Country Club, two northern Virginia regional parks, and more than 65 county parks, 7 of which have designated trail systems. Additionally, there are 5 mi of the 40-mi Washington and Old Dominion Bicycle Trail, which follows Four-Mile Run from Alexandria through the county to the city of Falls Church and

beyond, and a 5.5-mi bicycle trail along I-66 that joins the W&OD. Both are also used for hiking and jogging. (It is recommended that hikers unfamiliar with the parks in Arlington first go to the county's parks and recreation office at 300 N Park Dr for orientation and to see the public open-space map. The office also has current information on area campgrounds.) The first three trails listed have a terminus at the Potomac River. USGS quad maps for this area are Falls Church, Washington W, Annandale, and Alexandria.

▼ GULF BRANCH NATURE TRAIL   737

This hike extends 1.3-mi in a 37-acre dense forest with tall poplar, oaks, and maple along Gulf Branch to the Potomac River, 0.5 mi SE of the Chain Bridge. Strangely, this is a serene area amid the continual sounds of jetliners where chipmunks, squirrels, raccoons, owls, and songbirds ignore the noise pollution. Plenty of wildflowers. Gulf Branch Nature Center is an excellent educational facility.

Access: From junction of US 29-211, Lee Highway and Military Rd, follow Military Rd to 3608 Military Rd N. Tel: 703-558-2340.

▼ DONALDSON RUN TRAIL   738

This 1.1-mi trail leads under tall hardwoods, along a stream valley, to the Potomac River. The 44-acre Taylor Park has a 1.5-mi hiking and bicycle trail extending from Military Rd W to Yorktown Blvd. (Adjoining the park near the river is a northern Virginia regional park and the county's Marcey Park, with facilities for swimming and tennis on Marcey Rd.) Forest has understory of haw, maple, and spicebush.

Access: From junction of US 29-211, Lee Highway and Military Rd, follow Military Rd to 30th St. Turn R on 30th St to parking area.

▼ WINDY RUN NATURE TRAIL   739

In a park of 13 acres this 1.4-mi trail runs to the Potomac, only 1.5 mi from the Key Bridge. A remarkable trail, it begins from the parking area in a cul-de-sac of Kenmore St. It crosses a stream three times under large oaks, poplar, and beech. Wild hydrangea, spicebush, and goats beard adorn the trail border. A surprise awaits the hiker at the river, where a glistening stream of water falls 45 ft in a flume. A descent can be made on the R of the stream by a railing to an enchanting part of the forest below.

Access: From the G.W. Pkwy take Spout Run Pkwy to Larcom Lane and go 3 blocks to Kenmore St on R.

▼ LONG BRANCH NATURE TRAIL,
GLENCARLYN PARK TRAIL   740–741

With 98 acres, these two areas connect and provide 1.5 mi of trails to the 8-mi Arlington County Bicycle Trail. (The bicycle trail can also be hiked along Four-Mile Run to facilities including picnic areas, lighted tennis courts, and comfort stations in such parks as Barcroft, Bluemont, Bon Air, and East Falls Church.) Glencarlyn has a nature center with interpretive programs.

Access: 625 South Carlin Springs Rd, between Glencarlyn Elementary School and Doctors' Hospital off Arlington Blvd, S. Tel: 703-558-2742.

▼ LUBBER RUN TRAIL   742

Used both for hiking and bicycling, this short trail—only 0.6 mi—connects Arlington County Parks and Recreation Center at 300 N Park Dr to Arlington Blvd. A wood-chip trail extends downstream, R, from the parks and recreation center; terminus is on N Edison St and the corner of F711. Midway on F711 (parallel with Arlington Blvd), a sign marks entry to the trail.

Access: From Arlington Blvd junction with George Mason Dr, 5 blocks N on L.

Information: Contact Director, Arlington County Parks and Recreation, 300 N Park Dr, Arlington, VA 22203; tel: 703-558-2426.

Brookneal Recreation Park
Campbell County

The Brookneal Recreation Park is a joint project of the Virginia Outdoors Fund, the Town of Brookneal, the Commonwealth of Virginia Commission on Outdoor Recreation, and the Campbell County Recreational Department. Facilities include four tennis courts, two lighted baseball fields, volleyball courts, horseshoe pits, picnicking areas, nature study areas, and hiking trails. The county is in the process of developing a park along the Staunton River near Long Island. (Red Hill, the Patrick Henry Shrine, is located 3 mi E of the town on SR 600 and 2 mi S on SR 619. The restored family cottage and outbuildings are open daily. Tel: 804-376-2044.)

Access: On US 501 in Brookneal turn onto Caroline Ave, SR 1116, in front of the Ford Tractor Equipment Co, and go 0.2 mi to the park entrance.

▼ FALLING RIVER TRAIL   743

Length: 2.6 mi (4.2 km) rt; easy to moderate. *USGS Map:* Brookneal. *Trailhead:* Ballfield parking lot.

Directions and Description: From the baseball field descend through young mixed forest to stream, crossing an old jeep road at 0.1 mi. At 0.3 mi descend from the end of the old road through large trees of gum, birch, and poplar to the bank of Falling River. Turn L, and follow up the tranquil river of flat water to an underground gas pipeline at 1.1 mi. At 1.3 mi reach a rocky bluff area over the river amid mountain laurel and wildflowers. Backtrack.

▼ LAKE TRAIL   744

Length: 0.5 mi (0.8 km); easy. *USGS Map:* Brookneal. *Trailhead:* Ballfield parking area.

Directions and Description: Follow the trail in either direction around the lake, through the picnic area and for a short section upstream. Trail is well graded.

Information: Contact Director, Campbell County Dept of Recreation, PO Box 369, Rustburg, VA 24588; tel: 804-847-0961.

Rockwood Park
Chesterfield County

The 162-acre Rockwood Park, Chesterfield's first,

opened in 1975. Its facilities are expansive, with nine picnic areas; ball courts and fields; physical fitness trail and hiking trails; and areas for tennis, football, and volleyball. Unique features are an archery range and an area for community vegetable garden plots.

Access: From US 360 and SR 653 junction, SW of Richmond, take SR 653 N for 0.1 mi and turn R to park entrance. Continue for 0.4 mi to parking area for trail entrance.

▼ ROCKWOOD NATURE TRAILS   745–746

Length: 3.4 mi (5.4 km) rt, ct; easy. *USGS Map:* Chesterfield. *Trailhead:* Trails parking area.

Directions and Description: Enter at the YCC trails sign and follow white blaze. At 0.1 mi a blue-marked trail is on the L and a green-marked trail on the R. White-blazed trail ends at 0.3 mi; an orange-marked trail goes both L and R through mature hardwood forest, ferns, club mosses, and wildflowers. If taking the R, follow on the edge of the lake, reaching a paved road for the *Physical Fitness Trail* at 0.7 mi. Follow the road R back to the lake and pick up on the orange-marked trail at 1.2 mi. Pass marsh where there is evidence of former beaver activity. Pass yellow-, blue-, and green-marked trails on the L, reaching gravel road at 1.9 mi. Return to parking area at 2.1 mi. Spur trails make a total of 3.4 mi.

Point of Rocks Park

Opened in 1980, Point of Rocks Park has 182 acres of diverse natural areas and historic significance. The area has been the site of American Indian villages, a colonial plantation, a customs wharf, major Civil War encampments, and red-ochre mining. It now provides facilities for tennis, baseball, softball, basketball, a fitness walk, hiking, picnicking, heritage study, and nature study in the Ashton Creek Marsh. Trails constructed by the YCC in 1980.

Access: From I-95 junction with VA 10, take VA 10 E for 5 mi to SR 746 junction. Turn R and go 2 mi SW to park.

▼ ASHTON CREEK TRAIL, WOODTHRUSH TRAIL, COBB'S WHARF TRAIL   747–749

Length: 1.5 mi (2.4 km) rt, ct; easy. *USGS Maps:* Chester, Hopewell. *Trailhead:* At either of the picnic parking areas.

Directions and Description: Begin at the homestead display and enter the forest at the trail signs. Cross bridge at 0.1 mi and turn R through mature forest of oaks, hickory, beech, gum, holly, and pines. Pass junction where trail extends L and reach Ashton Creek Marsh at 0.4 mi. Follow spur trail on boardwalks to observation deck in marsh of arrow arums and cattails. Return to main trail and reach another observation deck at 0.8 mi with views of Ashton Creek Marsh, and again at 1.3 mi. View the Appomattox River before turning L and returning by a meadow on the L. Reach the other picnic area at 1.4 mi, returning to the parking area. Trails and observation decks well designed.

Information: Contact Director, Chesterfield County Parks and Recreation Dept, PO Box 40, Chesterfield, VA 23832; tel: 804-748-1623.

Fairfax County

The Fairfax County Park Authority, operating on an $11.4-million budget, has more than 925 permanent and seasonal employees to supervise and maintain 290 parks and recreational localities for one of the finest county park systems in the nation.

In 1950, when the Virginia General Assembly passed the Park Authorities Act, the Fairfax County Board of Supervisors lost no time in adopting a resolution to create a park authority. Since then land acquired has amounted to 14,000 acres, in the county's effort to provide the best in services to the citizens of the metropolitan area. The complex and extensive park system provides more than the usual sports facilities, bicycle routes, lakes, and nature preserves; it has parks with a model farm, cultural centers, photographic labs, indoor ice rink, restored landmarks, and historic sites. Along with an incomparable record of wise and effective management, the county has developed a master plan for facilities to serve future generations that is even more impressive. Hikers may wish to examine the master plans and the *Annual Register of Parks and Facilities* at the Park Authority headquarters.

There are 106 parks, which have three nature centers and nine exercise trails among them and, typically, short, unnamed trails of less than 1 mi; descriptions of the county's numerous trails would themselves suffice to fill a volume. For this guidebook a selection of some short and long trails suggested by the Park Authority are described to reflect trail, facility, and camping variety. (Covered in the regional-parks section of this guidebook, Chapter 13—under the Northern Virginia Regional Park Authority, of which Fairfax County is a member—are the *W&OD RR Trail*, Bull Run–Occoquan Regional Park trails, Fountainhead Park Trails, and Pohick Bay Trails. The Great Falls Park N trails and the *Mt Vernon Trail* are listed with national-park trails in Chapter 9, under George Washington Memorial Pkwy. Not covered, by specific request, are 26 trails under the aegis of the 112 private clubs and organizations in the county with recreational facilities.) The county's three nature centers are at Annandale Community Park (see entry); at Riverbend Park (see entry); and at Hidden Pond Park (8511 Greeley Blvd, Springfield, VA 22150; tel: 703-451-9588).

Access to the Park Headquarters: Near junction of I-495 and VA 236, Little River Turnpike, turn off VA 236 (2 blocks E of junction) on Hummer Rd N. Go 2 blocks to 4030 Hummer Rd, Annandale, VA 22003. See also access instructions for individual parks.

Information: See listings for some individual park descriptions that follow, or call park headquarters: 703-941-5000.

Annandale Community Park   750

This park, which adjoins the Park Authority head-quarters, has recreational facilities, the Hidden Oaks Nature Center, and the 0.3-mi loop interpretive *Old Oak Nature Trail*. The trailhead is on the approach R of the nature center, through large white oaks and by a small stream, with scattered gum, pine, mountain laurel, and wildflowers. (Other trails are proposed.)

Access to the Nature Center: The same as for the park headquarters (see preceding description), except on Hummer Rd go 3 blocks from VA 236 to Royce St,

Annandale Community Park, Fairfax County Park Authority.
Allen de Hart.

turn L and go to nature center parking on L at corner of
Linda Ln.

Information: tel: 703-941-5009.

Braddock Road Park

At present there is a 3.2-mi natural service trail for
equestrians and hikers, with plans for additional trails as
the 42-acre park is developed. Terrain is gentle and most
of the forest is young hardwood. The trailhead is at the
parking area on Braddock Rd, SR 620, near a sign for-
bidding unauthorized vehicles.

Access: From SR 620, 1.5 mi SE from US 29–211 in
Centreville, go to 13241 Braddock Rd (between Union
Mill Rd and Clifton Rd, which is SR 645).

Burke Lake Park

In the 883-acre Burke Lake Park a hiker has, in addition
to trails, facilities for tent or trailer camping, fishing (for
bass, walleye, and sunfish), and boating in the 218-acre
lake; also, picnicking, golfing, and bicycling. Open all
year.

Access: From Fairfax city junction of VA 123 and VA
236, Little River Turnpike, go S on VA 123, Ox Rd, for
6.5 mi to park on L. Another access route is from I-95
and Occoquan junction; take VA 123 N for 8 mi.

▼ BURKE LAKE TRAIL   751–752

Length: 6.1 mi (9.8 km); easy. *USGS Map:* Fairfax.
Trailhead: Family campground or marina.

Directions and Description: From the park entrance

and information center, follow road L for 1.2 mi to end of road, and park. Take *Beaver Cove Nature Trail,* hiking 0.7 mi to junction with lake trail. If turning R proceed along lake border through poplar, oaks, ferns, beech, and aspen, and occasional partridge berry beds. Pass family campground and begin gravel physical-fitness trail, which ends, or begins, E of par-three golf course. Cross stream near Burke Lake Rd at 1.8 mi and continue around the lake, reaching the marina at 2.9 mi. Follow trail to dam at 3.8 mi. After crossing the dam continue to follow along the lake edge in and out of coves through hardwoods and scattered pine. Complete loop at 5.4 mi, returning to trailhead on *Beaver Cove Nature Trail* at 6.1 mi.

Information: Contact Burke Lake Park, 7315 Ox Rd, Fairfax Station, VA 22039; tel: 703-323-6600.

Dranesville District Park

Halfway between the Arlington County line and the Great Falls Park on the Potomac River is Dranesville Park, with 337 acres. Mainly a conservation area, its major activities are fishing, hiking, and nature study. (This area is not to be confused with the Dranesville Tavern Park, near the Loudoun County line on VA 7, Leesburg Pike.)

Access: From junction of I-495 and VA 193 go W on Georgetown Pike for 0.7 mi to parking area on R by Scott Run. (Exit from parking area into traffic is dangerous.)

▼ SCOTT RUN TRAIL   753

Length: 2.9 mi (4.6 km) rt; easy. *USGS Map:* Falls Church. *Trailhead:* Parking area.

Directions and Description: Follow frequently used trail downstream near river birch, sumac, dogwood, basswood, and locust with spots of tag alder and redbud. Rock-hop across stream, but notice that the trail can be hiked on either side. Approach a defile with rocky terrain and a steep ascent to the ridge L offering a view of the Potomac. Descend to rocky gorge with pools and cascades. Under a heavy cover of hemlock, mountain laurel, and witchhazel, the mosses and lichens give the ambience of a Blue Ridge Mtns glen. Wildflowers bloom between the base of the cascades and the narrow Potomac River beach. Backtrack to parking area.

Ellanor C. Lawrence Park

This exceptionally beautiful 640-acre park, formerly the Walney Farm, was donated to the county in 1971 by Mrs. Ellanor C. Lawrence and her husband David, who was the founder and publisher of *U.S. News and World Report.* In accordance with Mrs. Lawrence's wishes the park offers a visitor center, sports facilities, historic buildings, archeological sites, and educational programs. A short interpretive trail is near the amphitheatre.

Access: From Centreville at junction of I-66 and Sully Rd, VA 28, go N on Sully Rd to first R, Walney Rd, and to visitor center.

Information: Contact Park Manager, 53300 Walney Rd, Centreville, VA 22020; tel: 703-631-0013 or 631-9566.

Holmes Run Parks I and III   754-755

The 1.3-mi *Holmes Run Stream Valley Trail I* goes from Hockett St parking area off Annandale Rd (which is 1.8

mi SW from Little River Turnpike, VA 236) to Sprucedale Dr off Fern Ln (which is 0.6 mi SE from Columbia Pike, VA 244). The 1.2-mi *Holmes Run Stream Valley Trail III* is a natural service pedestrian footpath running from Columbia Pike, VA 244 (1 mi W of Bailey's Crossroads at junction of VA 244, Columbia Pike, and VA 7) SE, past Glasgow Middle School to Glen Hills Park, E end of Larston Dr.

Lake Fairfax Park

Another of the county's excellent parks for camping is Lake Fairfax Park, with 476 acres, including a 30-acre lake. Open all year. A camp store for tent or trailer camping is on a seasonal schedule. There are 200 campsites, 92 of which have hookups. Other facilities are an Olympic-size swimming pool and areas for fishing and picnicking. At least 3.2 mi of unmarked equestrian, hiker, and cross-country ski trails currently exist, with additional development planned. Entrance to a 0.8-mi nature trail is at campsite C21 beyond the camp store.

Access: From I-495 take VA 7, Leesburg Pike, W for approximately 7 mi to junction of Baron Cameron Ave, and turn L. Go 0.5 mi to park entrance on L, Lake Fairfax Dr.

Information: For campsite information contact Lake Fairfax Park, 1400 Lake Fairfax Dr, Reston, VA 22090; tel: 703-471-5414.

Mason District Park

The uniqueness of this 121-acre park is in the distinctive emphasis here on the changing land, during its 400 years of use from Capt John Smith's occupancy to the construction of I-495. The park has tennis courts, ball fields, picnic areas, but no camping. Facilities are lighted until 11 P.M. A parcourse trail, a hiking trail, and a nature trail —all unnamed—provide a total of 1.9 mi.

Access: From I-495, exit 6E (Annandale), take Little River Turnpike, which is VA 236, E to Columbia Pike, which is VA 244. Turn L and go 1.2 mi to park entrance on R.

Information: Contact Park Manager, Mason District Park, 6621 Columbia Pike, Annandale, VA 22003; tel: 703-941-1730.

Riverbend Park

The 409-acre Riverbend Park is an outstanding preserve for maintaining the natural beauty of the Potomac River shoreline. It has a visitor center overlooking the river and a nature center tucked back in the forest. It is at the nature center that all trails can begin or connect.

Access: From I-495, exit 13, take VA 193, Georgetown Pike, W for 5 mi, and turn R on Riverbend Rd. Go 2 mi on Riverbend Rd to Jeffery Rd; turn R and proceed 1 mi into the park.

▼ PAW PAW PASSAGE TRAIL, POTOMAC HERITAGE TRAIL, UPLAND TRAIL, CENTER TRAIL, DUFF AND STUFF TRAIL 756–760

Length: 5.5 mi (8.8 km) rt, ct; easy. *USGS Maps:* Seneca, Rockville. *Trailhead:* Nature center.

Directions and Description: The green-blazed *Paw*

Paw Passage Trail is a 1.2-mi loop from the nature center connecting with the *Potomac Heritage Trail*. Go L at sign, descending to a spur trail on R for an exhibit area. Pass pond, turn sharply R, and follow the orange-blazed *Potomac Heritage Trail* down the river for 1.7 mi. Along the floodplain grow huge beech, poplar, elm, basswood, birch, and sycamore. In the understory are large patches of papaw (also spelled *paw paw*), holly, ironwood, and spicebush. Wildflowers and ferns are commonplace.

Pass the visitor center and picnic area on way to junction with the red-blazed *Upland Trail*, R. It can be followed back to the nature center on rolling terrain among tall trees and a number of spur trails R and L. Or, after 1 mi farther on Potomac Heritage Trail reach junction with the yellow-blazed *Center Trail* and take it 0.3 mi to the nature center. Back at the nature center the white-blazed *Duff and Stuff Trail* is a 0.2-mi paved, self-guiding walk.

Information: Contact Riverbend Park, 8814 Jeffery Rd, Great Falls, VA 22066; tel: 703-759-9018, or, for Nature Center, 759-3211.

Wakefield and Lake Accotink Parks

Wakefield Park and Lake Accotink Park are connected only by the *Wakefield-Accotink Trail*, which passes by Accotink Creek under the Braddock Rd bridge W near exit 5W of I-495. Wakefield Park's 290 acres provide an exceptionally broad list of outdoor and indoor activities —numbering at least 25. At Lake Accotink, which has 476 acres and is S of Wakefield, facilities emphasize outdoor water sports, picnicking, and hiking.

Access: To Wakefield Park take Woodlark Dr off VA 236, Little River Turnpike, W of I-495 junction, or enter from Braddock R, exit 5, near I-495. For Lake Accotink Park enter from Highland St, which is off Blacklick Rd near junction of I-495 and I-395, or follow Queenberry Ave from Braddock Rd to Henning Ave and turn R on Henning to marina.

▼ WAKEFIELD-ACCOTINK TRAIL   761

Length: 6.1 mi (9.8 km); easy. *USGS Map:* Annandale. *Trailhead:* End of Woodlark Dr.

Directions and Description: Begin hiking N, at the end of Woodlark Dr or from Americana Dr, which is 1.5 mi from the Little River Turnpike, VA 236. (If the latter, note the pedestrian overpass of I-495 prevents parking on Americana Dr near the overpass.) From the overpass the hiker can see the varied activities in the large park. Follow the trail by the recreation building to the parking area and into the forest on a wide trail. Go under the Braddock Rd bridge, following the Accotink Creek S through river birch, sycamore, oaks, ash, maple, poplar, basswood, and a wide range of wildflowers. Pass the marsh, and join the physical-fitness trail for the last 0.7 mi to the marina area.

Information: Contact Wakefield Park, 8100 Braddock Rd, Annandale, VA 22003; tel: 703-321-7080.

Waverly Park   762

The Waverly-Wolftrap Trail is a 6-ft-wide asphalt trail that begins at the Creek Crossing Rd W of Westwood Golf Course and N of the town of Vienna. The trail meanders N for 1 mi to the Old Courthouse Rd. (This trail is also called the *Wolfstream Valley Trail.*) Park address is 1801 Abbotsford Dr, Vienna, VA 22180.

Franklin County Recreation Park
Franklin County

The Franklin County Recreation Park has a playground and facilities for tennis, basketball, picnicking, and hiking.

Access: From junction of US 220 Bypass and VA 40 in Rocky Mount, go 3.8 mi S on US 220 Bypass to junction with SR 619 near the Minute Market. Follow SR 619 E to park entrance on R.

▼ FRANKLIN COUNTY NATURE TRAIL   763

Length: 1.2 mi (1.9 km); easy. *USGS Maps:* Rocky Mount, Gladehill. *Trailhead:* Parking lot.

Directions and Description: From the parking lot near the visitor center follow signs and make a loop around the park through young oaks, maples, and pines. Trail constructed by the YCC.

Information: Contact Franklin County Recreation Dept, Rte 2, Box 98-A, Rocky Mount, VA 24151; tel: 703-483-9293.

Tindall's Point Park
Gloucester County

▼ TINDALL'S POINT PARK NATURE TRAIL   764

Length: 0.5 mi (0.8 km), easy. *USGS Maps:* Claybank,

Yorktown. *Trailhead:* Parking area.

Access: From Yorktown cross the George P. Coleman Bridge on US 17 N and enter Gloucester County. Park on L immediately after crossing the bridge.

Directions and Description: From the parking area at Gloucester Point follow the trail signs to display stations with information on the Revolutionary and Civil war fortifications. A picnic area adjoins the trail.

Information: Contact Gloucester County Parks and Recreation Dept, PO Box 157, Gloucester, VA 23601; tel: 804-693-2355.

Grayson County Recreation Park
Grayson County   765

The Grayson County Recreation Park opened in the summer of 1980, its first phase focusing on a solar-heated swimming pool. A second-phase project involves completion of nearly $300,000 worth of other facilities by 1984. These facilities will include picnic areas, hiking and fitness trails, two lighted ball fields, and tennis courts. Phase-three construction begins in 1984 on a campground and par-three golf course. The current *Grayson County Nature Trail,* a 0.8-mi round trip, begins at the dam and descends to Peachbottom Creek. Backtrack. Vegetation includes birch, hemlock, white pine, rosebay rhododendron, maidenhair fern, and wildflowers.

Access: From the town of Independence go E for 1 mi on US 58 to Morton Rd, SR 1124, and turn L. Follow park signs to entrance.

Information: Grayson County Recreation Dept, PO Box 358, Independence, VA 24348; tel: 703-773-2471.

Poor Farm Park
Hanover County   766–767

The Poor Farm Park is located in the South Anna District near Stagg Creek, behind the Patrick Henry High School and the Liberty Junior High School. The gate at the end of SR 810 is locked at all times except when reservations have been made for use. The picnic and camping area is on a grassy hill with large trees providing a forest cover. Trail entrance is at the W end of the picnic area. Constructed two years ago, the trails are well designed for nature study. The *Patrick Henry Cross-County Trail* is used chiefly by the students at the high school, but others have used an orange-blazed trail as part of the *NRM Nature Trail.* These two trails connect to total 2.8 mi; and other trails, S in the park and up Stagg Creek, connect to 2-mi-plus old logging roads. The forest is mixed, and its understory has a wide range of plants and wildflowers.

Access: From junction of I-95 and VA 54 go W on VA 54 for 4.8 mi to SR 810 and turn L. Gated road is at the end of SR 810.

Information: Contact Director of Parks and Recreation, Hanover Courthouse, Hanover, VA 23069; tel: 804-798-6081.

Cheswick Park
Henrico County   768

Among the parks in Henrico County are Cheswick Park and Crump Park. These areas have trail signs, but the trails are not named. Connecting trails in Cheswick Park include a physical-fitness trail of 0.7 mi. There is also a picnic area and playground under large trees. Near the stream are stands of sweet pepperbush and the white fragrant Virginia sweetspier.

Access: At the junction of I-64 and Glenside NW of Richmond turn on Glenside SW and take Forest Ave, next R. Follow Forest Ave 0.9 mi past Henrico Doctors' Hospital to park entrance on R.

Meadow Farms Museum and Crump Park   769

A newly developed parkland, Meadow Farms Museum and Crump Park has 1.3 mi of red-blazed interconnecting trails. Begin at museum or across from the parking lot at the lake. Other trails are planned.

Access: NW of Richmond, at I-295 and Woodman Ave junction, take Woodman Ave S for 0.3 mi to Mountain Rd and turn R. Follow Mountain Rd through Glen Allen for 1.9 mi to park entrance, R, opposite Courtney Rd.

Information: Contact Henrico County Recreation and Parks Dept, PO Box 27032, Richmond, VA 23273; tel: 804-649-0566.

Carrollton Nike Park
Isle of Wight County

▼ NIKE PARK NATURE TRAIL   770

Length: 0.8 mi (1.3 km); easy. *USGS Map:* Benns Church. *Trailhead:* Near picnic shed.

Access: From junction of US 258 and VA 10–32 at Benns Church, go NE on US 258 to park sign. Turn L on SR 665 to Carrollton and go 3.2 mi; turn L on SR 669 and go 1 mi. Park entrance is on L.

Directions and Description: Follow the trail sign through forest of tall trees with wax myrtle understory to observation deck over marsh to view waterfowl. Return on loop. Facilities at the park include those for baseball, tennis, basketball, boating, fishing, hiking, and picnicking.

Information: Contact Carrollton Nike Park, Rte 1, Box 4, Carrollton, VA 23314; tel: 804-357-2291.

Lancaster County

▼ HICKORY HOLLOW TRAIL   771

Length: 4 mi (6.4 km); easy. *USGS Map:* Lancaster. *Trailhead:* Parking area.

Access: From the town of Lancaster go 0.6 mi E on VA 3 past the Lancaster High School. At junction with SR 604, turn L on SR 604 and go 0.3 mi to parking area on L.

Directions and Description: An exceptionally good example of a trail prepared for educational purposes, the trail has 45 different signs describing with unusual degree of detail the species of trees, shrubs and wildflowers. At 0.2 mi the trail forks L and makes a loop for a total of 4 mi.

Information: Contact Parks and Recreation Dept, PO Box 167, Lancaster VA 22503; tel: 804-462-5220.

Loudoun County

The *W&OD RR Trail* goes 22.4 mi, from Herndon in Fairfax County to Purcellville in Loudoun County. The Red Rock Wilderness Overlook Regional Park, offering a loop route, also is in this county. See descriptions of both of these (the latter under *Loblolly Trail*) under Northern Virginia Regional Parks Authority, Chapter 16.

Information: Contact County of Loudoun, Dept of Parks and Recreation, 18 N King St, Leesburg, VA 22075; tel: 703-777-0343.

Indiantown Park
Northampton County   772

The 52-acre Indiantown Park, on Virginia's Eastern Shore, is a converted US Government camera site. The area has a rich history and is adjacent to an old Indian village and the Pocahontas Farm. Financial assistance from a number of public and private sources as well as volunteer work made it possible for the park to open —the county's first park. Among its facilities are a recreational center, swimming pool for instruction, ball fields, picnic areas, and a nature trail.

The 1.5-mi *Indiantown Nature Trail* begins between the parking lot and the softball field. Forming a loop, the trail passes an Indian burial ground. Vegetation is mostly pine with some hardwoods. An exercise trail is also included.

Access: From US 13 in Eastville, turn E on SR 631 and drive 2 mi to the park entrance.

Information: Contact Director, Northampton County Parks and Recreation Dept, PO Box 847, Eastville, VA 23347; tel: 804-678-5179.

Prince William County

The Prince William Park Authority, created in 1977 from

the previous parks and recreation agency, has 11 completed recreational parks with 1,593 acres. An additional 56 associated recreational areas are at the public schools and Manassas. Veterans' Memorial Park, established in 1969, has a wide range of facilities—ball fields, community center, nature area, picnic grounds, lighted tennis courts, swimming pool, racquetball courts—on its 78.4 acres. No camping.

Access: From US 1 junction with Featherstone Rd in Woodbridge (at Featherstone Shopping Center) go on Featherstone Rd 1.9 mi to park.

▼ VETERANS' MEMORIAL PARK
NATURE TRAIL   773

Length: 0.8 mi (1.2 km); easy. *USGS Map:* Occoquan.
Trailhead: Entrance gate of park.

Directions and Description: The trail has 23 interpretive points with two decks for observation of migratory and local waterfowl, forest succession, wetland plants, flowers, and wildlife. White marsh mallow and water lilies are prevalent in the summer. The area borders the Mason Neck Wildlife Refuge.

Information: Contact Prince William County Park Authority, 12249 Bristow Rd, Bristow, VA 22013. Or, Veterans' Memorial Park, 14300 Featherstone Rd, Woodbridge, VA 22191; tel: 703-491-2183.

Roanoke County

Roanoke County has 40 parks, spread widely in the county on 850 acres. The park system is a combined effort of the Roanoke County School Board and the

Roanoke County Board of Supervisors. The resulting recreational areas have 40 tennis courts, 22 basketball courts, 47 ball fields, 10 football/soccer fields, 13 picnic areas, and 6 nature preserves with hiking trails. More are proposed. Described below are the areas that have hiking trails; brochures are available from the park service.

Cave Springs Nature Area   774

The 0.5-mi, self-guided *Nature Trail* winds through a deciduous forest and emphasizes the plant life used by early settlers for medicine and daily needs.

Access: Turn off VA 419 between US 221 and US 220, onto Chaparral Dr. Park behind the Cave Springs High School.

Glen Cove Nature Area   775

Another 0.5-mi, self-guided *Nature Trail* loops through a 15-acre forest and by a stream. Emphasis here is on herbaceous plants and small mammals.

Access: Via either Cove Rd or Peter's Creek Rd off VA 419 between US 460 and I-81.

Glenvar Nature Preservation Area   776

The county's largest natural area, with 60 acres, also has the longest combined trail mileage. If hiking from the Glenvar High School parking area go 0.4 mi to the N end of the ball field to trail entrance. Follow signs for *Nature Preservation Trail* on a well-graded gravel trail bordered with native stones. Forest cover is chiefly hardwoods and

Virginia pine. Return to the paved road at 0.8 mi, and follow the trail through the woods to the tennis court at 1.5 mi.

Access: From I-81, exit 40, take VA 112 for 0.4 mi to US 11–460. Turn R and go 2.1 mi to SR 643. Turn R and cross over I-81 to junction with SR 828. Turn L and go to school entrance.

Hidden Valley Nature Preservation Area   777–778

The *Six Oaks Trail* and the *Pine Ridge Trail* combine to make a 1.6-mi route excellent for study of forest life.

Access: From VA 419 (halfway between US 460 junction and US 221 junction) turn off VA 419 onto SR 9360, Hidden Valley School Rd. Follow SR 9360 to trail entrance parking area behind Hidden Valley School.

Information: Contact Director, Roanoke County Parks and Recreation Dept, 5929 Cove Rd NW, Roanoke, VA 24019; tel: 703-366-3481.

A. Willis Robertson Park
Rockbridge County

Named in honor of Senator A. Willis Robertson, a devoted conservationist, this park has 581 acres of hills and meadows and a 31-acre lake stocked with bass and sunfish on the E slopes of the Allegheny Mtns. Open from May 20 through September 10, the park has swimming pool and bathhouse, tennis courts, ball fields, and picnic areas. Also, it offers fishing, full-service camping, boating, hunting, and hiking. (One of the sponsoring agencies for the park in addition to the county is the

Virginia Commission of Game and Inland Fisheries.) There are two shelters on 7 mi of connecting trails.

Access: From US 11 junction with VA 251, in Lexington, take VA 251 W for 10.6 mi. Turn L over bridge on SR 770, go 1.3 mi, and turn R on SR 652 to park entry.

▼ SOUTH AND NORTH BOUNDARY TRAILS,
BRANCH TRAIL, RIDGE TRAIL,
LAKE TRAIL   779–783

Length: 7 mi (11.2 km) rt, ct; moderate. *USGS Maps:* Collierstown, Longdale Furnace. *Trailhead:* Between camping sites 25 and 26.

Directions and Description: From camping area pass through sites 25 and 26 to children's playground, where trail signs give directions. Ascend on *S Boundary Trail* for 1.1 mi to shelter, turn R, pass junction on R with *Branch Trail* (which leads in 1 mi to *Ridge Trail*), and reach second shelter at 1.7 mi (by junction with *Ridge Trail* R). Continue on *N Boundary Trail* (or return on *Ridge Trail* for 1.5 mi) to junction with *Lake Trail* at 2.8 mi and second junction with *Lake Trail* near the dam at 3.4 mi. A loop can be completed by taking the *Lake Trail* in either direction to the campground entrance. Among the species of trail vegetation are white and Virginia pine, cedar, oaks, locust, red raspberry, redbud, shagbark hickory, and wildflowers.

Information: Contact Supervisor, Lake A. Willis Robertson Park, Rte 2, Box 208-A, Lexington, VA 24450; tel: 703-463-4164. Or, Rockbridge County Parks and Recreation Dept, Court House Square, Lexington, VA 24450; tel: 703-463-9407.

Curtis Memorial Park
Stafford County

The 565-acre Curtis Memorial Park, dedicated to property donors Jesse and Emma Curtis, is Stafford County's answer to recreational needs for its citizens. The park is exceptionally well landscaped and meticulously maintained. Its facilities are expansive, with an Olympic-size swimming pool, picnic areas, tennis courts, playgrounds, ball fields, amphitheater, volleyball courts, a 91-acre stocked lake for fishing, nature trails, and a wide variety of youth recreation instructional programs. (In addition to Curtis Park, the county has 17 other parks, some affiliated with its public school system.) Paved hiking trails connect in the picnic area, where one section has a grove of large sassafras towering over other understory shrubs. A 1.7-mi exercise trail is planned to open in 1983.

Access: From junction in Fredericksburg of I-95 with US 17, go W 5.2 mi to SR 705. Turn R and drive 0.1 mi, where SR 612 forks; take SR 612 1.9 mi to park entrance, R. The office is 0.3 mi ahead.

▼ CEDAR PATH NATURE TRAIL   784

Length: 0.4 mi (0.6 km); easy. *USGS Map:* Storck. *Trailhead:* Park office parking area.

Directions and Description: For such a short trail this one has an exceptional display of vascular plants—pines, oaks, dogwood, ironwood, holly, gums, cottonwood, wild orchids, wild azalea, red cedar, huckleberry, mountain laurel, ferns, mosses, lichens, and running cedar.

Information: Contact Director, Stafford County Parks and Recreation Dept, Rte 6, Box 451, Hartwood, VA 22471; tel: 703-752-5611.

Alexandria

Although Alexandria was settled in 1670, it was not until surveyors John West, Jr. and George Washington had laid out the streets for the town in 1749 that the area became cosmopolitan, with handsome townhouses near the Potomac River. During the Civil War the city, occupied early by Federal forces, was spared destruction. An all-American city, it is advertised as "the most historic community in the nation." It has a number of museums, historic buildings, and monuments, and more than 30 parks. One of the parks is the 50-acre Dora Kelly Nature Park, with a splendid trail and Nature Center.

Dora Kelly Nature Park
▼ DORA KELLY NATURE TRAIL   785

Length: 1 mi (1.6 km); easy. *USGS Map:* Annandale. *Trailhead:* Parking area.

   Directions and Description: From the Ramsay Nature Center, at the W end of the William Ramsay School on Sanger Ave, follow the interpretive trail S from the parking area. The trail descends to rocky Holmes Run and turns R; it follows the stream and is partially on the bicycle trail. A guidebook describes the 28 numbered posts, which identify the trees, shrubs, flowers, and animal life in a loop of marsh and climax community of oaks and hickory.

Access: From junction of Shirley Memorial Highway, I-395, with Seminary Rd, go (NW) on Seminary Rd to Beauregard St. Turn L (SW) on Beauregard St and go 0.8 mi to Sanger Ave on R, then to parking area behind the Ramsay School.

Information: Contact Director, Ramsay Nature Center, 5700 Sanger Ave, Alexandria, VA 22311; tel: 703-838-4829.

Blacksburg 786

Settled in 1745, Blacksburg has become a university city, with more than 21,000 students enrolled in Virginia Polytechnic Institute and State University (founded 1872). Framed on the NW by the Jefferson National Forest, Blacksburg has a scenic backdrop to complement the pastoral surrounding farmlands. It is also noted for the Smithfield Plantation, the home of three state governors —James P. Preston, John Buchanan, and John Floyd, Jr. Among the facilities operated by the city's Parks and Recreation Dept are the nature center at 725 Patrick Henry Dr, the *Huckleberry Line Trail,* and Ellett Park. The 1-mi physical-fitness and bicycle trail on the old railroad grade—the Huckleberry Line—for which the trail is named extends from the junction of Harrell and Miller Sts to Southgate Dr. Ellett Park is described here.

Ellett Park

Access: From the junction of US 460 and SR 642, follow

SR 642 for 2.3 mi to narrow entrance on R. (Another route is from US 460 on Ellett Rd, SR 603, to junction of SR 642; turn R and go 0.2 mi to entrance on L.)

▼ TURTLE RIDGE TRAIL,
ROCKY RUN TRAIL, OLD FARM TRAIL   787–789

Length: 3.2 mi (5.1 km) ct; easy. *USGS Map:* Blacksburg. *Trailhead:* Parking area.

Directions and Description: From parking area go R on self-guiding blue-blazed *Turtle Ridge Trail* through mixed forest for 1.5 mi, to junction with *Rocky Run Trail.* Turn R on red-blazed trail, walking through a more mature forest with signs emphasizing geological features. Circle for 1 mi, returning to orange-blazed *Old Farm Trail* for a study of an old farm site. After 0.7 mi return to parking area.

Information: Contact Blacksburg Parks and Recreation, 300 S Main St, Blacksburg, VA 24060; tel: 703-961-1135.

Buena Vista

"Welcome to Buena Vista: 6,946 happy people and 4 old grouches," is the message on a commercial furniture sign near the city limit on US 501 South. Not only is it a happy town, at the base of the Blue Ridge Mtns, its name means "good view" in Spanish. Planned carefully by the city's founders, the streets running E and W all are numbered, and those running N and S all bear the names of trees—at least 35 of them. Even the city's main street is named Magnolia Ave. An industrial town, it is also home for Southern Seminary, a two-year private women's college operating successfully for 107 years, and for scenic Glen Maury Park.

Glen Maury Park

An extraordinarily large park for a small town, with 315 acres, the beautiful Glen Maury Park has the following facilities: Olympic-size swimming pool; fully equipped picnic areas; playgrounds; area for bird watching; river frontage; canoes; bicycle, horse, and foot trails; golf course; tennis courts; ball fields; fishing; full-service campsites; a laundry; concessions; a mountaintop pavilion; and an auditorium.

Access: In downtown Buena Vista take 10th St W from Magnolia Ave, US 501, for 0.3 mi to park across the Maury River bridge.

▼ GLEN MAURY NATURE TRAIL   790

Length: 2.2 mi (3.5 km); easy. *USGS Maps:* Buena Vista, Glasgow. *Trailhead:* Parking area at multipurpose building.

Directions and Description: Route follows an interconnecting system of sloping woodland trails that joins the Maury River campground with grassy balds, campsites, and swimming pool. Trail signs indicate direction at forest line.

Information: Contact Director, Glen Maury Park, Buena Vista, VA 24416; tel: 703-261-7321. Or, tel: 261-6121.

Charlottesville

Charlottesville, almost in the center of the state, is the

birthplace of Thomas Jefferson, whose accomplishments include the design and founding of the University of Virginia (1819). Having examined the classical architecture of Europe, Jefferson gleaned the best of what he'd seen and created an academic quadrangle with lawns, white colonnaded buildings, serpentine walls, gardens, and the inimitable rotunda. His home Monticello, 3 mi away, is one of America's most classic architectural designs. Hiking tours are provided at both places and at other historic sites in the area, including the Albemarle County Court House on Court Square. George Roger Clark, of Lewis and Clark fame, was born 2 mi N of the city.

Ivy Creek Natural Area

Charlottesville's Dept of Parks and Recreation and the Albemarle County Dept of Parks and Recreation jointly hold in perpetuity the 215 acres of the Ivy Creek Natural Area for free use by the public to hike and study nature. In addition, the private, nonprofit Ivy Creek Foundation assists the city and county in planning and protecting the preserve. The foundation's recent environmental education project resulted in a list of more than 400 species of plants and 78 species of birds. (A mammal list is being developed.) Garden clubs and civic clubs are also involved, providing community support for landscaping, an information kiosk, reference library, and birdhouses. The 6-mi trail system is graded, well designed, and, where across open fields, carefully mowed.

Access: From US 29, N in Charlottesville, take SR 743, Hydraulic Rd, W for 2.3 mi to entrance on L.

▼ IVY CREEK NATURE TRAIL   791

Length: 6 mi (9.6 km) rt, ct; easy to moderate. *USGS Maps:* Charlottesville W and E. *Trailhead:* Parking area.

Directions and Description: From parking area follow signs past Virginia's first public solar composting rest rooms to restored farm barn. Follow R on blue-marked loop interpretive trail for 0.7 mi, and connect with the white-marked trail. Pass a red-marked trail on L and descend to cascading stream at 0.8 mi. After taking a yellow-marked loop partly along the Rivanna Reservoir return to the white-marked trail at 1.3 mi. Reach junction of red and orange loop-trail markers at 1.4 mi. (If the white-marked trail is continued, pass the 0.1-mi green-marked loop trail at 1.5 mi and junction with the orange-marked trail at 1.6 mi.) To continue on the orange-marked trail follow it R through a mature forest to the peninsula loop and return R on the orange-marked trail to the red-marked loop trail at 3.2 mi. On the red-marked trail cross stream three times, and cross a pipe-line boundary. At 5.6 mi is another junction with the white-marked trail; turn R and return to the parking area.

Pen Municipal Park

Pen Park has 285 acres in a bend of the Rivanna River containing a nine-hole golf course, eight tennis courts, four picnic shelters, a children's playground, large, open playing fields, and a trail network of more than 4 mi.

Access: At the junction of US 250 and Park Street, SR 631, take Park St N, which becomes River Rd after 0.9 mi. Go another 0.6 mi and turn R on SR 768 at Pen Park Sign.

▼ DAN BEARD TRAIL, EAGLE TRAIL,
LIFE TRAIL, E.T. SECTOR TRAIL,
TENDERFOOT TRAIL, STAR TRAIL   792–798

Length: 4.2 mi (6.7 km) rt, ct; easy. *USGS Map:* Charlottesville E. *Trailhead:* Parking area near picnic shelter #1.

Directions and Description: From parking area near picnic shelter #1, go R by shelter on the *Dan Beard Trail* for 0.3 mi to flood plains of Rivanna River and junction with the 1.6-mi *Eagle Trail.* Turn L and follow downstream through elm, locust, cedar, sycamore, oak, sassafras, and honeysuckle to the 0.2-mi *Life Trail* on L. (It ascends to a junction with the 0.4-mi *E.T. Sector Trail,* extending R.) Continue downstream to the 0.8-mi *Tenderfoot Trail* and the junction of the 0.4-mi *Star Trail.* From here take the *Star Trail* L, returning to picnic shelter #2 and the 0.5-mi *Unknown Scout Trail.* Cross field to origin of the hike. (The Boy Scouts of America, Troop 36, placed the trail signs.)

Information: Contact Superintendent, Charlottesville Dept of Parks and Recreation, 1300 Pen Park Rd, Charlottesville, VA 22901; tel: 804-295-7170.

Northwest River Park
Chesapeake

Carefully planned to protect the natural environment and to provide a wide variety of outdoor recreation for the entire family, the 763-acre Northwest River Park was opened on December 4, 1976 by the city of Chesapeake.

Located in the southern area of the city, reaching almost to the North Carolina state line, the park is bounded on the W by Indian Creek, on the S by the

Northwest River, and on the E by Smith Creek. It is an extraordinary laboratory for nature study, with 160 species of birds, 150 species of herbaceous plants (including 7 species of wild orchids), 18 species of ferns and club mosses, 40 species of shrubs, 60 species of trees, and 18 species of vines. Wild mammals are chiefly deer, squirrel, mink, nutria, raccoon, gray fox, otter, and bobcat. There are 18 species of snakes (including 3 species of poisonous reptiles), 9 species of turtles, and 16 species of fish.

Facilities include those for fishing, hiking, nature study, and boating (with access to Chesapeake's 30-mile Scenic Water Trail System); equestrian trails; picnic grounds; a children's play area; a visitor center and museum; and a 104-site campground. The campground is equipped with modern bathhouses, hot showers, laundry facilities, drinking water, and electric outlets.

Access: From the junction of I-64 and VA 168, exit on VA 168 S, Battlefield Blvd, and go 10.3 mi to Indian Creek Rd on L at Green Thumb Market. Turn L and go 4.1 mi to entrance of park on R.

▼ INDIAN CREEK TRAIL   799–800

Length: 4.2 mi (6.7 km) rt; easy. *USGS Map:* Moyock. *Trailhead:* Visitor center parking area.

Directions and Description: From the visitor center follow the trail sign, cross bridge over lake at 0.2 mi, and continue R at junction with *Deer Island Trail*. Cross bridle trail at 0.7 mi, and reach proposed Indian Creek Overlook at 1.4 mi. Pass through large Christmas fern patch and, at 1.6 mi, Moonshine Meadow bridge. Cross Eagle Bridge, and exit at 2 mi at the *Shuttle Trail*,

Southern Terminal. Backtrack, or return on one of the connecting trails.

▼ DEER ISLAND TRAIL   801–802

Length: 2.2 mi (3.5 km) rt; easy. *USGS Map:* Moyock.
Trailhead: Visitor center parking area.

Directions and Description: Follow same route as for preceding *Indian Creek Trail*, but turn L after crossing bridge at 0.2 mi, following old service road. At 0.7 mi cross another bridge and notice sign to Southern Terminal. At 1 mi is junction with *Otter Point Trail* and at 1.1 mi is junction with *Wood Duck Slough Trail*. Backtrack, or return on one of the connecting trails.

▼ MOLLY MITCHELL TRAIL,
WOOD DUCK SLOUGH TRAIL   803–804

Length: 3.2 mi (5.1 km) rt; easy. *USGS Map:* Moyock.
Trailhead: Visitor center parking area.

Directions and Description: Follow trail sign E of the visitor center for 0.1 mi, passing R of Picnic Area #4 at 0.2 mi. Follow trail in low areas sometimes flooded in wet seasons. (The park elevation ranges between 8 and 11 ft.) Tall beech, sweet gum, and oaks have small bamboo as understory. Cross bridge at 1.2 mi, leaving the *Molly Mitchell Trail* at 1.3 mi for *Wood Duck Slough Trail*. Cross the Blue Heron Bridge at 1.4 mi, and reach trail end at the *Shuttle Trail* at 1.6 mi. Backtrack, or return on one of the connecting trails.

▼ FRAGRANCE TRAIL   805

Length: 210 yds (0.16 km); easy. *USGS Map:* Moyock.

Trailhead: Visitor center parking area.

Directions and Description: On the E side of the visitor center the loop *Fragrance Trail* has Braille signs for the visually handicapped. Approximately 35 flowering trees and shrubs have been labeled, some of them planted by the Chesapeake Council of Garden Clubs. (Contact the council at 2108 Haywood Ave, Chesapeake, VA 23324; tel: 804-545-7223.)

Information: Contact City of Chesapeake, Dept of Parks and Civic Center, PO Box 15225, Chesapeake, VA 23320; tel: 804-547-6411. Or, Northwest River Park System, 1733 Indian Creek Rd, Chesapeake, VA 23322; tel: 804-421-7151, or 421-3145.

Colonial Heights

Although not named or designated, there are 2 mi of trails within two Colonial Heights parks—Fort Clifton and White Bank. In historic Fort Clifton interconnecting trails are well designed and maintained under large oaks and pines. Park also has picnic grounds. White Bank has 23 acres by Swift Creek, with playgrounds and facilities for picnicking, tennis, boating, and fishing.

Access: From US 301-1 turn on Ellerslie Ave and go 1.1 mi; turn L on Conduit St and go 1.6 mi to Rockwell St. Turn R and go 0.3 mi to parking area for Fort Clifton. To reach White Bank follow above route except go 1.7 mi on Conduit St and turn L at park sign.

Information: Contact Recreation and Parks Dept, PO Box 62, Colonial Heights, VA 23834; tel: 703-526-3388.

Ballou Park
Danville

An industrial city, Danville is the home for Dan River,

Inc, the largest single-unit textile mill in the world, and is one of the nation's largest bright leaf tobacco markets. The last capital of the Confederacy, April 3–10, 1865, Danville has a museum at 975 S Main St. Its Ballou Park has a playground and municipal rose garden, plus facilities for picnicking, arts and crafts, tennis, and baseball.

Access: On W Main St, US Bus 29, enter Ballou Park and drive to the N end of the park. Watch for trail signs.

▼ BALLOU PARK NATURE TRAIL   806

Length: 0.5 mi (0.8 km); easy. *USGS Map:* Danville. *Trailhead:* Park road.

Directions and Description: Follow signs on a 19-station interpretive loop trail through large hornbeam, sycamore, poplar, gum, and oak forest. Large banks of wild hydrangea, black cohosh, and other wildflowers.

Information: Contact Danville Parks and Recreation, PO Box 3300, Danville, VA 24541; tel: 804-799-5212.

Pinnacles Hydro Development

The Pinnacles Hydro Development is owned by the city of Danville and supervised by the Electric Dept. Two dams—Talbott and Townes—on the Dan River prevent the river from flooding. At the Townes Dam an aqueduct tunnel channels water through the scenic Pinnacles of Dan to the Pinnacles Power Plant downstream. Hiking trails in the development are open to the public, during daylight hours, but a written permit is required. Camping is not usually allowed; however, exceptions are made for experienced hikers and campers. Hikers are reminded by the city of Danville that they enter the gorge at their own risk and hazard.

Access: From US 58 in Meadows of Dan take SR 614 for 3.8 mi to junction with SR 602. Take SR 602 L for 1 mi to parking area for descent to Townes Dam. Another access route is to continue ahead on SR 614 for 1.3 mi to junction with SR 724. Turn L and follow SR 724 for 0.6 mi to a parking area near the edge of the forest. It is also possible to take SR 648 and SR 773 up Kibler Valley from VA 103 to hike up the gorge from the Pinnacles Power Plant.

▼ AQUEDUCT TRAIL   807

Length: 6 mi (9.6 km) rt; strenuous. *USGS Map:* Meadows of Dan. *Trailhead:* Parking area at the end of SR 602.

Directions and Description: From the parking area at the end of SR 602, descend on the paved road for 0.7 mi to the Townes Dam. Climb down the steps to the aqueduct and follow the pipeline to a large trestle over Barnard Creek at 1.7 mi. Follow trail up switchbacks by hemlocks and mixed hardwoods to the intersection with the *Pinnacle Trail* at 2.1 mi. Begin the descent on switchbacks to Kibler Valley and the power plant at 3 mi. Backtrack, or use vehicle switching.

▼ PINNACLE TRAIL   808–809

Length: 2.8 mi (4.5 km) rt; strenuous. *USGS Map:* Meadows of Dan. *Trailhead:* Parking area on SR 724.

Directions and Description: From the parking area on

SR 724 at the edge of the forest, hike on an old jeep road E through rhododendron and hardwoods. As this is the *Old Appalachian Trail* some white blazes may be seen. Follow old jeep road for 0.4 mi, turn off road L, and descend on the trail. Cross the road again at its terminus. Descend steeply to junction with *Aqueduct Trail* at 0.7 mi. (To the R it is 0.9 mi to the Pinnacles Power Plant in Kibler Valley; to the L it is 1.4 mi, descending, to Townes Dam.) Continue ahead on the ridge, crossing a saddle, and begin to climb steeply over precipitous rocks. Reach the highest pinnacle (2,662 ft) at 1 mi. Vegetation consists of scrub pine, mountain laurel, bleeding hearts, galax, serviceberry, ferns, and mosses. The trail is dangerous in wet or icy weather.

Descend, following the *Old A.T.* E over large boulders to the Dan River at 1.4 mi. Elevation loss from the highest pinnacle is 1100 ft. Backtrack. (From here the *Old A.T.* ascends on a steep rocky spine—the Devil's Stairsteps—for 0.8 mi to an old road now called the Busted Rock Wilderness Rd, which is privately owned. The road extends 3.8 mi to state maintenance SR 610, which leads out to US 58. This route should not be hiked unless permission is granted from a resident and the hiker is familiar with the terrain.)

Support Facilities: A nearby commercial campground is Daddy Rabbit's Campground, Rte 3, Box 199, Willis, VA 24380; tel: 703-789-4150. To locate it turn off the Blue Ridge Pkwy at mp 174, near Mabry Mill, onto SR 799. Go 7 mi on SR 799 and SR 727. Full service, recreational facilities. Open April 15–October 31.

Information: Contact Superintendent, Pinnacles Hydro Development, Rte 1, Box K33, Ararat, VA 24053; tel: 703-251-5141. Or, contact John T. Bowman, Ranger,

Rte 2, Box 114, Meadows of Dan, VA 24120; tel: 703-952-2615.

Falls Church

The *W&OD RR Trail* goes for 1.3 mi through Falls Church on its route from Arlington to Purcellville. (See Northern Virginia Regional Park Authority, chapter 16.) The city also has a short hiking trail in Berman Park.

Information: Contact Dept of Recreation and Parks, 223 Little Falls St, Falls Church, VA 22046; tel: 703-241-5077.

Fredericksburg

The area of Fredericksburg was visited in 1608 by Capt John Smith, who recommended it be settled. In 1727 the Virginia General Assembly authorized it to become a town and named it in honor of the Prince of Wales. The town was among the first in 1775 to declare independence of England, and in the Civil War the city was the center of four bloody major battles, changing hands between sides seven times. Many pre-Revolutionary and Civil war buildings remain standing, however, and their grandeur is maintained by the townspeople.

Saint Clair Brooks Memorial Park

The Saint Clair Brooks Park has 211 acres on the N side of the Rappahannock River with facilities for picnicking, fishing, tennis, ball games, and hiking. The trails are unnamed and unmarked but easy to follow. The most scenic, 1.2 mi long, begins at the N corner of the parking area for Picnic Area B. Go to the corner of the woods under a power line and cross a wide bridge. Descend into a deep ravine near a stream where a heavy canopy is formed of tall beech; red, black, and white oaks; and poplar. Beds of skunk cabbage, papaw, and mountain laurel are part of a light understory. Exit at the River Rd, or return. Other paths are along the riverfront, where tall ash, elm, and sycamore tower over a grassy 0.5 mi before trail ascends to connect with the administrative building.

In 1975 Old Mill Park, with 50 acres, was established across the river on Caroline St, and in 1981 a 65-acre complex of ball fields was created on the SE of St Clair Brooks Memorial Park. It was named in honor of John Lee Pratt.

Access: To Saint Clair Brooks Memorial Park in Falmouth, turn off US 1 onto Prince St, then to Butler Rd (junction of US 17 W) and park entrance. For Old Mill Park take Caroline St E off US 1 on S side of Rappahannock River bridge. To John Lee Pratt Memorial Park take River Rd on Carter St, R on Gordon St, L on King St to River Rd and park entrance on L.

Information: Contact Fredericksburg-Stafford Park Authority, PO Box 433, Fredericksburg, VA 22404, tel: 703-373-7909.

Alum Spring Park

The 40-acre Alum Spring Park has facilities for picnicking, a physical-fitness trail, and unnamed trails for exploring the park's unique sandstone cliffs. In the 18th and 19th centuries the area had a water gristmill, flour mill, and sawmill. Water dripping from under the cliffs carries alum, being deposited in crystalline pink, white, and yellow layers on the ground. During Revolutionary times alum was used to preserve meat. A pedestrian swing bridge is over Hazel Run near the park gate to prevent hikers from wetting their feet on the road.

Access: At junction of Alt US 1 and VA 3, William St, take VA 3 for 0.1 mi E to Greenbriar Dr, R. Follow Greenbriar for 0.4 mi to park.

Motts Run Park   810–811

Motts Run Park has an effulgent 126-acre lake where, according to some anglers, the bass, pike, and sunfish always bite, but catching them may be another matter. The orange-blazed *Motts Run Trail*, a 2 mi round trip, was designed and constructed by the YACC (Young Adults Conservation Corps). Its winding and dipping route in an 870-acre hardwood forest begins at the end of the picnic area. At 0.3 mi the trail ascends steeply under a power line; it crosses a bridge at 0.8 mi and officially ends at 1 mi on a precipitous bluff by the lake. The forest walk has huckleberry, filbert, ginger, and trailing arbutus with scattered mountain laurel. Descent to Motts Run is R for 0.1 mi on a faint but scenic trail—an unfinished trail that fell victim to federal cuts in YACC funding.

Access: From I-95 and VA 3 go W on VA 3 for 0.8 mi to Bragg Rd, SR 639, R. Follow SR 639 for another 0.8 mi to SR 618, L. Follow River Rd, SR 618, for 2.3 mi to Motts Reservoir; park is on L.

(A more challenging hike, nearly 14 mi, is *Rappahan-*

nock River Trail. It follows along city property, with few exceptions, on the N bank near an old canal. For ingress to the Rapidan-Rappahannock confluence take US 17 W of I-95 for 6.2 mi to SR 752. Turn L, and go 2.6 mi to end of paved SR 752. Turn R on narrow gravel road for 0.2 mi to major power-line route. From this point access under the power line or on the mud-hole routes is difficult even for some four-wheel-drive vehicles. Obtaining information from the Fredericksburg parks office is recommended before attempting to hike this route.)

Information: For all but Saint Clair, contact Fredericksburg Dept of Parks and Recreation, 408 Canal St, Fredericksburg, VA 22401; tel: 703-373-9411.

Hampton

Settled in 1610, Hampton is a historic city with the claim of being the oldest English-speaking settlement in America. Caught, because of its strategic location, in the wars of 1776, 1812, and 1861, it survived them all. Now it is a center for commercial fishing, national defense, and industry. Langley Air Force Base and the Research Center for NASA are here. It is also known for Hampton Institute (founded 1868), Fort Monroe and the Fort Monroe Museum, and the Syms-Eaton Museum. Its hiking areas are mainly on the beach, at Buckroe Beach, Fort Monroe, and Grandview Preserve.

▼ GRANDVIEW PRESERVE TRAIL   812

Along the Chesapeake Bay beach, this superb trail extends more than 2 mi to Back River, for a round trip of nearly 4.5 mi. The trailhead is at the double-gated entrance at the end of State Park Dr. From here follow the service road through a channel of sumac, myrtle, cattails, and cane past Hawkins Pond R to the beach at 0.6 mi. Turn L along beach to Back River. Backtrack.

Access: At junction of I-64 and Mallory St, near Fort Monroe, go NE on Mallory St to Mercury Blvd and turn L. From here go to Old Buckroe Rd; turn R and follow it to Beach Rd. Turn R on Beach Rd and proceed to State Park Rd on the L.

Information: Contact Dept of Recreation, City Hall, Hampton, VA 23369; tel: 804-727-6197. For Fort Monroe, contact Public Affairs Office, Dept of the Army, HHC Fort Monroe Bldg, Fort Monroe, VA 23551; tel: 804-727-2092.

Herndon   813

The *W&OD RR Trail* has a 2.4-mi stretch through Herndon on its way from Arlington to Purcellville. (See Northern Virginia Regional Park Authority, Chapter 16.) The 0.7-mi *Sugarland Run Trail* connects SR 606, Elden St, to the *W&OD Trail*.

Information: Contact Town of Herndon, Parks and Recreation, 703 Elder St, PO Box 427, Herndon, VA 22070; tel: 703-437-1000.

Hopewell   814

Founded in 1613, the inland port of Hopewell, first named City Point, is the second oldest permanent settlement established by the English in America. Now an industrial city, it also has city parks. One recreational area is Atwater Park, with facilities for picnicking and hiking. A loop trail extends there through a forest of oaks, maple, holly, and mountain laurel for 0.8 mi. This path also serves as a physical-fitness trail.

Access: On VA 36, S Mesa St, in the city, turn on River Rd at WHAP radio station and go 1.3 mi to Atwater Park on R at the city limits.

Information: Contact Dept of Recreation and Parks, Randolph Rd and Main St, Hopewell, VA 23860; tel: 804-458-3211.

Lexington

Founded in 1777, Lexington is the historic county seat of Rockbridge County. It is the home of Washington and Lee University (founded 1749), the nation's sixth oldest, where Robert E. Lee served as president from 1865 until his death in 1870, and also home of Virginia Military Institute (VMI, founded 1839), the nation's oldest state-supported military college, where Thomas J. "Stonewall" Jackson taught military tactics and math for 10 yrs before the Civil War. Both of these Confederate heroes are buried in Lexington.

▼ WOODS CREEK PARK TRAIL   815

Length: 1.3 mi (2.1 km); easy. *USGS Map:* Lexington. *Trailhead:* Parking area SE side of Waddell School.

Directions and Description: From Main St go NW on Jordan St to Highland Rd and turn L to parking area at corner of Pendleton Place near Waddell School. Notice sign and follow wide, graded trail clockwise around the playfield to Woods Creek. Follow downstream, crossing streets, through ash, locust, sycamore, walnut, and scattered pines to the VMI Athletic Field. Continue to connection with the *Chessie Trail* at VMI Island. Backtrack, or use vehicle shuttle.

▼ LEE-JACKSON AND VMI-MARSHALL
TOUR TRAIL   816–817

Length: 2 mi (3.3 km) rt, ct; easy. *USGS Map:* Lexington. *Trailhead:* Visitor parking area on Washington St.

Directions and Description: From Main St go 1½ blocks E on Washington St to the visitor information center and parking area. After receiving guide maps follow 8 blocks of historic Lexington on the Lee-Jackson route to Lee's and Jackson's homes, colleges, churches, and burial shrines. Pass the front campus of Washington and Lee University, regarded as one of the most beautiful campuses in the nation. Continue on the hike to VMI's George C. Marshall Museum and the parade ground to form a loop back to Washington St. A 16-block hike tracing 200 yrs of American history can continue (see guide map) in the residential and business area. Approximate time for combined urban hike is 5 hrs. (See *Chessie Trail* under VMI in Chapter 18.)

Support Facilities: Natural Bridge KOA, Box 148, Natural Bridge, VA 24578; tel: 703-291-2770. Open all year, full service, recreational facilities. Access is at 8 mi S of Lexington at junction of I-81—exit 50—and US 11.

Information: Contact Visitor Information Center, 107 E Washington St, Lexington, VA 24450; tel: 703-463-3777.

Lynchburg

Lynchburg, settled in 1786, overlooks the James River. It was initially a tobacco community; among its first buildings were a ferryhouse and a tobacco warehouse built by John Lynch. An important supply depot during the Civil War, it was successfully defended by General Jubal A. Early in June 1864 from a Union attack.

Now a city of diversified industries, Lynchburg is also the home of five colleges, including Randolph-Macon Women's College (founded 1891), the first accredited college for women in Virginia.

The citywide park system provides a wide range of outdoor recreational activities. Among the parks are Blackwater Creek Athletic Area, with 19.5 acres; Blackwater Creek Natural Area, with 288 acres; Miller Park, with 37 acres; Peaks View Park, with 115 acres; Riverside Park, with 47 acres; and Jefferson Park, with 23 acres. Neighborhood parks provide another 100 acres.

Blackwater Creek Natural Area

This carefully planned and constructed area for preserving the natural environment is located in the heart of the city. A basically undisturbed area, its facilities allow hiking, bicycling, picnicking, and nature study. A proposed natural area would extend upstream to Dreaming Creek and to Burton Creek. (A special athletic area, which includes ball fields, is off Monticello Ave in the natural area.)

The Ruskin Freer Nature Preserve has 115 acres near the center of the natural area. It provides a good example of forestry succession. In this and other sections along the creek and high bluffs of the gorge are oaks, pines, tulip poplar, hickory, beech, dogwood, redbud, syca-more, locust, willow, ironwood, black walnut, maple, ferns, mountain laurel, Scotch broom, and a wide range of wildflowers.

Access: To enter the Ruskin Freer Nature Preserve and Blackwater Creek Natural Area go to the junction of US 29 and 501 and take US 501 N for 0.8 mi to Tate Spring Rd. Turn R and go 0.2 mi to Thomson Dr on L. Follow Thomson Dr to end of street for trail entry on R. No parking in the cul-de-sac. Hiking hours are from 8 A.M. to sunset.

Another access is from the junction of US 29 and Bus 29; take Bus 29 W for 0.9 mi to junction with US 501 Alt, Rivermont Dr. Continue on US 501, Rivermont Dr, for another 0.9 mi to Bidford Ave, and turn L. After 0.7 mi turn L again on Hollins Mill Rd and go for 0.7 mi to the Blackwater Creek Natural Area parking lot. (Other access points are at Cabell St, Jefferson Park, and E Randolph Pl.)

Information: Contact Director, Lynchburg Dept of Recreation and Parks, PO Box 60, Lynchburg, VA 24505, tel: 704-847-1484.

▼ BLACKWATER CREEK TRAIL   818–820

Length: 8.6 mi (13.7 km), easy to moderate. *USGS Map:* Lynchburg. *Trailhead:* Hollins Mill Rd parking area.

Directions and Description: From the Hollins Mill Rd parking area, hike upstream on the paved, wide bikeway. Vehicle shuttle contact can be made at Jefferson Park, off York St; or farther upstream at the trailheads of *Upper Loop Trail* (which is 1.2 mi) or *Creek Loop Trail* (itself 1 mi), at the Thomson Dr access. Hiking is also possible downstream on the bikeway, to Cabell St, downtown.

After hiking and observing this area it is easy to see why the *Blackwater Creek Trail* was designated a national recreation trail by the US Dept of Interior in 1981.

Riverside Park

▼ ALPINE TRAIL   821

Length: 0.25 mi (0.4 km), easy. *USGS Map:* Lynchburg. *Trailhead:* Rivermont Ave parking area.

Directions and Description: From the Rivermont Ave parking area follow the *Alpine Trail* signs overlooking the James River. This is one of the city's oldest parks, and the Miller-Clayton House (1791) and the packet boat *Marshall* are located here. This 47-acre park has facilities for basketball, tennis, and picnics.

Access: From junction of US 501 Alt and US 29 Bus downtown Lynchburg, go W on US 501 Alt, Bedford Ave, until Bedford Ave becomes Rivermont Ave. Look for sign of park on R.

Newport News

A city of more than 150,000 people, Newport News is the base for the Newport News Shipbuilding Co, the largest in the world. Two other cities nearby, Hampton and Norfolk, are together the site of Port of Hampton Roads, one of the world's best deep and natural harbors.

The famed Wars Memorial Museum of Virginia and the Mariners Museum are here. Newport News Park, with 8,500 acres, is the largest municipal park E of the Mississippi River.

Newport News Park

Newport News Park has more than 200 campsites, laundry facilities, picnic shelters, two golf courses, a playground, boat and bike rentals, bike trails, horse trails, an arboretum, horse shows, concerts, hiking trails, and an interpretive center. Nature walks and birding are activities here. Park is open year round. No swimming.

Access: From SR 105, Fort Eustis Blvd, crossing of parallel routes I-64 and SR 143, turn N on SR 143, Jefferson Ave, to park entrance on R.

▼ WHITE OAK NATURE TRAIL, WYNN'S MILL
LOOP TRAIL, TWIN FORTS LOOP TRAIL   822–825

Length: 4.6 mi (7.4 km); easy. *USGS Map:* Yorktown. *Trailhead:* Interpretive center.

Directions and Description: From interpretive center secure a trail guidebook for the 63 stations, follow trail signs for 0.4 mi to the 360-acre Lee Hall Reservoir, and reach the Swamp Bridge at 1 mi. (Notice extensive environmental change and range of flora and fauna.) *Wynn's Mill Loop Trail* (1.1 mi) turns R, rejoining main trail near Old Homesite. At 3.7 mi the *Twin Forts Loop Trail* (0.7 mi), with well-preserved Confederate forts, bears R. Return, crossing long boardwalk at Dam #1 Bridge to regain interpretive center at 4.6 mi.

White Oak Trail, Newport News Park. Mike Poplawski.

Other trails include an *Exercise Trail* of 0.8 mi, with 14 exercise points. Access is from the parking area for fishing—the first entrance on L after entering the park. Fire trails also can be hiked; check park headquarters for regulations.

Information: Contact Park Supervisor, Newport News Park, 13564 Jefferson Ave, Newport News, VA 23603; tel: 804-877-5211.

Norfolk

One of the great seaports of the world, Norfolk also has a great history. Settled in the 17th century, by 1736 it was Virginia's largest town. The British shelled it in 1776, and it fell to Union forces in 1862. By the end of the 19th century it was a prosperous industrial city and, with its sister city, Portsmouth, became the headquarters for the Atlantic Fleet. The city has three large educational institutions—Old Dominion University (founded 1930), Norfolk State College (1935), and Virginia Wesleyan College (1961). Its museums, memorials, historic buildings, festivals, and recreational areas are numerous. An example is the Norfolk Botanical Gardens, described here. Other large parks are Northside and Indian River, neither of which has a designated trail system.

Norfolk Botanical Gardens   826–827

Unsurpassed in beauty, scope, and design, the 175-acre Norfolk gardens-by-the-sea has been home for the annual International Azalea Festival since 1954. There are more than 30 special gardens here, with 12 mi of intertwining trails. Flowering plants are seen throughout the year. This horticultural center for the tidewater area has a quarter-million azaleas of almost every known variety, 700 varieties of camellias, and 150 varieties of rhododendron. Also located here is the Norfolk Public Schools Center for Horticulture.

The gardens were established in 1931 and expanded in 1958. In 1962 a Japanese garden was created, and in 1976 a rose garden was dedicated, with more than 250 varieties and 4,000 rose plants. In addition, the site offers hikers access to the *R. W. Cross Nature Trail* and to the shorelines of Lake Whitehurst and Mirrow Lake. And at least 145 species of birds have been sighted, either as residents or as migratory fowl.

Tidewater-district garden clubs contribute to projects within the gardens; they also sponsor a number of annual flower shows, and they have sponsored the "Sculptures of Nature's Living Things" and a *Fragrance Garden Trail* for the visually handicapped.

A large berm has been constructed on the S side of the gardens' main parking area to reduce the noise from the Norfolk International Airport. Hours of operation of the gardens are weekdays, 8:30 A.M. to 5 P.M., and weekends and holidays, 10 A.M. to 5 P.M. Entrance fee is $1 per person.

Access: Turn off I-64 at Northview Ave and go 1 mi to Azalea Gardens Rd, VA 192, on the L. After 0.6 mi turn R into the Botanical Gardens. Access is also from US 60; turn off on VA 170, Little Creek Rd, and going 1.1 mi, then turn L on the Azalea Gardens Rd, VA 192.

Information: Contact the Norfolk Dept of Parks and Recreation, East Wing, City Hall, Norfolk, VA 23501; tel: 804-441-2400. For the Botanical Gardens administrative office, tel: 804-853-6972.

Norton

Scenic Flag Rock Park's picnic area overlooks the town of Norton, and its unnamed and unmarked trails lead to outstanding views from rock outcroppings with guard rails. A short trail past caves and crevices leads to a view of the American flag high on a large rock formation. Vegetation is mostly hardwoods, rhododendron, galax, mountain laurel, blueberry, and wintergreen.

Access: From downtown Norton at junction of US 58–23 and SR 619 over the railroad bridge, go 2.1 mi on steep, winding SR 619 to park entrance on L.

Information: Contact City Parks and Recreation, PO Box 618, Norton, VA 24273; tel: 703-679-0754.

Poquoson   828

From I-64 and US 17 junction (exit 9), go N on US 17 (Morris Blvd) for 2.5 mi to VA 171 (Yorktown Rd). Turn R on VA 171 and go to junction with VA 172; turn R, then turn L on VA 172 E (Poquoson Ave) to the Municipal Bldg. Turn R, go behind the police station, and enter the Poquoson City Park. Park has excellent swimming pool facilities, plus areas for picnicking, baseball, and hiking. The 0.5-mi *Poquoson Nature Trail* is a serpentine pea-gravel loop trail through forest of gums, oaks, and pines.

Information: Contact Poquoson Parks and Recreation, 830 Poquoson Ave, Poquoson, VA 23662; tel: 804-868-7151.

Portsmouth

Founded in 1752 and taking its name from the town in

England, Portsmouth had a British naval repair station until the Revolution. Since then the station has become the Norfolk Naval Shipyard, the largest in the world. The drydock, still in use, is the nation's oldest (1831); the famous *Merrimac* was built there. It is a city of history and pride, and many of its historic Colonial, Revolutionary, and Civil War period homes are open for tours. It also takes pride in its parks. An example is Sleepy Hole Park.

Sleepy Hole Park

The city of Portsmouth maintains the 18-hole Sleepy Hole Golf Course and Recreation Park, which is actually in the northern area of Suffolk. Facilities in the park include those for boat rental, picnicking, camping, fishing, hiking, and nature study, as well as a playground. The Westwood Garden Club of Portsmouth (associated with the Tidewater District of the Virginia Federation of Garden Clubs, Inc) plans to provide design and maintenance direction for the trails in the park.

Access: From junction of VA 337 and US 58–460–13, in metropolitan Suffolk, take VA 337 N on Nansemond Pkwy. At 4.7 mi turn L on SR 627, cross VA 126 at 6.1 mi, and turn L off SR 627 at 6.7 mi on Sleepy Hole Rd, SR 629. At 6.9 mi reach the Sleepy Hole Golf Course on R; go straight ahead for another 0.6 mi and turn R on SR 749 into the park. If from downtown Portsmouth, take VA 337, Portsmouth Blvd, W for 12 mi and turn R on SR 629.

▼ SPECIAL POPULATION TRAIL   829

Length: 0.2 mi (0.3 km) rt; easy. *USGS Map:* Chuckatuck. *Trailhead:* Parking area.

Directions and Description: After entering the park, drive to the parking area at picnic shelters #10 and #12. The paved trail to the Nansemond River, with benches and observation points, is designed for the handicapped. Flora is chiefly oaks, sassafras, sweet gum, grapevines, and honeysuckle.

▼ MARSH TRAIL   830

This route on an unmarked trail with numerous spurs can begin at the parking area near picnic shelters #22 and #24, near the exit of the *Special Population Trail*, or from the parking area near the park headquarters. Area has great potential; the boardwalk trail in the marsh near the Nansemond River could be reconstructed. Abundant waterfowl seen in the area.

Information: Contact Portsmouth Parks and Recreation Dept, 430 High St, Portsmouth, VA 23704; tel: 804-397-9403.

Wildwood Park
Radford

In the heart of Radford is 32-acre Wildwood Park, a preserve for nature study and hiking. It has four structured, color-coded trails and a number of spurs, which were mostly constructed by a creative YACC in 1980 with a grant from the Virginia Commission of Outdoor Recreation in cooperation with the city's Recreation and Parks Dept.

Access: From I-81 and VA 177 junction, exit 35, go 4.2 mi on VA 177 to US 11 in downtown Radford. Turn L and go a few blocks to the park entrance on the L, immediately past the Tyler Motel entrance.

▼ PINE RIDGE TRAIL,
RABBIT RUN TRAIL, CAVE CIRCLE TRAIL,
MOUNTAIN SPRING TRAIL   831–834

Length: 4.5 mi (7.2 km) rt, ct; easy. *USGS Maps:* Radford N and S. *Trailhead:* Park parking area.

Directions and Description: (If gate is locked go by the Dept of Parks and Recreation for permission.) It is easy to veer off to L at the park entrance and arrive in front of the Tyler Motel, so examine the coded trail design at the R of the entrance before hiking. Begin on the *Pine Ridge Trail* and connect with *Rabbit Run,* where a lookout platform provides a good view. Examine the area for Civil War bunkers, and descend to the creek. Cross the bridge and connect with *Cave Circle Trail*, which later connects with *Mtn Spring Trail*. Depending upon loop completions the mileage will vary. Return to the parking area on the Leisure Ln. Among the vascular plants seen on the trails are hickories, oaks, yellow buckeye, Virginia pine, white pine, locust, white ash, cucumber tree, poplar, mulberry, honeysuckle, bee balm, maples, coltsfoot, and sumac.

Information: Contact Director, Radford Dept of Parks and Recreation, 29 1st St, Radford, VA 24141; tel: 703-639-3051, or 639-4452.

Richmond

Richmond, founded in 1737 by William Byrd, became the state's capital in 1780. Patrick Henry made his famous "give me liberty or give me death" speech here at St. John's Church in 1775. Richmond is a city of extraordinary history; the capitol building's design was

St. John's Church, Old Dominion Trail, Richmond.
Virginia State Travel Service.

selected by Thomas Jefferson, and it houses the oldest continuous legislative body in the nation. The governor's mansion is also in the capitol square. The city was the capital of the Confederacy from 1861 to 1865, and more than 18,000 Confederate soldiers and Jefferson Davis are buried in the Hollywood Cemetery.

Now a modern city of skyscrapers, Richmond continues to be a historic city of Southern pride. It is an educational center—the home for Virginia Commonwealth University (founded 1838), including the Medical College of Virginia; the University of Richmond (1830); Virginia Union University (1865); and Union Theological Seminary (1812). It is an industrial center—for tobacco products, chemicals, textiles, machinery, and printing and publishing—and it is a cultural center, with such museums as the Valentine, Fine Arts, and Edgar Allen Poe, as well as the Museum of the Confederacy.

There are 54 metropolitan parks and recreational areas managed by the Richmond Dept of Recreation and Parks in City Hall. The major parks that have hiking trails are the ones described.

James River Park

Main Section: The James River Park has five riverside and island segments in the western and central areas of the city. Wildlife and botanical variety are abundant, fishing is excellent, and the quality of whitewater sports is superior to that of any metropolitan area in the nation. Picnic facilities are provided, but camping and fires are not permitted. A visitor center, accessible only by foot, is halfway between 22nd St and 42nd St on Riverside Dr.

Access: From junction of Lee Bridge, US 1-301, and Riverside Dr, take Riverside Dr W for 0.3 mi to the parking area on the R.

▼ RIVERSIDE TRAIL, MEADOW TRAIL,
BUTTERMILK TRAIL   835–837

Length: 2.8 mi (4.5 km) rt, ct; easy to moderate. *USGS Maps:* Richmond, Bon Air. *Trailhead:* 22nd St parking area.

Directions and Description: For the *Riverside Trail* begin on the E end of the parking area, climb steps to pedestrian bridge over the Southern Railway, and descend steps at 0.1 mi. Turn L, cross canal bridge at 0.3 mi, and pass the dam crossing to Belle Isle on the R at 0.4 mi. Cross canal bridge on L and turn R on gravel park service road to the visitor center at 0.8 mi. The well-maintained *Meadow Trail* loops the visitor center. Continue ahead and enter forest at 1 mi, pass picnic area at 1.3 mi, and climb the cement steps to the pedestrian bridge at 1.4 mi on the L. (Trail to the R continues to a picnic area at 0.3 mi and to the "Nickel Bridge" at 0.5 mi.)

After crossing the pedestrian bridge, turn R and enter the *Buttermilk Trail.* (A climb up the rock steps leads to the 42nd St parking area.) Follow the *Buttermilk Trail* by the old Netherwood Granite Quarry at 1.7 mi, and cross the park service road at 2 mi. Continue through mature forest, cross Reedy Creek, pass Buttermilk Spring on the R, and complete the loop of 2.8 mi at the 22nd St parking area. Some of the vegetation along the trail consists of red elm, sumac, green ash, papaw, oaks, hackberry, ivy, periwinkle, club mosses, honeysuckle, and tree of heaven.

▼ GEOLOGY INTERPRETIVE TRAIL   838

Length: 0.8 mi (1.3 km) rt; easy. *USGS Map:* Richmond. *Trailhead:* 22nd St parking area.

Directions and Description: Follow the *Riverside Trail* up the steps, across the pedestrian bridge over the railroad, and down the spiral steps. Turn R, follow a cement walkway in places, and end at the abandoned railroad bridge to Belle Isle. Backtrack.

▼ BELLE ISLE LOOP TRAIL   839

Length: 1.7 mi (2.7 km) rt; easy to moderate. *USGS Map:* Richmond. *Trailhead:* 22nd St parking area.

Directions and Description: Follow the *Riverside Trail* up the steps, across the pedestrian bridge, and down to the base. Turn L, and follow up the river to Belle Isle dam at 0.3 mi. Turn R to the Belle Isle Loop Trail by crossing the river rocks or on the rim of the dam to abandoned hydroelectric power plant strainer mechanism at 0.4 mi. Turn L, pass the old picnic site and the quarry pit lake. Follow scenic island edge, where whitewater rapids —some class 4 and 5—can be seen. Reach the remains of the Old Dominion Iron and Steel Factory and the area of the notorious Civil War prison for Federal enlisted men at 1 mi. Pass the site of an 1815 snuff factory, and arrive at the old VEPCO hydro power plant. (A spur trail on the R ascends to the top of the hill.) Return to the "rusty roof" entrance by the strainer mechanism, and descend to the river. (A guide for this trail is available from the visitor center.)

Pony Pasture Section: This area is popular for sunbathing, fishing, hiking, nature study, birding, and innertubing. There are rest rooms and drinking water at the ranger station.

Access: From the junction of Huguenot Rd at the Huguenot Bridge and Riverside Dr take Riverside E, downstream, for 1.8 mi to the James River Park parking area on the L.

▼ PLEASANT CREEK TRAIL,
QUIET WOODS TRAIL, FOREST TRAIL,
RIVER ACCESS TRAIL   840–843

Length: 1.3 mi (2.1 km) rt, ct; easy. *USGS Maps:* Richmond, Bon Air. *Trailhead:* Riverside parking area.

Directions and Description: Begin at the entrance to the wide *Pleasant Creek Trail,* which has jewelweed, spicebush, and young mixed forest. Pass junction with *Quiet Woods Trail,* extending L, at 0.4 mi. Continue ahead in a mature forest of sycamore, poplar, and river birch to the James River at 0.7 mi. Turn L on the spur *Forest Trail* at 0.9 mi for return. Continue ahead on a wide trail in the old Pony Pasture area to the *River Access Trail* and the parking area.

Huguenot Annex Section: Access: From the Huguenot Bridge descend the ramp to Riverside Dr and go upriver to Southampton St parking area. Parking is also possible downriver opposite Oxford Pkwy.

▼ HUGUENOT BRIDGE TRAIL   844

Length: 1.5 mi (2.4 km) rt; easy. *USGS Maps:* Richmond, Bon Air. *Trailhead:* Southampton St parking area.

Directions and Description: From parking area go out to observation point, then follow the river's edge down-river through a mature floodplain forest for 0.5 mi to Rattlesnake Creek. Backtrack. There is also a 0.2-mi spur trail halfway along the trail.

Maymont Park   845–848

Formerly Crenshaw's Dairy Farm, the 105 acres on the edge of Richmond purchased by Maj James H. Dooley in 1886 became his estate, which he renamed in honor of his wife, the former Sallie O. May. At the death of the Dooleys in 1925 this magnificent English country estate was willed to the city of Richmond for "the pleasure of its citizens." It is operated by the private, nonprofit Maymont Foundation and is open free to the public. There are four distinctive trails in the park, totalling approximately 4 mi. The *Historic Walk* has 7 major points of interest, beginning at the carriage entrance and including the Dooley Mansion. On the *Garden Walk* are 15 major areas, which include the Italian garden, Japanese garden, and wildflower garden. More than 50 trees are labeled on the *Tree Walk,* and the *Animal Walk* includes an aviary, small and large mammal habitat, and other zoo features. A detailed map and walking-tour guide is available at the nature center information desk at the entrance from Hampton St.

Access: From the Boulevard, VA 161, in Byrd Park, follow the signs to Hampton St and go S to the park entrance on L. (Trail entrances begin here.) There is also the Spottswood entrance from Shirley St, off the Boulevard in Byrd Park.

Information on Maymont Park: Contact Maymont Foundation, 1700 Hampton St, Richmond, VA 23220; tel: 804-358-7166.

Forest Hill Park

Forest Hill Park adjoins James River Park on the N side and Forest Hill Ave and US 60 on the S side. Forest Hill is one of Richmond's famous seven hills. It has a lake, picnic area with pavilions, tennis court, and nature study area. Unmarked and unnamed trails extend along Reedy Creek, which flows through the park. A 1.2-mi trail follows the old road below the dam to Riverside Dr, where a connection could be made with *Buttermilk Trail.* The park has large poplar and beech trees with banks of wildflowers and shrubs. No vehicles are allowed in the park.

Access: At junction of US 1–301 and US 60, on S side of the Robert E. Lee Bridge, take US 60 W to Forest Hill Ave and 41st St R. Enter near 41st St and Springfield.

Information: There are other parks in the city that have unmarked trails. For example, the beautiful 279-acre Joseph Bryan Park at the corner of I–95 and I–64 W has walkways through gardens of more than 50,000 azaleas. For information on all the preceding city parks except Maymont contact Director, Richmond Dept of Recreation and Parks, City Hall, 900 E Broad St, Richmond, VA 23219; tel: 804-780-8677.

Capitol Square Area

Richmond has three urban trails, with a common focus on Capitol Square. *Old Dominion Trail,* the oldest, is a linear trail of 7.5 mi designed by the Robert E. Lee

Council of the Boy Scouts. The *Richmond Walking Trail* has been designed by the Chamber of Commerce to loop around the Capitol Square at 10 historic sites. For the *Downtown Richmond Trail,* the design has been proposed by Hank Harman, regional director, and Tom Driscoll, treasurer, of the Virginia Trails Association in the summer of 1981. The design is to create a triple loop trail for western, midtown, and eastern areas to emphasize "both the historic and natural interests."

Access: From any of the expressways such as I-95, I-64, I-195, turn off at the proper interchange which has signs for downtown. Follow sign to Broad St and Capitol Square.

▼ OLD DOMINION TRAIL   849

Length: 7.5 mi (12 km); easy to moderate. *USGS Maps:* Richmond, Bon Air. *Trailhead:* Corner 24th St and Broad.

Directions and Description: Begin at the St. John's Church (established 1741) at 24th St and Broad. (It was in this church, in 1775 when George Washington, Thomas Jefferson, and other patriots were assembled at the Virginia Convention to discuss independence, that Patrick Henry made his famous "liberty or death" speech.) After visiting inside the church hike W on Broad to 12th St at 0.9 mi, and turn R to Marshall St, where a R turn leads half a block to the Egyptian Building (the only architecture of its type in America). Backtrack to junction of 12th St, proceed on Marshall St to 11th St, and take a L to Capitol Square. Reach the governor's mansion at 1.2 mi. After leaving the mansion enter the Capitol Building at 1.3 mi. Visit the Old Bell Tower at 1.6 mi, and leave the Capitol grounds by the side gate, which exits on 9th St.

Leaving capitol grounds, turn L and proceed down 9th St to Main St. Turn R and hike on Main St to Monroe Park at 2.4 mi. From Monroe Park pass the Mosque and turn L on S Cherry St. Follow S Cherry St to the entrance of Hollywood Cemetery at 3 mi. Visit the burial sites of James Monroe, John Tyler, and Jefferson Davis. Backtrack to Main St and turn L at 5 mi. Follow Main St to the Boulevard, and turn L on the Boulevard at 6.3 mi. Stay on the Boulevard (VA 161) past the carillon through Byrd Park, and to Shirley St. Turn L on Shirley St at 7.4 mi and turn R for entry into Maymont Park parking area at 7.5 mi. Vehicle shuttle is necessary.

Information: Contact the Boy Scouts of America, Robert E. Lee Council, 900 Westover Rd, Richmond, VA 23220; tel: 804-355-4306 or 804-270-3191.

▼ RICHMOND WALKING TRAIL   850

This loop walk through midtown can take 2 hrs, visiting the 10 historic sites and walking from the origin, at the State Capitol, to the John Marshall House. Circle east on Governor St and to the James River, and return by way of St Paul's Episcopal Church on E Grace, for approximately 1.5 mi. The detailed information and map from the state's Visitor Bureau is a must for this urban hike.

Information: Contact Richmond Convention and Visitor Bureau, 201 E Franklin St, Richmond, VA 23219; tel: 804-649-0373.

▼ DOWNTOWN RICHMOND TRAIL   851

Length: 9.5 mi (15.2 km) rt; easy to moderate. *USGS Map:* Richmond. *Trailhead:* Capitol Square.

Directions and Description: The western loop begins

at the zero mileage marker on the Grace St entrance to Capitol Square. Go W on Grace St, passing St Paul's Episcopal Church and St Peter's Catholic Church. Turn L (S) on 8th St to the Robert E. Lee House (on E Franklin St), and reach the pedestrian bridge over Canal St to Kanawha Plaza at 0.4 mi. Turn R (W) on Byrd St to 5th St; turn L (S) on 5th St through Gamble's Hill Park and to 2nd St. Then turn L (S) on 2nd St, and go to the Virginia War Memorial at 1.2 mi.

Cross the Robert E. Lee Bridge to Riverside Dr and turn R. Follow Riverside Dr to 22nd St entrance of James River Park at 2.7 mi. Continue on the James River Park trails (as described in preceding entry for James River Park) to Westover Hills Blvd and cross the "Nickel Bridge" at 5.6 mi. After another 0.4 mi turn R on Shirley St to the Spottswood entrance of Maymont Park. Follow the park's trails to the Hampton St entrance at 6.4 mi (as described in preceding Maymont Park entry). Turn L (N) on Hampton St to Colorado Ave and go R (E) on Colorado Ave to merge into Harrison St and reach junction with Idlewood Ave. Turn R (E) on Idlewood Ave to Cherry St, where a turn R (S) leads into the Hollywood Cemetery (as previously described for the *Old Dominion Trail,* also in Richmond).

Backtrack on Cherry St to Main St and to Virginia Commonwealth University at 8.1 mi. Turn R (E) on Main St to the Mosque and Monroe Park; pass the park diagonally L to the corner of Belvedere and Franklin Sts. Turn R (E) on Franklin St, passing Hotel Jefferson, the Richmond Public Library, and the Richmond Times-Dispatch Bldg to 4th St. Turn L (N) on 4th St, and after 1 block turn R (E) on Grace St. Reach the Virginia Center for the Performing Arts at 9.3 mi; finish at Capitol Square at 9.5 mi. (The design for the midtown and eastern loops will likely be completed by the time this book is published.)

Information: Contact Virginia Trails Association, 13 West Maple St, Alexandria, VA 22301, tel: 703-548-7490 or 804-264-8524.

Bennett's Creek Park
Suffolk

Bennett's Creek Park, a former US Army Nike Missile Installation, features picnic areas and shelters, boat ramp, fishing and crabbing pier, hiking area, and children's playground. Boat access is from either the Nansemond River or the Hampton Rds areas. Permits and fees are required for use of picnic shelters, and the park is fully open from May 1 through September 30. (Visitors may wish to check on the schedule, as park has been closed on Mondays and Tuesdays in the past.) No camping is allowed.

Access: From the E take Portsmouth Blvd, VA 337, W to Shoulders Hill Rd, SR 626, and turn R. Go 2.2 mi to SR 757, Bennett's Creek Rd, and turn L. Follow SR 757 for 0.9 mi to the entrance of Bennett's Creek Park. From the N, at US 17 and SR 626 junction, go S on SR 626 for 0.9 mi and turn R on SR 757 to the park. From the S, in Suffolk, at the junction of Business US 58-460-13 and VA 337, Nansemond Pkwy, turn N on VA 337 and go to the junction of SR 626, Shoulders Hill Rd. Turn L and go 2.2 mi to SR 757. Turn L on SR 757 to the park.

▼ FLORIDA MAPLE TRAIL   852

Length: 0.9 mi (1.4 km) rt; easy. *USGS Map:* Chuckatuck. *Trailhead:* Parking area.

Directions and Description: From the parking area headquarters, hike on an unmarked but well-graded trail along Bennett's Creek. Cross Locust Bridge; at 0.1 mi cross Gunsmoke Bridge and hike through a grove of beautiful Florida maple trees. Pass through stands of holly, dogwood, sycamore, cedar, locust, sweet gum, water oak, and mountain laurel. From the Upcreek Lookout turn L, and reach the park road at 0.4 mi. Return on the gravel road to the parking area.

Lone Star Lakes

The four manmade Lone Star Lakes—Crane, Butler, Annette, and Crystal—are the focus of a water-resource and recreation project acquired by the city of Suffolk in 1975 from Lone Star Industries. The park area has 490 acres of lake surface and 682 acres of land surface. Developed from marl mining pits, the lakes have freshwater fish, such as largemouth bass, bluegill, and crappie. In addition to facilities for fishing, others are for boating, picnicking, bicycling, horseback riding, birding, and hiking. Hiking is allowed over 10 mi of unpaved roads. The park is open all year but usually is closed on Mondays and Tuesdays. Fees and permits are required. Swimming and camping are not allowed.

Access: From Suffolk follow VA 10–32 N from the junction of US 58 and the 460 Bypass for 5.8 mi to SR 741, Pembroke Ln, across from the Oakland Elementary School. Turn R on Pembroke Ln. Drive 1.9 mi to Lone Star Lakes entrance. From the N, follow VA 10–32 S to Chuckatuck. In Chuckatuck continue on VA 10–32 0.9 mi from the Holiday Food Store to SR 741, Pembroke Ln, and turn L.

▼ LONE STAR LAKES NATURE TRAIL   853

Length: 0.5 mi (0.8 km) rt; easy. *USGS Map:* Chuckatuck. *Trailhead:* Parking area near park headquarters.

Directions and Description: From the park headquarters begin the hike on R of entrance road, and follow
loop. At 0.2 mi there is an excellent overlook on the R
toward the canal and the marshlands. Ascend and
descend on the dunes, reaching a loop at 0.3 mi. Return
to the road and to the parking area. Among the trees here
are beech, cedar, oaks, locust, sweet gum, and holly.

Support Facilities: A commercial campground near
Bennett's Creek Park and Lone Star Lakes is American
Sportsman Family Campground, Rte 3, Box 92A, Windsor, VA 23487; tel: 804-357-7211. Open all year. Full service, recreational facilities. To reach it, from junction of
US 258 and US 460 go NW 6.5 mi on US 460 to SR 644;
turn L, go 0.7 mi. Turn L on SR 649 and go 2 mi, then
turn L on SR 646. This is about 12 mi W of Smithfield.

Information: Contact the Suffolk Dept of Parks and
Recreation, Rm 203, 441 Market St, Suffolk, VA 23434;
tel: 804-484-3984, ext 322.

Vienna

The *W&OD RR Trail* goes 2 mi through Vienna in Fairfax County. (See Northern Virginia Regional Park
Authority, Chapter 16.) Also some short loop trails exist
in the Vienna city parks.

Information: Contact Dept of Parks and Recreation,
Vienna Community Center, 120 Cherry St SE, Vienna,
VA 22180; tel: 703-938-8000.

Williamsburg

Settled in 1633, Williamsburg is the site of America's

finest Colonial restoration. Restoration was made possible when, in 1926, John D. Rockefeller, Jr and Dr. W. A. R. Goodwin, rector of Bruton Parish Church, shared their visions of archeological development. Now, after years of personal attention and the donation of more than $90 million by Rockefeller, the historical research and construction is nearly complete. Home for the College of William and Mary (founded 1693) and a wide range of historical homes, museums, gardens, and entertainment centers, the city is a must visit. Its Warner Mill Park is particularly attractive.

Warner Mill Park

Warner Mill Park, with 2,000 acres and a 365-acre dual lake, is open for fishing, boating, and canoeing. (A tunnel under SR 645 connects the lakes.) Other activities are picnicking, hiking, and nature study, and the facilities include playfields. A 12-station physical-fitness trail of 0.8 mi begins from parking lot. Park is also a haven for wildlife.

Access: At junction of I-64 and SR 143, Camp Perry exit, turn W and immediately turn R on Rochambeau Dr. Go 1.2 mi, turn L on SR 645, Airport Rd, and go 0.4 mi to entrance on L. (SR 645 connects with US 60.)

▼ LOOKOUT TOWER TRAIL,
DOGWOOD TRAIL   854–855

Length: 6.6 mi (10.6 km) rt, ct; easy. *USGS Map:* Williamsburg. *Trailhead:* Parking lot.

Directions and Description: At lower end of parking lot follow trail signs; at 0.1 mi trails fork. Take *Lookout*

Tower Trail L across old railroad grade to edge of lake, climb L to observation deck in stand of tall beech for view of lake at 0.3 mi, and then continue for loop. At 3.5 mi return to *Dogwood Trail,* cross road, follow loop along northern section of lake, and return to parking lot after 3 mi.

▼ BAYBERRY NATURE TRAIL   856

Length: 1.6 mi (2.6 km); easy. *USGS Map:* Williamsburg. *Trailhead:* Parking lot.

Directions and Description: Begin at the boat dock on floating bridge and hike on self-guided trail with 54 interpretive stakes describing trees, shrubs, and wildflowers. Bayberry, also called wax myrtle, is prominent.

Support Facilities: Numerous commercial campgrounds are in the area. Contact Colonial Williamsburg Foundation, PO Box C, Williamsburg, VA 23185; tel: 804-229-1000.

Information: Contact Dept of Parks and Recreation, 412 N Boundary St, Williamsburg, VA 23185; tel: 804-229-4821 or 229-2855.

Part Five

Regional, Military, College, and Private Trails

Grand Caverns Regional Park
Augusta County

The Grand Caverns Regional Park is one of two regional parks in the Shenandoah Valley. (See following description of Natural Chimneys Regional Park.) Its recreational facilities include a swimming pool, tennis courts, picnic shelters, concession stand, softball field, nature center, and bicycle and hiking trails. Spectacular in subterranean beauty is the Grand Cavern with its 5,000-sq-ft Grand Ballroom, an area visitors have admired since 1806 and the scene of early-19th-century dances. Geologists find some of the formations in the caverns a mystery. All facilities, including the caverns, are open from March 20 to November 30.

Access: From I-81 exit 60 and US 11, go E 6 mi on VA 256 to the town of Grottoes, and turn R on SR 825. Park is to R, across the S River.

▼ GRAND CAVERN NATURE TRAIL   857

Length: 0.8 mi (1.3 km) rt; easy. *USGS Map:* Grottoes. *Trailhead:* Parking area near caverns.

Directions and Description: From parking area near the cavern walkway ascend at trail sign on white-blazed trail through basswood, redbud, oaks, locust, bluebells, goats beard, and honeysuckle. Reach overview of S River valley and the Blue Ridge Mtns at 0.3 mi. A second overview is 200 yds farther. Backtrack.

Information: Contact Grand Caverns Regional Park, Grottoes, VA 24441; tel: 703-249-5705. Or, Upper Valley Regional Park Authority, Rm 205, Professional Bldg, 340 Ohio Ave, Harrisonburg, VA 22801.

Natural Chimneys Regional Park
Augusta County

The Natural Chimneys Regional Park at Mt Solon and the Grand Caverns Regional Park at Grottoes are both owned by the Upper Valley Regional Park Authority of Augusta and Rockingham counties and the cities of Harrisonburg and Staunton. The two parks are a model of regional-park-systems management; user fees make them almost self-supporting. Full-service camping is available from March 19 through November 30. Facilities include swimming pool, picnic shelters, camping store, laundry, and bicycle and hiking trails. The 127-acre park is also an excellent place for birdwatching, with more than 125 species of birds.

The park has two outstanding features. One is a pair of events: the Annual National Jousting Hall of Fame Tournament, held each third Saturday in June, and the Annual Natural Chimneys Jousting Tournament— America's oldest continuously held sports event, staged

Natural Chimneys Regional Park. Allen de Hart.

since 1821—held annually on the third Saturday in August. The other special feature is the group of seven natural limestone chimneys ranging from 65 ft to 120 ft high. More than 500 million yrs old, the majestic chimneys contain iron, magnesium, and chert on the top.

Access: From I-81, exit 61, go 3.5 mi W on VA 257 to Bridgewater. Turn L on VA 42 for 3.8 mi to SR 747. Turn R, go 3.5 mi to Mt Solon and then R on SR 731 for 0.6 mi to park entrance.

▼ NATURAL CHIMNEYS NATURE TRAIL   858

Length: 3 mi (4.8 km) rt; easy. *USGS Map:* Parnassus. *Trailhead:* Visitor center parking area.

Directions and Description: From the visitor center parking area follow sign on R, ascending on graded trail. Pass shelter and a ski slope, and reach chimneys overlook at 1.5 mi. Descend to picnic shelter and parking area. Turn R to follow trail through and around the chimneys where six exhibit signs explain the unique rock formations. Return on road from parking area to visitor center.

Information: Contact Natural Chimneys Regional Park, Mt Solon, VA 22843; tel: 703-350-2510.

Northern Virginia Regional Park Authority
Arlington, Fairfax, and Loudoun Counties, and Cities of Alexandria, Fairfax, and Falls Church

The Northern Virginia Regional Park Authority is the result of combined efforts in the 1950s of a small group of citizens plus the local governments of Arlington and

Fairfax counties and the city of Falls Church. They united to protect some of the natural heritage from suburban encroachment, and their remarkable wisdom and foresight led to organizing the Authority in 1959 under the Virginia Park Authorities Act. Since then Loudoun County and the cities of Fairfax and Alexandria have been added. Functioning under a 12-member board, the Authority plans, acquires, develops, and operates regional parks and other sites, which now number 15. It has an annual budget of $3 million, 63% of which is from revenue-producing sources. Management employs a professional staff of 62, plus more than 200 part-time employees.

The parks provide an extraordinary variety of public recreational activities, ranging from a visit to the historic Carlyle House to swimming, camping, picnicking, fishing, canoeing, and hiking in Bull Run Regional Park. Conventional car camping is also allowed, in Pohick Bay Park. Fountainhead Park has a primitive campground backpackers must hike in to reach. Hikers have a choice of more than 60 mi of forest trails near streams and meadows and rolling countryside, and 44 mi of additional hiking on the *W&OD RR Trail*. A guidebook, the third edition of *Happy Trails*, was published in 1983 with detailed maps; hikers should purchase it from the Authority headquarters to receive maximum benefits from the parks' services.

Access to NVRPA Headquarters: From I-66 junction with VA 123 in the city of Fairfax, go 4.3 mi on VA 123, Ox Rd, to junction of Popes Head Rd, SR 654. Sign is on the corner. (For trailhead access, see note with each trail description.)

Information: Contact Northern Virginia Regional

Park Authority, 11001 Popes Head Rd, Fairfax, VA 22030; tel: 703-278-8880. (See individual trail descriptions for some additional resources.)

▼ WASHINGTON AND OLD DOMINION
RR TRAIL   859–860

Length: 44 mi (70.4 km); moderate. *USGS Maps:* Washington W, Falls Church, Vienna, Sterling, Leesburg, Purcellville, Herndon, Waterford. *Trailhead:* Corner of 19th Rd N and Van Buren Sts in Falls Church.

Directions and Description: (Before planning to hike the entire distance, the hiker should purchase the *W&OD RR Trail Guide*, which has detailed maps to indicate trail access points, parking areas, comfort stations, welcome centers, police stations, fire and rescue departments, and mileage markers. The 48-page guidebook is available from the Authority headquarters.) Begin in Falls Church at junction of N Washington St (Lee Hwy, US 29–211, near I-66) and 19th Rd N to junction with Van Buren St. (A connection can be made here to the *Arlington Four-Mile Run Trail* to connect with the *Mt Vernon Trail*, and to Rosslyn, paralleling I-66.) For the first 16 mi the trail has an 8-ft-wide tread of asphalt, making it easy for hikers, bicyclists, and joggers. Through Loudoun County the surface is bluestone dust. The trail name is from the Washington and Old Dominion RR line, "The Virginia Creeper," whose trains ran this route from 1859 to 1968. The park area is a 100-ft corridor, the slenderest in the state. Vistas along the trail range from views of high-rise condominiums, shopping centers, suburban backyards, and gardens to forests, ponds, bridges, streambeds, meadows, and farms. More than 450 wildflower species and 100 bird species have been identified on or near the trail. Western terminus of the trail is at O St and 21st St (SR 690) in Purcellville, Loudoun County, only 10 mi from the *Appalachian Trail*.

▼ UPTON HILL TRAIL   861

Entry to this 1-mi trail can be either E of the reflecting pool or E of the swimming pool complex, in the 26-acre Upton Hill Park. In a densely populated area the tall poplars and oaks provide a forest oasis.

Access: Enter park on Patrick Henry Dr off 6060 Wilson Blvd in Arlington, near Arlington-Fairfax county line.

Information: Tel: 703-534-3437 (see also for NVRPA).

▼ POTOMAC OVERLOOK TRAILS   862–863

At least 2 mi of trails—one green blazed and joined by an interpretive trail R from parking area, and one blue-blazed trail L that adjoins Arlington's *Donaldson Run Trail*—are in the park's 100 acres. Large oaks and poplars tower over an understory of haw, maple, and dogwood, where rock outcroppings and the Potomac palisades (offering views of Georgetown) are only 5 mi away from the Washington Monument. The park has a nature center.

Access: From the George Washington Pkwy N exit at Spout Run, turn R on Lorcom Ln and go 4 blocks, turning R on Nellie Custis Dr, which becomes Military Rd. After 3 blocks on Military Rd turn R on Marcey Rd into park.

Information: Tel: 703-528-5406 (see also for NVRPA).

▼ LOBLOLLY TRAIL, HEMLOCK TRAIL, HOLLY TRAIL,
SPRUCE TRAIL, WHITE PINE TRAIL,
SWEETBAY TRAIL   864–869

The loop *Loblolly Trail* has five connector trails, for a
total of 3 mi; the trails follow ridges and converge at a
small stream flowing into the Potomac River in the
67-acre Red Rock Wilderness Overlook Regional Park in
Loudoun County. At the NE point of the *Loblolly Trail*
are three overlooks from the sheer cliffs of the Potomac.
A true nature preserve, the area is away from the urban
noise in a tranquil forest with plentiful wildflowers.
USGS quad map, Leesburg.

Access: From US 15 in Leesburg go 1.5 mi E on SR
773, Edward Perry Rd, to park on L. Tel: 703-278-8880.

▼ POHICK BAY TRAILS   870

Two trails, a yellow-blazed one 1.4 mi long, beginning
near park gatehouse, and a blue-blazed one 1.6 mi long,
provide the hiker a loop through a hardwood forest with
scattered pines and laurel in Pohick Bay Regional Park.
Another trail, 0.8 mi and orange blazed, connects the
parking area with the blue-blazed trail between campsites
118 and 119. A number of spur trails connect near the
campground and tidal shore of the bay. ("Pohick" is the
Algonquin Indian word for "water place.") In addition to
hiking, the park has excellent facilities for boating, sailing, birding, and camping. (See Gunston Hall in Chapter
13 and Mason Neck National Wildlife Refuge in Chapter
8 for other trails nearby.)

Access: From US 1 junction with VA 242 in Fairfax
County, go 3.2 mi on VA 242 to park entrance.

Bull Run–Occoquan Regional Parks

The 5,000-acre park and recreational complex of Bull Run–Occoquan is northern Virginia's largest system; it includes four separate areas: Bull Run, Bull Run Marina, Fountainhead, and Sandy Run, stretching 22 mi. Among the facilities are those for hiking and nature study plus 25 mi of shoreline for fishing, boating, lake cruises, and rowboat rentals; picnic grounds; visitor centers; playgrounds; swimming pool; skeet and trap-shooting center; bridle trails; and concerts are held. Camping is allowed in Bull Run, Bull Run Marina, and Fountainhead. (Consult *Happy Trails*, available from Authority office, for specific facilities and activities in each park.) The connecting parks offer more than recreation; they have forest and marshes and lakes both for preserving wildlife and as the water supply for a large segment of the people in the regional-parks area.

▼ BULL RUN–OCCOQUAN TRAIL   871

Length: 17.5 mi (28 km), moderate. *USGS Maps:* Manassas, Independent Hill, Occoquan. *Trailhead:* Between Group Camps B and C in Bull Run Regional Park.

Directions and Description: In Bull Run Regional Park drive to parking area near Group Camps B and C. Begin hike on the blue-blazed trail on the riverside, downstream. A pair of "Siamese sycamores" are joined near the river bank in a forest of ash, walnut, elm, and birch. Cross Cub Run on footbridge, continuing downstream for 8 mi to Hemlock Overlook Park. Pass Civil War sites, and cross state roads and streams to the site of the Orange and Alexandria RR, dating from 1844. Some of the streams (called "runs" or "rundles" if the water channels are above the tidal level) may be difficult to ford in rainy seasons. At Hemlock Overlook the trail is on steep grade, often rocky in hemlock groves. Follow downstream for 3.5 mi to Bull Run Marina, with an exit at the boat ramp or between the visitor center and parking area. From here pass through a group picnic and camping area on an unmarked trail for 6 mi to Fountainhead Park.

Access: From junction of VA 28 and US 29–211 in Centreville, go W 3 mi on US 29–211 to Bull Run Park sign on Bull Run Post Office Rd, SR 621, L, and then 2 mi to park entrance.

Information: Tel: 703-621-0550 (see also for NVRPA).

▼ BULL RUN NATURE TRAIL   872

This 1.5-mi yellow-blazed trail may be the most beautiful wildflower trail in Virginia each April, when Virginia bluebells carpet the forest floor. Many other wildflowers are also in profusion. The trail begins near the visitor center at Bull Run Regional Park and forms a loop by Cub Run and Bull Run. It touches another loop trail—a 1.8-mi white-blazed trail that circles the campground pool and azalea garden. Also, it connects with the blue-blazed Bull Run–Occoquan Trail.

Access: See directions for preceding *Bull Run–Occoquan Trail.*

▼ HEMLOCK OVERLOOK TRAILS   873

At least five short trails totaling 3 mi may be hiked in Hemlock Overlook Park. One extends from the parking lot past the pond. Others, on steep terrain, are spurs from the blue-blazed *Bull Run–Occoquan Trail* at the riverside, and one connects from the Yates Ford Rd to the Old Power Plant and Dam site.

Access: From the Lee highway, US 29–211, junction with Clifton Rd, go S on SR 645 through the small town of Clifton and on to SR 615, 0.7 mi beyond. Turn R and follow SR 615, Yates Ford Rd, to park.

Information: Tel: 703-631-1220 (see also for NVRPA).

▼ BULL RUN MARINA TRAILS   874

Three trails—a 1.3-mi section of the blue-blazed *Bull Run–Occoquan Trail*; a 1.3-mi, orange-blazed trail from the Kincheloe Rd junction with Old Yates Ford Rd parking area; and a 1.2-mi, yellow-blazed trail forming a loop from the visitor center—total 3.8 mi for this park. Both orange- and yellow-marked trails connect with the *Bull Run–Occoquan Trail*. Here, as at other places along the run, is evidence of deer, beaver, wild turkey, raccoon, squirrel, reptiles, and wildfowl.

Access: From the junction in Fairfax City of Ox Rd, which is also VA 123, and VA 236, the Little River Turnpike, go 8 mi S on VA 123 to Henderson R, SR 643. Turn R on Henderson Rd and go 5 mi to Old Yates Rd; turn L on SR 612 and go 1 mi to the park.

Information: 12619 Old Yates Ford Rd, Clifton, VA 22024; tel: 703-631-0549 (see also for NVRPA).

▼ FOUNTAINHEAD PARK TRAILS   875

In Fountainhead Park a 1-mi, yellow-blazed trail, L, and a 2-mi, white-blazed trail, R of parking lot, are circular paths and self-guiding. Hikers wishing to backpack and camp, can take the yellow-blazed trail entry to the 3-mi blue-blazed trail, then follow the blazes over hillsides in the forest, sometimes rocky, to a primitive campground near Lake Occoquan. (Campers must have reservations from the NVRPA headquarters and must register at the park's visitor center.) Vegetation includes river birch, beech, hemlock, hickory, oaks, ash, rhododendron, laurel, ferns, club mosses, and wildflowers. (A 6-mi unmarked trail proceeds upstream to Bull Run Marina. Requiring fords, Wolf Run and other tributaries may be formidable obstacles; request advice from the NVRPA.

Access: From Fairfax City, go 8 mi S on VA 123, Ox Rd, to Henderson Rd, SR 643, and turn R. Go 1.9 mi and turn L on SR 647, Hampton Rd, and continue 1.7 mi to park on R.

Information: 10875 Hampton Rd, Fairfax Station, VA 22039; tel: 703-250-9124 (see also for NVRPA).

15 · US Army Corps of Engineers and Military Areas

US Army Corps of Engineers Areas

John H. Kerr Dam and Reservoir
Mecklenburg and Charlotte Counties

Constructed by the US Army Corps of Engineers, this 50,000-acre lake and 800 miles of shoreline in Virginia and North Carolina provides recreational facilities for camping, boating, and other water sports, fishing, hunting, picnicking, and hiking. A special nature trail is operated by the Corps at the dam.

Access: From US 58, 6 mi E of Boydton, take VA 4 S for 6 mi to the dam. Cross and park at S end of dam near Liberty Hill Cemetery.

▼ LIBERTY HILL TRAIL   876

Length: 0.7 mi (1.1 km); easy. *USGS Map:* Kerr Dam.
Trailhead: Parking lot.

Directions and Description: From the parking lot at the Liberty Hill Cemetery follow the 15 interpretive signs on a loop down to the riverbank through forest of hardwoods including stands of hickory and gum. Scenic views are of Buggs Island and the river channel below the dam.

Information: Contact Resource Manager, John H. Kerr Reservoir, Rte 1, Box 76, Boydton, VA 23917; tel: 804-738-6662 or 738-6633.

North Fork of Pound Reservoir
Wise County

The 4,500-acre North Fork of Pound Reservoir was authorized by Congress in 1960; construction began in 1963, and it became operational in 1966. Operated for the purpose of flood control, it also offers considerable recreational activities—fishing and boating at a 154-acre lake, picnicking, hiking, camping, and nature study—in one or more of nine locations. The two locations which have trails are described below. This mountain area of the North Fork figures in the literary folklore of John Fox's 1908 *The Trail of the Lonesome Pine.*

Hopkins Branch and Laurel Fork Areas

Access: From junction of US 23 and VA 630 (1 mi W of Pound on US 23) go 0.7 mi on VA 630 to the dam and operations headquarters parking area.

▼ LAKESIDE TRAIL   877

Length: 0.5 mi (0.8 km) rt; easy; *USGS Maps:* Jenkins W, Flat Gap; *Trailhead:* Parking area across the dam.

Directions and Description: Ascend a steep slope at the trail sign on a graded area and hike through redbud, sumac, white pine, hemlock, and hardwoods. After ascending a high bluff descend to a grassy and open view of the lake. Backtrack.

▼ HOPKINS BRANCH TRAIL, ACORN RIDGE TRAIL, LAUREL FORK TRAIL, PINE MTN TRAIL   878–881

Length: 6.6 mi (10.6 km) rt, ct; moderate to strenuous; *USGS Maps:* Jenkins W, Flat Gap; *Trailhead:* Parking area at Pound Launching and Picnic Area.

Directions and Description: On the west slope of the mountain near the rest rooms, begin hike on the *Hopkins Branch Trail*. Ascend on it for 0.7 mi, then turn sharply L to Hopkins Branch and a primitive campsite. Turn R; at 1.2 mi *Acorn Ridge Trail* goes L. (*Acorn Ridge Trail* ascends for 0.1 mi, where it forms a loop that leads to scenic overlooks and returns after 1.5 mi.) Continue ahead on *Hopkins Branch Trail* over the ridge, and down to Laurel Fork Primitive Area at 1.7 mi. Good campsite here. *Laurel Fork Trail* crosses both creeks W and, at 0.5 mi, forks L. (To the R fork is *Pine Mtn Trail*, a loop trail.) Follow L for 0.4 mi to Laurel Fork stream, cross, and face a T junction. The trail to the R is *Pine Mtn Trail*; it goes to the top of Pine Mtn, then loops back to *Laurel Fork Trail* after 2.3 mi; to the L the trail descends to the lake. Turn R and ascend on the *Pine Mtn Trail* where numerous northern plants grow, uncommon in Virginia. Descend to return junction with *Laurel Fork Trail*. Turn L and follow trail back to the Pound Launching and Picnic Area for a total of 6.6 mi.

Phillips Creek Day Use Area

The other location of the nine recreational facilities in the

North Fork of Pound Reservoir area that has trails is the Phillips Creek Day Use Area. It has swimming, picnicking, nature study, and hiking.

Access: In Pound on US 23, go W 6 mi on SR 671; turn R to entrance of the facility.

▼ PINE MOUNTAIN TRAIL   882

Length: 1 mi (1.6 km); easy; *USGS Map:* Flat Gap; *Trailhead:* End of picnic area.

Directions and Description: (This trail is not to be confused with the other *Pine Mtn Trail* described above in the Hopkins Branch area, or the *Pine Mtn Trail* in the adjoining Clinch Ranger District of the Jefferson National Forest.) This unique interpretive route has been a National Recreation Trail since 1980. A large directional sign for it is at the end of the picnic area. From here go 1 mi on the loop trail that has an emphasis on a wildlife food plot of autumn olive, bicolor lespedeza, persimmon, and walnut; an old homestead; a white-pine stand; a whiskey-still site; waterfalls; Indian history; and a narrow-gauge railroad bed.

Information: Contact Resource Manager, North Fork of Pound Reservoir, Rte 1, Box 369, Pound, VA 24279; tel: 703-796-5775.

Philpott Lake and Park
Franklin, Henry, and Patrick Counties

The 10,000 acres of Philpott Lake and surrounding lands were authorized by Congress in 1944 to be developed for flood control, hydroelectric power generation, and recreation. Construction by the US Army Corps of Engineers began in 1948, and the project went into full operation in 1953. The clear, blue-green lake encompasses 3,000 acres, stretching 15 miles up the Smith River, and has a shoreline of 100 miles. A total of 5,000 acres are leased to the Virginia Game Commission for wildlife management purposes. Fairy Stone State Park adjoins the area on the W.

Public facilities include boat-launching ramps, nature trails, and areas for fishing, water skiing, picnicking, camping, hunting, and nature study. Camping is allowed in 10 of the 15 recreational areas. Four areas have hiking trails.

Access: From downtown Bassett go W on VA 57 for 2 mi to junction with SR 904. Turn R on SR 904 and go 0.9 mi to park sign and resource manager's office. For the dam and the lake, go another 0.3 mi to the parking area for Dam Overlook.

Philpott Park and Overlook

▼ SMITH RIVER TRAIL   883

Length: 1.4 mi (2.2 km) rt; moderate to strenuous. *USGS Map:* Philpott Reservoir. *Trailhead:* Parking area at Dam Overlook.

Directions and Description: From the scenic Overlook parking area follow the sign, descending on switchbacks, for 0.1 mi to the top of the dam. Continue descending the switchbacks, reaching the base of the dam at 0.3 mi. Follow the 21 interpretive trail signs down the Smith River with a guide booklet provided by the resource manager's office. Reach the end of the trail at 0.7 mi at a large, nine-pronged sycamore. Other vegetation on the trail includes hemlock, beech, poplar, hornbeam, and rhododendron. Backtrack or use vehicle switching.

▼ FISHING BARGE TRAIL   884

Length: 1.6 mi (2.6 km) rt; easy to moderate. *USGS Map:* Philpott Reservoir. *Trailhead:* Parking area at Dam Overlook.

Directions and Description: Walk W, passing the rest rooms on the L, and descend to a parking area at 0.1 mi. Reach the boat-launching site at 0.2 mi, and follow R along the lake on a steep slope in a white-pine stand. Reach the end of the trail at a group campsite, at 0.6 mi, but continue another 0.2 mi to the Group Camp Swim Area. Backtrack. (Camping at Philpott Park requires reservation.)

Goose Point Recreation Area

▼ GOOSE POINT TRAIL   885

Length: 0.5 mi (0.8 km); easy. *USGS Map:* Philpott Reservoir. *Trailhead:* Parking area for swimming.

Directions and Description: From downtown Bassett go W on VA 57, 7.5 mi to SR 822. Turn R and take SR 822 for 5.3 mi to Goose Point Recreation Area. The area has public boat ramps, campground, picnicking, swimming, hot showers, and hiking trails. The trail is from the campground along the lake to the amphitheater for 0.5 mi. Area has mixed forest with scenic views on a peninsula. Portions of this area are open all year.

Jamison Mill Recreation Area

▼ JAMISON MILL TRAIL   886

Length: 0.7 mi (1.1 km) rt; easy to moderate. *USGS Maps:* Ferrum, Philpott Reservoir. *Trailhead:* Picnic area near entrance.

Directions and Description: From the town of Ferrum take SR 623 SW for 3.8 mi to junction with SR 605. Turn L on SR 605 and drive 2.2 mi to junction with SR 778. Turn R on SR 778 and drive 1.9 mi to Jamison Mill. Park at the picnic area on the L by the river. Begin hike across the road on the R side of the river against a rocky bluff. Cross a small bridge in an area of trout lilies, spring beauty, may-apples and ground cedar. Ascend through hemlock forest and, at 0.2 mi, join an old road. Turn L for excellent view of campground below. At 0.4 mi reach paved area for camping, return to the bridge over the river and to the picnic area at 0.7 mi. In addition to picnic grounds and campsites the area also provides swimming and fishing areas, and hot showers. Full service is available from May 28 through September 6.

Salthouse Branch Recreation Area

▼ SALTHOUSE BRANCH NATURE TRAIL   887

Length: 0.5 mi (0.8 km); easy. *USGS Map:* Philpott Reservoir. *Trailhead:* Parking area.

Directions and Description: From the town of Henry drive W on SR 605 for 1.7 mi to junction with SR 798. Take SR 798 on L for 1.4 mi to junction with SR 773. Take SR 773 for 0.4 mi and enter the Salthouse Branch

Recreation Area. Pass the swim area and comfort stations to park near a campsite area. Follow the trail signs on R, crossing three streams and completing a loop of 20 interpretive points at 0.5 mi. Vegetation includes oaks, maple, poplar, birch, rhododendron, pines, cedar, and beech. Other facilities in this area are for picnicking, swimming, hot showers, and boating. Portions of this area are open all year.

Information: Contact the Resource Manager's Office, Philpott Lake, Rte 6, Box 140, Bassett, VA 24055; tel: 703-629-2703.

Military Installations

Virginia has 372,692 acres of military lands, of which 174,198 are often available for public hunting, fishing, and hiking. Another 1,141 acres are designated for other recreational activities. Fort A. P. Hill and Fort Pickett, with a combined total of 154,353 acres, are the two largest of nine US Army installations in the state. Hunting, fishing, and hiking are also allowed on portions of the 54,000-acre US Marine Corps Base at Quantico. For information on camping, trailer, travel, and recreational activities at eight of Virginia's military installations, request the *Armed Forces Recreation Areas Travel Guide,* DOD PA-15, from any of the addresses below.

Fort A. P. Hill Military Reservation
Caroline County 888

The A. P. Hill military installation, named in honor of

Civil War general Ambrose Powell Hill, includes a 200-acre tract of land set aside for the utilization of the Boy Scouts. In this area, hiking is permitted once requests to use the facility are received, programmed, and approved. Group participation in hiking exercises is allowed in designated areas during specific times of the year if such activities do not interfere with training of military personnel. Written requests are mandatory. Individual hiking is discouraged. No hiking is allowed during hunting seasons or during Reserve Component Training. The Wildlife Section has constructed the 0.5-mi *Fort A. P. Hill Nature Trail* at Beaverdam Pond, and it is open to the public daily. Inquiry may also be made about other potential trails, and the MP's at the base entrance can give directions. *USGS Maps:* Rappahannock Academy, Port Royal, Bowling Green.

Access: From junction of VA 2 and US 301 in Bowling Green go NE 2 mi to main entrance, on L.

Information: Contact Adjutant, Hqs US Army Garrison, Fort A. P. Hill, Bowling Green, VA 22427; tel: 804-633-5041.

Fort Belvoir
Fairfax County

Fort Belvoir has the 700-acre Accotink Bay Wildlife Refuge and Nature Study Area with 7 mi of hiking trails. The preserve's wildlife is abundant, including deer, opossum, beaver, mink, osprey, and more. The area is available during daylight hours only. Outside the refuge there is a campground on the base large enough to accommodate 750 Boy Scout groups. Camping is also allowed for active-duty and retired military personnel, as well as civilians who work for the Armed Services.

Access: One access point is off US 1, 8 mi S of Alexandria. Another is E of Lorton from I-95 and US 1.

Information: Contact Public Affairs Officer, Community Relations Branch, Fort Belvoir, VA 22060; tel: 703-664-1180 or 664-2821.

Fort Pickett Military Reservation
Nottoway, Brunswick, and Dinwiddie Counties

Named in honor of Civil War general George Edward Pickett, this large military installation in the heart of Virginia has nearly 45,000 acres of land set aside for recreational use, mainly for hunting. Although designated hiking trails have not been developed, at least 10 mi can be hiked near areas set aside for hunting, fishing, field trials, and boating. Hikers should write for a copy of Fort Pickett Regulations 210–11.

Access: In Blackstone enter the reservation on VA 40, E. Another entrance is on VA 40 W from McKenny, at US 1 and I-95.

Information: Contact Director of Personnel and Community Activities, Hqs US Army Garrison, Fort Pickett, Blackstone, VA 23284; tel: 804-292-2613.

Quantico Marine Base
Stafford, Prince William, and Fauquier Counties

Quantico Marine Base has 61,000 acres of woodlands and 807 acres of lakes. Designated areas around the lakes and 13 mi of streams are open to the public for hunting in season and for fishing year round. Hiking or camping is limited, and all uses of the properties require permits. Each visitor is subject to special restrictions.

Access: Off I-95 or US 1 on SR 619 near Triangle, 35 mi S of Washington, DC.

Information: Contact Marine Corps Development and Education Command, Quantico, VA 22134; tel: 703-640-2121.

16 · Colleges and Universities

College of William and Mary

The nation's second-oldest college (founded 1693) has three self-guiding tours, which provide short hikes on the campus for botanical observation. The college-plant tour begins at the Sir Christopher Wren Building, on the corner of Richmond and Jamestown Rds, and takes a clockwise direction around the quadrangle. At plant label #31, a turn L leads across Blair Rd to Wildflower Refuge, and opposite the refuge across Old Campus Rd is John Millington Hall, which houses the Dept of Biology. On the roof of this building is a self-guiding tour of 96 plants in the greenhouse. Other unnamed walks are around the wooded area of Lake Matoaka, W of the Commons.

Information: Contact Director of Communications, College of William and Mary, Williamsburg, VA 23185; tel: 804-253-4000. Or, Dr. Martin Mathes, botanist, 804-253-4240.

Hollins College

▼ HOLLINS COLLEGE HISTORICAL WALK   889

Directions and Description: N of Roanoke, at exit 43,

turn off I-81 on VA 115; go 1 mi to junction of VA 115 and US 11–220. Turn L on US 11–220 for 0.5 mi to entrance. Park at visitor parking area. The historical walking-tour loop route extends 0.7 mi from here, then returns. Follow the location directory to Main Building for the brochure *Around the Quadrangle.* The trail of history circles 15 historic buildings, of which East Building (1856) is the oldest; its architectural style is Jeffersonian. Listed in the National Register of Historic Places, the quadrangle is resplendent with towering ash trees, elegant buildings, and manicured landscaping.

Information: Contact Information Office, Hollins College, Hollins College, VA 24020; tel: 703-362-6000.

Lynchburg College

▼ LYNCHBURG COLLEGE BOTANICAL TRAIL   890

Directions and Description: From US 29 Expressway turn on US 221 and go W for 2.3 mi. Turn L on College Dr and go 0.3 mi; make sharp R on Vernon St, and then L on College St to corner of Westwood. Park in parking lot near Science Building. If gate to the arboretum is locked, request key from receptionist in first room on R inside the Science Building. Follow well-graded interpretive trail for 0.3-mi loop through stand of mature trees and wide variety of understory shrubs and wildflowers.

Information: Contact Biology Dept, Lynchburg College, Lynchburg, VA 24501; tel: 804-845-9071.

New River Community College

▼ NEW RIVER COMMUNITY COLLEGE TRAIL   891

Well designed for hiking and jogging, this 0.8-mi loop

trail has large oaks, hickory, and a stand of white pine. Under the forest canopy are dogwood, maple, and wildflowers such as cohosh and may-apple, with large beds of Virginia creeper. Access is, from US 11 in Dublin, 0.4 mi on VA 100 to the campus entrance on L. Go to parking area; trailhead is R of yield sign. *USGS Map:* Dublin.

Information: Contact Information Officer, New River Community College, Box 1127, Dublin, VA 24084; tel: 703-674-4121.

Rappahannock Community College, South

▼ RAPPAHANNOCK COMMUNITY COLLEGE
NATURE TRAIL   892

This is a forested, 0.9-mi loop trail through hardwoods and pines, with a carpet of leaves and pine needles for a pleasant hike. Understory has dogwood, blueberry, and wildflowers. Access is from the town of Glenns on VA 33; go W for 0.7 mi from junction with US 17. Park in parking area of college, examine directional sign near the main building, turn L, and enter gate of recreational area. Turn R on unmarked but wide trail. *USGS Maps:* Shackleford, Saluda.

Information: Contact Recreation Dept, Rappahannock Community College, South, Saluda, VA 23149; tel: 804-758-5324.

University of Virginia

▼ UNIVERSITY OF VIRGINIA ACADEMIC WALK   893

In 1975 Mary Hall Betts designed and compiled a 0.6-mi guide for a walking tour on the grounds of Thomas Jefferson's "Academic Village" of 1819. The trail covers 22 major points of academic and architectural interest. Among them are the Rotunda; the Lawn, formed by two parallel rows of buildings connected by the Colonnades and the five Pavilions on each side; the 10 formal gardens, each designed differently but enclosed by the serpentine walls behind the Ionic, Doric, or Corinthian Pavilions; and the East and West Ranges, where student rooms are connected with a series of arches framing a covered walkway. The walk begins at the south portico of the Rotunda and turns L between Pavilions II and IV. A loop is formed by touring the East Range and gardens and the statue of Homer near Cabell Hall, with a return on the West Range. Request a guide map in the Rotunda.

Information: Contact Director of Information Services, University of Virginia, Charlottesville, VA 22903; tel: 703-924-0311.

Virginia Military Institute

▼ CHESSIE NATURE TRAIL   894

Length: 7.3 mi (11.7 km); easy. *USGS Maps:* Lexington, Glasgow, Buena Vista. *Trailhead:* VMI Island.

Directions and Description: Of all the college and university trails, the Chessie is the longest and most scenic. It is owned, developed, and maintained by the VMI Foundation, Inc, a private endowment agency for VMI. A great source of pride for the foundation, the trail is also a source of pride for others, such as the citizens of Lexington, the Chesapeake and Ohio RR (whose old railroad grade it follows), and the Virginia Environmental Endowment. In Lexington, from N Main St at VMI (near junction of US 11-A) take side street down to Woods Creek and parking area on VMI Island. Follow trail signs, cross pedestrian bridge over the Maury River, and pass under US 11 bridge. At 0.8 mi enter tunnel of ash, sycamore, and mulberry. Chicory and thistle border the trail in the open spaces in summer. In the spring the high cliffs on the L at 1 mi are pocketed with bloodroot, trillium, columbine, and meadow rue. A bamboo copse is R at 2.4 mi. Go under I-81 bridge. Cross small bridge on the trail at 2.7 mi, and then pass through gates three times between 2.8-mi and 4-mi points. At 4.1 mi is South River Lock on R, the site of an old canal. Cross the South River on a skillfully constructed 235-ft footbridge on a C&O steel truss. At 5.4 mi there is evidence of beavers, both on the trail and by the river. Enter field of flowers—Virginia bluebells, phlox, thistle, black-eyed Susan, chicory, blueweed, soapwort, and nodding onion. On the R at 5.9 mi are the remains of the Ben Salem Lock. Pass cliff of limestone veined with calcite and quartz on L at 6.4 mi. And at 6.6 mi pass the Zimmerman's Lock remains. Cross road at 6.9 mi, and at 7.3 mi go under the US 60 bridge to parking area in Buena Vista. Vehicle shuttle necessary.

Information: Contact VMI Foundation, Inc, Virginia Military Institute, Lexington, VA 24450; tel: 703-463-6287.

17 · Private Holdings

Virginia has hundreds of private trails, many of which are short but formal and elegant, with august land-scaping; a number of these are open to the public only during the April Historic Garden Week or for special guests. Other trails are less sublime, and some are only paths behind homes to points of respite. A few are long treks on the firelines of private paper and timber companies.

In addition to the trails described in this chapter is the category of scenic, well-maintained trails at private resorts, where hikers are expected to be paying guests or to request permission to hike the trails or use other facilities. A primary example of this category is The Homestead, at Hot Springs, where well-designed and graded trails blend into the 16,000-acre estate (write Hot Springs, VA 24445; tel: 703-839-5500). Others are the 13,000 acres of Wintergreen near Reeds Gap (Winter-green, VA 22938; tel: 804-361-2200), Graves Mountain Lodge at Syria (Syria, VA 22743; tel: 703-923-4231), and Mountain Lake Resort at Newport (Mountain Lake, VA 24136; tel: 703-626-7121).

Most of the trails described in this section are open to the public. Restrictions that apply are noted.

Buena Vista

▼ MINERAL RIDGE TRAIL   895

Used by local hikers, joggers, and equestrians, many of them from Southern Seminary Junior College, this 1.2-mi-round-trip trail is along an old mining railroad grade on the slope of Mineral Ridge. Hardwoods and wildflowers. (It is more than 2 mi if the entire road is followed to US 60 and back.)

Access: Enter by a steep path at the end of 21st St E below the water tower in Buena Vista. *USGS Maps:* Buena Vista, Cornwall.

Information: Contact the owner, J. T. Lewis Dickinson, Jr., 2253 Maple Ave, Buena Vista, VA 24416; tel: 703-261-3495.

Charlottesville

▼ JEFFERSON HISTORICAL TRAIL   896

This 16-mi trail from the University of Virginia to Ash Lawn, the home of James Monroe, is for Boy Scouts only. It is a moderately rugged trail as it crosses Carters Mtn, Patterson Mtn, and by Monticello. Campsites have been designated. It was built by Scout Troop 19 and sponsored by the St Paul's Memorial Episcopal Church in Charlottesville. Reservations are required.

Information: Contact Stonewall Jackson Area Council, Inc, BSA, 633 Greenville Ave, Staunton, VA 24401; tel: 703-885-1595. Or, Landscape Div, Dept of Physical Plant, University of Virginia, 575 Alderman Rd, Charlottesville, VA 22903; tel: 804-924-7771.

Chesapeake

▼ COPPER TRAIL   897

A 0.8-mi loop trail goes from the red barn through a forest of cedar, ash, maple, sweet gum, cypress, and pin oak. Along the way are a wide variety of wildflowers, and near the lake are mallard, black, wood, ring-necked, and redhead ducks. A handsome golden retriever named "Copper" is always ready to accompany the hiker around the lake.

Access: From junction of I-64 and VA 168, Battlefield Blvd, go S on VA 168 for 5 mi and turn L on Mt Pleasants Rd. After 0.9 mi turn R on Fentress Rd, and go 0.1 mi to residence on R. Request permission to hike.

Information: Contact Robert Old, 721 Fentress Rd, Chesapeake, VA 23320; tel: 804-482-1132.

There are seven major forest-industry companies in Virginia that manage lands intensively to produce lumber and fiber. Additionally, the lands provide desirable wildlife habitat and recreational opportunities. Designated areas allow hunting, fishing, hiking, and nature study. A few offer limited backpacking and primitive camping. One of the largest such corporations is Union Camp, with 345,000 acres in Virginia and North Carolina. The company has designated open to the public some areas that have forest roads to hike, though these are not named as trails. Contact Land Manager, Union Camp Corp, Franklin, VA 23851; tel: 804-569-4321.

Another land-managing corporation is Owens-Illinois, with hundreds of miles of logging roads in seven counties that can be used for hiking. Permits and fees are necessary for hunting or fishing. Hiking without firearms does not require a permit. Contact Forest Management, Owens-Illinois, Big Island, VA 24526; tel: 804-299-5911.

The Glatfelter Pulp Wood Co also allows hiking on designated wildlife tracts and firelines. Hunters must pay fees and have a permit. Contact The Glatfelter Pulp and Paper Wood Co, PO Box 868, Fredericksburg, VA 22404; tel: 703-373-9431. In addition to the three companies named are two that put special emphasis on their lands' trails; these two, Evington and West Point, are described below.

Evington

▼ BUFFALO CREEK TRAIL   898

When it comes to wildflower pilgrimages, none does it better than WESTVACO (West Virginia Pulp and Paper Company). An example is WESTVACO's Wildflower-Woodlands Tours each April in the Buffalo Creek Nature Area. Here in the 1,049-acre Irvine Tract grow more than 70 species of wildflowers in a regal natural display. During the period of April tours reservations are required; use the address given here. Otherwise, the area is open to the public year round. A network of interpretive trails is planned in the area.

Access: From US 29 go W 6.2 mi to Evington on VA 24. From Evington continue W for 1.8 mi to gated entrance on L, or go another 0.7 mi to Campbell and Bedford county line. Park on R; enter gated meadow on L and go to forest edge near Buffalo Creek. (It is 19.3 mi

W to US 460 in Bedford.) *USGS Maps:* Forest, Lynch Station. Hunters, fishermen, backpackers, and students of nature will find that the 110,000 acres of forests divided among 25 counties are exceptionally inviting. However, write to the company for information on fees and specific locations.

Information: Contact WESTVACO Timberland Div, PO Box WV, Appomattox, VA 24522; tel: 804-846-5291.

West Point

▼ CHESAPEAKE NATURE TRAIL   899

The Chesapeake Corp of Virginia, with 245,000 acres, has designed and constructed a 1.5-mi loop trail through a portion of its 565-acre complex near West Point. An exceptionally educational trail, it has 44 observation markers, and a guidebook describes the trees, shrubs, ferns, and forest orchards. Open to the public year round. *USGS Map:* West Point.

Access: From I-64 take VA 33 for 3.8 mi toward West Point. Parking area on R.

Information: Contact Public Relations Office, The Chesapeake Corp, West Point, VA 23181; tel: 804-843-5000.

Marion

▼ WILDERNESS NATURE TRAIL   900

A project planned and designed by the Wilderness Rd Garden Club has yielded an attractive botanical trail paralleling an old mill race along the Holston River Middle Fork for 0.6 mi. Large ash, maple, poplar, sycamore, and elm shade the path, with locust and ironwood making a partial understory. Wildflowers are prominent, and many are labeled near a picnic area. Assistance comes from the city government and from Boy Scouts and other citizens. Open to the public. *USGS Map:* Marion.

Access: Off US 11–VA 16, Main St, at Campbell St to corner of Wilderness Rd.

Information: Contact Mrs. J. D. Killinger, 522 E Main St, Marion, VA 23454; tel: 703-783-4303.

The Nature Conservancy

The Nature Conservancy, formed in 1950, is a private conservation organization with more than 100,000 members dedicated to the preservation of natural environments. Through its action and cooperation with public and private agencies it maintains more than 1.7 million acres of natural diversity in more than 700 natural sanctuaries in all 50 states, The Virgin Islands, Canada, and elsewhere. The conservancy acquires funding from individual contributors, foundation grants, corporate gifts, and investments. It publishes *The Nature Conservancy News*.

In 1960 the Virginia chapter was established, and since then its 3,760 members have been active in acquiring and protecting more than 114,000 acres of forest, islands, wetlands, and significant wildlife sanctuaries. Of the 44 separate projects in which the chapter has been involved, 12 have been retained and managed by the chapter. Those with trails open to the public are listed here. Other trails are planned.

• The "Uplands" section of 713 acres in the 841-acre Alexander Berger Memorial Sanctuary in Caroline and Spotsylvania counties.
   Information: Contact Steve Linderer, Preserve Mgr, 1 Rainier Lane, Fredericksburg, VA 22401; tel: 703-898-3138.

• The 655-acre Falls Ridge Preserve in Montgomery County.
   Information: Contact William Bradley, Preserve Mgr, Rte 2, Box 289, Christiansburg, VA 24073; tel: 703-382-2220.

• The 63-acre Fernbrook Preserve in Albemarle County.
   Information: Contact Mrs. George Paschal, Rte 4, Fernbrook Farm, Charlottesville, VA 22901; tel: 804-973-6602. (Open to the public by permission.)

   Other Information: Contact Southeast Regional Office, 35 South King St, Leesburg, VA 22075; tel: 703-777-7760. Or, Virginia Field Office, 619 E High St, Charlottesville, VA 22901; tel: 804-295-6106.

Newport News

▼ LAKE MAURY TRAIL   901

On a former bridle trail and on forest paths, this 7-mi route along combined trails follows near the shoreline of Lake Maury in the Mariners Museum Park. Although it is not marked or maintained, its use by fishermen has made the route easy to follow through jack pine, gum, oaks, locust, magnolia, and bayberry. More than 437 species of plants and 112 species of birds have been catalogued in this park. *USGS Map:* Newport News N.

Access: From the junction of US 60 and Warwick Blvd enter on Museum Dr; go to visitor center.

Information: Contact the Superintendent of Bldg and Grounds, Mariners Museum, Museum Dr, Newport News, VA 23601; tel: 804-595-0368.

▼ WOODLAND ECOLOGY TRAIL   902

This 0.8-mi trail has 16 stations to describe the trees, ground-covering plants, shrubs—such as the devil's walking stick, nonvascular plants, and ferns—and animal life near a winding stream. It is part of the Peninsula Nature and Science Center, which houses special educational programs, a planetarium, displays, and an aquarium.

Access: From junction of US 60 and VA 312, Clyde Morris Blvd, go E 0.7 mi to center on R.

Information: Contact Director, Peninsula Nature and Science Center, 524 Clyde Morris Blvd, Newport News, VA 23601; tel: 804-595-1900 or 599-4897.

Studley

▼ SWEET PEPPERBUSH TRAIL   903

Winding gently through fern beds and partridgeberry patches, this 0.3-mi loop trail passes under a huge poplar at the edge of Mantilo Branch. Bunches of glabrous, ovate sweet pepperbush wave in the breeze. Leaving the stream, the trail slightly ascends under a canopy of oaks, hickory, and pines, with holly, dogwood, mountain laurel, and maple forming an understory. Among wildflowers, complete the circle around the house and return to the street.

Access: E of Richmond on I-295 take SR 627, Meadowbridge Rd, E exit; go 5.5 mi to SR 615, then L 2.7 mi to junction with SR 606. (Here, to R, is Studley, where—to the E, 0.5 mi on SR 606—the birthplace of Patrick Henry is located.) Cross SR 606 and go 0.3 mi to SR 1610, Santa Maria Dr, R. Go 0.4 mi to SR 1611, Nina Ct, and turn L. Trail begins at end of cul-de-sac at footbridge.

Information: Contact owners, 104 Nina Ct, Mechanicsville, VA 23111.

Vesta

▼ FIRE PINK TRAIL   904–905

Following a steep road, this 0.8-mi round-trip trail ascends to the summit of De Hart Mtn for sweeping views of Smith River Valley and Rocky Knob on the Blue Ridge Pkwy. Fire pink, purple rhododendron, columbine, mountain laurel, serviceberry, galax, and crested dwarf iris grow in abundance on the precipitous rock outcroppings. *USGS Map:* Stuart.

Access: From Vesta go 4 mi E on US 58 (8 mi W from Stuart) to horseshoe curve with two driveways on L. Park at first (which is second driveway from Stuart), and hike past the cable gate, following road with two major switchbacks to top of peak. No camping. The adjoining 2.5-mi *Wildwood Trail*, which descends to the valley on other private property, is no longer maintained.

Information: Contact Mr. and Mrs. Arthur Belcher, Rte 4, Box 183, Stuart, VA 24171; tel: 703-930-2285.

Maps

The Virginia Commission of Outdoor Recreation has divided the Commonwealth into 11 regions. These regions were determined by urban-rural and physiographic distinctions. Within the regions are 21 planning districts of counties and cities.

Following are an index map, 11 regional maps, and maps of the Washington, D.C. area and the Richmond area. The trail numbers on the maps correspond with those on the right side of each trail description in the text. Detailed trail outlines would require another volume the size of this guidebook. It is hoped therefore that the trail descriptions in the chapters are sufficiently clear to guide you to, and along, the trails of your choice.

The maps are printed by permission of the Virginia Department of Conservation and Economic Development, Division of Parks and Recreation. Source maps appear in *1979 Virginia Outdoors Plan*.

Legend

🛡17 Federal highways

🛡95 Interstate highways

🛡2 State highways

 National parks and forests

● 48 Trail numbers

– · – County line

– · · – State line

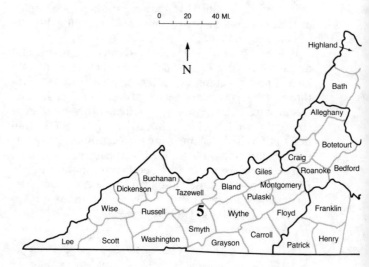

THE COUNTIES
AND REGIONS OF VIRGINIA

0 20 40 Mi.

↑
N

Highland

Bath

Alleghany

Botetourt

Craig

Giles

Roanoke Bedford

Buchanan

Dickenson Tazewell Bland Montgomery

Pulaski

5

Wise Russell Wythe Floyd Franklin

Smyth

Lee Scott Washington Carroll

Grayson Patrick Henry

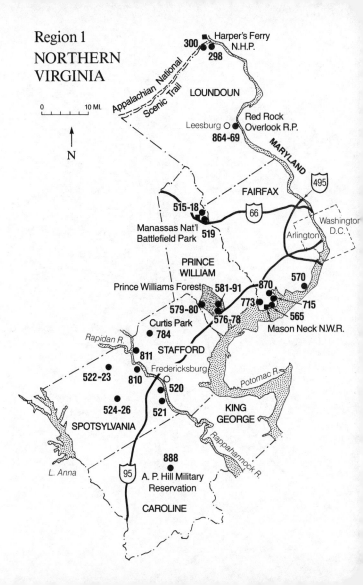

Region 1
NORTHERN
VIRGINIA

0 ___ 10 MI.

N

Harper's Ferry
N.H.P.
300
298

LOUNDOUN

Appalachian National Scenic Trail

Leesburg O • Red Rock
Overlook R.P.
864-69

MARYLAND

495

FAIRFAX

66

Washington
D.C.

Arlington

515-18

519

Manassas Nat'l
Battlefield Park

PRINCE
WILLIAM

Prince Williams Forest

581-91

570

579-80

870

773

715

565

Mason Neck N.W.R.

576-78

Curtis Park
• 784

Rapidan R.

811

STAFFORD

810

Fredericksburg O

520

522-23

524-26

521

SPOTSYLVANIA

L. Anna

95

Potomac R.

KING
GEORGE

Rappahannock R.

888

A. P. Hill Military
Reservation

CAROLINE

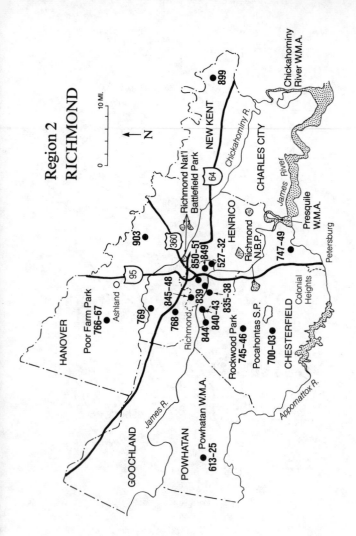

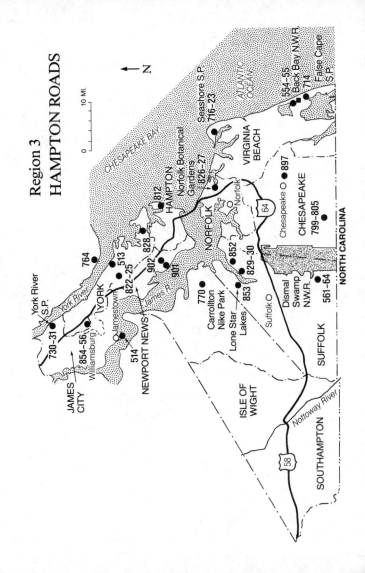

Region 3
HAMPTON ROADS

← N

0   10 MI.

CHESAPEAKE BAY

ATLANTIC OCEAN

York River S.P.
730-31

JAMES CITY

Williamsburg
854-56

Jamestown

514

YORK

822-25

764

513

902

828

901

812

HAMPTON

Norfolk Botanical Gardens
826-27

Seashore S.P.
716-23

VIRGINIA BEACH

554-55
Back Bay NWR
714
False Cape S.P.

NEWPORT NEWS

770

Carrollton

Nike Park

853

Lone Star Lakes

852

829-30

NORFOLK

Norfolk

64

Chesapeake O 897

CHESAPEAKE

799-805

NORTH CAROLINA

Suffolk O

Dismal Swamp NWR.

561-64

SUFFOLK

ISLE OF WIGHT

Nottoway River

58

SOUTHAMPTON

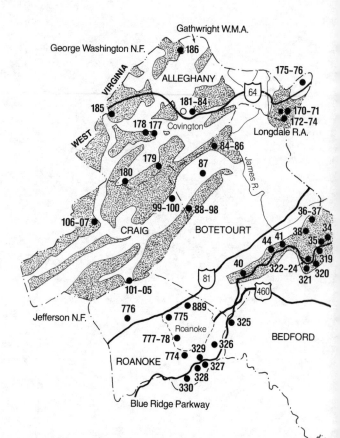

Region 4
ROANOKE-LYNCHBURG

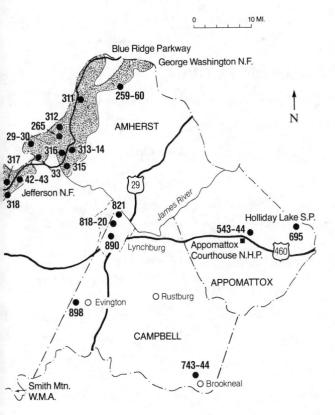

0   10 MI.

Blue Ridge Parkway
George Washington N.F.

259-60

311

312
265
29-30
316   313-14
317
315
33
42-43
318
Jefferson N.F.

AMHERST

N

29

James River

821
818-20
890   Lynchburg

Holliday Lake S.P.

543-44
695
Appomattox
Courthouse N.H.P.   460

APPOMATTOX

O Evington
898   O Rustburg

CAMPBELL

743-44
O Brookneal

Smith Mtn.
W.M.A.

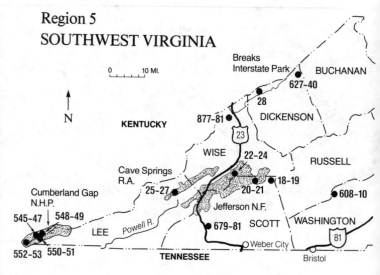

Region 5
SOUTHWEST VIRGINIA

0   10 MI.

N

KENTUCKY

Breaks
Interstate Park

BUCHANAN

627-40

28

877-81

DICKENSON

23

WISE

22-24

RUSSELL

Cave Springs
R.A.

25-27

20-21

18-19

608-10

Jefferson N.F.

Cumberland Gap
N.H.P.

545-47   548-49

LEE   Powell R.

679-81

SCOTT

WASHINGTON

81

552-53   550-51

Weber City

TENNESSEE

Bristol

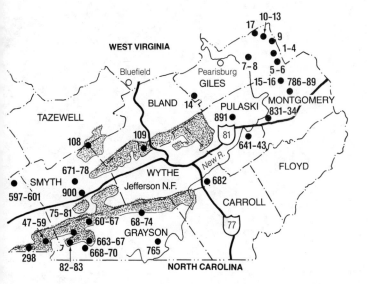

Region 6
SHENANDOAH VALLEY

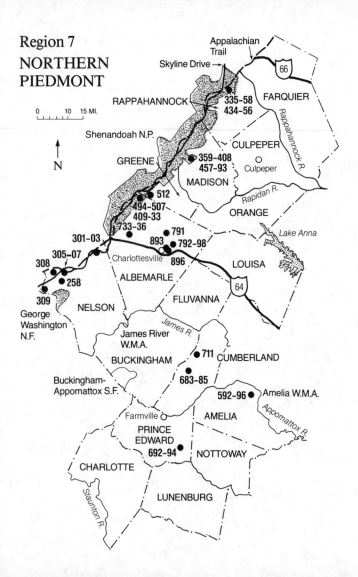

Region 7
NORTHERN PIEDMONT

0   10   15 MI.

N

RAPPAHANNOCK

FARQUIER

66

Appalachian Trail

Skyline Drive →

335-58
434-56

Shenandoah N.P.

CULPEPER

GREENE

Culpeper

MADISON

359-408
457-93

Rapidan R.

Rappahannock R.

512

ORANGE

494-507
409-33

733-36

Lake Anna

301-03

791

893   792-98

305-07

Charlottesville

896

308

258

ALBEMARLE

LOUISA

309

64

George
Washington
N.F.

NELSON

FLUVANNA

James R.

James River
W.M.A.

BUCKINGHAM

711   CUMBERLAND

Buckingham-
Appomattox S.F.

683-85

592-96   Amelia W.M.A.

Farmville

AMELIA

Appomattox R.

PRINCE
EDWARD

692-94   NOTTOWAY

CHARLOTTE

LUNENBURG

Staunton R.

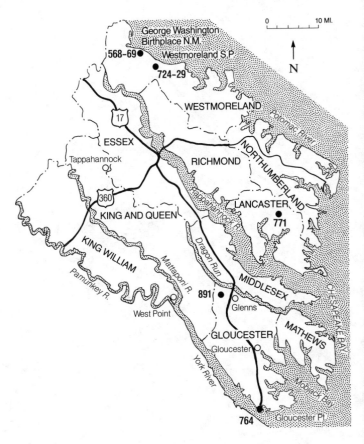

Region 8
TIDEWATER

0   10 MI.

N

George Washington
Birthplace N.M.
568-69
Westmoreland S.P.
724-29

WESTMORELAND

Potomac River

17

ESSEX

Tappahannock

RICHMOND

NORTHUMBERLAND

Rappahannock R.

360

LANCASTER

771

KING AND QUEEN

Dragon Run

KING WILLIAM

Mattaponi R.

Pamunkey R.

West Point

891

Glenns

MIDDLESEX

MATHEWS

CHESAPEAKE BAY

GLOUCESTER

Gloucester

York River

Mobjack Bay

764

Gloucester Pt.

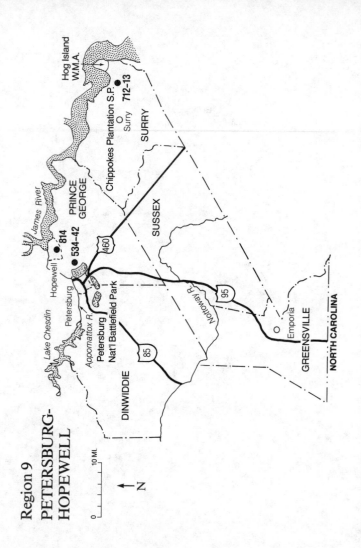

Region 9
PETERSBURG-
HOPEWELL

N

0   10 Mi.

Hog Island W.M.A.

James River

PRINCE GEORGE

Hopewell

814
534-42

Lake Chesdin

Petersburg

Appomattox R.

Petersburg Nat'l Battlefield Park

DINWIDDIE

85

95

Chippokes Plantation S.P.

Surry

712-13

SURRY

460

SUSSEX

Nottoway R.

Emporia

GREENSVILLE

NORTH CAROLINA

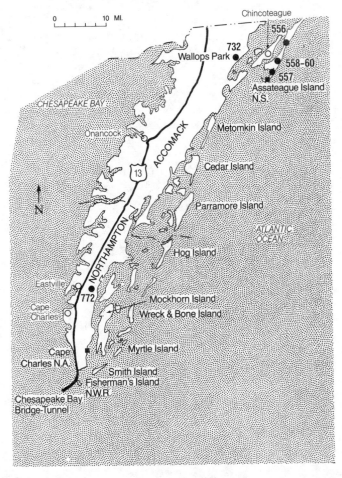

Region 10
EASTERN SHORE

0   10 MI.

Chincoteague

556

732

Wallops Park

558-60

557

Assateague Island
N.S.

CHESAPEAKE BAY

Onancock

Metomkin Island

ACCOMACK

Cedar Island

US 13

Parramore Island

NORTHAMPTON

ATLANTIC
OCEAN

Hog Island

Eastville

772

Mockhorn Island

Cape
Charles

Wreck & Bone Island

Cape
Charles N.A.

Myrtle Island

Smith Island

Fisherman's Island
N.W.R.

Chesapeake Bay
Bridge-Tunnel

N

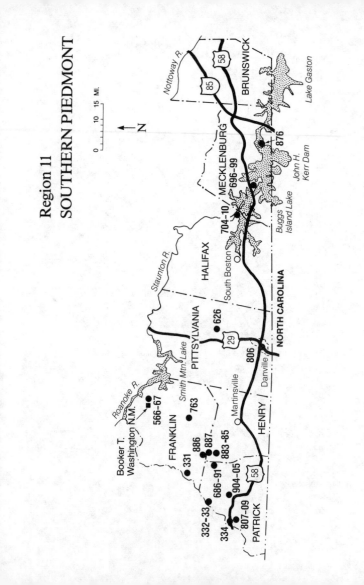

Region 11
SOUTHERN PIEDMONT

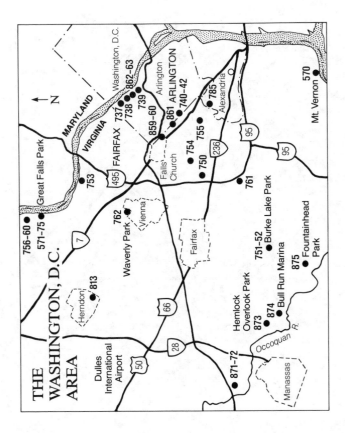

Resources

1. Organizations and Clubs

Virginia Trails Association

The Virginia Trails Association, a tax-exempt, nonprofit organization, is composed of trail users and clubs, planners, managers, landowners, and others interested in nonmotorized trails. Its purpose is to promote trails, their proper use, and trail facilities throughout Virginia, and to cooperate with those working for trails within other states and on a nationwide basis. It does this by providing information; the association collects and publishes in a newsletter information from private and public agencies about trails.

The association also provides assistance to existing outing groups and works to establish outing groups in areas that do not have them. These groups are needed to meet the challenge to existing trails from private developers and public road or bridge construction; to increase urban trails; to alert trail users to opportunities to establish trails, such as those offered by abandoned railroad rights-of-way; and to provide leadership for volunteers to fill the gap resulting from government cuts on trail development and maintenance support.

VTA dues are $5 for an individual, $10 for a family, and $10 for a club or organization, payable to the Virginia Trails Association, 13 W Maple St, Alexandria, VA 22301; tel: 703-548-7490.

—Jeannette Fitzwilliams

The following nine Class A clubs assist in maintaining the 543.2 mi of the Appalachian National Scenic Trail in Virginia.

Kanawha Trail Club

The Kanawha Trail Club began as the Charleston Daily Mail Hiking Club in July 1942. Sol Padlibsky of the *Charleston Daily Mail* collaborated with H. M. F. Kinsey, a Boy Scouts executive, in organizing group hiking. In September 1944 the group reorganized with 54 charter members and changed the club name to the Kanawha Trail Club. Three years later the club was incorporated and a charter obtained. Plans followed for a lodge on the Middle Lick Fork of Davis Creek, 7 mi from Charleston, and the lodge that was then built has been in use since October 1948.

The KTC is the largest hiking club in West Virginia, with a present membership of 140, and it maintains 20.7 mi of the *A.T.*, from the New River north to the Stony Creek Valley. About 80% of the KTC's outings are in the 9,000-acre Kanawha State Forest, which is only 6 mi from Charleston. In 1978 several club members, including Charlie Carlson and Howard and Dorothy Guest, were active in lobbying for a state bill that prohibits commercial timber cutting in this forest.

Membership is open to all ages. For information write

or call Dr. George Becker, 207 28th St SE, Charleston, WV 25304; tel: 304-343-1662.

Mount Rogers Appalachian Trail Club

The Mt Rogers Appalachian Trail Club was organized February 29, 1960, after the Roanoke Appalachian Trail Club agreed to relinquish 32 mi of the *A.T.* between Damascus and US 16 south of Marion, Virginia. In September of the same year the Appalachian Trail Conference made the formal transfer, and the MRATC became an authorized *A.T.*-maintaining club. Louise and George Hall, of Damascus, and Nerine and David Thomas, of Abingdon, provided the animating spirit for the club's organization.

The original 32-mi segment has grown through relocations to more than 64 mi; the MRATC's maintenance responsibilities are for sections 35 through 38 in the *A.T.* guidebook. This segment provides access to Virginia's two highest peaks, Mt Rogers (5,729 ft) and Whitetop Mtn (5,520 ft).

The MRATC also provides trail maintenance for 17 mi of the *Iron Mtn Trail* (the old *A.T.*) and *Elk Garden Trail* (the old SR 600, a good cross-country ski route). The club publishes a quarterly bulletin listing regular scheduled hikes and maintenance work projects. The club's address is Rte 7, Box 248, Abingdon, VA 24210; tel: 703-628-2601.

—*David O. Thomas*

Natural Bridge Appalachian Trail Club

The Natural Bridge Appalachian Trail Club (NBATC)

was formed in Lynchburg on October 2, 1930 under the sponsorship of the local Lions Club and with the encouragement of the Potomac Appalachian Trail Club. At that time the Potomac club maintained the *A.T.* from Rockfish Gap to the Peaks of Otter. Fred M. Davis, secretary of the Lions Club, and Dr. Ruskin S. Freer, professor of biology at Lynchburg College, were among the sponsors and charter members. Myron H. Avery, president of the PATC, acted as advisor at the organization meetings.

Because of the construction of the Blue Ridge Pkwy, sections of the *A.T.* had to be relocated; the NBATC sections were completed in 1951. Again, help was provided by Myron Avery, as well as crews from PATC and the National Forest Service. (The NBATC celebrated its 50th anniversary in 1980.)

Club activities range from short walks to weekend outings, canoe trips, rock climbing, and educational nature studies. An annual dinner meeting is held in October. Membership, which is by invitation, is open to people over 18 years of age; experience also is necessary. The club's address is PO Box 3012, Lynchburg, VA 24503; tel: 804-384-7791.

The Old Dominion Appalachian Trail Club

The Old Dominion Appalachian Trail Club was founded in 1968 by a group of Richmond hikers, headed by Tom Pearson. At that time the club was allotted a 10-mile section of the *A.T.* by the Natural Bridge Appalachian Trail Club, and the ODATC also jointly maintained a second section with the Shenandoah-Rockfish A.T. Club. Upon the dissolution of that club, ODATC was

Theresa Duffey
266-7913

granted sole maintenance responsibility for this section. The club currently manages 15.4 mi of the *A.T.* near the Blue Ridge Pkwy.

As with the other clubs maintaining the *A.T.,* work is done by volunteers, who clear out summer growth, reblaze and reroute, and improve the treadway. The ODATC also maintains a four-season outing schedule. Hikes range from short family walks to week-long excursions for experts. There are special-interest groups within the club that organize bicycle, canoe, cross-country ski, snowshoe, and caving trips. Club members offer programs to community groups on special camping techniques and environmental awareness.

Membership in the ODATC is open to anyone interested in the management and protection of the *Appalachian Trail*. The club's address is PO Box 25283, Richmond, VA 23260; tel: 804-264-8524 or 321-5933.

—*Lynne Overman*

Piedmont Appalachian Trail Hikers

The Piedmont Appalachian Trail Hikers (PATH) was organized in 1965 with the assistance of Tom Campbell, an Appalachian Trail Conference board member and a member of the Roanoke Appalachian Trail Club. The Roanoke Club relinquished 27 miles of the *A.T.*, from US 21–52 at Walker Mtn to VA 16, to the Potomac Appalachian Trail Hikers. Almost immediately a portion of the trail was relocated to bypass Mtn Empire Airport. Several other relocations have been made, including the major shift of the *A.T.* from Walker Mtn to Garden Mtn. This rerouting has added 13 miles of the 40 that constitute sections 32, 33, and 34 as described in the 1980 *A.T.* guidebook.

PATH has been fortunate to be associated with the Jefferson National Forest and its personnel in the Wythe Ranger District. The two have worked together in scouting and relocating trails, selecting shelter sites, and arranging management plans. PATH's membership includes volunteer workers from locales including Greensboro, Winston-Salem, Burlington, Asheboro, Wadesboro, and Raleigh, to name a few. The territory's expanse requires members to drive from 120 to 220 mi (260 mi to the most distant trail points) to scout, flag, build, and maintain the *A.T.*

The club has an annual meeting in January and publishes periodic newsletters. Membership is open to all who are interested. The club's address is 124 Lawrence St, Greensboro, NC 27406; tel: 919-272-8965.

—Ken Rose

Potomac Appalachian Trail Club

The Potomac Appalachian Trail Club, the largest of the Class A clubs in the Virginia area, has 3,100 members and was established in 1927. In its first year it had 7 members and built 19 mi of the *A.T.* By 1936 it had completed 250 mi of the *A.T.*, from the Susquehanna River in Pennsylvania to Rockfish Gap in Virginia. Today it maintains 231 mi of the *A.T.*, of which 155.7 are in Virginia. In addition the club maintains approximately 600 mi of other foot trails in the area, including Pennsylvania, Maryland, the District of Columbia, northern Virginia, and West Virginia.

Exceptionally active, the club maintains 15 primitive cabins and 22 shelters for *A.T.* hikers, as well as several trail work centers; provides roving *A.T.* patrols to help hikers in the peak season; and supervises the hut system for long-distance hikers in the Shenandoah National Park.

In addition to the PATC's wide range of services to hikers and of outdoor recreational activities, it publishes detailed guidebooks, maps, brochures, and other informational materials, on such topics as land acquisition for protecting the *A.T.* and government policies and agencies.

For information contact the main headquarters at 1718 N St, NW, Washington, DC 20036. This office is open to the public from 7 to 10 P.M., Monday through Friday. Tel: 202-638-5306.

—William E. Hutchinson

Roanoke Appalachian Trail Club

The Roanoke Appalachian Trail Club was founded by Donald Gates, a Roanoke College professor of economics, in 1932. The club accepted as its initial responsibility the planning of the *A.T.* south of the city toward Fancy Gap. By 1940 the 72 mi of trail that had been arranged, mostly on secondary roads, were in route conflict with the construction of the Blue Ridge Pkwy. By 1947 the club had located a new route, extending 150 mi SW and again mostly on secondary roads, through large segments of the Jefferson National Forest. Under the leadership and influence of Jim and Molly Denton and Tom and Charlene Campbell, considerable progress was made in relocating the *A.T.* off the roads. Meanwhile another *A.T.* segment, a stretch of 41 mi NE of the city, was accepted by the club; the result was a monumental task of maintenance. Fortunately for the hiking community four other *A.T.* clubs became responsible for SW sections, leaving the RATC with two segments comprising 117 mi of trail. Severe storm damage and further trail relocations during the 1970s in the Catawba Mtn area have led the RATC to appeal for assistance in improving the trail route. Coming to their aid are Old Dominion Appalachian Trail Club and faculty and students of Roanoke College (an auxiliary affiliate). The current address for information is 4551 Nelms Ln NE, Roanoke, VA 24019; tel: 703-366-3508.

Tidewater Appalachian Trail Club

The Tidewater Appalachian Trail Club (TATC) was founded in 1972 and, like the other hiking organizations that are affiliated with the umbrella Appalachian Trail Conference, the maintenance of the *A.T.* is its primary function. Membership is more than 250. The club holds monthly meetings, and its activities include hiking, backpacking, canoeing, rappelling, and caving. Social events are also held.

In addition to maintaining the *A.T.* from the Tye River to Reeds Gap, the TATC also maintains other trails, in the Blue Ridge Mtns and in the tidewater area of Virginia and the NE area of North Carolina.

The TATC has published a hiking guide to the trails in the tidewater area, *Tidewater Hiking Trails*, which is available at area camping stores and from the club. It is also constructing a stone cabin off the Blue Ridge Pkwy for use by members and guests. Membership is open to the public. The club's address is PO Box 8246, Norfolk, VA 23503; tel: 804-340-5948.

—Reese F. Lukei, Jr.

Virginia Tech Outing Club

The Virginia Tech Outing Club was initially established to help organize trips for hiking, backpacking, rock climbing, canoeing, kayaking, and cross-country skiing. Subsequently, other organizations at the university and in Blacksburg became the primary area sponsors of some of these and other outdoor sports activities. Now, as a Class A member of the Appalachian Trail Conference since 1973, the VTOC maintains 27.8 mi of the *A.T.* in Bland County. Current club membership is 45.

In addition to trail maintenance VTOC's activities include the completion of one of three guidebooks on trails in Southwest Virginia; environmental action; and weekly meetings and programs, usually each Thursday at the university. Membership is open to anyone interested in the club's activities. The current address for the club's president is PO Box 459, Blacksburg, VA 24060; tel: 703-389-1573. Another address is PO Box 538 in Blacksburg; tel: 703-552-3747 or 961-6712.

2. Agencies and Other Sources of Information

United States Government Departments

Dept of Agriculture
Forest Service
PO Box 2417
Washington, DC 20013 (Tel: 202-447-3957 and 447-3760 for information)

Dept of Agriculture
Regional Forester #8, Southern
1720 Peachtree Rd, NW
Atlanta, GA 30309
(Tel: 404-881-4177)

Dept of Agriculture
Natural Resources and
  Environment
14th St and Jefferson Dr, SW
Washington, DC 20250 (Tel:
  202-655-4000, ext 77173)

Dept of the Interior
Bureau of Land Management
Washington, DC 20240
  (Tel: 202-343-1100
  for information)

Dept of the Interior
Fish and Wildlife Service Area
  Manager
1825 Virginia St
Annapolis, MD 21401
  (Tel: 301-269-6324)

Dept of the Interior
National Park Service
Interior Bldg
Washington, DC 20240
  (Tel: 202-343-4747)

Dept of the Interior
National Parks Regional
  Director
75 Spring St, SW
Atlanta, GA 30303
  (Tel: 404-221-5185)

United States Congressional Committees

Committee on Agriculture
  (House)
Rm 1301, Longworth House
  Office Bldg
Washington, DC 20515
  (Tel: 202-225-2171)

Committee on Agriculture,
  Nutrition and Forestry
  (Senate)
Rm 322, Russell Bldg
Washington, DC 20510
  (Tel: 202-224-2035)

Committee on Environment
  and Public Works (Senate)
Rm 4204, Dirksen Bldg
Washington, DC 20510
  (Tel: 202-224-6176)

Committee on Interior and
  Insular Affairs (House)
Rm 1324, Longworth House
  Office Bldg
Washington, DC 20515
  (Tel: 202-225-2761)

National and Regional Organizations and Clubs

American Camping
 Association, Inc
Bradford Woods
Martinsville, IN 46151
 (Tel: 317-342-8456)

American Forestry
 Association
1319 18th St NW
Washington, DC 20036
 (Tel: 202-467-5810

American Hiking Society
1701 18th St NW
Washington, DC 20009
 (Tel: 202-234-4610)

Appalachian Mountain Club
5 Joy St
Boston, MA 02108
 (Tel: 617-523-0636)

Appalachian Trail
 Conference, Inc
PO Box 807
Harpers Ferry, WV 25425
 (Tel: 304-535-6331)

Boone and Crockett Club
205 S Patrick St
Alexandria, VA 22314
 (Tel: 703-548-7727)

Boy Scouts of America
Southeast Region
500, 300 Interstate N Pkwy
Atlanta, GA 30099
 (Tel: 404-955-2333)

Camp Fire, Inc
4601 Madison Ave
Kansas City, MO 64112
 (Tel: 816-756-1950)

Center for Environmental
 Education, Inc
625 9th St NW
Washington, DC 20001
 (Tel: 202-735-6300)

Clean Water Action Project
1341 G St NW
Washington, DC 20005
 (Tel: 202-638-1196)

Conservation Foundation
1717 Massachusetts Ave NW
Washington, DC 20036
 (Tel: 202-797-4300)

Defenders of Wildlife
1244 19th St NW
Washington, DC 20036
 (Tel: 202-659-9510)

Ducks Unlimited, Inc
PO Box 66300
Chicago, IL 60666
 (Tel: 312-438-4300)

Friends of the Earth
1045 Sansome St
San Francisco, CA 94111
 (Tel: 415-495-4770)

Girl Scouts
of the United States
830 3rd Ave
New York, NY 10022
(Tel: 212-940-7500)

Green Mountain Club, Inc
PO Box 889
Montpelier, VT 05602
(Tel: 802-223-3463)

Izaak Walton League
of America, Inc
1800 N Kent St, Suite 806
Arlington, VA 22209
(Tel: 703-528-1818)

National Audubon Society
950 Third Ave
New York, NY 10022
(Tel: 202-832-3200)

National Campers and Hikers
Association, Inc
7172 Transid Rd
Buffalo, NY 14221
(Tel: 716-634-5433)

National Geographic Society
17th and M Sts NW
Washington, DC 20036
(Tel: 202-857-7000)

National Parks and
Conservation Association
1701 18th St NW
Washington, DC 20009
(Tel: 202-265-2717)

National Speleological
Society, Inc
Cave Ave
Huntsville, AL 35810

National Trails Council
13 West Maple St
Alexandria, VA 22301
(Tel: 703-548-7490)

National Recreation and
Park Association
1601 N Kent St
Arlington, VA 22209
(Tel: 703-525-0606)

National Wildlife Federation
1412 16th St NW
Washington, DC 20036
(Tel: 202-797-6800)

The Nature Conservancy
Suite 800, 1800 N Kent St
Arlington, VA 22209
(Tel: 703-841-5300)

The Ruffed Grouse Society
994 Broadhead Rd, Suite 304
Coraopolis, PA 15108
(Tel: 412-262-4044)

Sierra Club
Washington Office
330 Pennsylvania Ave SE
Washington, DC 20003
(Tel: 202-547-1144)

The Wilderness Society
1901 Pennsylvania Ave, NW
Washington, DC 20006
(Tel: 202-828-6600)

Virginia Government Agencies

Commission of Game and
Inland Fisheries
4010 W. Broad Street
Richmond, VA 23230
(Tel: 804-257-1000)

Commission of Outdoor
Recreation
101 N. 14th Street,
James Monroe Bldg
Richmond, VA 23219
(Tel: 804-225-3030)

Council on the Environment
903 Ninth Street Office Bldg
Richmond, VA 23219
(Tel: 804-786-4500)

Department of Conservation
and Economic
Development
1100 Washington Bldg,
Capitol Square
Richmond, VA 23219
(Tel: 804-786-2121)

Division of Forestry
Box 3758
Charlottesville, VA 22903
(Tel: 804-977-6555)

Division of State Parks
1201 Washington Bldg,
Capitol Square
Richmond, VA 23219
(Tel: 804-786-2132)

Virginia State Travel Service
9th Street Office Bldg
Richmond, VA 23219
(Tel: 804-786-2051)

Department of Highways
and Transportation
1221 East Broad Street
Richmond, VA 23219
(Tel: 804-786-2838)

State Water Control Board
2111 N Hamilton Street
Richmond, VA 23230
(Tel: 804-257-0056)

Virginia Citizens' Groups

Izaak Walton League
of America
Virginia Chapter
308 Kerfoot, Front Royal, VA
(Tel: 703-636-1617)

Piedmont Environmental
Council
28-C Main Street
Warrenton, VA 22186
(Tel: 703-347-2334)

Trout Unlimited
  Virginia Council
Route 1, Box 12
Fisherville, VA 22939
  (Tel: 703-825-6660)

Virginia Association
  of Soil and Water
Conservation Districts
Suite 800, 830 E Main St
Richmond, VA 23219
  (Tel: 804-786-2064)

Virginia Forestry Association
One North Fifth St
Richmond, VA 23219
  (Tel: 804-644-8462)

Virginia Society
  of Ornithology
615 Carolina Ave
Norfolk, VA 23503
  (Tel: 804-625-6082)

Virginia Wildlife Federation
314 W Bute St
Norfolk, VA 23501
  (Tel: 804-627-0055)

Virginia Outdoor Clubs and Organizations

(See also addresses of clubs that begin Resources.)

Virginia Recreation and Park
  Society
Route 4, Box 155
Mechanicsville, VA 23111
  (Tel: 804-730-9447)

Virginia Trails Association
13 West Maple St
Alexandria, VA 22301
  (Tel: 703-548-7490)

Colleges and Universities

Ski and Outing Club
Bridgewater College
Bridgewater, VA 22812

Ski and Outing Club
College of William and Mary
Williamsburg, VA 23185

Outing Club
Eastern Mennonite College
Harrisonburg, VA 22801

George Mason Union
  Outing Club
4400 University Dr
Fairfax, VA 22030

Outsiders Club
Box 92, Hampden-Sydney
 College
Hampden-Sydney, VA 23943

Hollins Outdoor Program
Hollins College
Hollins College, VA 24020

Outdoor Recreation Club
PO Box 3624
James Madison University
Harrisonburg, VA 22807

Outdoor Recreation
Dept of Physical Education
Longwood College
Farmville, VA 23901

Recreation Association
Mary Baldwin College
Staunton, VA 24401

Intrepid Travelers
200 Webb Center
Old Dominion University
Norfolk, VA 23508

Outing Club
WC 3254
University of Richmond
Richmond, VA 23173

Virginia Commonwealth
 Union Outing Club
Outing Venture Center, VCU
916½ W Franklin St
Richmond, VA 23284

Outing Club
Newcomb Hall Station,
 Box 101X
University of Virginia
Charlottesville, VA 22901

Cadet Recreation Committee
Lejeune Hall
Virginia Military Institute
Lexington, VA 24450

Sierra Club Local Chapters

Old Dominion Chapter,
 Sierra Club
Rte 2, Box 385
Blacksburg, VA 24060

Sierra Club Blue Ridge Group
Rte 1, Box 305-B
Faber, VA 22938
 (Tel: 804-361-1420)

Sierra Club Chesapeake Bay
 Group
210 87th St
Virginia Beach, VA 23451
 (Tel: 804-428-1509)

Sierra Club Falls of the James
Group
6408 Morningside Dr
Richmond, VA 23226
  (Tel: 804-285-4989)

Sierra Club Piedmont Group
Rte 1, Box 149
Esmont, VA 22937
  (Tel: 804-296-0487)

Sierra Club New River Group
500 Linkous Cr
Blacksburg, VA 24060
  (Tel: 703-552-2092)

3. Trail Supplies

The following stores, listed by city, have a partial or complete range of supplies and equipment for hiking, backpacking, and camping.

Greensprings Sports Center
Hwy 75 S
Abingdon, VA 24210

Wilderness-Murphy
VHCC I-81 Exit 7
Abingdon, VA 24210

Canterbury Tales, Inc
Britches of Georgetowne
1321 Leslie Ave
Alexandria, VA 22301

Memco
6600 Richmond Hwy
Alexandria, VA 22306

Memco
655 Little River Turnpike
Alexandria, VA 22312

Recreation Services
884 S Pickett
Alexandria, VA 22304

Ski Shop of Old Town, Inc
821 S Washington
Alexandria, VA 22314

Team Sports Inc
5641 Q Gen Washington
Alexandria, VA 22312

Annandale Surplus
4220 Annandale Rd
Annandale, VA 22003

Marine Corps Exchange 0111
Hqs Batallion HOMC
Henderson Hall
Arlington, VA 22214

The Surplus Center
3451–5 North
Washington Blvd
Arlington, VA 22201

Camping Sites
121 N Bridge St
Bedford, VA 24523

Backcountry Ski & Sport
3710 S Main St
Blacksburg, VA 24060

Blue Ridge Mountaineering
211 Draper Rd
Blacksburg, VA 24060

Blaustein & Reich, Inc
424 N Main St
Blacksburg, VA 24060

Eagle Associates Inc
424 N Main St
Blacksburg, VA 24060

Mountain Sports, Ltd
1010 Commonwealth Ave
Bristol, VA 24201

Blue Ridge Mountain Sports
1417 Emmett St (Highway 29)
Charlottesville, VA 22901

Blue Ridge Mountain Sports
115 Elliewood Ave
Charlottesville, VA 22903

Bare Essentials, Inc
#2 Ivy Square
Charlottesville, VA 22901

Booth White Village Sports
3298 Riverside Shopping
    Center
Danville, VA 24541

Camper's World
2852 Riverside Dr
Danville, VA 24541

Herman's
Fair Oaks Mall
12005 Lee Jackson Hwy
Fairfax, VA 22033

Hudson Bay Outfitters
9683 Lee Hwy
Fairfax, VA 22033

Hudson Bay Outfitters, Ltd
Fair Oaks Mall
Fairfax, VA 22033

Memco
3201 Old Lee Hwy
Fairfax, VA 22030

The Great Outdoors
533 Jefferson Davis Blvd
Fredericksburg, VA 22401

J C Penney Co
2023 Coliseum Dr
Hampton, VA 23666

Land/Sea Passages
14 E Water St
Harrisonburg, VA 22801

Marks Bike Shop
1094 S College Ave
Harrisonburg, VA 22801

Rockbridge Outfitters, Inc
The Outfitters
785 E Market St
Harrisonburg, VA 22801

Outdoor School, Inc
1050 Knight Ave
Herndon, VA 22070

Colorado East Ltd
51 S King St
Leesburg, VA 22075

Harvest Trading Company,
  Inc
23–25 S King St
Leesburg, VA 22075

Ara-Virginia Skyline
21 N Broad St
Luray, VA 22835

Old Dominion Outfitters
PO Box 678
Madison Heights, VA 24572

Francis Brothers
315 N Main St
Marion, VA 24354

Summit Sports
517 N Main St
Marion, VA 24354

Bowman's Surplus Sales
7515 Centerville Rd
Manassas, VA 22110

The Outdoorsman
15 E Main St
Middleburg, VA 22117

Bike and Hike
434 Warwick Village Center
Newport News, VA 23601

Blue Ridge Mountain Sports
871 N Military Hwy
Norfolk, VA 23502

Bob's Gun & Tackle
746 Granby St
Norfolk, VA 23510

M & G Sales Co, Inc
2609–17 Granby St
Norfolk, VA 23517

Navy Exchange
Hampton Blvd
Bldg CD-1
Norfolk, VA 23511

Appalachian Outfitters
Box 249
2938 Chain Bridge Rd
Oakton, VA 22124

Wild River Outfitters, Inc
5921 Churchland Blvd
Portsmouth, VA 23703

Memco
1651 Reston Ave
Reston, VA 22090

Alpine Outfitters, Inc
11010 Midlothian Turnpike
Richmond, VA 23235

Alpine Outfitters, Inc
7107 W Broad St
Richmond, VA 28229

Blue Ridge Mountain Sports
Gayton Crossing Shopping
    Center
13 Gaskins Rd
Richmond, VA 23233

J C Penney Co
7301 Midlothian Turnpike
Richmond, VA 23225

Memco
5501 Midlothian Turnpike
Richmond, VA 23225
    and
6301 West Broad St
Richmond, VA 23230

Steruheimer Bros
A & N Stores
PO Box 26926
Richmond, VA 23261

CMT Sporting Goods
3441 Brandon Ave SW
Roanoke, VA 24018

Graves Humphreys Inc
4001 Avenham Ave SW
Roanoke, VA 24014

Valley Marine Center
2620 Broadway SW
Roanoke, VA 24015

Blue Ridge Mountain Sports
Wintergreen Resort
Roseland, VA 22967

Great Outdoors
Rte 3, Box 7A
Salem, VA 24153

Herman's
6787 Springfield Mall
Springfield, VA 22150

Springfield Surplus
6530 Backlick Rd
Springfield, VA 22150

Hermans-Tyson Corner
8204 Leesburg Park
Vienna, VA 22180

Bay Camping
3757 Bonney Dr
Virginia Beach, VA 23452

The Old Mountain Man
55909 Clearspring Ct
Virginia Beach, VA 23462

R & M Supply Co
1378 Baker Rd
Virginia Beach, VA 06714

Clark Bros
Rte 2, Hwy 295
Warrenton, VA 22186

The Outdoor Place
Rte 3, Box 167, Hwy 340N
Waynesboro, VA 22980

Bell's Dept Store
122 N Loudoun
Winchester, VA 22601

Blue Ridge Mountain Sports
Wintergreen Resort
Wintergreen, VA 22958

Index

Bold face type indicates trail numbers.

Acorn Ridge Trail, *412*, **879**
Allegheny Trail, *44*, **17**
Alpine Trail, *372*, **821**
American Historical Trails, *198*
Animal Walk, *386*, **848**
Anthony Knobs Trail, *107*, **174**
Appalachian National Scenic
    Trail, *16, 19–20, 23, 35–38,
    41–44, 50–51, 54–57, 59, 64–67,
    70–72, 77–80, 84, 115, 117, 134,
    136–37, 150–60, 163–64,
    167–69, 174, 177–86, 191, 263,
    269, 281–82, 362, 404, 298*
Apple Orchard Falls Trail/West,
    53, **34**
Apple Orchard Falls Trail/East,
    167, **317**
Appomattox History Trail, *211*,
    543
Appomattox NESA Trail, *211*,
    544
Aqueduct Trail, *361*, **807**
Arlington Four-Mile Run Trail,
    403, **860**
Arrowhead Trail, *264*, **616**
Ashton Creek Trail, *328*, **747**
Atwater Park Trail, *367*, **814**
Austin Mountain Trail, *183*, **416**
Awareness Trail, *300*, **703**

Back Bay Trail, *219*, **555**
Back Creek Gorge Trail, *142*, **283**
Back Draft Trail, *93*, **138**

Backway Hollow Trail, *276*, **648**
Balcony Falls Trail, *50*, **29**
Bald Cypress Nature Trail, *312*,
    716
Bald Mountain Trail, *132*, **251**
Bald Ridge Trail, *88*, **122**
Bald Ridge Trail, *98*, **152**
Ballou Park, *359–360*
Ballou Park Nature Trail, *360*,
    806
Bark Camp Lake Trail, *46*, **21**
Barn Wharf Trail, *310*, **715**
Battery 5 Spur Trail, *209*, **536**
Battery 7 Trail, *209*, **537**
Bayberry Nature Trail, *395*, **856**
Beach Trail, *316*, **729**
Bear Draft Trail, *98*, **151**
Beards Gap Hollow Trail, *277*,
    651
Bearfence Hut Trail, *182*, **405**
Bearfence Trail, *182*, **398**
Bear Rock Trail, *45*, **19**
Bear Rock Trail, *143*, **285**
Beartree Gap Trail, *62*, **58**
Bearwallow Run Trail, *138*, **276**
Bear Wallow Spur Trail, *128*, **221**
Beaver Cove Nature Trail, *333*,
    752
Beaver Dam Trail, *316*, **726**
Beaver Lake Nature Trail, *299*,
    700
Beecher Ridge Trail, *185*, **439**
Beech Grove Trail, *60*, **50**

Beldor Ridge Trail, *183,* **409**
Belfast Trail, *51,* **31**
Bell Cover Trail, *136,* **264**
Belle Isle Loop Trail, *384,* **839**
Berry Hollow Trail, *187,* **469**
Betty's Rock Trail, *182,* **397**
Big Bend Trail, *189,* **493**
Big Blue Trail (GWNF), *115,* **187**
Big Blue Trail (SNP), *178,* **349**
Big Devil Stairs Trail, *177,* **337**
Big Hollow Trail, *102,* **160**
Big Mama Trail, *111,* **183**
Big Meadow Trail, *315,* **724**
Big Oak Trail, *298,* **699**
Big Pinnacle Trail, *281,* **665**
Big Ridge Trail, *97,* **150**
Big Run Loop Trail, *183,* **417**
Big Run Loop Trail (part), *189,* **498**
Big Run Portal Trail, *189,* **497**
Big Schloss Trail, *124,* **226**
Big Spy Mountain Trail, *165,* **308**
Big Survey Trail, *321,* **736**
Bird Knob Trail, *120,* **210**
Black Rock Hut Trail, *184,* **429**
Black Rock Trail, *182,* **403**
Blacks Creek Trail, *57,* **45**
Blackwater Creek Trail, *371,* **818**
Bloody Angle Loop Trail, *202,* **525**
Blueberry Trail, *105,* **167**
Blue Spur Trail, *122,* **218**
Blue Suck Trail, *107,* **173**
Blue Suck Trail, *276,* **650**
Bluff Trail, *185,* **435**
Boardwalk Trail, *225,* **563**
Bobcat Ridge Trail, *239,* **580**
Bogan Run Trail, *141,* **280**
Bolshers Run Trail, *92,* **135**
Boone Run Trail, *121,* **216**

Boston Knob Trail, *166,* **310**
Braley Branch Trail, *88,* **123**
Braley Pond Loop Trail, *88,* **121**
Branch Trail, *209,* **535**
Branch Trail, *348,* **781**
Breakthrough Point Trail, *204,* **528**
Broad Hollow Trail, *179,* **362**
Brown Gap Trail, *190,* **501**
Brown Mountain—Rocky Mountain Trail, *183,* **412**
Browntown Trail, *185,* **437**
Brumley Creek Trail, *258,* **608**
Brumley Rim Trail, *258,* **610**
Brushy Hollow Trail, *278,* **656**
Brushy Ridge Trail, *94,* **140**
Brushy Ridge Trail, *144,* **290**
Buchanan Trail, *54,* **36**
Buck Hollow Trail, *179,* **359**
Buck Lick Trail, *279,* **662**
Buck Mountain Trail, *171,* **330**
Buck Ridge Trail, *179,* **360**
Buck Run Spur Trail, *137,* **269**
Buck Run Trail, *137,* **268**
Buffalo Creek Trail, *429,* **898**
Bullpasture Mountain Trail, *261,* **612**
Bull Run Marina Trail, *408,* **874**
Bull Run Nature Trail, *407,* **872**
Bull Run—Occoquan Trail, *406,* **871**
Bunny Trail, *245,* **594**
Burke Lake Trail, *332,* **751**
Buttermilk Trail, *383,* **835**
Butterwood Branch Trail, *177,* **344**
Buzzard Rock Trail, *116,* **191**

Cabin Creek Nature Trail, *283,* **668**

California Ridge Trail, *101,* 157
Campground Trail, *303,* 709
Camp Hoover Trail, *188,* 478
Captain Staunton's Loop Trail, *303,* 710
Cascades Trail, *38,* 7
Cat Knob Trail, *182,* 401
Catlett Mountain Trail, *179,* 364
Catlett Spur Trail, *179,* 363
Cave Circle Trail, *380,* 834
Cave Springs Nature Trail, *346,* 774
CCC Fire Trail, *260,* 611
CCC Trail, *264,* 622
CCC Trail, *284,* 673
Cedar Creek Trail, *124,* 231
Cedar Path Nature Trail, *349,* 784
Cedar Run Trail, *180,* 379
Cellar Mountain Trail, *133,* 256
Center Creek Trail, *273,* 633
Center Trail, *336,* 760
Charcoal Passage Creek Trail, *115,* 189
Chesapeake Nature Trail, *430,* 899
Chessie Nature Trail, *424,* 894
Chestnut Flat Spring Trail, *85,* 112
Chestnut Ridge Trail, *61,* 53
Chestnut Ridge Trail, *96,* 146
Chestnut Ridge Trail, *170,* 329
Chestnut Ridge Trail, *273,* 627
Cheswick Park Trail, *341,* 768
Chimney, Hollow Trail, *86,* 118
Chippokes Plantation Loop Trail, *307,* 712
Christian Run Trail, *137,* 275
Claytor Lake Trail, *275,* 641
Cliff Trail, *130,* 242
Cliffside Trail, *70,* 78

Clinch Mountain Trail, *248,* 598
Cobb's Wharf Trail, *328,* 749
Cock's Comb Trail, *107,* 171
Cold Harbor Trail, *204,* 527
Cold Springs Run Trail, *138,* 273
Cold Spring Trail, *84,* 111
Cold Spring Trail, *274,* 640
Comers Creek Trail, *66,* 64
Compton Gap Trail, *186,* 456
Compton Peak East Trail, *178,* 358
Compton Peak West Trail, *178,* 357
Conservancy Trail, *40,* 8
Conway Trail, *188,* 484
Copper Trail, *428,* 897
Corbin Cabin Cutoff Trail, *179,* 369
Corbin Hollow Trail, *180,* 373
Corbin Mountain Trail, *179,* 372
Cornelius Trail, *54,* 35
Cotoctin Trail, *164,* 303
Cove Mountain Trail, *54,* 37
Crabtree Falls Trail, *133,* 258
Craig Creek Trail, *75,* 87
Crane Trail, *147,* 295
Crater Spur Trail, *209,* 542
Crawford Knob Trail, *86,* 117
Crawford Mountain Trail, *86,* 116
Creasy Hollow Trail, *62,* 57
Creek Loop Trail, *371,* 820
Crescent Rocks Trail, *182,* 400
Crow's Nest Trail, *302,* 706
Crump Park Trail, *342,* 769
Crusher Ridge Trail, *179,* 367
Curry Creek Trail, *56,* 40

Dam Spillway Trail, *291,* 690

Dan Beard Trail, *346,* **792**
Dark Hollow Falls Trail, *181,* **383**
Deadening Trail, *191,* **512**
Deep Cut Trail, *196,* **517**
Deer Island Trail, *358,* **801**
Deer Ridge Trail, *239,* **579**
Deer Trail, *79,* **103**
Deer Trail, *275,* **643**
Dickey Gap Trail, *64,* **61**
Dickey Hill Trail (part) *186,* **452**
Dickey Knob Trail, *66,* **65**
Dickey Ridge Trail, *177,* **335**
Dickey Run Trail, *160,* **299**
Difficult Run Trail, *236,* **575**
Discovery Way Trail, *120,* **208**
Dismal Branch Trail, *42,* **13**
Divide Trail, *69,* **73**
Dixon Branch Trail, *42,* **12**
Dogwood Trail, *264,* **619**
Dogwood Trail, *394,* **855**
Donaldson Run Trail, *323,* **738**
Dora Kelly Nature Trail, *350,* **785**
Dowells Draft Trail, *87,* **120**
Downtown Richmond Trail, *389,* **851**
Doyle River Cabin Trail, *184,* **428**
Doyle River Trail, *183,* **418**
Dragon's Tooth Trail, *79,* **102**
Dry River Ranger District, *11, 84, 95–106*
Dry Run Trail, *111,* **182**
Dry Run Trail, *189,* **491**
Duff and Stuff Trail, *336,* **757**
Duncan Hollow Trail, *118,* **202**

Eagle Trail, *219,* **554**
Eagle Trail, *356,* **793**

Eastern National Chilfens Forest Trail, *110,* **179**
Elephant Mountain Trail, *135,* **263**
Elk Run Trail, *169,* **322**
Elkwallow Trail, *178,* **347**
Elmore Trail, *75,* **92**
Encampment Trail, *209,* **540**
E.T. Sector Trail, *356,* **795**
Exercise Trail, *375,* **825**

Fairview Trail, *201,* **523**
Falling River Trail, *326,* **743**
Fallingwater Cascades, *168*
Fallingwater Cascades Trail, *168,* **320**
Falls Hollow Trail, *86,* **115**
Falls Ridge Trail, *127,* **236**
False Cape Trail, *309,* **714**
Farm to Forest Trail, *239,* **578**
Fat Pat Trail, *111,* **184**
Feathercamp Branch Trail, *60,* **51**
Fenwick Nature Trail, *77,* **99**
Ferrier Trail, *77,* **98**
Ferris Hollow Trail, *86,* **114**
Fescue Trail, *264,* **613**
Fire Pink Trail, *434,* **904**
Fire Trail, *246,* **596**
Fire Trail, *249,* **600**
Fire Trail, *321,* **734**
Fishing Barge Trail, *415,* **884**
Flat Peter Trail, *41,* **11**
Flat Top Trail, *168,* **319**
Florida Maple Trail, *391,* **852**
Fore Mountain Trail, *111,* **181**
Forest Trail, *385,* **841**
Fork Moorman River Trail, *190* **504**

Fork Mountain Road Trail, *188,* **481**

Fork Mountain Trail, *177,* **342**

Fork Mountain Trail, *188,* **482**

Fort A. P. Hill Nature Trail, *417,* **888**

Fort Darling Trail, *204,* **531**

Fort Drewry Trail, *204,* **532**

Fort Harrison Trail, *204,* **529**

Fountainhead Park Trail, *408,* **875**

Fox Hollow Trail, *191,* **508**

Fox Run Trail, *313,* **723**

Fragrance Garden Trail, *376,* **827**

Fragrance Trail, *358,* **805**

Franklin Trail, *264,* **620**

Franklin County Nature Trail, *339,* **763**

Fridley Gap Trail, *121,* **214**

Friend Trail, *209,* **538**

Furnace Mountain Summit Trail, *184,* **420**

Furnace Mountain Trail, *183,* **419**

Gap Creek Trail, *119,* **203**

Gap Run Trail, *183,* **410**

Garden Walk, *386,* **846**

Gasline Road Trail, *190,* **507**

Geological Trail, *273,* **628**

Geology Interpretive Trail, *384,* **838**

George Washington Birthplace Nat'l Monument, *232–33*

George Washington Memorial Parkway, *234–38*

Gibson Gap Trail, *215,* **549**

Gilliam Run Trail, *144,* **292**

Glass House Trail, *123,* **222**

Glencarlyn Park Trail, *324,* **741**

Glen Cove Nature Trail, *346,* **775**

Glen Maury Nature Trail, *353,* **790**

Goodwin Lake Trail, *294,* **694**

Goose Point Trail, *415,* **885**

Goshen-Little North Mtn WMA, *253–56*

Grand Cavern Nature Trail, *398,* **857**

Grandview Preserve Trail, *366,* **812**

Grassy Branch Trail, *72,* **81**

Grassy Creek Trail, *273,* **634**

Grassy Overlook Trail, *273,* **629**

Gravel Springs Hut Trail, *178,* **353**

Graves Mill Trail, *188,* **486**

Grayson County Nature Trail, *340,* **765**

Green Leaf Nature Trail, *217,* **550**

Greenstone Trail, *164,* **304**

Grooms Ridge Trail, *97,* **149**

Ground Pine Nature Trail, *300,* **701**

Grouse Trail, *79,* **104**

Guest Lodge Trail, *279,* **661**

Gulf Branch Nature Trail, *323,* **737**

Gunter Ridge Trail, *51,* **32**

Guys Run Trail, *254,* **606**

Habron Gap Trail, *117,* **197**

Hale Lake Trail, *68,* **72**

Hammond Hollow Trail, *56,* **41**

Hancock Trail, *202,* **526**

Handicapped Trail, *292,* **691**

Hankey Mountain Trail, *96,* **147**

Hannah Run Trail, *179,* **365**

Hardscrabble Knob Trail, *90,* **128**

Harkening Hill Trail, *169,* **323**
Harris Hollow Trail, *185,* **436**
Harrison Creek Trail, *209,* **541**
Hawksbill Trail, *180,* **381**
Hazel Mountain Trail, *187,* **460**
Hazel River Trail, *187,* **461**
Hazel Spur Trail, *187,* **459**
Heiskell Hollow Trail, *185,* **440**
Helms Trail, *75,* **90**
Helton Creek Loop Trail, *72,* **82**
Hemlock Overlook Trails, *407,* **873**
Hemlock Trail, *405,* **865**
Henley Hollow Trail, *69,* **68**
Henry Hill Trail, *196,* **515**
Hensley Church Trail, *181,* **390**
Hiawatha Nature Trail, *268,* **626**
Hickerson Hollow Trail, *186,* **448**
Hickory Hollow Trail, *343,* **771**
Hidden Valley Trail, *141,* **279**
High Knob Lake Shore Trail, *46,* **23**
High Knob Trail, *46,* **22**
High Top Fire Trail, *253,* **602**
Hightop Hut Trail, *184,* **431**
Hightop Road Trail, *184,* **430**
Historic Walk, *386,* **845**
Hogback Spur Trail, *178,* **356**
Hollins College Historical Walk, *421,* **889**
Hollow Trail, *321,* **735**
Holly Trail, *264,* **617**
Holly Trail, *405,* **866**
Holmes Run Stream Valley Trail I, *334,* **754**
Holmes Run Stream Valley Trail III, *334,* **755**
Hone Quarry Ridge Trail, *102,* **159**
Honey Tree Spur Trail, *217,* **551**

Hoop Hole Trail, *72,* **86**
Hopkins Branch Trail, *412,* **878**
Horse Heaven Trail, *69,* **70**
Hot Mountain—Short Mountain Trail, *179,* **368**
Huckleberry Line Trail, *351,* **786**
Huckleberry Ridge Trail, *41,* **10**
Huffs Trail, *276,* **649**
Huguenot Bridge Trail, *385,* **844**
Hull School Trail, *185,* **444**
Humpback Mountain Trail, *164,* **302**
Hunkerson Gap Trail, *128,* **239**
Hunting Creek Trail, *56,* **42**
Hurrican Creek Trail, *65,* **62**
Hurrican Knob Nature Trail, *64,* **60**

Indian Creek Trail, *357,* **799**
Indian Gap Trail, *135,* **261**
Indian Gap Trail, *166,* **311**
Indian Grave Ridge Trail, *117,* **196**
Indian Run PATC Maintenance Hut Trail, *178,* **352**
Indian Run Trail, *179,* **371**
Indiantown Nature Trail, *344,* **772**
Iron Mine Trail, *290,* **687**
Iron Mountain Trail, *60,* **49**
Iron Ore Trail, *73,* **85**
Ivy Creek Nature Trail, *355,* **791**
Ivy Creek PATC Maintenance Trail, *184,* **427**

Jack-O-Lantern Branch Trail, *231,* **567**
Jackson Trail, *200,* **522**
James River Trail, *167,* **315**
Jamestown Colony Trail, *194,* **514**
Jamison Mill Trail, *416,* **886**

Jefferson Historical Trail, *427,* **896**

Jenkins Gap Trail, *185,* **434**

Jeremys Run Trail, *178,* **345**

Jeremys Run Trail, (part), *186,* **447**

Jerkemtight Creek Trail, *94,* **142**

Jerry's Run Trail, *89,* **126**

Jerry's Run Trail, *112,* **185**

Jingling Rocks Trail, *109,* **178**

John's Creek Mountain Trail, *37,* **5**

John's Creek Trail, *38,* **6**

Johnson Farm Loop Trail, *169,* **324**

Jones Mountain Cabin Trail, *182,* **395**

Jones Mountain Trail, *182,* **396**

Jordan River Trail, *186,* **451**

Kelly Trail, *75,* **94**

Kemp Hollow Trail, *186,* **450**

Kennedy Peak Trail, *118,* **199**

Kennedy Ridge Trail, *133,* **255**

Keokee Trail, *47,* **27**

Keyser Run Trail, *185,* **441**

King Fisher Trail, *313,* **720**

Kitchen Rock Trail, *46,* **20**

Knob Mountain Cutoff Trail, *178,* **346**

Knob Mountain Trail, *185,* **442**

Lagoon Trail, *312,* **718**

Lake Maury Trail, *432,* **901**

Lake Shore Nature Trail, *296,* **695**

Lakeside Trail, *130,* **241**

Lakeside Trail, *288,* **685**

Lakewide Trail, *411,* **877**

Lake Trail, *245,* **593**

Lake Trail, *274,* **639**

Lake Trail, *284,* **674**

Lake Trail, *321,* **733**

Lake Trail, *326,* **744**

Lake Trail, *348,* **783**

Lands Run Trail, *186,* **455**

Laurel Bed Creek Trail, *248,* **597**

Laurel Branch Trail, *273,* **635**

Laurel Fork Trail, *137,* **267**

Laurel Fork Trail, *412,* **880**

Laurel Point Trail, *316,* **727**

Laurel Prong Trail, *181,* **392**

Laurel Prong Trail, (part), *188,* **479**

Laurel Run Trail, *127,* **234**

Laurel Run Trail, *254,* **603**

Laurel Spur Trail, *127,* **235**

Laurel View Trail, *277,* **654**

Leading Ridge Trail, *179,* **366**

Lee Drive Trail, *200,* **521**

Lee-Jackson Tour Trail, *369,* **816**

Lewis Falls Spur Trail, *181,* **385**

Lewis Fork Trail, *70,* **77**

Lewis Hollow Trail, *215,* **548**

Lewis Mountain East Trail, *181,* **389**

Lewis Mountain West Trail, *181,* **388**

Lewis Peak Trail, *183,* **415**

Lewis Spring Falls Trail, *181,* **384**

Liberty Hill Trail, *410,* **876**

Lick Branch Trail, *77,* **97**

Life Trail, *356,* **794**

Lighthouse Trail, *222,* **559**

Lignite Trail, *77,* **100**

Limberlost Trail, *180,* **378**

Lion's Tail Trail, *118,* **201**

Listening Rock Trail, *283,* **669**

Little Cove Mountain Trail, *55,* **38**

Little Devil Stairs Trail, *177,* **339**
Little Dry Run Trail, *69,* **74**
Little Mare Mountain Spur Trail, *144,* **294**
Little Mare Mountain Trail, *144,* **293**
Little Mountain Trail, *61,* **54**
Little North Mountain Trail, *255,* **607**
Little Rocky Row Run Trail, *137,* **266**
Little Sluice Mountain Trail, *124,* **230**
Little Stony Creek Trail, *45,* **18**
Little Stony Creek Trail, *124,* **229**
Little Stony Man Trail, *182,* **402**
Little Tumbling Creek Trail, *249,* **599**
Living Forest Trail, *239,* **577**
Loblolly Trail, *302,* **708**
Loblolly Trail, *405,* **864**
Locust Gap Trail, *277,* **652**
Locust Spring Run Spur Trail, *138,* **271**
Locust Spring Run Trail, *137,* **270**
Lone Star Lakes Nature Trail, *393,* **853**
Long Arm Hollow Trail, *258,* **609**
Long Branch Nature Trail, *324,* **740**
Long Creek Trail, *313,* **722**
Lookout Mountain Trail, *96,* **148**
Lookout Tower Trail, *394,* **854**
Loop Trail, *75,* **91**
Loop Trail, *273,* **636**
Loudoun Heights Trail, *160,* **300**
Lower Chippokes Creek Trail, *307,* **713**
Lower Trail, *286,* **681**
Lubber Run Trail, *325,* **742**

Lum Martin Trail, *60,* **47**
Lunchburg College Botanical Trail, *422,* **890**

Madison County Route 649 Trail, *188,* **485**
Madison Run Trail, *190,* **500**
Main Trail, *313,* **719**
Manassas Battlefield Historical Trails, *197,* **519**
Marshall Draft Trail, *92,* **136**
Marsh Point Trail, *246,* **595**
Marsh Trail, *379,* **830**
Massanutten Mountain East Trail, *116,* **190**
Massanutten Mountain South Trail, *119,* **207**
Massanutten Mountain West Trail, *122,* **219**
Massanutten Story Book Trail, *120,* **209**
Matthews Arm Trail, *185,* **438**
Meadow Ground Trail, *254,* **604**
Meadow School Trail, *188,* **487**
Meadow Trail, *383,* **837**
McDaniel Hollow Trail, *181,* **394**
Middle Mountain Trail, *119,* **205**
Middle Mountain Trail, *137,* **274**
Middle Mountain Trail, *144,* **288**
Middle Mountain Trail, (Douthat), *276,* **646**
Milford Gap Trail, *117,* **194**
Millers Head Trail, *182,* **399**
Mill Mountain Trail, *93,* **137**
Mill Mountain Trail, *124,* **225**
Mill Mountain Trail, *147,* **296**
Mill Prong Horse Spur Trail, *188,* **480**
Mill Prong Trail, *181,* **386**

Mill Run Trail, *118,* **200**
Mills Creek Spur Trail, *130,* **248**
Mills Creek Trail, *130,* **247**
Mine Bank Trail, *132,* **252**
Mineral Ridge Trail, *427,* **895**
Mines Run Trail, *102,* **158**
Molly Mitchell Trail, *358,* **803**
Molly's Knob Trail, *284,* **672**
Molly's Pioneer Trail, *284,* **671**
Morgan Run Trail, *121,* **213**
Morning Knob Tower Trail, *109,* **177**
Mossy Creek Trail, *298,* **697**
Motts Run Park, *365–66*
Motts Run Trail, *365,* **810**
Mountain Farm Self-Guiding Trail, *163,* **301**
Mountain Fork Trail, *46,* **24**
Mountain Side Trail, *278,* **660**
Mountain Spring Trail, *380,* **833**
Mountain Top Trail, *278,* **657**
Mount Marshall Trail, *185,* **445**
Mount Pleasant Trail, *134,* **259**
Mount Rogers National Recreation Trail, *69,* **76**
Mount Vernon Trail, *235,* **570**
Muddy Run Trail, *141,* **281**
Mud Pond Gap Trail, *105,* **168**
Mullins Branch Trail, *66,* **67**
Muskrat Run Trail, *317,* **731**

Naked Top Trail, *180,* **380**
Natural Chimneys Nature Trail, *401,* **858**
Nature Preservation Trail, *346,* **776**
Nature Trail, *264,* **615**
Neighbor Mountain Trail, *186,* **446**
Nelson Draft Trail, *92,* **134**

New Market Battlefield Trail, *205,* **533**
New River Community College Trail, *422,* **891**
Nicholson Hollow Trail, *179,* **370**
Nike Park Nature Trail, *342,* **770**
North Boundary Trail, *348,* **780**
North Fork and South Trail, *190,* **503**
North Mountain Trail, *58,* **46**
North Mountain Trail, *127,* **233**
North Mountain Trail/Central, *106,* **170**
North Mountain Trail/North, *84,* **110**
North Mountain Trail/South, *78,* **101**
North River Gorge Trail, *99,* **153**
NRM Nature Trail, *341,* **767**

Oak Hickory Trail, *290,* **686**
Old Appalachian Trail, *362,* **809**
Old Carriage Trail, *236,* **573**
Old Chestnut Trail, *36,* **2**
Old Dominion Trail, *388,* **849**
Old Farm Trail, *352,* **787**
Old Hazel Trail, *187,* **457**
Old Oak Native Trail, *330,* **750**
Old Plantation Trail, *297,* **696**
Old Rag Trail, *187,* **466**
Old Shawnee Trail, *285,* **677**
Olinger Trail, *47,* **26**
Oliver Mountain Trails, *113,* **186**
One-Mile Run Trail, *184,* **426**
Onion Mountain Loop Trail, *168,* **318**
Ore Bank Trail, *147,* **297**
Orkney Springs Trail, *128,* **238**
Osmanthus Trail, *312,* **717**
Otter Creek Trail, *166,* **313**

Otter Lake Trail, *166,* **314**
Otter Point Trail, *358,* **802**
Otter's Path Trail, *293,* **693**
Overall-Beecher Ridge Trail, *178,* **351**
Overall Run Trail, *178,* **348**
Overlook Trail, *273,* **630**
Overlook Trail, *275,* **642**
Overtop Mountain Trail, *177,* **343**

Paddy Knob Trail, *140,* **277**
Paddy Knob Spur Trail, *140,* **278**
Paine Run Trail, *190,* **502**
Pandapas Pond Trail, *43,* **15**
Pass Mountain Hut Trail, *178,* **354**
Patowmack Canal Trail, *236,* **572**
Patrick Henry Cross-Country Trail, *341,* **766**
Patterson Mountain Trail, *75,* **88**
Patterson Ridge Trail, *189,* **496**
Paw Paw Passage Trail, *336,* **756**
Peak Trail, The*177,* **336**
Peer Trail, *125,* **228**
Perkins Knob Trail, *67,* **69**
Petersburg Battlefield National Recreation Trail, *208,* **534**
Physical Fitness Trail, *327,* **746**
Pig Iron Trail, *115,* **188**
Pinefield Hut Trail, *184,* **432**
Pine Grove Forest Trail, *238,* **576**
Pine Hill Gap Trail, *187,* **462**
Pine Knob Trail, *288,* **684**
Pine Mountain Trail, *49,* **28**
Pine Mountain Trail, *71,* **80**
Pine Mountain Trail, *254,* **605**
Pine Mountain Trail, *412,* **881**
Pine Mountain Trail, *413,* **882**
Pine Ridge Trail, *347,* **778**
Pine Ridge Trail, *380,* **831**

Pine Trail, *264,* **618**
Pine Tree Trail, *277,* **653**
Piney Branch Trail, *177,* **338**
Piney Branch Trail, (part), *186,* **449**
Piney Mountain Trail, *143,* **284**
Piney Ridge Trail, *53,* **33**
Piney Ridge Trail, *177,* **341**
Pinnacle Trail, *361,* **808**
Pitt Spring Lookout Trail, *120,* **212**
Plantation Trail, *231,* **566**
Pleasant Creek Trail, *385,* **840**
Pocosin Cabin Trail, *182,* **406**
Pocosin Hollow Trail, *181,* **391**
Pocosin Horse Trail, *189,* **490**
Pocosin Trail, *189,* **489**
Pohick Bay Trails, *405,* **870**
Pole Bridge Link Trail, *177,* **340**
Pompey Loop Trail, *134,* **260**
Pond Knob Trail, *106,* **169**
Pond Run Trail, *125,* **227**
Pony Trail, *222,* **560**
Poquoson Nature Trail, *377,* **828**
Possums Rest Trail, *178,* **355**
Potomac Heritage Trail, *336,* **758**
Potomac Overlook Trails, *404,* **862**
Potts Mountain Trail, *36,* **3**
Potts Mountain Trail, *110,* **180**
Potts Mountain Trail/West, *79,* **107**
Potts Mountain Trail/East, *79,* **106**
Poverty Creek Horse Trail, *43,* **16**
Powell Mountain Trail, *181,* **387**
Powell's Mountain Trail, *123,* **223**
Power Line Trail, *264,* **625**
Price-Broad Mountain Trail, *77,* **96**

Price Mountain Trail, *75,* **93**
Priest Trail, The, *164,* **305**
Prospectors Trail, *273,* **637**
Punch and Judy Creek Trail,
   80, **108**

Quiet Woods Trail, *385,* **843**

Rabbit Run Trail, *380,* **832**
Raccoon Branch Trail, *66,* **66**
Raider's Run Trail, *285,* **678**
Railroad Ditch Lane Trail,
   225, **564**
Ramsey's Draft Nature Trail,
   89, **125**
Ramsey's Draft Trail, *89,* **124**
Ranger Station Trail, *184,* **433**
Rapidan Trail, *188,* **475**
Rappahannock Community
   College Nature Trail, *423,* **892**
Rappahannock River Trail,
   365, **811**
Red Branch Trail, *250,* **601**
Redbud Trail, *264,* **621**
Red Gate Trail, *187,* **471**
Red Oak Trail, *264,* **624**
Reservoir Hollow Trail, *135,* **262**
Rhododendron Trail, *71,* **79**
Rhododendron Trail, *281,* **664**
Ribble Trail, *42,* **14**
Rich Hold Trail, *108,* **175**
Richmond Walking Trail,
   389, **850**
Ridge Trail, *180,* **375**
Ridge Trail, *215,* **545**
Ridge Trail, *236,* **574**
Ridge Trail, *284,* **675**
Ridge Trail, *348,* **782**
Riprap Trail, *184,* **422**
River Access Trail, *385,* **842**
River Bank Trail, *302,* **704**

Riverside Trail, *383,* **836**
River Trail, *236,* **571**
River Trail, *204,* **530**
River Trail, *273,* **638**
River Trail, *316,* **728**
Roanoke Mountain Loop Trail,
   170, **328**
Roanoke River Trail, *170,* **326**
Roanoke Valley Horse Trail,
   170, **327**
Roaring Run Trail, *73,* **84**
Roaring Run Trail, *120,* **211**
Robertson Mountain Trail,
   180, **374**
Robin's Roost Trail, *302,* **707**
Rock Castle Gorge Trail,
   172, **332**
Rock House Ridge Trail, *283,* **670**
Rock Shelter Trail, *141,* **282**
Rock Springs Cabin Trail,
   182, **404**
Rocks Mountain Trail, *184,* **423**
Rockwood Nature Trail, *327,* **745**
Rocky Knob Self-Guiding Trail,
   173, **333**
Rocky Mount Run Trail, *183,* **413**
Rocky Mount Trail, *183,* **411**
Rocky Run Trail, *103,* **161**
Rocky Run Trail, *352,* **789**
Rockytop Trail, *183,* **414**
Rose River Loop Trail, *181,* **352**
Rose River Trail, *187,* **472**
Ross Camp Hollow Trail,
   278, **658**
Round Meadow Creek Trail,
   173, **334**
Running Cedar Trail, *288,* **683**
Rush Trail, *61,* **55**
Ruskin Freer Nature Preserve,
   370–71

R. W. Cross Nature Trail, *376,* **826**

Saddleback Mountain Trail, *182,* **408**
Saddle Gap Trail, *136,* **265**
Saddle Trail, *180,* **376**
Saint Mary's Falls Trail, *132,* **254**
Saint Mary's Trail, *132,* **253**
Salthouse Branch Nature Trail, *416,* **887**
Salt Pond Ridge Trail, *144,* **291**
Salt Stump Trail, *276,* **647**
Sams Ridge Trail, *179,* **361**
Sand Spring Mountain Trail, *100,* **155**
Sandy Gap Trail, *144,* **289**
Scothorn Gap Trail, *119,* **204**
Scott Run Trail, *333,* **753**
Second Battle of Manassas Trail, *198,* **520**
Sensitivity Trail, *222,* **558**
Sharp Top Trail, *169,* **321**
Shaw Gap Trail, *60,* **52**
Shawl Gap Trail, *116,* **192**
Shaw's Ridge Trail, *91,* **131**
Shelton Trail, *121,* **215**
Shenandoah Mountain Trail/North, *90,* **129**
Shenandoah Mountain Trail/South, *91,* **132**
Short Loop Trail, *209,* **539**
Short Ridge Trail, *94,* **141**
Shot Tower Historical Trail, *287,* **682**
Shuttle Trail, *357,* **800**
Signal Corps Knob Trail, *92,* **133**
Signal Knob Trail, *122,* **217**
Simmons Gap Trail—East/West, *189,* **495**

Sinclair Hollow Trail, *91,* **130**
Six Oaks Trail, *347,* **777**
Skyland—Big Meadows Horse Trail, *187,* **465**
Skyland Trail, *187,* **463**
Skylight Cave Trail, *215,* **546**
Slabcamp Run Trail, *137,* **272**
Slacks Overlook Trail, *131,* **250**
Slate Springs Mountain Trail, *103,* **162**
Slate Springs Trail A, *103,* **165**
Slate Springs Trail AA, *103,* **163**
Slate Springs Trail B, *103,* **164**
Slate Springs Trail BB, *103,* **166**
Slaughter Trail, *189,* **488**
Smart View Loop Trail, *171,* **331**
Smith River Trail, *414,* **883**
Smith Roach Gap Trail, *189,* **494**
Snyder Trail, *129,* **240**
South Boundary Trail, *348,* **779**
South River Falls Trail, *182,* **407**
South River Trail, *189,* **492**
Special Population Trail, *378,* **829**
Specs Mines Trail, *57,* **44**
Spillway Trail, *284,* **676**
Spotsylvania Battlefield History Trail, *202,* **524**
Springhouse Ridge Trail, *90,* **127**
Spring House Road Trail, *186,* **453**
Spruce Trail, *405,* **867**
Squirrel Ridge Trail, *264,* **614**
Stack Rock Trail, *127,* **237**
Stampers Branch Trail, *281,* **667**
Star Trail, *356,* **797**
Staunton River Trail, *181,* **393**
Stephens Trail, *118,* **198**
Stewarts Knob Trail, *170,* **325**

Stone Bridge—Van Pelt Trail, *196,* **516**
Stone Mountain Trail, *47,* **25**
Stony Fork Trail, *80,* **109**
Stony Hill Loop Trail, *130,* **244**
Stony Man Horse Trail, *187,* **464**
Stony Man Trail, *191,* **510**
Stony Mountain Trail, *188,* **473**
Stony Run Trail, *133,* **257**
Stony Run Trail, *276,* **644**
Story of Forest Trail, *191,* **511**
Straight Branch Trail, *60,* **48**
Stuart's Knob Trail, *291,* **688**
Stull Run Trail, *190,* **499**
Sudley Springs Trail, *196,* **518**
Sugarland Run Trail, *367,* **813**
Sugar Maple Loop Trail, *72,* **83**
Sulphur Ridge Trail, *75,* **95**
Sulphur Spring Trail, *50,* **30**
Sunken Road Trail, *199,* **520**
Sweetbay Trail, *405,* **869**
Sweet Pepperbush Trail, *433,* **903**

Tanners Ridge Horse Trail, *188,* **476**
Tanners Ridge Trail, *188,* **477**
Taskers Gap Trail, *123,* **220**
Taskinas Creek Trail, *317,* **730**
Taylor Hollow Trail, *86,* **113**
Tenderfoot Trail, *356,* **796**
Terrapin Mountain Trail, *57,* **43**
Third Branch Trail, *300,* **702**
Thompson Hollow Trail, *178,* **350**
Thornton River Trail, *185,* **443**
Tibbet Knob Trail, *127,* **232**
Timber Ridge Trail, *100,* **154**
Tindall's Point Park Nature Trail, *339,* **764**
Tobacco House Ridge Trail, *277,* **655**

Todd Lake Trail, *95,* **143**
Tolliver Trail, *117,* **195**
Toms Cove Nature Trail, *222,* **557**
Torry Ridge Spur Trail, *130,* **245**
Torry Ridge Trail, *130,* **246**
Tower Hill Mountain Trail, *143,* **286**
Towers Trail, *273,* **631**
Tower Tunnel Trail, *273,* **632**
Traces Trail, *191,* **509**
Trail of Trees, *167,* **316**
Trayfoot Mountain Trail, *184,* **421**
Tree Walk, *486,* **847**
Trimble Mountain Trail, *95,* **144**
Tri-State Trail, *217,* **552**
T-Trails, *240,* **581–91**
Tucker Trail, *75,* **89**
Tunnel Hill Trail, *286,* **680**
Turk Branch Trail, *190,* **506**
Turkey Neck Trail, *315,* **725**
Turkey Trail, *79,* **105**
Turk Gap Trail, *190,* **505**
Turk Mountain Trail, *184,* **425**
Turtle Ridge Trail, *352,* **788**
Tuscarora Overlook Trail, *276,* **645**
Tutelo Trail, *302,* **705**
Twin Beech Trail, *293,* **692**
Twin Forks Loop Trail, *373,* **824**
Twin Pinnacles Trail, *281,* **666**

Unaka Native Trail, *68,* **71**
University of Virginia Academic Walk, *423,* **893**
Unknown Scout Trail, *356,* **798**
Upland Trail, *336,* **759**

Upper Dark Hollow Trail, *188,* **474**
Upper Lake Trail, *130,* **243**
Upper Loop Trail, *371,* **819**
Upper Trail, *286,* **679**
Upton Hill Trail, *404,* **861**

Veach Gap Grail, *116,* **193**
Veterans' Memorial Park Nature Trail, *345,* **773**
Virginia Creeper Trail, *62,* **59**
Virginia Division of Forestry, *12,* **306**
Virginia Division of State Parks, *17*
Virginia Highlands Horse Trail, *65,* **63**
Virginia's Nature Trail, *41,* **9**
VMI-Marshall Tour Trail, *369,* **817**

Wagon Road Trail, *123,* **224**
Wakefield-Accotink Trail, *338,* **761**
Walker Mountain Trail, *93,* **139**
Wallops Park Nature Trail, *320,* **732**
Warm Springs Mountain Trail, *143,* **287**
Warrior Path Trail, *298,* **698**
War Spur Trail, *36,* **1**
Washington and Lee University, *368–69*
Washington Ditch Trail, *225,* **561**
Washington Historic Trail, *233,* **568**
Washington Nature Trail, *233,* **569**
Washington & Old Dominion Railroad Trail, *403,* **859**

Waterfall Mountain Trail, *119,* **206**
Waverly-Wolftrap Trail, *338,* **762**
Weakley Hollow Trail, *187,* **468**
Weddlewood Trail, *186,* **454**
West Naked Creek Road, *188,* **483**
Whiskey Run Trail, *291,* **689**
Whispering Water Trail, *69,* **75**
White Lake Trail, *313,* **721**
Whiteoak Canyon Trail, *187,* **470**
White Oak Draft Trail, *87,* **119**
White Oak Flats Trail, *166,* **312**
White Oak Nature Trail, *373,* **822**
Whiteoak Ranger Station Trail, *187,* **467**
Whiteoak Trail, *180,* **377**
White Oak Trail, *364,* **623**
White Pine Trail, *405,* **868**
White Rock Falls Trail I, *164,* **306**
White Rock Falls Trail II, *165,* **307**
White Rocks Gap Trail, *131,* **249**
White Rocks Trail, *37,* **4**
White Rocks Trail, *187,* **458**
White Rock Tower Trail, *108,* **176**
Wildcat Mountain Trail, *55,* **39**
Wildcat Ridge Trail, *184,* **424**
Wilderness Nature Trail, *430,* **900**
Wilderness Road Trail, *217,* **553**
Wildlife Trail, *221,* **556**
Wild Oak Trail, *96,* **145**
Wildwood Trail, *434,* **905**
Willis River, *304,* **711**
Wilson Creek Trail, *278,* **659**
Wilson Creek Trail, *281,* **663**
Windy Run Nature Trail, *324,* **739**
Wolf Ridge Trail, *100,* **156**
Woodcock Trail, *245,* **592**
Wood Duck Slough Trail, *358,* **804**

Woodland Ecology Trail, *433,* **902**
Woodmarsh Trail, *228,* **565**
Woods Creek Park Trail, *368,* **815**
Woodson Gap Trail, *215,* **547**
Woodthrush Trail, *328,* **748**
Wright Trail, *62,* **56**
Wynn's Mill Loop Trail, *373,* **823**

YACC's Run Trail, *107,* **172**
Yankee Horse Trail, *165,* **309**
Yorktown Battlefield Trail,
     193, **513**